RESPONSA IN A HISTORICAL CONTEXT
A VIEW OF POST-EXPULSION
SPANISH-PORTUGUESE JEWISH COMMUNITIES
THROUGH SIXTEENTH- AND SEVENTEENTH-CENTURY
RESPONSA

Studies in Orthodox Judaism

Series Editor
  Marc B. Shapiro (University of Scranton, Scranton, Pennsylvania)

Editorial Board
  Alan Brill (Seton Hall University, South Orange, New Jersey)
  Benjamin Brown (Hebrew University, Jerusalem)
  David Ellenson (Hebrew Union College, New York)
  Adam S. Ferziger (Bar-Ilan University, Ramat Gan)
  Miri Freud-Kandel (University of Oxford, Oxford)
  Jeffrey Gurock (Yeshiva University, New York)
  Shlomo Tikoshinski (Jerusalem)

RESPONSA IN A HISTORICAL CONTEXT

A VIEW OF POST-EXPULSION
SPANISH-PORTUGUESE JEWISH COMMUNITIES
THROUGH SIXTEENTH- AND SEVENTEENTH-CENTURY
RESPONSA

DEBBY KOREN

BOSTON
2024

Copyright © Academic Studies Press, 2024
Copyright ©Debby Koren, translation rights

ISBN 9798887193595 (hardback)
ISBN 9798887193601 (adobe pdf)
ISBN 9798887193618 (epub)

Library of Congress Cataloging-in-Publication Data
Names: Koren, Debby, 1951- author.
Title: Responsa in a historical context: A view of post-expulsion Spanish-Portuguese Jewish communities through sixteenth- and seventeenth-century responsa / Debby Koren.
Description: Boston: Academic Studies Press, 2024. | Series: Studies in Orthodox Judaism | Includes bibliographical references.
Identifiers: LCCN 2023036603 (print) | LCCN 2023036604 (ebook) | ISBN 9798887193595 (paperback) | ISBN 9798887193601 (adobe pdf) | ISBN 9798887193618 (epub).
Subjects: LCSH: Responsa—History and criticism. | Jews—Ottoman Empire—History—16th century. | Jews—Ottoman Empire—History—17th century. | Jews—Netherlands—History—17th century. | Jews—Brazil—History—17th century.
Classification: LCC BM523.K67 2024 (print) | LCC BM523 (ebook) DDC 296.1/850896—dc23/eng/20230914
LC record available at https://lccn.loc.gov/2023036603
LC ebook record available at https://lccn.loc.gov/2023036604

Book design by Sally M. Freedman
Cover design by Ivan Grave
   Cover: Map of Jewish expulsion at end of 15th century is a remix of the following image, available under the Creative Commons license: https://commons.m.wikimedia.org/wiki/File:Expulsion_judios-en.svg#
   Background: Ms. Heb. 128=8, Responsa of Radbaz, 16th century MS, from the collection of the National Library of Israel, Ktiv Project. Reproduced by permission.

Published by Academic Studies Press
1577 Beacon Street
Brookline, MA 02446 USA
press@academicstudiespress.com
www.academicstudiespress.com

Contents

Acknowledgments VI

Introduction VII
    Overview VII
    The Halakhic Discourse in Responsa VIII
    Translation and Presentation X
    The Eight Responsa XI
    Notes on Translation, Transliteration, and Citations XV
    Glossary XVII
    Abbreviations XVII
    Further Reading XVIII

On Excommunication 1

Responsa

1. Divorce out of Love: A Sixteenth-Century Woman's Story—
   Rabbi David ben Solomon ibn Abi Zimra Responsum 1,398 9

2. The Tax Cut Lobby—Rabbi Joseph ibn Lev Responsum 4:14 47

3. Are You Calling Me a Heretic?!—*Zᵉqan Aharon* 25 85

4. Families Torn Apart—Rabbi Moses ben Joseph di Trani
   Responsum 1,142 119

5. What's in a Name?—Rabbi Samuel de Medina *Yo-re Deʿa* 199 139

6. Is Your Blood Any Redder? The Case of an Informer in the
   Venetian Inquisition—Rabbi Solomon ben Abraham Ha-Kohen
   Responsum 4,31 155

7. Excommunication in Amsterdam—Baḥ (*Ha-Yᵉshanot*) 5 187

8. South of the Equator, in the New World—*Torat Ḥayyim* 3,3 209

Index 243

Acknowledgments

I'd like to express my gratitude to my editorial consultant, Sally Freedman, whose suggestions went way beyond the call of duty. Sally served as a critical reader, patiently letting me talk through my thoughts to arrive at a more effective way to write them.

Sincere appreciation to the scholars of the H-Judaic Jewish Studies Network, whose suggestions for references for some obscure points allowed me to feel part of a community of people who love knowledge and generously share it.

Introduction

Overview

Responsa literature is vast and varied—vast in the time that it spans, vast in its geographical origins; in fact, as vast as the history of the Jewish people and their presence, in communities large or small, across the globe. It is varied in the range of topics that it addresses, from religious minutia about the laws of the Sabbath and dietary laws, to medical questions, to issues of Jewish identity, to torts and inheritance disputes, to halakhic questions about the use of modern technology. The cases can be somber, sometimes political in nature, at times reflective of the darkest times in Jewish history. Or, they can be spicy, bordering on the stuff of soap operas.

While some questions might have been asked at any time in any place, others are a product of their time: they arose as a result of the historical experience of the Jewish community in a particular location. In the latter case, we can better appreciate the questions and their answers when we understand their historical context.

This book contains a collection of eight annotated translations of responsa, alongside the original Hebrew texts, focusing on the post-expulsion Spanish-Portuguese communities of the sixteenth to seventeenth centuries. This collection of responsa will acquaint the reader with Jews who, following their expulsion, settled in the Ottoman Empire, in Palestine under the Mamluks, in Amsterdam and in Brazil. Among them are both Jews who left their homes in Spain or Portugal immediately upon the expulsion decree,[1] and Jews who lived as New Christians, conversos, and returned to Judaism only later (as well as some who did not). The period of the expulsion of the Jews from the Iberian Peninsula was a tragic time in Jewish history, but the revitalization of the post-expulsion Spanish-Portuguese Jewish communities in new locales is testimony to the human spirit and determination.

---

1 The Portuguese expulsion decree was issued in December 1496; the Jews were permitted eleven months to convert or leave, but were blocked at the ports and forcibly converted. Though "the majority of Jews preferred to leave rather than convert," "the vast majority of Jews in Portugal were forcibly converted and never left the kingdom" ([Soyer], ch. 4). However, "some Jews succeeded in leaving Portugal before the mass conversions of 1497, while others managed to escape as Conversos immediately thereafter" ([Ray], 41). The borders were "never hermetically" closed (Miriam Bodian, "Hebrews of the Portuguese Nation: The Ambiguous Boundaries of Self-Definition," *Jewish Social Studies: History, Culture, Society* 15, no. 1 [Fall 2008]: 67).

The volume includes eight chapters, each built around one responsum from one of the great halakhic authorities of the time, covering topics that include excommunication in Amsterdam, 'agunot,[2] inheritance rights of a converso son, obligatory contracts and breach of agreement, heresy and humanist scholarship, informing on someone to the Venetian Inquisition, and more. A preparatory chapter addresses the topic of excommunication, a recurring concept among the responsa.

The halakhic authorities whose responsa are presented include six of the great Sephardic rabbis of the time, one rabbi of the Eastern Mediterranean group known as the Romaniots, and one Ashkenazi rabbi to whom former Crypto-Jews and conversos in Amsterdam—now Jews—turned to settle a dispute. The focus on Sephardic rabbis, natural for this period in Jewish history, is valuable for the illumination of the scholarly facet of Sephardic culture. Sephardic culture should not be known only for its Ladino songs and delicious cuisine, but also for the great scholarship of the prolific rabbis who served the Sephardic communities in their new locales. They bequeathed a myriad of responsa, which have served as sources for generations of scholars.

The responsa present a variety of issues characteristic of Jewish life in the sixteenth and seventeenth centuries, in some cases specifically as a result of the expulsion, while in others merely as a reflection of Jewish communal life at that time. Further, they contain varied halakhic themes, to expose the readers to several halakhic concepts and to a selection of examples of codified halakha.

The Halakhic Discourse in Responsa

In modern times, scholars have been mining the responsa literature for historical and sociological data and for use as source material for books and courses on Jewish history.[3] My goal, conversely, is to delve into the halakhic discourse,

---

2   'Aguna (pl. 'agunot; lit., an anchored or chained woman) is a halakhic term for a woman who is "chained" to her marriage, whether because her husband has disappeared and his death cannot be verified or because her husband refuses to grant her a divorce.

3   Early examples of this type of work include Morris S. Goodblatt, *Jewish Life in Turkey in the XVIth Century as Reflected in the Writings of Samuel De Medina* (New York: JTSA, 1952) and Israel M. Goldman, *The Life and Times of Rabbi David Ibn Abi Zimra: A Social, Economic and Cultural Study of Jewish Life in the Ottoman Empire in the 15th and 16th Centuries as Reflected in the Responsa of the RDBZ* (New York: JTSA, 1970). Works on women's lives, in particular, in which responsa literature is used as historical evidence include Elisheva Baumgarten, *Mothers and Children: Jewish Family Life in Medieval Europe* (Princeton: Princeton University Press, 2007), Avraham Grossman, *Pious and Rebellious: Jewish Women in Medieval Europe*, trans. Jonathan Chipman (Waltham: Brandeis University Press, 2004), and others. A wealth of responsa literature is analyzed and woven into the work of the eminent historian Jacob Katz. Matt Goldish, *Jewish Questions* (Princeton: Princeton University Press, 2008) contains

which was, of course, the focus of the responsum's author, while using what is known of the historical and sociological context to enrich our appreciation of the worlds of the questioner and of the halakhic authority, the challenges each faced, the knowledge and precedents available at the time, and the needs of the community. By means of a close, contextualized reading, we can enhance our understanding of how historical and social conditions might come into play in the halakhic process. And we can appreciate the scholastic achievement that the responsa embody. What makes these halakhic authorities great is not how historically interesting the questions they were asked were. Rather, it is their erudition, their ability to present careful, detailed halakhic arguments, with respect for the practical needs of the Jewish community and often with ingenuity.

When learning Talmud, it can be delightful to use one's imagination to envision what it must have been like to live in those times and to be sitting in the *bet midrash*—the study hall—listening to the discussion. Understanding the technology of the time, the monetary system, what people ate, and so on, is often essential in understanding the reasoning of the discussions. But the other essential element required to follow the discussion is, of course, familiarity with the rabbinic language and references.

Similarly, to be able to follow the discourse in the responsa literature, it is essential to be familiar with the halakhic foundations upon which the discussion is based, so that the halakhic references (which are assumed by the author to be known to the reader, who originally was typically another rabbi) can be considered. Without this knowledge a person attempting to read a responsum, even if he or she reads Hebrew (or another Judeo language in which the responsum is written) will get lost rather quickly. The question might make sense and be of interest in its own right, but the reader might be intimidated by the details of the answer. Nevertheless, it is by reading the answers that we can understand how the halakhic process has operated over the centuries, how the halakhic foundations laid down in the Talmud and interpreted by the Rishonim have been applied through the centuries.

By digesting the responses we can come to appreciate the erudition of the rabbis who wrote them, and, sometimes, how creative they were in their application of the halakhic sources available to them. We may also be impressed and delighted by their use of language: biblical and Talmudic phrases can be woven into the text, almost seamlessly, demonstrating mastery of the texts, even when

---

a collection of translations of responsa aimed at using them as source material for historical purposes, but only the questions are translated, while the responses are summarized in one or two sentences. Goldish provides some historical background in the introduction to each of his translations. A predecessor to this genre was Samuel Freehof, *A Treasury of Responsa* (Philadelphia: JPS, 1963), in which the author briefly introduces each responsum, which is translated in abridged form.

the author did not have all the texts available at his fingertips, as was frequently the case.

In the collection of responsa presented here, the aim is to provide not only a translation of the text, but also enough background material and annotations to enable readers to be able to immerse themselves in this complex material, follow the discourse, and appreciate the immense knowledge displayed and methods used in applying this knowledge.

For each responsum, a selection of basic halakhic sources is provided, with translation and annotation. Other halakhic aspects are elucidated and referenced in the annotations, which can be used for further study of the halakhic issues at stake for a particular topic.

Translation and Presentation

Accepting the encumbrance of clumsiness that sometimes comes with fidelity in translation, I have generally favored a literal or near literal rendering of the texts to English. In this way I hope to encourage readers to use the translations to facilitate their reading of the original text, rather than as a replacement for it. So that the reader can more easily find a citation from the Talmud (and look up any corresponding passages from the Talmud that I chose to include in the related Halakhic Background), the page in the Vilna edition is included in square brackets following the translation of chapter names or numbers that appear in the responsa.[4]

Hebrew is more concise than English, and given that some of the authors tend to be quite verbose, sometimes citing more citations than necessary to make their point, sometimes referring to esoteric references that would be challenging to follow in translation, and sometimes using some convoluted logic, there is a risk that absolutely complete translations will lose the interest of the reader.

However, I chose to take that risk so that I might provide a complete and rich source. Translating only excerpts while summarizing the remainder, as is found in some other collections of translated responsa,[5] presents a different danger: shortchanging some of the richest Jewish literature.

Each responsum is introduced with some historical information, but readers who wish to attain a broader background can refer to the bibliography provided for each responsum. References to books in the bibliographies are indicated by [Author] (in brackets). At the end of this introduction there are several biblio-

---

4   The pagination of the Vilna edition is in accordance with the 1523 Bomberg edition of the Talmud.
5   Such as Freehof, *A Treasury of Responsa*.

graphic suggestions for general background about the expulsion of the Jews from Spain and Portugal—appropriate for all of the responsa—chosen (with difficulty) from the large corpus of literature about this period in history.

Questions for further discussion are offered after each responsum is presented and discussed. Some of these questions enable the reader to discover the current relevance of the ideas contained in the halakhic themes, while others can provoke consideration of halakhic methods and attitudes.

In addition to those who might read the book for independent study, or informal study groups, the target audience for this volume includes students, teachers, and rabbis in either formal or informal classes in areas of Jewish law, comparative legal systems, halakha, Jewish history, Sephardic culture, and Jewish ethics. A portion of the content is appropriate for Jewish gender studies. The book can be used to teach a halakhic concept, such as excommunication, breach of agreements, or the 'aguna, by considering its application in an actual historical example, or to examine the impact of historical events on the Jewish experience.

The Eight Responsa

1. Divorce out of Love: R. David ben Solomon ibn Abi Zimra (1479–1573) Responsum 1,398

This responsum revolves around the plight of a woman in Jerusalem around the turn of the sixteenth century, whose husband has disappeared. He had sent her a writ of divorce (*get*), by messenger, but this document was lost when she fled, following the expulsion of the Jews from Spain. Is she free to remarry?

The responsum sheds light on a facet of divorce that is not commonly considered today: divorce employed to avoid 'iggun (the state of being an 'aguna). Because of the complexity of this woman's case, the responsum presents a microcosm of Jewish divorce laws: divorce by proxy, conditional divorce, a woman's testimony about her marital status and other factors come into play. Questions for discussion invite the readers to explore application of these laws to modern situations, such as the case of the wives whose husbands apparently—but not definitely—perished in the 9/11 World Trade Center tragedy.

2. The Tax Cut Lobby: R. Joseph ibn Lev (1505–1580) Responsum 4,14

The question posed in this responsum provides a window into the methods of survival of Jewish communities in the sixteenth century. Where Jews were allowed to reside, heavy taxes and high customs duties were levied on their communities in exchange for the privilege of living under the ruler's protection. Offering gifts and other favors so as to reduce those taxes or customs duties was a common practice.

The response introduces the readers to Jewish contract law and demonstrates some interesting aspects of the Sages' attitudes towards obligatory contracts and breach of agreements. Had Antonio in *The Merchant of Venice* studied Jewish law, he would have been able to tell Shylock and the Venetian court that in Jewish law the principle of *pacta sunt servanda* (agreements must be kept) is not sacrosanct, and Antonio's agreement to Shylock's stipulation in the event that he cannot repay the loan would have been considered *asmakhta*, a type of conditional contract that would not be upheld in a Jewish religious court of law.

3. Are You Calling Me a Heretic?!: *Zᶜqan Aharon* 25 (authored by R. Elijah ben Benjamin Ha-Levi, 1481–after 1540)

When Spanish and Portuguese Jewish exiles arrived in Constantinople (Istanbul) following the expulsions from Spain and Portugal, they found an established, thriving and intellectual community of Romaniot Jews, Greek-speaking Jews who lived under Byzantine rule. When the Romaniot rabbi Ha-Levi, a member of the highest rabbinical court in the city, and, following the death of R. Elijah Mizraḥi in c.1526, the head of that rabbinical court, was asked about a man who is derided because of his study of philosophy, he not only comes to the man's defense, but to the defense of all those Jewish scholars who came before him, maintaining that such was always the Jewish tradition, from Talmudic times.

There is no indication of whether the plaintiff and defendant in the case were of Iberian origins or Romaniot (or one of each, possibly playing out some cultural conflict), but the tragedy of the expulsion was in his mind when Ha-Levi wrote his response. This responsum provides a fascinating view of the cultural life of Jews in the Ottoman Empire, where so many of the exiles found refuge, and serves as a springboard for discussion about the centuries-old tension between secular knowledge and religion.

4. Families Torn Apart: R. Moses ben Joseph di Trani (1500–1580) Responsum 1,142

This responsum tells of a family that was torn apart in the upheavals of the expulsion of the Jews from Iberia. Some family members chose to stay in Iberia or return there and live as Christians. Some returned to their Jewish faith in the Ottoman Empire. How does such a divide affect familial relationships? How does this affect inheritance of family property? In preparation for reading this responsum, inheritance laws, laws about a last will and testament, and legal loopholes in Jewish law will be explored.

5. What's in a Name?: R. Samuel de Medina (1506–1589) Responsum Yo-re De'a 199

A Portuguese Jew who was a former converso and now resides in the Ottoman Empire inquires about the use of his Christian name in correspondence with business connections and family who are located in Iberia. His concern is that the appearance of his Jewish name in any correspondence might endanger the recipient, or his own property being managed there. Does the use of his Christian name indicate a lack of loyalty to his Jewish faith? This is a simple, but touching, question about a Jew's identity and the travails of life under the Inquisition. Though the halakhic aspects are marginal (so that the chapter requires only a brief Halakhic Background), and the response could have been trivial, de Medina responds with gravity, respect for the questioner, and ample halakhic sources so as not to dismiss the question lightly. The discussion touches on some ethical questions that arise in the response and on questions of Jewish names and Jewish identity.

6. Is your Blood Any Redder? The Case of an Informer in the Venetian Inquisition: R. Solomon ben Abraham Ha-Kohen (c.1520–c.1601) Responsum 4,31

The responsum to be studied in this chapter—which relates events that took place in Venice—is fascinating from a historical perspective because it corroborates one of the trial records, or *processi*, from the Venetian Inquisition. The details of the case presented in a question to Ha-Kohen of Salonica are so consistent with the Inquisition records for the case of someone by the name of Filippo de Nis, who informed on the physicians who circumcised him and his nephew, that there can be little doubt that this responsum is in fact an epilogue to the de Nis case.

The texts upon which Ha-Kohen relies in his halakhic discussion include some of the most foundational and classic writings in Jewish ethics, which address moral questions that are frequently raised and debated in courses on the philosophy of law, political philosophy, and similar fields.

7. Excommunication in Amsterdam: Baḥ (*Ha-Yᵉshanot*) 5 (authored by R. Joel Sirkes, 1561–1640)

Towards the end of the sixteenth century, the Netherlands enjoyed a relatively tolerant atmosphere and offered economic opportunity. As such, it became a haven to descendants of Jews who were expelled from Spain and Portugal, or who became conversos, and to Crypto-Jews from Portugal who wished to return to Judaism in a society that would tolerate them.

The responsum deals with an unnamed physician in the Amsterdam community who is accused of holding heretical views and of giving permission to an (allegedly) unqualified man to serve as a ritual slaughterer. The possible outcome is shunning and excommunication of the accused. The fact that the dispute is addressed by R. Sirkes is of interest, as well, considering that he is an Ashkenazi rabbi situated in Poland.

8. South of the Equator, in the New World: *Torat Ḥayyim* 3,3 (authored by R. Ḥayyim Shabbetai, before 1555–1647)

Though the Netherlands became a haven to Jews and descendants of Jews, some felt compelled to emigrate from there to Brazil in the early seventeenth century.

The traditional liturgy regarding rainfall in the thrice-daily prayer assumes that the seasons occur according to the northern hemisphere, in particular the Middle East. Shabbetai was asked to respond to a liturgical question about these prayers from Jews who are in locations that were not even known to the Sages.

This responsum is also of interest because it is the first known responsum sent from the New World, and is one indication of the Jewish character of this new community. Though the Recife community was disbanded, R. Shabbetai's responsum would serve as a resource when other Jewish communities arose south of the equator.

Notes on Translation, Transliteration, and Citations

The translations are my own, other than most of the translations of verses from the Bible, which are usually from one of the JPS translations or the Jerusalem Bible,[6] according to the most suitable interpretation. However, sometimes the translations are my own. Biblical citations are in parentheses and are always an addition to the author's original text (he assumed the reader would know where the text is from). In the English, words in square brackets are explanatory insertions or fill in omissions made by the author of the responsum. (If omissions in quotations are not critical to understanding the responsum, an ellipsis indicates that the rabbi himself omitted some of the original text.) In the Hebrew texts, acronyms and words abbreviated by apostrophes are spelled out in square brackets.

The responsa often have nested quotes. For example, the author of the responsum cites a selection from the Talmud that, in turn, contains a quote. To reduce confusing nests of quotation marks in the translations, biblical quotations are in italics and Talmudic quotes are in a sans serif font, without quotation marks. For example:

> [There is] proof in what [is found] in chapter "The gold" [*Bava Mᵉtsi'a* 58b]: *Do not defraud one another* (Lev. 25:17)—the text refers to [defrauding] by insulting words. [... How?] Do not say [to a penitent] "remember your previous deeds."

And:

> The essence of this matter is [found] in *Bava Batra* chapter "Partners" [3a]. We say there: R. Yoḥanan said: "Our mishna is [the case of a courtyard] when it is not subject to the law of division," but if it is subject to the law of division, even though they do not want [i.e., agree] to divide [the courtyard], they divide [it].

For Talmudic Sages, I use common spellings rather than strict transliterations. Names and dates of post-Talmudic rabbinic figures are given in accordance with the *Encyclopaedia Judaica*, 2nd ed. (EJ),[7] or, if the name does not appear there, with the *Jewish Encyclopedia* of 1906.[8]

Transliteration conventions follow the *SBL Handbook of Style*,[9] with some exceptions.

---

6   Jewish Publication Society (Philadelphia, 1955 and 1962) and The Jerusalem Bible (Jerusalem: Koren, 1992).
7   Michael Berenbaum and Fred Skolnik, eds. *Encylcopaedia Judaica*, 22 vols., 2nd ed. (Detroit: Macmillan Reference, 2007).
8   Isidore Singer et al., eds., *The Jewish Encyclopedia*, 12 vols. (New York: Funk & Wagnalls, 1906).
9   *The SBL Handbook of Style*, 2nd ed. (Atlanta: SBL Press, 2014).

Source Texts

The following editions are used for the source texts:

Mishna:[10] MS Kaufmann A 50[11] (with numbering according to the common printed editions).

Babylonian Talmud (BT): Vilna edition, with some significant variants noted. The Friedberg Project for Talmud Bavli Variants is relied on for comparison with manuscripts and early printed editions. Tractates referenced with no indication of which Talmud are from the Babylonian Talmud.

Jerusalem Talmud (JT): *Talmud Yerushalmi* (Jerusalem: Academy of the Hebrew Language, 2016). This edition is according to the MS Leiden Or. 4720. The convention for citation is tractate chapter:halakha (page column), such as JT M^egilla 3:2 (74a).

R. Asher ben Jehiel (on BT): Vilna edition.

Maimonides, *Mishne Torah*: Yitzhak Shilat, *Rambam M^eduyyaq* (Maale Adumim: M^ekhon Ma'aliyot and Shilat, 2004-2018) for all the volumes that have been published. For those volumes that have not yet been published: Maimonides, *Mishne Torah*: Yosef Qafiḥ (Qiryat Ono: M^ekhon Mishnat Ha-Rambam, 1984–1996).

R. David ben Solomon ibn Abi Zimra Responsum 1,398: Venice, 1749 (first printing of this volume), with a few very minor obvious errors corrected. No discrepancies of any significance are found between that and the more accessible Warsaw, 1882 edition.

R. Joseph ibn Lev Responsum 4,14: Amsterdam, 1726. In addition, the editions published in Kuru Tshesme (near Constantinople) (1597), Venice (1606), and Fuerth (1692) were used to resolve some corruptions in the text.

R. Elijah ben Benjamin Ha-Levi, *Z^eqan Aharon* 25: Constantinople, 1734, with a few minor corrections.

R. Moses ben Joseph di Trani Responsum 1,142: Venice, 1629, with a few very minor obvious typographical errors corrected.

R. Samuel de Medina *Yore De'a* 199: Salonica, 1594-1598, with a few minor obvious typographical errors corrected.

R. Solomon ben Abraham Ha-Kohen Responsum 4,31: Salonica, 1730 printing, with a few very minor obvious typographical errors corrected.

---

10 The word Mishna with an uppercase M refers to the entire code—all six "orders." The word *mishna* with a lowercase *m* refers to one unit of law in the Mishna. One *mishna* (pl. *mishnayot*) may contain several halakhic statements or opinions.

11 Considered to be one of the most reliable extant manuscripts of the Mishna.

R. Joel Sirkes Responsum (*Ha-Yᵉshanot*) 5: Frankfurt-am-Main, 1697, which is the first printed edition of this collection of responsa. I made some minor corrections to what are obvious typographical errors. In the Frankfurt edition, the responsum number is 4, but the number 5 is in accordance with the more ubiquitous photo offsets of the Ostrog 1834 edition (such as New York, 1966).

R. Ḥayyim Shabbetai, *Torat Ḥayyim* 3,3: Salonica, 1722 printing, with a few obvious errors corrected.

R. Asher ben Jehiel (Rosh) 4,10: Yitshak Yudlov, ed. (Jerusalem: Machon Yerushalayim, 1993). (This responsum is included in the Halakhic Background for the previous one in this list.)

Glossary

Some commonly used terms:

Amora'im (sg.: *amora*) Sages in the Talmud during the time after the compilation of the Mishna.

bar (Aramaic), ben (Hebrew) "the son of."

baraita Tannaitic text that is not in the Mishna.

gᵉmara The portion of the Talmud that is the discussion and elaboration of each *mishna* by the Amora'im.

Geonim (sg.: Gaon) The heads of the academies in Babylonia, recognized as the highest halakhic authorities approximately between the end of the sixth century to the middle of the eleventh century.

Rishonim (lit., "first ones") The name given to medieval Jewish scholars who lived after the Geonim approximately up to the time of R. Joseph Caro (1488–1575), author of the *Shulḥan ʿArukh*.

Tanna'im (sg.: *tanna*) Sages from the period of Hillel until the compilation of the Mishna, from about 20–200 CE.

Abbreviations

BT Babylonian Talmud
EH Even Ha-ʿezer
ḤM Ḥoshen Mishpat
JT Jerusalem (Palestinian) Talmud
MT Mishne Torah (authored by Maimonides)
OḤ Oraḥ Ḥayyim
SA Shulḥan ʿArukh (authored by R. Joseph Caro)
YD Yo-re Deʿa

Further Reading

[Beinart] Beinart, Haim. *The Expulsion of the Jews from Spain*. Portland: Littman Library of Jewish Civilization, 2002.

[Marx] Marx, Alexander. "The Expulsion of the Jews from Spain" *Jewish Quarterly Review* 20, no. 2 (January 1908): 240-271.

[Marx2] ———. "The Expulsion of the Jews from Spain (Additions and Corrections to "JQR.", XX, 240-71)." *Jewish Quarterly Review*, n.s. 2, no. 2 (October 1911): 257-258.

[Perez] Perez, Joseph. *History of a Tragedy: The Expulsion of the Jews from Spain*. Urbana: University of Illinois Press, 2007.

[Ray] Ray, Jonathan. *After Expulsion: 1492 and the Making of Sephardic Jewry*. New York: New York University Press, 2012.

[Soyer] Soyer, François. *The Persecution of the Jews and Muslims of Portugal: King Manuel I and the End of Religious Tolerance (1496–7)*. Leiden: Brill, 2007.

On Excommunication

Introduction

This brief preparatory chapter explores the concepts of *niddui* (shunning) and *ḥerem* (excommunication),[1] and the halakhic basis for this method of punishment in Jewish communities.

> The most effective punishment and method of enforcement wielded by the Jewish communal authorities was excommunication. ... There were two forms of excommunication: the milder form was known as *niddui*, and the more severe type as *ḥerem*. The severity of each type again differed in degree according to the culpability of the offender. When the ban of *niddui* was imposed on a guilty person ... no one was to speak or deal with him for a period ranging in duration from seven to thirty days. When the ban was more rigorous, the following penalties were imposed: the culprit was required to change his permanent seat in the synagogue and was denied the honor of being called up to the Torah; for a period of a number of years he was not to be counted in the quorum of three that is necessary for grace after meals, nor in the quorum of ten worshippers that constitute a congregation... After this came the most rigorous form of the ban, the *ḥerem*, a solemn anathema of indefinite duration. The penalties of the *ḥerem* usually required that the culprit be completely isolated from his fellow Jews. ... Like a heathen, his bread and wine were forbidden. He was denied burial in a Jewish cemetery, and no one was to perform the ceremony of circumcision on his children. ... The severity of the ban was determined by the nature of the offense.[2]

---

1   These are both forms of excommunication. Though there is a technical distinction, at times the terms are used interchangeably. The Aramaic *shamta* (excommunication) is sometimes used to mean *niddui*.

2   Morris Goodblatt, *Jewish Life in Turkey in the XVIth Century as Reflected in the Legal Writings of Samuel De Medina* (New York: Jewish Theological Seminary of America, 1952), 88-89. See 88-90 for further discussion of these forms of punishment. See also [Kaplan], 115. Kaplan states: "It does not appear to me that, in imposing excommunications the leaders of the Portuguese Jewish community in Amsterdam distinguished among the various stages of *nidui*, *ḥerem* and *shamta*" (139n78).

In several of the responsa in this book, this type of punishment is proposed for the defendant in the case under discussion. However, it is not really what the author of the responsum is seeking. Rather, he is seeking some kind of reconciliation or compromise, and hoping that the threat of shunning or excommunication will bring this about.

Halakhic Background

Selections from the Talmud, the Rishonim and the halakhic codes elucidate the halakhic basis of excommunication and the views of the Sages on such punishment.

In *Mo'ed Qatan*, a discussion about the suspension of mourning customs for a mourner during a festival (including the intermediary days) leads to a question about whether shunning is suspended during these days; Rav Yosef concludes, using an a fortiori argument, that it is not. From this brief excerpt we learn that excommunication was a method used to enforce a court decision.

Mo'ed Qatan 14b	מועד קטן י"ד ב'

A mourner does not observe the mourning customs during a festival, as it says *You shall rejoice in your feast* (Deut. 16:14). ... [Regarding] one who is shunned—should he abide by [the restrictions of] his shunning during the festival? Rav Yosef said: "Come and hear:[3] 'Capital cases, [offenses subject to] flogging, and monetary cases are judged [during the festival].' And if he does not heed the [court's] ruling, we excommunicate him [even during the festival].[4] If you would think that one is not [obligated to] abide by the restrictions of shunning during the festival, [so that] the festival comes [and] suspends for one who is already excommunicated [from before the festival], would we excommunicate someone [during the festival]?!"[5]

אבל אינו נוהג אבילותו ברגל שנאמר ושמחת בחגך ... מנודה מהו שינהוג נידויו ברגל אמר רב יוסף תא שמע דנין דיני נפשות ודיני מכות ודיני ממונות ואי לא ציית דינא משמתינן ליה ואי סלקא דעתך אינו נוהג נידויו ברגל משומת ואתי מעיקרא אתי רגל דחי ליה השתא משמתינן ליה אנן

---

3 The expression *ta sh'ma'* introduces a Tannaitic source.

4 Scriptural allusion for this practice is offered in *Mo'ed Qatan* 16a: And from where [do we know] that we shun [one who refuses to appear in court]? As it is written: *Curse Meroz* (Jud. 5:23) [who did not come to aid].... And from where [do we know] that we excommunicate? As it is written: *bitterly curse* (ibid.).

5 So, concludes Rav Yosef, since we do have the option to excommunicate during the festival, a fortiori it must be that the festival does not suspend the excommunication.

The following statement, also from *Mo'ed Qatan*, gives some details about the procedure.

Mo'ed Qatan 16a	מועד קטן ט"ז א'
Rav Yehuda, the son of Rav Shmuel bar Shelat [said] in the name of Rav: "We immediately shun [one who refuses to appear in court] and repeat this after thirty days, and excommunicate him after sixty."	אמר רב יהודה בריה דרב שמואל בר שילת משמיה דרב מנדין לאלתר ושונין לאחר שלשים ומחרימין לאחר ששים

Rulings by Maimonides, based on several pages in *Mo'ed Qatan*, fill in some details.

Maimonides *MT Hilkhot Talmud Torah* (The Laws of Torah Study) 7	רמב"ם משנה תורה הלכות תלמוד תורה ז
4 What is the practice that one who is shunned [must] observe himself, and what practice is done to him [by others]? A person who is shunned is forbidden to cut his hair or launder his clothes, like a mourner, all the days of his ostracism. He is not included in the quorum of three for the grace after meals, and he is not included in the quorum of ten for any matter that requires ten.[6] One should not sit within four cubits of him. But he [may] teach others, and they may teach him; he [may be] hired and hire [others]. If he dies	ד מה הוא המנהג שינהוג המנודה בעצמו ושנוהגין עמו, מנודה אסור לספר ולכבס כאבל כל ימי נידויו, ואין מזמנין עליו, ולא כוללין אותו בעשרה לכל דבר שצריך עשרה, ולא יושבין עימו בארבע אמות. אבל שונה הוא לאחרים, ושונין לו, ונשכר, ושוכר. ואם מת בנידויו, בית דין שולחין ומניחין אבן על ארונו, כלומר שהן רוגמין אותו, לפי שהוא מובדל מן הציבור. ואין צריך לומר שאין מספידין אותו, ואין מלוין את מיטתו:

while in his state of shunning, the religious court sends and places a stone on his coffin, that is to say, they stone him, because he separated from the community. Needless to say, he is not eulogized, nor is his bier accompanied.

---

6 Such as public reading of the Torah, or public repetition of the silent prayer.

5 One who is excommunicated [has] more stringent [restrictions] than him. He may not teach others, nor may they teach him, but he [is permitted] to teach himself so that he will not forget what he has learned. He may not be hired, and he may not hire [others]. It is not [permitted] to trade or do business with him, but only a small amount of business for his livelihood.

6 One who remains ostracized for thirty days and does not request a release from shunning [by appearing in court, as required] is shunned a second time. If he remains another thirty days and does not request a release, he is excommunicated.[7]

ה יתר עליו המוחרם, שאינו שונה לאחרים, ואין שונין לו, אבל שונה הוא לעצמו כדי שלא ישכח תלמודו, ואינו נשכר, ואין נשכרין לו, ואין נושאין ונותנין עמו, ואין מתעסקין עמו אלא מעט עסק כדי פרנסתו:

ו מי שישב בנידויו שלשים יום ולא ביקש להתירו, מנדין אותו שנייה. ישב שלושים יום אחרים ולא ביקש להתירו, מחרימין אותו:

The following passage from *Mo'ed Qatan* (cited in the responsum in "Excommunication in Amsterdam") elucidates a further application of shunning and excommunication: making certain that scholars adhere to the standard of behavior expected of them.

Mo'ed Qatan 17a   מועד קטן י״ז א׳

There was once a young scholar about whom bad word was going around. Said Rav Yehuda [bar Ezekiel]: "What shall be done in this case? Shall we excommunicate him? The rabbis need him! But if we do not excommunicate him, the name of Heaven will be desecrated!" ... Rav Huna said: "It was enacted in Usha that if the head of a court should sin,[8] [the first time] he should not be shunned, but only be told: *Be dignified and stay at home.* (2 Kings 14:10)

ההוא צורבא מרבנן דהוו סנו שומעניה אמר רב יהודה היכי ליעביד לשמתיה צריכי ליה רבנן לא לשמתיה קא מיתחיל שמא דשמיא ... אמר רב הונא באושא התקינו אב בית דין שסרח אין מנדין אותו אלא אומר לו הכבד ושב בביתך

---

7   This is how Maimonides interprets "sixty" in the statement attributed to Rav in *Mo'ed Qatan* 16a.

8   Lit., "stank" in a manner deserving of shunning or excommunication.

But if he sins a second time, he should be shunned, lest the name of Heaven be desecrated." This is not in accordance with the following statement of Resh Laqish:[9] "A scholar who sins is not shunned publicly, for it is written: *Therefore shalt thou stumble in the daytime, and the prophet also shall stumble with thee in the night* (Hosea 4:5), [which means] cover him as the night."[10] When a young scholar was deserving of excommunication, Mar Zutra the Pious first put himself under excommunication and then the young scholar. When he [Mar Zutra] entered his residence, he first absolved himself and then the young scholar. Rav Giddel said in the name of Rav: "A scholar may first make himself shunned and afterward absolve himself from it." Said Rav Pappa: "[Perhaps] I am deserving [of a reward from God], for I have never excommunicated a young scholar." Rather, when a young scholar was deserving of excommunication, what did he do? Like what they did in the West:[11] they would vote [and decide] to give lashes[12] to young scholars [who sinned]; and they did not opt to excommunicate them.

חזר וסרח מנדין אותו מפני חילול השם ופליגא דריש לקיש דאמר ריש לקיש תלמיד חכם שסרח אין מנדין אותו בפרהסיא שנאמר וכשלת היום וכשל גם נביא עמך לילה כסהו כלילה מר זוטרא חסידא כי מיחייב צורבא מרבנן שמתא ברישא משמית נפשיה והדר משמית לדידיה כי הוה עייל באושפיזיה שרי ליה לנפשיה והדר שרי ליה לדידיה אמר רב גידל אמר רב תלמיד חכם מנדה לעצמו ומיפר לעצמו אמר רב פפא תיתי לי דלא שמיתי צורבא מרבנן מעולם אלא כי קא מיחייב צורבא מרבנן שמתא היכי עביד כי הא דבמערבא מימנו אנגידא דצורבא מרבנן ולא מימנו אשמתא

It is not clear from the previous passage what the inappropriate behavior might be, but the following commentary from R. Asher ben Jehiel (Rosh)[13] explains.

---

9   Shimon ben Laqish.
10 Just as the darkness of night keeps things hidden, the sins of a scholar should not be made public.
11 I.e., the Land of Israel (west, from the perspective of Rav Pappa, who lived in Babylon).
12 See discussion for an elaboration.
13 C. 1250–1327.

Rosh *Mo'ed Qatan* 3:11 — רא״ש מסכת מועד קטן ג׳ י״א

"There was once a young scholar about whom bad word was going around."—Rashi explained[14] that because of him "the name of Heaven was desecrated," such as what we learn in chapter "The Day of Atonement" [*Yoma* 86a]: What is the case of profanation of the name of Heaven? [...] Anything for which his friends are embarrassed by what is being said about him, [... or] such [things] as [make] people say 'may God forgive him,' or such [behavior] as [that of] Elisha Aḥer[15] who engaged himself with heretical books, and [frequented places] with drink and improper song; and all young scholars who act such are called "those about whom a bad word is going around."

ההוא צורבא מדרבנן דהוו סנו שומעניה פרש״י [פירש רש״י] שהיה שם שמים מתחלל על ידו כגון הא דגרסי׳[נן] בפרק יום הכפורים היכי דמי חילול השם כל שחביריו מתביישים משמועתו או דקא אמרי אינשי שרא ליה מרא לפלניא וכגון אלישע אחר שהיה מתעסק בספרי מינין ושותה במיני זמר וכל צורבא מדרבנן דהכי עובדיה מיתקרי סנו שומעניה

The previous two selections are codified in the *Shulḥan 'Arukh* as follows:

Shulḥan 'Arukh YD 334:42 — שולחן ערוך יורה דעה של״ד מ״ב

A scholar, a wise elder, or a head of a court who sinned is never publicly shunned, unless he behaved like Jeroboam, son of Nebat,[16] and his cohorts. But if he [the scholar, etc.] sinned any other sin, he is given lashes in private. Similarly, for any Torah scholar who is deserving of shunning, it is forbidden for the court to jump quickly to shun him; rather they should flee and stay away from him. The righteous among the Sages were proud of

חכם, זקן בחכמה, או אב בית דין שסרח, אין מנדין אותו בפרהסיא לעולם, אלא אם כן עשה כירבעם בן נבט וחביריו. אבל כשחטא שאר חטאות, מלקין אותו בצינעא. וכן כל ת״ח [תלמיד חכם] שנתחייב נידוי, אסור לב״ד [לבית דין] לקפוץ ולנדותו במהרה, אלא בורחים ונשמטים ממנו. וחסידי החכמים היו משתבחים שלא

---

14 *Yoma* 86a at *be'emor lahem*.

15 Elisha ben Avuya, known as Aḥer (other), was a scholar who adopted views considered heretical by the Sages.

16 Jeroboam not only sinned, but led others to sin; see 1 Kings 12:25-33.

themselves for never deciding to shun a Torah scholar, even though they might decide he deserved lashes or a blow for rebelliousness. But if a bad word is heard [about the scholar, etc.], such as [that] he engages himself with heretical books or [frequents places] with drink and improper song, or that his friends are ashamed of him and by his actions the name of Heaven is desecrated, then he is excommunicated.

נמנו מעולם לנדות תלמיד חכם, ואף ע״פ [על פי] שנמנים להלקותו אם נתחייב מלקות או מכת מרדות. ואי סני שומעניה כגון שמתעסק בספרי אפיקורוסין ושותה במיני זמר, או שחביריו מתביישין ממנו ושם שמים מתחלל על ידו, משמתינן ליה.

Discussion

This last passage from the Talmud suggests that lashes could be applied instead of excommunication, and that flogging was considered preferable by some Sages. The flogging in this context would be *makkat mardut*, a blow for rebelliousness, as the inappropriate behavior is not a Toraitic transgression, rather than the Toraitic punishment of thirty-nine lashes, for such sins as eating carrion.[17]

As difficult as the concept of corporal punishment might be to us, particularly when it is being applied to enforce religious law, in the minds of the Sages these punishments were never meant to be cruel, uncontrolled violence, but rather to keep the wayward from sinning.

Questions for Further Discussion

Should scholars (or budding scholars) be held to a different standard than other members of a community? If scholars are deserving of punishment, should their punishment be different from that of other community members? If so, should it be stricter or more lenient?

Discuss the ruling of the *Shulḥan ʿArukh YD* 334:42, quoted above. Compare it with the excerpt from *Moʿed Qatan* 17a. Would you have ruled the same way, based on that selection?

Try to imagine yourself in the time of the Sages, or perhaps even one thousand or five hundred years ago. Which seems harsher to the person considered wayward—excommunication or flogging?

---

17   See Deut. 25:3. From Mishna *Makkot* 3:10-11, it is clear that the Sages understood that the Toraitic punishment of flogging should never be lethal. Corporal or capital punishment for transgression of Torah law was not applicable unless there were two witnesses to the transgression, who warned the offender before the transgression was committed, informing them of the punishment to which they would be subject, and the offender responded to the warning by saying, "Nevertheless, I will do it." Only then would such a punishment be inflicted.

Why do you think the rabbis in the autonomous Jewish courts relied on excommunication as a method to either enforce their judgments or to inflict punishment? You may wish to read [Kaplan], in which the author discusses the applications of excommunication in Amsterdam in the period beginning shortly after the events in the responsum in "Excommunication in Amsterdam."[18]

Further Reading

[Kaplan] Kaplan, Yosef. "The Social Functions of the *Herem* in the Portuguese Jewish Community of Amsterdam in the Seventeenth Century." In *Dutch Jewish History, Proceedings of the Symposium on the History of the Jews in the Netherlands*, edited by Jozeph Michman, 111-155. Jerusalem: Institute for Research on Dutch Jewry, 1984.

---

18 Though Kaplan focuses on a particular community in a particular time frame, excommunication was also used in Ashkenazi Jewish communities. See Moshe Greenberg and Haim Hermann Cohn, "Ḥerem," in EJ, 9:10-16, particularly the section "In Post-Talmudic Law."

1.
Divorce out of Love: A Sixteenth-Century Woman's Story

Rabbi David ben Solomon ibn Abi Zimra
Responsum 1,398

Historical Background

The responsum to be studied in this chapter, written by R. David ben Solomon ibn Abi Zimra,[1] revolves around the plight of a woman in Jerusalem around the turn of the sixteenth century. Her husband, who has disappeared, had sent her a *get*, a writ of divorce, but the document has been lost, and the woman wants to know if she is now allowed to remarry.

The woman, Hanna, describes how her husband, who was traveling, had sent her a *get* by messenger, but the *get* was lost when she fled into exile. She had thought this left her an *'aguna*,[2] but now she wishes to know whether she may nevertheless be free to remarry. She brought her question regarding her marital status to the rabbinic authorities—the *ḥakhamim*[3]—of Jerusalem, who deliberated it and then sent it on to Abi Zimra.

Though the responsum is not dated by its author, we can fairly closely estimate the year it was written and when the events described in it took place. Based on her recounting of the events that led to her situation, the woman arrived in Jerusalem sometime after the expulsion from Spain (1492) or Portugal (1497).[4]

---

1   Known by the acronym Radbaz, 1479–1573.
2   Pl. *'agunot*; lit., an anchored or chained woman. This is the halakhic term for a woman who is not allowed to remarry, whether because her husband has disappeared and his death cannot be verified or because her husband refuses to grant her a divorce.
3   The term *ḥakham* is used throughout the responsum, as is common in the Sephardi communities, rather than the term *rav*, which is used in the Ashkenazi communities.
4   See introduction, note 1.

Her husband left "to bring citrons"⁵ and sent her the *get* by messenger, all before her expulsion. When the *get* was presented to her, she was told that she must wait four years before remarrying, but those four years were not completed before she was expelled (and subsequently lost the *get*), which would imply that the *get* was presented to her not earlier than approximately 1488. When she relates the events, after she is in Jerusalem, she states that more than ten years have passed since she received her *get*, which would mean that it must have been around 1500 when the question was sent to Abi Zimra, or perhaps a few years later, allowing for the deliberations that took place among the authorities in Jerusalem before the question was sent to him.

In 1500 Abi Zimra was a young man, situated most likely in Safed, but perhaps in Jerusalem.⁶ However, he already was a recognized scholar; by the time he arrived in Egypt (in approximately 1514) he was appointed to the court of the Nagid, the highest Jewish judicial court in Egypt. Therefore we can say that at the time that Abi Zimra wrote this responsum, he and the woman in question were living under the rule of the Mamluk sultanate, shortly before its conquest by the Ottomans in 1516.

Halakhic Background

The details surrounding the presentation of the *get* are not certain, and the only witness is the woman herself, whose voice we hear in the question. Because of the complexity of her case, the responsum presents a microcosm of the laws of *gittin*:⁷ divorce by proxy,⁸ conditional divorce, a woman's testimony about her marital status and requirements of the *get* itself. All these laws come into play.

There is a question whether the divorce the woman was given was conditional, and therefore it is important to become acquainted with the laws of con-

---

5   Presumably, he brought the citrons from Spain, Portugal, or another Mediterranean country where citrons grow, to a more northern Jewish community to sell them (for Sukkot). The husband may have gone to one of the Ashkenazi Jewish communities in the Holy Roman Empire, or perhaps in Lithuania or Poland. We learn in the responsum that it was known to the parties involved that the *get* was written by a court where Ashkenazi custom prevailed and was delivered according to that custom.

6   Abi Zimra left Spain with his family in 1492. By the age of thirteen he and his family were living in Safed. He later moved to Jerusalem, but by 1514 had moved to Egypt, where he spent forty years before returning to the Land of Israel.

7   Plural of *get*.

8   Divorce by messenger, like any transaction by messenger, is based on the legal principle of "a man's agent is like himself" (*shʿluḥo shel adam kʿmoto*). For further discussion of this principle, see Rakover, Nahum and Michael Wygoda, "Agency," in EJ, 1:449-454.

ditional divorce. There is also a problem in that the woman lost her *get*, and so we need to consider the laws of a woman whose *get* is lost and, in particular, the laws relating to a woman's testimony about her marital status.

As in other legal systems, such as Roman law,[9] Jewish law provides for conditional contracts, including conditional betrothal or divorce. Divorce, however, is substantially different from other conditional agreements, in that, until the ordinance (*taqqana*) of Rabbenu Gershom at the turn of the eleventh century,[10] it could be unilateral. A man could divorce his wife, whether she agreed to it or not, and he could impose conditions on the divorce, whether she agreed to them or not. For example, he could say: "This is your *get* from this moment under the condition that I do not return within one year from now."[11] However, in many cases, the conditions might have been agreed to by the wife, such as "this is your *get* under the condition that you give me two hundred *zuz*."[12]

Many conditional divorces were initiated when husbands traveled far from home, went to war, were entering some other dangerous circumstance, or were in danger of dying from a serious illness. The husband did not really want to divorce his wife, nor did the woman want to be divorced, but wished to avoid the pitfalls of *'iggun* (the state of being an *'aguna*) or, if widowed, either levirate marriage[13] or *ḥalitsa*.[14] Because the couple did not really want to divorce, making the divorce conditional meant that the divorce would only be in effect if the unfortunate scenario took place. If the husband recovered from the illness, or if he returned from the front or from overseas within the specified time, then the divorce would not take effect.

Though the responsa literature is replete with cases of conditional divorce, the Ashkenazi rabbis, apparently around the thirteenth and fourteenth centuries, began to view the practice with disfavor. They preferred an absolute divorce, even

---

9   On conditional contracts in Roman law, see [Stein].
10 This decree, which included a prohibition to divorce a woman against her will, was only binding on Ashkenazic communities.
11 *Gittin* 76b.
12 *Gittin* 74a. A *zuz* is a silver coin, also called a dinar, and equal to 1/25 of a gold dinar.
13 Maimonides wrote: "It is beneficial to most women not to be subject to levirate marriage" (*MT Hilkhot Gerushin* [The Laws of Divorce] 9,21, based on *Yᵉvamot* 118b).
14 *Ḥalitsa* is the rite for release of a widow whose deceased husband has no living descendants from the obligation to marry her brother-in-law. The word refers to her removal of his sandal, as described in Deut. 25:7-10.

when the hope was for husband and wife to be reunited. R. Perez of Corbeil[15] wrote in his glosses on the *Sefer Mitsvot Qatan* (184:9): "My teacher, our Rabbi Jehiel [of Paris][16] would usually require with the *get* of a critically ill husband that he divorce absolutely, without any condition, so as to relieve him of any doubt or hesitation. However, he would require that they [the husband and wife] accept the ordinance of the communities, enforceable by excommunication[17] (*ḥerem*), that he remarry her as soon as he recovered."

R. Jehiel's requirement is not referred to here as an ordinance (*taqqana*),[18] and it is mentioned specifically in connection with a divorce given by a critically ill husband. However, the term *taqqana* is used in later references to R. Jehiel's practice.[19] In the codes, the context of this practice is specified as that of a *get* given by a critically ill husband.[20] However, it seems that in the fifteenth and sixteenth centuries there was disagreement in the Ashkenazi communities as to whether or not the same practice should be applied to all cases of a *get* written to avoid problems of *'iggun* or levirate marriage.[21] Modern responsa attest that unconditional divorce in such cases became the norm in Ashkenazi practice.[22]

With the "ordinance of the communities," a wife could not be expected to wait indefinitely for her former husband to return to remarry him (otherwise, she was being asked to live as though she were an *'aguna*, though in actuality she

---

15 D. 1295.

16 D. c. 1265.

17 For Halakhic Background and discussion of this form of enforcement, see the chapter "On Excommunication."

18 Which would be more authoritative and binding.

19 See R. Samuel Edels (known as Maharsha, 1555–1631), *Ḥiddushei Halakhot, Gittin* 90b, at *lᵉma'an yedᵉ'u ha-dorot*; R. Joel Sirkes (known as Baḥ, 1561–1640), *Bayit Ḥadash, EH* 145:4, at *vᵉdin*; and R. David ben Samuel Ha-Levi (known as Taz for his commentary, 1586–1667), *Turei Zahav, EH* 145:6.

20 *Bayit Ḥadash, EH* 145:4, at *vᵉdin* and 148:4, at *katav ba-Smaq*; R. Moses Isserles (known as Rma) *EH* 145:9; and R. Abraham Hirsch b. Jacob Eisenstadt (1812–1868), *Pitḥei Tᵉshuva, EH* 145:5.

21 And not only for a critically ill husband. See Menahem Mendel ben Abraham Krochmal, *Tsemaḥ Tsedeq Ha-Qadmon* 38, approving the application of R. Jehiel's "ordinance" to a case of a husband going to war and citing fifteenth- and sixteenth-century precedents. Edels (*Ḥiddushei Halakhot, Gittin* 90b, at *lᵉma'an yedᵉ'u ha-dorot*), too, understood the ordinance as applying not only to critically ill husbands.

22 See, e.g., R. Eliezer Waldenberg, *Tsits Eli'ezer* 15:57; and R. Joseph Elijah Henkin, "He'arot Nosafot 'Al Dᵉvar Gittin Linshei Ha-yotsᵉim La-milḥama," *Hapardes* 16, no. 2 (May 1942): 16-18.

was a divorcee). Some reasonable waiting period had to be defined, after which, if her former husband did not reappear, she was permitted to marry someone else.

In an actual thirteenth-century case, R. Elazar[23] of Verona[24] maintained that a woman who did not receive a *get*, but whose husband apparently had drowned without a trace in a shipwreck, was permitted to remarry, when, after four years, there was still no sign of him being alive. Though the Talmud's ruling would have forbidden the wife to remarry,[25] R. Elazar maintained that "forbidden" does not mean "forever forbidden" and four years was long enough for her to wait. He sought support for this assessment (*umdana*) from contemporaneous rabbis in the Rhine and Cologne communities, but they did not agree. R. Joseph Caro[26] also vehemently opposed R. Elazar's ruling. Several other authorities[27] were more inclined to a positive view of R. Elazar's ruling, but given all the opposition, were hesitant to rely solely on it.[28]

Nevertheless, R. Elazar's ruling has been cited many times in buttressing a complex argument to permit an *'aguna* to remarry.[29] In light of R. Elazar's assessment, four years would seem to be a reasonable number of years to expect a woman with an unconditional divorce to wait in case her former husband should return.[30]

Among the details of conditional divorce that the Sages and later authorities deliberated is the exact language that must be used when presenting the *get*. The

---

23 Often referred to as Eliezer.
24 And not Vardun, as appears in a commonly perpetuated mistake.
25 See Y*vamot* 121a.
26 *Bet Yosef, EH* 17.
27 R. Jacob Berav, *Mahari Berav* 13; R. Moses ben Joseph di Trani, *Mabit* 1,187.
28 See E. E. Urbach, *Ba'alei Ha-tosafot*, 2 vols., 6th ed. (Jerusalem: Bialik Institute, 1995), 1:433-435; also R. Isaac Herzog, *Heikhal Yitshak, EH* 1,23.
29 See, e.g., *Heikhal Yitshak, EH* 1,23; *Tsits Eli'ezer* 3,25 iv; and R. Ovadiah Yosef, *Yabia' Omer, EH* 6,4 §10 and 7,15 §12, citing many more examples.
30 See, e.g., R. Menahem Mendel Krochmal, *Tsemah Tsedeq Ha-Qadmon* 38; R. Jacob Isaiah Blau, *Ts*e*daqa U-mishpat, EH* 6; R. Ezekiel Landau, *Noda' BiYhuda Tinyana, EH* 47; R. Zevi Pesah Frank, *Har Ts*e*vi, EH* 65; *Heikhal Yitshak, EH* 2,1; and *Tsits Eli'ezer* 15,57. In some of these cases, less than four years sufficed; and in *Heikhal Yitshak, EH* 2:1, R. Herzog, writing around 1948, states that over twelve months in our time is equivalent to four years in R. Elazar's time. By contrast, in fifteenth-century Muslim society, conditional divorces could come into effect after an absence of as short as two months or even ten days; see [Rapoport2]: 34n167. However, the practice of using an unconditional divorce presents a difficulty for a *kohen*, a descendant of a priestly family, who may not marry a divorcee, even his own ex-wife (in the event that he returns), and so an exception is made for *kohanim*, who may use a conditional divorce (Rma *EH* 145:9).

validity of a *get* that is either written or presented improperly might later be called into question, which could have extremely serious consequences. If the woman has meanwhile remarried, she might be considered an unwitting adulteress, and the children of the second marriage would have the status of *mamzerim*.[31] The proper wording is further complicated when the *get* is delivered to the woman by proxy, as was the situation in the case presented to Abi Zimra.

These two topics—the laws of divorce by an agent and the laws of conditional divorce—are primarily, but not exclusively, discussed in the sixth and seventh chapters of tractate *Gittin*. However, the discourse in the Talmud leaves many details open to interpretation, so that we find among the Rishonim multiple opinions about the law. This may be why Abi Zimra does not cite directly from the Talmud when discussing the laws of conditional divorce. It is likely that Maimonides's *Mishne Torah*, the authoritative halakhic code at that time, had a strong influence on Abi Zimra's interpretation of the law. Therefore, we will rely on a selection of laws from *MT Hilkhot Ishut* (The Laws of Personal Status) and *MT Hilkhot Gerushin* (The Laws of Divorce) to present the background for issues of conditional divorce and divorce by proxy that shall be seen in the responsum. This selection of laws constitutes the first three sources in this section.

To consider the legal value of a woman's testimony about her own marital status, we will examine the Tannaitic legal principle "the mouth that prohibited is the mouth that permitted,"[32] that is, the court admits unverifiable testimony that simultaneously self-incriminates and exonerates the witness. The reasoning is that since this testimony is not verifiable—because there are no other witnesses or evidence—the witness could have remained silent if he wished to be deceitful.[33] So for example, if someone admits to a claimant in court, "This field was your father's, but I purchased it from him," he is believed, even though he does not have proof of purchase, in the event that the claimant has no proof that the

---

31 A *mamzer*, who is a person born of an incestuous relationship or a sexual relationship between a married woman and a Jewish man other than her husband, is allowed to marry only converts or other *mamzerim* (and their children would be *mamzerim*).

32 Lit., the mouth that bound is the [same] mouth that unbound. This principle also appears in Mishna *Dᵉmai* 6:11, *Kᵉtubbot* 2:2 and 2:5 and *ʿEduyyot* 3:6; Tosefta (Lieberman) *Dᵉmai* 1:4 and 1:6, *Maʿaser Sheni* 5:13, *Kᵉtubbot* 2:2, *Bava Mᵉtsiʿa* 1:10, and (Zukermandel) *Tohorot* 8:5.

33 The *gᵉmara* (*Kᵉtubbot* 22a) states that this principle is established by reason. The reasoning explained above—that the witness could have remained silent if he wished to be deceitful—is in accordance with the approach of the Tosafot (*Kᵉtubbot* 22a at *minayin*).

field did belong to his father.³⁴ After all, if the claimant accuses someone of stealing a field that the claimant maintains he inherited from his father, the person holding the field could just say, "Prove it"!

Abi Zimra cites application of this legal principle to a woman's testimony about her own marital status from *Kᵉtubbot*.

Maimonides *MT Hilkhot Gerushin* (The Laws of Divorce) 8	רמב״ם הלכות גירושין ח

1 One who divorces on condition—if the condition is upheld, then she is divorced, but if the condition is not upheld, she is not divorced. And we have already explained the laws of conditions in their entirety in chapter six of The Laws of Personal Status.³⁵ It is explained there that one who divorces on condition—when the condition is upheld, she is divorced at the time that it is upheld and not at the time that the divorce was placed in her hand. [...] But if the husband dies or the *get* was lost or burned before the condition is upheld, she is not divorced. [...] If he said to her, "You are divorced from now" or "From today, on this and this condition," or if he said to her, "Behold, you are divorced, under condition that such and such," once the condition is fulfilled, then she is divorced from the time that the *get* was placed in her hand. [...] If [the *get*] is lost or burned, [or] even if the husband dies before the condition is fulfilled, so that she fulfills the condition after his death, she is already divorced from the time the *get* was placed in her hand. [...]

א המגרש על תנאי, אם נתקיים התנאי הרי זו מגורשת, ואם לא נתקיים התנאי אינה מגורשת. וכבר בארנו בפרק ששי מהלכות אישות משפטי התנאין כולן. ושם נתבאר שהמגרש על תנאי כשיתקיים התנאי תהיה מגורשת בשעה שיתקיים לא בשעת נתינת הגט לידה. [...] ואם מת הבעל או אבד הגט או נשרף קודם שיתקיים התנאי אינה מגורשת. [...] שאם אמר לה הרי את מגורשת מעכשיו, או מהיום, על תנאי כך וכך, או שאמר לה הרי את מגורשת על מנת כך וכך, כשיתקיים התנאי תהיה מגורשת משעת נתינת הגט לידה. [...] ואם אבד או נשרף אפילו מת הבעל קודם שיתקיים התנאי, הרי זו מקיימת התנאי אחרי מותו, וכבר נתגרשה משעת נתינת הגט לידה. [...]

---

34   This case is presented in Mishna *Kᵉtubbot* 2:2.
35   An excerpt from *Hilkhot Ishut* (The Laws of Personal Status) will follow this excerpt.

3 How does one divorce on condition? He does not say, "Write a *get* for my wife on this condition," or "write and give her on condition," and it is needless to say that he should not write [the condition] in the *get*, [such as]: "On this condition so-and-so divorced so-and-so." Rather, how does he do it? He says to the scribe to write and to the witnesses to sign,[36] and they write a proper *get* without any condition in the world. Afterwards, he gives her the *get* and says to her: "Behold, this is your *get*" or "behold, you are divorced with this, on condition that such and such." Or, he should say to them [the scribe and witnesses] or to a messenger, "Give her this *get* with the condition that such and such."

ג כיצד מגרש אדם על תנאי, לא שיאמר כתבו גט לאשתי על תנאי, או כתבו ותנו לה על תנאי, ואין צריך לומר שלא יכתוב בתוך הגט על תנאי זה גירש פלוני את פלונית. אלא כיצד עושה, אומר לסופר לכתוב ולעדים לחתום, וכותבין גט כשר בלא שם תנאי בעולם. ואחר כך נותן לה הגט ואומר לה, הרי זה גטיך, או הרי את מגורשת בזה, על מנת כך וכך. או יאמר להם, או לשליח תנו לה גט זה על מנת כך וכך.

Maimonides *MT Hilkhot Ishut* (The Laws of Personal Status) 6   רמב״ם הלכות אישות ו

---

1 One who betroths [a woman] on condition—if the condition is upheld, she is betrothed, but if it is not upheld, then she is not betrothed, whether the condition was [stipulated] by the man or by the woman. Any condition whatsoever, whether in [matters of] betrothal or in [matters of] divorce, or in [matters] of commercial transaction, or in any other monetary laws, requires four factors in the condition.

א המקדש על תנאי, אם נתקיים התנאי מקודשת, ואם לא נתקיים אינה מקודשת. בין שהיה התנאי מן האיש, בין שהיה מן האשה. וכל תנאי שבעולם, בין בקידושין, בין בגירושין, בין במקח וממכר בין בשאר דיני ממון, צריך להיות בתנאי ארבעה דברים.

---

36   This is the same procedure as for an unconditional divorce.

2 These are the four factors of every condition: that it should be a twofold condition;[37] that its positive [i.e., the condition that must be fulfilled][38] should precede the negative [i.e., what constitutes nonfulfillment of the condition]; that the condition should be [stated] prior to the [actual] deed; and that it is feasible to uphold the condition.[39] If any one of these [factors] is absent from the condition, then the condition is null, as if there were no condition at all. Rather, she would be betrothed or divorced, and the transaction or gift would take place immediately, as if he did not stipulate a condition at all, since the condition is missing one of the four [required factors].

3 How [is this done]? [For example,] if one says to a woman: "If you give me two hundred *zuz*, behold you are betrothed to me with this dinar, and if you do not give [it to] me, you shall not be betrothed to me," and after he stipulated this condition, he gave her the dinar, then the condition is valid, and thus she is conditionally betrothed. If she [then] gives him two hundred *zuz*, then she would be betrothed, but if she does not give him two hundred *zuz*, then she would not be betrothed.

ב ואלו הן הארבעה דברים של כל תנאי. שיהיה התנאי כפול. ושיהיה הין שלו קודם ללאו, ושיהיה התנאי קודם למעשה. ושיהיה התנאי דבר שאפשר לקיימו. ואם חסר התנאי אחד מהן הרי התנאי בטל וכאלו אין שם תנאי כלל, אלא תהיה זו מקודשת או מגורשת, ויתקיים המקח או המתנה מיד, וכאלו לא התנה כלל, הואיל וחסר התנאי אחד מן הארבעה.

ג כיצד, האומר לאשה אם תתני לי מאתים זוז הרי את מקודשת לי בדינר זה, ואם לא תתני לי לא תהי מקודשת. ואחר שהתנה תנאי זה נתן לה הדינר, הרי התנאי קיים והרי זו מקודשת על תנאי. ואם נתנה לו מאתים זוז תהיה מקודשת, ואם לא נתנה לו אינה מקודשת.

---

37 I.e., if A then B, and if not-A then not-B. In paragraph 14 of this chapter, Maimonides states that there are some Geonim who did not require the twofold condition, other than in matters of betrothal and divorce, but Maimonides disagrees and explains the foundation of his opinion.

38 A "positive" condition that must be fulfilled may be expressed in a negative statement, such as "if I do not return within a year."

39 The classic example of an infeasible condition is "if you go up to the sky" (*Gittin* 84a).

| Maimonides *MT Hilkhot Gerushin* (The Laws of Divorce) 9 | רמב״ם הלכות גירושין ט |

1 One who divorces his wife [with the divorce to take effect] after a specified time—she is divorced when the specified time has elapsed.⁴⁰

2 How? One who says to his wife: "Behold, this is your *get*, but you will not be divorced with it until after thirty days," she is not divorced until after thirty days. Therefore, if the husband dies or the *get* was lost or burned within thirty days, she is not divorced.⁴¹

א המגרש את אשתו לאחר זמן קבוע, הרי זו מגורשת כשיגיע הזמן שקבע.
ב כיצד, האומר לאשתו הרי זה גטיך ולא תתגרשי בו אלא לאחר שלשים יום, אינה מגורשת בו אלא לאחר שלשים יום. ואם מת הבעל או אבד הגט או נשרף בתוך שלשים יום אינה מגורשת.

| K'tubbot 22a | כתובות כ״ב א׳ |

mishna: The woman who said "I was a married woman, but I am divorced" is believed, because the mouth that prohibited is the mouth that permitted. However, if there are witnesses that she was married and she says "I am divorced," she is not believed. [...]

g'mara: Rav Asi said: "From where [do we know that the principle] 'the mouth that prohibited is the mouth that permitted' is from the Torah? ...

מתני׳ האשה שאמרה אשת איש הייתי וגרושה אני נאמנת שהפה שאסר הוא הפה שהתיר ואם יש עדים שהיתה אשת איש והיא אומרת גרושה אני אינה נאמנת [...]
גמ׳ א״ר [אמר רב] אסי מנין להפה שאסר הוא הפה שהתיר מן התורה

---

40 This halakha is truncated here, the remaining portion being less relevant for this responsum.

41 If a husband gave his wife such a *get*, for example, before leaving to war with the purpose that she not be left an *'aguna*, if he dies before the time elapses, presumably with witnesses to that effect, she would not be an *'aguna* but a widow. If his whereabouts are unknown (perhaps he did die, but there are no witnesses), then after thirty days she would be divorced, and therefore not an *'aguna*—the *get* would have accomplished its task. However, if the purpose was (also) to avoid levirate marriage or *ḥalitsa*, then if he dies before the time elapses, with witness to that effect, she would not be absolved of levirate marriage or *ḥalitsa*, because "there is no divorce after death" (*Gittin* 73b). The way to avoid such a bind is to give a divorce stating, "Behold, this is your *get* **from now**, if I do not return during the next thirty days." In that case, as we saw in *Hilkhot Gerushin* (The Laws of Divorce) 8,1 above, even if the husband dies within that time, she is divorced. Similarly, even if the *get* is lost, she is divorced.

Why do I need a verse from the Torah [to prove this]?! There is an argument based on reason! He made her forbidden, and he made her permitted! ... Our Rabbis taught [in a *baraita*]: "The woman who said 'I am a married woman' and then said 'I am single' is believed. [The *gᵉmara* challenges:] But she has made herself forbidden![42] [How can she now permit herself merely by contradicting her own words?] Rava bar Rav Huna explains: [This rule is so] in the case that she gives an *amatla*[43] to [explain the contradiction in] her statements." [Corroboration of Rava bar Rav Huna's explanation] is taught in another [*baraita*]: "If she said 'I am a married woman' and then said 'I am single' she is not believed, but if she gave an *amatla* to [explain the contradiction in] her statements, she is believed."

... ל"י [למה לי] קרא סברא היא הוא אסרה והוא שרי לה ... ת"ר [תנו רבנן] האשה שאמרה אשת איש אני וחזרה ואמרה פנויה אני נאמנת והא שויה לנפשה חתיכה דאיסורא אמר רבא בר רב הונא כגון שנתנה אמתלא לדבריה תניא נמי הכי אמרה אשת איש אני וחזרה ואמרה פנויה אני אינה נאמנת ואם נתנה אמתלא לדבריה נאמנת ומעשה נמי באשה אחת גדולה שהיתה גדולה בנוי וקפצו עליה בני אדם לקדשה ואמרה להם מקודשת אני לימים עמדה וקידשה את עצמה אמרו לה חכמים מה ראית לעשות כן אמרה להם בתחלה שבאו עלי אנשים שאינם מהוגנים אמרתי מקודשת אני עכשיו שבאו עלי אנשים מהוגנים עמדתי וקדשתי את עצמי וזו הלכה העלה רב אחא שר הבירה לפני חכמי'[ם] באושא ואמרו אם נתנה אמתלא'[א] לדבריה נאמנת

Further [corroboration is found in the following] incident: There once was an important woman, who was very beautiful, and men were ardent[44] to betroth her, and she told them "I am betrothed." After some time, she betrothed herself. The Sages said to her: "Why did you think [it was acceptable] to do this?" She said to them: "At first, when these unseemly men came to me, I said I was betrothed. Now that seemly men have come to me, I went and betrothed myself." And Rav Aḥa, Chief of the Temple Mount, proposed this law before the Sages in Usha, and they said: "If she gave an *amatla* for her statements, she is believed."

---

42   Lit., "a piece of prohibition."
43   An *amatla* is a plausible reason for a contradiction in testimony.
44   Lit., jumped on her.

Discussion

In the last source, *Kᵉtubbot* 22a, the first case in the *mishna* is of a woman who cannot prove that she is divorced. Perhaps she lost her *get* and there are no witnesses that the divorce took place. If there is no one to testify that she was married, she is believed, because she did not need to offer any information about her marital status. By saying she was married, she would be prohibited to another man, and so the court believes that she is telling the truth both about having been married and being divorced. However, if there are witnesses that she was married, she could not have pretended to have never been married. Therefore, without providing a *get* or witnesses to the divorce, her statement that she is divorced is not sufficient to permit her to marry another man.

The first *baraita* cited in the *gᵉmara* is similar to this first case in the *mishna*, but not identical. If we read both of them together, it is reasonable to say that in the *mishna*, the woman stated both claims—that she was married and that she is a divorcee—at the same time,[45] while in the *baraita*, it appears that there was some time lapse between making each of the claims. First she said she was married, and then later she said she was single.[46] However, some commentators did not limit the first case in the *mishna* to apply only when the woman makes both claims "in the course of speaking."[47] By stating that the woman is believed, even if there is a time lapse between claims, those commentators are more lenient in defining conditions under which a woman who claims she is divorced is believed. In the responsum, Abi Zimra considers both of these interpretations.

---

45 The legal term used here is *tokh kᵉdei dibbur* (in the course of speaking). This concept is found in numerous places in the Talmud (e.g., *Nᵉdarim* 87a and *Nazir* 20b). It is used in the following manner: If a person gives testimony and corrects himself "in the course of speaking," then his words are considered as one statement rather than two contradictory statements. This rule is stated as *tokh kᵉdei dibbur kᵉdibbur damei* ([whatever is said] in the course of speaking is like a [single] statement). The term is quantified as the time that it takes for a student to say, "Peace be with you, my rabbi." (*Nazir* 20b; see *MT Hilkhot Shᵉvuʿot* [The Laws of Oaths] 2,17]) If two claims are not made within the specified time frame, then the second claim is said to be *lᵉaḥar dibbur*—"after speaking."

46 The language in the *baraita* is *ḥazᵉra vᵉamᵉra*, which can be understood in several ways, such as "she returned and said," "she changed her mind and said," "she reiterated and said," etc.

47 Among them are R. Jacob ben Asher (*Tur EH* 152) and R. Vidal of Tolosa (*Maggid Mishne* on *MT Hilkhot Gerushin* [The Laws of Divorce] 12,1), each of whom cites both approaches, but maintains that the *mishna* does not require the woman to make both her claims "in the course of speaking," considering that the latter statement does not contradict the first.

Tractate *Gittin* opens with a *mishna* about a *get* brought by a messenger from a husband who is far away from his wife. Why, one wonders, does the tractate on divorce start this way? Why wouldn't it begin with what we might consider the more usual case of a husband and wife who were living together and are now divorcing due to friction in the marriage? How common was the situation of a writ of divorce being sent by messenger, perhaps from overseas? And why would a husband send a divorce from a remote locale? His having met another woman would not have been a problem in Mishnaic times, when polygyny was permissible; and given the distance between them, it cannot be said that the couple must have gotten into a bad spat, so that the husband decided to divorce his wife in anger.

Men often traveled for their livelihood, risking the dangers that were part and parcel of travel in those times. People were taken captive; ships sank; roads were not safe. A traveling husband—or a man who went to war—might not return. So that his wife would not be left an *'aguna* in such an event, a husband might leave her with a conditional *get*, stipulating that it would come into effect if he did not return within a specified amount of time. Except in some very rare cases, Jewish law did not provide for a judicial annulment, such as exists in Muslim law, in which courts can annul the marriage of an abandoned wife.[48]

The question, then, ought to be: Why didn't every husband who embarked on a dangerous voyage or mission leave such a *get* with his wife?[49] We have no answer for this, but we do know, from responsa and other rabbinic literature and

---

48 For a discussion of the conditions under which a marriage might be annulled by a Jewish court, see [Westreich]. In Muslim law, a judicial divorce (*faskh*) can be granted to a deserted wife, who is defined in the Mamluk legal texts as a woman whose husband has been absent for at least six months, leaving her without property or financial support; see [Rapoport], 76. Since our responsum was written during the time of the Mamluk sultanate in Palestine, comparison to Mamluk practice is of interest.

49 Indeed, we find an agreement to do so stipulated in some *k^etubbot* (marriage contracts). See, for example, [Lamdan2], 53 and 83-87. The practice of a husband giving his wife a conditional *get* in case he did not return within a specified amount of time was common among both Jews and Muslims. See [Goitein], 155 and 189-190; [Rapoport2]: 34; and [Rapoport], 77. R. S. A. Pardes, "Ki Tetse La-milḥama," *Hapardes* 16, no. 2 (May 1942): 2-3 and Henkin, "He'arot Nosafot 'Al D^evar Gittin Linshei Ha-yots^eim La-milḥama," *Hapardes* 16, no. 2: 16-18, encouraged men to give divorces to their wives before departing to fight in World War II, and instructed rabbis how to arrange such divorces. In the second half of the twentieth century we find individual cases, but not such a broad instruction. For example, *Tsits Eli'ezer* 11:90 was written about a case that took place prior to the Six-Day War (June 1967). *Tsits Eli'ezer* 15:57, written as a follow up (but not dated), states, "in our time, this question arises among many of those who are going to war."

from medieval documents left in the Cairo Geniza,[50] that men did send divorces by proxy after their departure on a voyage or to battle.[51] Perhaps they realized that their situation was becoming more precarious. Perhaps, in the case of a husband who had no offspring (whether from this marriage or from another relationship), he had become ill and did not want to leave his wife a widow, subject to levirate marriage. He may have realized or suspected that the obligated brother-in-law was not accessible, old enough, or willing either to marry the widow or to perform *halitsa*. For these latter reasons, it was also common for a critically ill man to write a divorce for his wife, which might be subject to the condition that he died from the illness.

Given the opening of Tractate *Gittin* with a *get* being delivered from a remote locale, it is conceivable that in the experience of the Tanna'im, such divorce represented a greater number of cases than those produced by dysfunctional marriages. Every husband who needed to travel, certainly every considerate one, might either write a divorce for his wife before he left or send one with a messenger if he saw he might be delayed or in danger.

Responsum

Radbaz Responsum 1,398	שו״ת רדב״ז חלק א סימן שצח
Question: "I, Hanna,[52] came to Jerusalem (may it be built and reestablished speedily in our days), and as soon as I arrived, I responded to men and women who spoke with me of marriage, telling them to leave me alone with such things, as I am an *'aguna*, because my *get* was lost before the completion of the	**שאלה** אני חנה באתי לירושלים תוב״ב [ותיבנה ותיכונן במהרה בימינו] ותכף שבאתי השבתי לאנשים ונשים שדברו עמי כדי לינשא ואמרתי להם הניחו אותי בדברים כאלה שאני עגונה מצד שנאבד הגט שלי קודם שעבר הזמן שגזר עלי החכם

time that the *hakham*[53] decreed that I wait [before being free to marry again].

---

50 See [Lamdan2], 110-123; on the Geniza documents, [Goitein], 189-195.
51 A woman might also send a request for a divorce, after finding it difficult to be married to a man who was absent for so long, but, given the unilateral nature of divorce in Jewish law, she was at the mercy of her husband in this regard. See, for example, [Goitein2], 220-226.
52 As usual in responsa literature, this is a pseudonym.
53 I.e., the rabbi who officiated over the delivery of her *get*.

Regarding this matter, I have many men and women who [can] testify that from the day I arrived in Jerusalem I spoke these words, and that such is the word that has gotten around Jerusalem. After I was in Jerusalem for approximately five years—always maintaining that I was an *'aguna*, as I understood [to be the case], and [during which time] I also spread the word myself, intentionally, because I needed to go to the market-place[54] to support myself, and if I were considered a single woman, there would have been slander about me, and I would not have been so protected—by and by, I told a particular *ḥakham* a bit of my troubles. He said to me: 'Tell me in every detail, in solemn truth,[55] the matter of the presentation of the *get*.' I responded in solemn truth that this was how it happened: My husband went with some other Jews to distant places to bring citrons. Afterwards, those same other Jews returned, and they brought me the *get*. The *ḥakham* of the city immediately went and collected all the learned men that were there with all of the influential men,[56] and they

להמתין ועל דבר זה יש לי הרבה אנשים ונשים שמעידים עלי שמיום בואי לירושלים דברתי זה הלשון ושכך יצא הקול בירושלים ואחרי שהייתי בירושלים כערך ה' שנים והחזקתי תמיד עצמי לעגונה כמו שהייתי סבורה וגם בכונה הוצאתי את הקול כי הוצרכתי לצאת לשוק כדי לפרנס את עצמי ואם הייתי בחזקת פנויה היו מרננים עלי ולא הייתי בחזקת שימור כל כך. ספרתי דרך מקרה לפני חכם א'[חד] קצת מצרותי ואמר לי תספרי לי העניין אות באות על פי נשמתך ויהדותך ענין נתינת הגט והשבתי לו על פי נשמתי ויהדותי שכך היה העניין. בעלי הלך למרחקים להביא אתרוגים עם יהודים אחרים אחר כך חזרו אותם היהודים והביאו לי הגט הלך חכם העיר א'[חד] וקבץ את כל הבעלי תורה שהיו לשם עם בעלי בתים ובאו לביתי ואמרו לי לקבל הגט התחלתי להיות בוכה וצועקת ואמרתי מה מצא בי בעלי עול לגרש אותי. השיב לי החכם וכל אותם שהיו לשם ואמרו לי עניה עניה זה הגט הוא לטובתך

came to my house and told me to accept the *get*. I started to cry and wail, and I said: 'What grievance did my husband find with me to divorce me?!' The *ḥakham* and all the others who were there responded and told me: 'You poor thing, you poor thing, this *get* is for your benefit, because your husband went by sea to distant places, and if he would drown or die,[57] you would be an *'aguna* for all of

---

54 *Shuk* can also refer to a street or other open public place.
55 Lit., "according to your soul and your Jewishness."
56 Lit., "householders."
57 Without adequate evidence of his death for the court to declare her a widow.

your days. Therefore, accept it for your benefit.' And so I did. After I accepted the *get*, that same *ḥakham* decreed that I am 'not to marry until four years have passed, because such has your husband stipulated.' Afterwards, due to their many sins, the Jews were expelled from that land, and I was exiled with them, and the *get* was lost in exile before the four years had passed. Because of this I am forbidden to marry, and because of this I requested a number of times that the *ḥakhamim* write for me and investigate the whereabouts of my husband so that he might release me. This is what I told that *ḥakham* here in Jerusalem, and he questioned me on other details, and I told him: 'These are the things that I remember. The rest of the details I forgot, because it is more than ten years [since this happened], and also at that time I was stricken with grief and crying, so that I could not pay attention to the details.' That *ḥakham* [then] said to me: 'Are there witnesses here that know that you were married?' I replied to him that no such word has been heard other than from me. He said to me: 'You poor thing, you poor thing, in my opinion, you are permitted [to remarry] according to the law of our holy Torah. Go to the *ḥakhamim* and ask them, because in my opinion they would all permit you, because it is a simple matter.' Therefore I came before Your Honor to respond to me with a ruling according to our Torah, according to this information, because God knows that I did not change one letter, because I am not someone with a reputation for lying, as you know about me now for several years. I also have

כי בעליך הלך דרך ים למרחקים ואם יטבע או ימות תהיי עגונה כל ימיך לכן קבלי אותו לטובתך וכן עשיתי אחר שקבלתי הגט גזר עלי אותו חכם שלא לינשא עד שיעברו ד' שנים שכן התנה בעליך. אחר כך נתגרשו היהודים בעוונות הרבים מכל אותה המדינה ואני עמהם בגולה ונאבד הגט בגלות קודם שעברו הד' שנים ובעבור זה אני אסורה לינשא ובעבור זה בקשתי כמה פעמים את החכמים שיכתבו בעבורי ויחקרו באי זה מקום בעלי שיפטור אותי ע"כ [עד כאן] ספרתי לפני אותו חכם פה בירושלים וחקר אותי בדברים אחרים ואמרתי לו אלה הדברים אני זוכרת שאר הדברים שכחתי כי הוא יותר מי' שנים וגם אני הייתי באותה שעה בצער ובבכיה שלא דקדקתי כ"כ [כל כך] ואמר לי אותו חכם יש בכאן עדים שיודעים שהיית נשואה והשבתי לו לא יצא הקול אלא ממני. אמר לי עניה עניה לפי דעתי את מותרת בדין תורתינו הקדושה לכי אל החכמים ושאלי להם כי לפי דעתי כולם יתירו אותך כי הוא דבר פשוט לכן באתי לפני כ"ת [כבוד תורתו] להשיב לי דין תורתינו על פי אלו הדברי[ם] כי ה' יודע שלא שניתי אות א[חת] כי איני מוחזקת לשקר כמו שאתם מכירים אותי זה כמה

witnesses that would testify about me that I am, praise to God, truthful in all my words, always maintaining an honest reputation." Up to here are the words of the question [from Hanna].

They [the ḥakhamim of Jerusalem] questioned the witnesses whom she specified, and their testimony was found to be consistent with hers, according to what she has continually stated. However, she differed from the language of the witnesses in that they testified that she always said that she had received a conditional divorce, while she said that she had received a divorce with no qualification, and [only] afterwards did they impose the condition upon her, because the meaning of her words is that he [the ḥakham] gave her the *get* unconditionally, and only afterwards did he stipulate that she should not marry until four years had passed, according to the custom in Ashkenaz.[58] They also asked her: "Why does your statement differ from that of the witnesses?" She replied "Heaven forbid, I did not change anything. Rather, such a *get* I call a conditional divorce. Is it not a conditional divorce? Was I permitted to marry immediately? I do not know what to call such a *get*. So long as I was not permitted to marry, I call it a conditional divorce." They made her take an oath about everything written above, by placing her hand on a Torah.[59] There was then a dispute among

שנים וגם יש לי עדים שמעידים עלי שאני ת"ל [תהילות לאל] נאמנת על כל דברי ובחזקת הכשרות אני תמיד. עכ"ל [עד כאן לשון] השאלה
ושאלו את פי העדים אשר שמעו מפיה ונמצאו דבריהם מכוונים עם דבריה כמו שאמרה תמיד אלא ששנתה מלשון העדים כי הם העידו בשמה שהיא ספרה תמיד שקבלה גט תנאי והיא אמרה שקבלה גט סתם ואחר כך הטילו עליה התנאי דמשמעות לשונה הוא שנתן לה הגט מכל וכל אלא שאח"כ [שאחר כך] התנה עליה שלא תנשא לאחר עד ד' שנים כמנהג אשכנזים. עוד שאלוה למה שנית דבריך מדברי העדים. השיבה ח"ו [חס ושלום] לא שניתי אלא לזה הגט אני קורא גט תנאי וכי אינו גט תנאי וכי הייתי מותרת לינשא מיד איני יודע באי זה לשון יקרא זה הגט כל זמן שלא הייתי מותרת לינשא אני קורא לו גט תנאי והשביעוה על כל הכתו[ב] לעיל בנקיטת חפץ. ונפל מחלוקת בין חכמי ירושלים אם אשה זו מותרת לינשא

---

58 Though the questioner states that it was an Ashkenazi custom to wait four years before remarrying, there is no record of such a custom. Rather, I believe that the questioner and Abi Zimra are referring to the Ashkenazi custom of using unconditional divorce and then requiring, on pain of excommunication, that the couple remarry in the event that the (now ex-) husband does return. However, by relying on R. Elazar's assessment to define the length of time a woman should wait before despairing of her husband's return, she must wait four years before remarrying to another man. See Halakhic Background.

59 Lit., "holding an object," that is, placing one's hand on a Torah, as was done for certain types of oaths.

the ḥakhamim in Jerusalem as to whether this woman is permitted to marry or not, and the woman came to us. *I also will express my opinion* (Job 32:10) that the one who permits did not want to permit until three distinguished and important ḥakhamim agreed with him.

Response: I am neither distinguished nor important, but, nevertheless, I, by myself, permit this woman to remarry, for a number of reasons. [1][60] First, I will clarify whether this presumption under which she has considered herself for several years, the presumption that she is an 'aguna, is indeed established or not. I say that this is a mistaken presumption and has not been established, because women have not learned the law, [and she would not know] until a ḥakham comes along to tell her, as is [stated] in the first chapter of *Qiddushin* [13a],[61] that [hers] is not [a case of] 'iggun. Further, there is no greater *amatla*[62] than this [i.e., hers], and even those who are aware [of the law] err in this [matter]: She thought that, because the *get* was lost before the condition [to wait four years] was met, she remains an 'aguna. [There is] evidence [that her *amatla* cancels out this mistaken presumption] from the precedent [in Kᵉtubbot 22a] of the woman who, when unseemly men were ardent to betroth her, said that she was [already] betrothed, and yet after some time she betrothed herself [implying that she had been free to marry], and the Sages said that if she gave an *amatla* for her [previous] words, she is believed.

או לא ובאת האשה אצלנו אחוה דעי גם אני כי המתיר לא רצה להתיר עד שיסכימו עמו שלשה חכמים רשומים וחשובים עכ״ל [עד כאן לשונו].

תשובה אני איני לא רשום ולא חשוב ואעפ״י [ואף על פי] כן אני לבדי מתיר אשה זו לינשא מכמה טעמי[ם].

וראשונה אבאר אם חזקה זו שהחזיקה עצמה כמה שנים בחזקת עגונה אם היא חזקה או לא. ואומר כי חזקה זו בטעות היא ואינה חזקה דנשי לאו דינא גמירי עד דמתרמי לה חכם כדאיתא בפ״ק [בפרק קמא] דקדושין ואמר לה דליכא הכא עגון. ותו דאין לך אמתלאה גדולה מזו ואפי׳[לו] היודעים יטעו בזה שחשבה כי באבדן גיטה בתוך זמן התנאי נשארה עגונה וראיה מהך אתתא דקפצו עליה בני אדם שאינם מהוגנים ואמרה מקודשת אני לימים קדשה את עצמה ואמרו חכמים אם נתנה אמתלאה לדבריה נאמנת.

---

60 Numbers are inserted to facilitate reading the discussion following the responsum.

61 In a discussion of how a woman should respond in certain unusual circumstances to an offer of betrothal, Rav Aḥai asks rhetorically: "Are all women learned in the law?" His point is that since they are not, they might not know the consequences of certain actions.

62 See Halakhic Background.

The definition of *amatla* is an explanation that is recognizably plausible, and all the rabbinic authorities wrote thus.[63] Therefore, in our case, can there be a greater *amatla* than this, that she said: "I cannot marry, because my *get* was lost"?! This [case] is even stronger than that [case], where she [the beautiful woman] certainly lied [to the unseemly men], and because of her *amatla* we declare that what she said at the outset was a lie [and therefore she was free to marry], whereas in our case, she told the truth both at the outset and afterwards, but, rather, she was mistaken about the law. For this reason, alone, even if the word that got around [that she is an 'aguna] were relevant, its cancellation accompanies it![64] For she says that she is an 'aguna, because her *get* [indicating the opposite, that she is free to marry] was lost. But the truth of the matter is that in our case any word that got around is not relevant, because there are no witnesses, but rather she spread

ופי[רוש] אמתלאה טענה הנכרת שהיא כדאי לסמוך עליה וכתבוה כל פוסקי הלכות. הילכך בנ"ד [בנידון דידן] היש לך אמתלאה גדול[ה] מזו שאמרה מפני שאבד גיטי איני יכולה לינשא. ועדיפא מהך דאלו התם ודאי משקרא וע"י [ועל ידי] האמתלאה אנו אומרים דשקרא אמרה בתחלה ואלו בנ"ד [בנידון דידן] קושטא אמרה בתחלה ובסוף אלא שהיתה טועה בדין. ומזה הטעם בעצמו אפי[לו] אי הוה שייך הכא קול הרי שוברו עמו שאומרת שהיא עגונה מפני שאבד גטה אבל קושטא דמלתא דלא שייך בנ"ד [בנידון דידן] קול כיון שאין שם עדים אלא על פיה והחזיקה עצמה עגונה בטעות. וכיון דברירנא דליכא הכא לא חזקה ולא קול אלא משום דשויתה אנפשה חתיכא דאיסורא הדבר ברור שהיא מותרת דהפה שאסר הוא הפה שהתיר דתנן בפרק ב' דכתובות האשה שאמרה אשת איש הייתי וגרושה אני נאמנת שהפה

the word herself and maintained, mistakenly, that she was an 'aguna. And since I have clarified that there is neither an established presumption nor any [supported] rumor [that she is an 'aguna], but rather [this impression arose] because she had "made herself forbidden," it is clear that she is permitted [to marry], because "the mouth that prohibited is the mouth that permitted,"[65] as is taught in chapter two of *K^etubbot* [22a]: The woman who said: "I was a married woman, but I am divorced" [in the absence of any witnesses to confirm either claim] is

---

63 For example, *MT Hilkhot Ishut* (The Laws of Personal Status) 9,31.

64 *Gittin* 88b–89a. The legal concept of *qol v^eshov^ero 'imo* (a report accompanied by its cancellation) is parallel to that of *sh^etar v^eshov^ero 'imo* (a promissory note accompanied by its receipt, which cancels the promissory note).

65 See Halakhic Background.

believed, because the mouth that prohibited [by making the first claim] is the mouth that permitted [by making the second claim], but if there are witnesses that she was a married woman, and she said: "I am divorced," she is not believed. In our case, too, because there are no witnesses that she was a married woman, she is believed if she says "I am divorced," and just as she is believed if she says "I am divorced," she is trusted to tell the manner of her divorce; and it is in the course of speaking[66] that she says [both things]: "I am an *'aguna*, because my *get* was lost," and, also, the witnesses who heard her testify that she always stated this reason that, to her, she is an *'aguna*. Even for those who say that there is a bit of a contradiction between what she says and what the witnesses say—and this is not true in my opinion, and, with God's help I will clarify this below—in any event, the witnesses admit that they always heard her say the reason for being an *'aguna*, which is that the *get* was lost. Even if she said: "I am an *'aguna*," and

שאסר הוא הפה שהתיר ואם יש עדים שהיא אשת איש ואמרה גרושה אני אינה נאמנת ובנ״ד [ובנידון דידן] נמי כיון דליכ׳[א] סהדי שהיא אשת איש נאמנת לומר גרושה אני וכי היכי דהיא נאמנת לומר גרושה אני נאמנת לומר אופן גירושיה. ובתוך כדי דבור אומרת עגונה אני לפי שנאבד גיטי וגם העדים אשר שמעו מפיה מעידין שלעולם היא אומרת הסבה שבשבילה היא עגונה. ואפילו לדעת האומרי[ם] שיש קצת הכחשה בין דבריה לדברי העדים מה שאינו אמת לדעתי כאשר אבאר לקמן ב״ה [בעזרת ה׳] מ״מ [מכל מקום] הא מודים העדים שלעולם שמעו מפיה סבת עגונה דהיינו שאבד הגט. ואפי[לו] אם אמרה עגונה אני ולאחר זמן אמרה מפני שאבד גטי אפי[לו] בכה״ג [בכהאי גוונא] אני מתירה לינשא ולא מיבעיא לדעת האומרי[ם] דמשנתינו איירי אפילו לאחר כדי דבור אלא אפילו לדעת האומרים דמשנתינו בתוך כדי דבור מודו בנ״ד [בנידון דידן] דבשלמא במתני׳[תין]

then after some time she said, "because my *get* was lost"—even in such a case—I permit her to marry. There is no need to rely on [the opinion of] those who say that our *mishna* [in K*e*tubbot] relates to a situation [in which she changes her testimony] even after speaking.[67] Rather, even according to those who say that our *mishna* [relates only to a situation in which she makes both claims] in the course of speaking, in our case they would concur [that the woman is believed]. In the *mishna*, the one who says: "I was a married woman, but I am divorced" is believed not because [she has] an *amatla* [for the change in her testimony],

---

66 *Tokh k*e*dei dibbur* is explained in note 45.
67 *L*e*aḥar dibbur*.

but even without a reason, because "the mouth that prohibited is the mouth that permitted." Because that [is the basis for believing her], it is reasonable for us to require [that she state both claims] in the course of speaking. But in our case, since [we believe her] because of an *amatla*, we rely on her [testimony] even after some time has passed [between her making the two claims], if her explanation makes sense to the court. So wrote Maimonides (may his memory be blessed) [in] chapter nine of The Laws of Personal Status: "Word got around that she was betrothed to so-and-so and after some days an *amatla* was given [for the rumor]. If what is said [in the *amatla*] makes sense to the court that it is so, they rely on the *amatla* and she is not considered betrothed."[68] And if you should say that there is a difference between [that case of] word getting around and our case, where she said she is a married woman—look, there is no [difference], because in the above-cited *baraita* [in *K^etubbot* 22a] she said she is betrothed and then after some days she gave an *amatla* [of why she said that, and she is believed]. And so wrote the Ran[69] (may his memory be blessed): "Since she gave an *amatla* for her [first] statement, she is believed even after speaking." [This is so, even] though he [the Ran] wrote at the end of *K^etubbot*[70] that we only say "the mouth that prohibited etc." [if the correction to the testimony is] in the course of speaking, in con-

שאמרה אשת איש הייתי וגרושה אני לא הוי טעמא משום אמתלאה אלא בלא טעם נמי נאמנת דהפה שאסר הוא הפה שהתיר ומשום הכי בעי'[נן] תוך כדי דבור. אבל בני"ד [בנידון דידן] דהוי מטעם אמתלאה אפי'[לו] לאחר זמן אם נראה לב"ד [לבית דין] שהטעם הוא נכון סומכים עליה. וכן כתב הרמב"ם ז"ל [זכרונו לברכה] פרק ט' מהלכות אישות יצא עליה קול שנתקדשה לפלוני ולאחר ימים אמרו אמתלאה אם נראין הדברים לב"ד [לבית דין] שהוא כן סומכין על האמתלאה ולא הוחזקה מקודשת ע"כ [עד כאן]. וכ"ת [וכי תאמר] דיש חילוק בין קול לני"ד [לנידון דידן] שאמרה שהיתה אשת איש הא ליתא דהא בהך ברייתא דמייתי'[נן] לעיל אמרה מקודשת אני ולאחר ימים אמרה האמתלאה וכן כתב הר"ן ז"ל [זכרונו לברכה] הואיל ונתנה אמתלאה לדבריה נאמנת לאחר כדי דבור ע"כ [עד כאן] אעפ"י [אף על פי] שכתב בסוף כתובות דלא אמרי'[נן] הפה שאסר וכו'[לי] אלא תוך כדי

---

68   *MT Hilkhot Ishut* 9,24.
69   R. Nissim Gerondi (1310?–1375?), *K^etubbot* 9b on the pages of the Rif (R. Isaac Alfasi, 1013-1103) at *im nat^ena amatla lidvareha*.
70   *K^etubbot* 64b on the pages of the Rif at *ne'eman*.

nection with the *mishna* where he made it a [boundary] mark for another.⁷¹ [It would seem then,] perforce we must agree to such a distinction [between "during the course of speaking" versus "after speaking"], because otherwise there is a conflict between the *mishna* [in Kᵉtubbot that was just referred to] and the *baraita*, which teaches [that] If she said "I am a married woman" and then said "I am single" she is not believed, but if she gave a reasonable explanation for [the contradiction in] her statements, she is believed. [The *gᵉmara* continues there with further corroboration]: There once was …⁷² Here you clearly have evidence [in the *baraita*] that an *amatla* is effective, even after speaking, if there is reason upon which to rely. And I think no one disputes this. But the dispute about the interpretation of the *mishna* [Kᵉtubbot 22a about the woman who changed her testimony]—whether it is dealing with [a situation of] "during the course of speaking" or "after speaking"—arises because her latter statement [in the testimony] contradicts the first with no reason, and therefore it is necessary that it be "during the course of speaking," to cancel her first statement. In this manner, it makes sense to me, that when there is an actual contradiction, as the case in the *baraita* where she said "I am a married woman" and then said "I am single," but did not give an *amatla*—in such a case she is believed only [if she alters her testimony] "in the course of speaking." But in a case such as in the *mishna* [where] she said "I was a married woman,

דבור עלה דמתני׳[תין] דעשאה סימן לאחר. ועל כרחינו צריכין להודות חילוק זה דאם לא קשיא מתני׳[תין] אברייתא דתניא אמרה אשת איש אני וחזרה ואמרה פנויה אני אינה נאמנת ואם נתנה אמתלאה לדבריה נאמנת ומעשה וכו׳[לין] הרי לך בהדיא דהאמתלאה אפי׳[לו] לאחר זמן תועיל אם יש בה טעם לסמוך ואני חושב שאין בזה חולק. ומה שנחלקו בפירושא דמתנן אי אייר תוך כדי דבור או אחר כדי דיבור הוא מפני שדבריה האחרונים מכחישים הראשונים בלא טעם ומשום הכי בעי׳[נן] תוך כדי דבור לבטל דבריה הראשונים והכי מסתברא לי דבזמן דאיכא הכחשה ממש כגוונא דברייתא שאמרה אשת איש אני וחזרה ואמרה פנויה אני ולא נתנה אמתלאה בכה״ג [בכהאי גוונא] אינה נאמנת אלא בתוך כדי דבור אבל כגונא דמתני׳[תין] דאמרה אשת איש הייתי וגרושה אני

---

71 He is referring to the *mishna* on Kᵉtubbot 109a. The situation is a case of someone who contests the ownership of a field for which he signed as a witness on the deed of sale. In his explanation, the Ran states that the rule "the mouth that prohibited is the mouth that permitted" only applies if the correction to testimony is during the course of speaking.

72 Kᵉtubbot 22a. See Halakhic Background.

but I am divorced"—she is believed, even "after speaking," which is a middle course, and the *mishna* teaches a clear-cut case. Likewise, the meaning of the *baraita* that teaches and then [said] is after some time. Because this is not relevant to our question, I will not elaborate further, because [with] our case there is an *amatla*, which would be effective even after some time [has passed], and even more so when it was in the course of speaking, as was stated in the question and in the testimony of witnesses.[73]

Further, there is another reason to be lenient, because she never claimed that she was a married woman, but rather a divorcee whose *get* was lost, and when she would find her *get*, she would be divorced even in her opinion. Therefore, when a *ḥakham* would be found who would say that [the absence of] the *get* is not a hindrance [to her being able to remarry], we would have [a situation] as if she had found her *get*. What difference does it make to me if she found her *get*, or if she found someone who would say it is not needed? Since there is no definite presumption of a prohibition [for her to remarry], but only a doubtful prohibition, when the doubt disappears, the prohibition will disappear.

[2] There is further reason to permit [her to marry] on the basis of her statement that he gave her the *get*, and [only] after she accepted it did the *ḥakham* decree that she is "not to marry until four years have passed, because such has your husband stipulated." Note, this language is entirely contradictory. Because, since he

נאמנת אפי׳[לו] אחר כדי דבור דהוי מלתא מציעתא ומתני׳[תין] מלתא פסיקתא קתני. וכן ברייתא דקתני וחזרה משמע לאחר זמן. ומפני שאין זה מעניין שאלתינו לא אאריך בו כי נ״ד [נידון דידן] הוי אמתלאה ותועיל אפי׳[לו] אחר כמה זמן וכ״ש [וכל שכן] שהיא בתוך כדי דבור כפי מה שבא בשאלה והעדאת העדים.

תו איכא טעמא אחרינא להקל שהרי לא החזיקה עצמה באשת איש אלא במגורשת שאבד גיטה ובזמן שתמצא גטה היא מגורשת אפי׳[לו] לפי דעתה. הילכך כשימצא חכם שיאמר לה שהגט אינו מעכב ה״ל [הוה לן] כאלו מצאה את גטה מה לי שתמצא הגט ומה לי שתמצא מי שיאמר לה שאינו צריך וכיון שאין כאן חזקת איסור ודאי אלא איסור ספק בהסתלק הספק יסתלק האיסור

ותו איכא טעמא להיתר לפי דבריה שנתן לה הגט ואחרי שקבלתו גזר עליה החכם שלא תנשא עד שיעברו ד׳ שנים שכך התנה בעליך והרי זה

---

73 Abi Zimra is claiming that the woman's situation is even stronger than a scenario in which the woman's claims are contradictory, and the second claim is made "after speaking," but she has an *amatla*. In our case, both of the woman's claims were made "in the course of speaking," and she has an *amatla*.

did **not** say [this] to her at the time the *get* was given, and also since the expression "decreed that I [wait]" [was used],[74] it means that there was no actual condition [to the divorce]. But what he [the ḥakham] said—"so stipulated your husband"—means that there was an actual condition. We do not suspect that the court erred, because there is no one who is experienced with the nature of divorces and marriages but does not know that stipulations must be made at the time that the *get* is given. Even more so, because the ḥakham of the city collected all the learned men, according to what was submitted in the question, and it cannot be said that they all erred on this. If this event had occurred in those lands where there is no custom [to give only an unconditional divorce], then there would be reason to say that there was an actual condition at the time the *get* was given, considering that the witnesses testified that she herself had told them she

הלשון מכחיש קצתו אל קצתו כי ממה שלא אמר לה בשעת נתינת הגט גם מלשון גזר עלי משמע שלא היה תנאי ממש. וממה שאמ[ר] כי כן התנה בעליך משמע שהיה תנאי גמור ולב"ד [ולבית דין] טועין לא חיישי[נן] דאין לך מי שיש לו עסק בטיב גיטין וקדושין שאינו יודע שצריך להתנות בשעת נתינת הגט וכ"ש [וכל שכן] שקבץ חכם העיר את כל הבעלי תורה כפי מה שבא בשאלה וליכא למימר דכולהו טעו בהכי. ואם היה המעשה בארצות אלו שאין בהן מנהג היה מקום לומר תנאי גמור היה בשעת נתינת הגט כאשר העידו העדים מפיה שהיתה מספרת להם שקבלה גט תנאי ועתה מתקנת דבריה שאחר שקבלה הגט סתם גזר עליה להמתין ד' שנים אבל כיון שמנהג אשכנז הוא שלא תנשא עד ד' שנים איפשר לקיים את דבריה כי נתנו לה הגט סתם ואחר כך גזר עליה שתמתין ד' שנים כמנהג. ומה שאמר לה שכן התנה בעליך

received a conditional divorce, and now she corrects her statement [to say] that she received a *get* with no qualification [and that it was the ḥakham who] decreed that she wait four years. But since the custom in Ashkenaz is not to [re]marry until four years [have passed], it is possible to uphold her statement, in the sense that they gave her an unqualified *get* and afterwards decreed that she wait four years according to custom. What he [the ḥakham] said to her that "your husband stipulated as such"—he [the husband] did not actually stipulate; rather [the husband requested that] he [the ḥakham] should stipulate to her according to the custom. It can [therefore] be concluded that this woman is prevented [from remarrying] because of the custom, not because of a condition on the divorce. What does it matter to me if [the *get*] was lost? Considering that four years have

---

74   In Hanna's own narrative.

passed for her, and the matter is clear that there is no contradiction between her and the witnesses, because it was from what the ḥakham said to her—"so has your husband stipulated"—that she learned to call it a conditional divorce. You should know that there was no absolute condition, because he did not double it,[75] and we do not suspect that the court erred. It cannot be said that it was an absolute condition, like all conditions [that are twofold, as required], and that she does not remember. [For] one [thing], we are not concerned about such a suspicion, which would make her an 'aguna,[76] for did the Sages[77] not advocate for the interest of permission so as to avoid the 'iggun of a woman?[78] So, should **we** be concerned with suspicions that would make her an 'aguna?! Further, since there are no witnesses that she was a married woman, we rely on her word,[79] for we have only what she herself said. And if you say [in an attempt to prove that the divorce was conditional] that, if the get had been totally unconditional, why did they not tear it, as is the custom[80]—and according to you, is it convenient that the get should not exist unless

לא שהתנה ממש אלא שיתנוהו לה כפי המנהג נמצאת אשה זו מעוכבת מפני המנהג לא מפני תנאי הגט ומה לי שאבד כיון שעברו עליה ד' שנים והדבר ברור כי אין הכחשה בינה לבין העדים כי מדברי החכם שאמר לה כי כן התנה בעליך למדה היא לקרות אותו גט תנאי. תדע שלא היה שם תנאי גמור שהרי לא כפל אותו ולב״ד [ולבית דין] טועין לא חיישי[נן] וליכא למימר תנאי גמור היה ככל תנאין והיא אינה זוכרת חדא דלא חיישינן להאי חששא כדי לעגן אותה דלא קמאי צדדו צדדי[ם] אאנפי דשריותא משום עגונא דאתתא ואנן נחוש חששות כדי לעגנה. ותו כיון דליכא סהדי שהיתה אשת איש מפיה אנו חיים ואין לנו אלא מה שאמרה היא. וא״ת [ואם תאמר] כיון שהגט היה לחלוטין למה לא קרעוהו כמנהג

---

75 I.e., state a twofold condition; see Halakhic Background.
76 I.e., we are not looking for excuses to make her an 'aguna.
77 Lit., "the first ones."
78 There are several instances in the Talmud where the Sages show leniency for the sake of avoiding 'iggun; e.g., Yᵉvamot 88a and Gittin 3a.
79 Lit., "we live from her mouth." In the Mishna and Talmud, this expression arises in disputes about whether a woman's word about herself is believed or not ("we do not live by her mouth"); see, for instance, Mishna Kᵉtubbot 1:7 and 1:8, Kᵉtubbot 12b. In responsa literature the expression is also used when a woman's testimony about herself is accepted, so that "we live from her mouth"; see, for instance, Joseph Caro, Avqat Rokhel 181.
80 The custom of tearing the writ of divorce after given will be addressed further on in the responsum.

it was conditional?![81] Do they ever write the condition on the *get*?! Rather, they write and give her a [record of the] judgment of the religious court [stating] "[the woman] so-and-so was divorced in our presence on condition such-and-such." And if you say that such was the condition, that she should not divorce with it [the *get*] until four years have passed, and therefore we require that the *get* be in existence at that time, if so, what did they accomplish with their ordinance[82] "if he should die or drown in the sea"? "There is no divorce after death"![83] Rather, it [the divorce] was certainly "from now," as has been the practice in all [communities of] Israel, and if so, why did they not tear it? Rather, the reason is that in case she wanted to go to another city, she would have it in her hand as proof that she was divorced. Also, if she found that he had property, she could collect her *kᵉtubba*,[84] and she would not need to look for witnesses that she was divorced. Perhaps there is some other reason, but we should not make the woman an *'aguna* because we do not know [why the *get* was not torn]. On the contrary, an intact *get* is preferable to a torn *get*, but they already customarily do [tear it], and Our Teacher Rabbi Israel[85] gave two reasons [for this], see there.[86] And I have

ולדידך מי ניחא לא יהיה אלא שהיה על תנאי כלום כותבין התנאי בגט אלא מעשה ב״ד [בית דין] כותבין ונותנין לה פלונית נתגרשה בפנינו על תנאי כך וכך וכי״ת [וכי תאמר] שכך היה התנאי שלא תתגרש בו אלא עד ד׳ שנים ולפיכך בעי׳[נן] שיהיה הגט קיים באותי[ה] שעה א״כ [אם כן] מה הועילו בתקנתם אם ימות או יטבע בים הרי אין גט לאחר מיתה אלא ודאי מעכשיו היה כאשר נהגו בכל ישראל וא״כ [ואם כן] למה לא קרעוהו. אלא טעמא הוי כי שמא היתה רוצה ללכת לעיר אחרת ותהיה בידה לראיה שנתגרשה. א״נ [אי נמי] שאם תמצא לו נכסים תגבה כתובתה ולא תצטרך לבקש עדים שנתגרשה או שמא היתה שם סבה אחרת ולא מפני שלא נדענה נעגן את האשה כי אדרבה גט שלם עדיף מגט קרוע אלא שכבר נהגו ומהרי״ר [ומורינו הרב רבי]

---

81 No, they do not! See *MT Hilkhot Gerushin* (The Laws of Divorce) 8,3, in Halakhic Background.

82 This question is a paraphrase of the expression "what have the Sages accomplished with their ordinance?" (*Kᵉtubbot* 10a, *Gittin* 17b, and other locations in the Talmud)

83 *Gittin* 73b.

84 The sum owed her according to her marriage contract if widowed or divorced.

85 R. Israel Isserlein, 1390–1460.

86 *Tᵉrumat Ha-Deshen, Pᵉsaqim Ukhtavim* 40. R. Isserlein states that he learned from his teacher, Maharil (R. Jacob ben Moses Moellin 1360?–1427), that the reason is so that a woman would not come to claim her marital settlement (even though it was already paid); this is based on

added a new reason, which is that it is necessary to be accurate with regard to all the details specified about *gittin*, because if [the *get*] was written by the husband, or by a scribe as dictated by him, the husband might [later] come and disqualify it, by saying: "I [intentionally] invalidated [the *get*] in these details,[87] and I intended to ruin her."[88] For this reason they tear it, because that way the husband cannot come [afterwards] to invalidate it in one of these details, which do not hinder [release of the woman] according to the Torah, but [are such that] she may not marry on its basis a priori. [This applies] even more strongly according to [the view of] those who say [in such a case] that even if she did marry, she should leave [the new husband]. If the [first] husband knows that they will tear [the *get*] immediately and he can no longer ruin her, he will just finish and divorce her completely, and would not intend to ruin her, or he would not divorce her at all, since he knows that he cannot ruin her. So it is a nice custom, but it is clear that if it was not torn, we did not lose anything because of that. I say [an] even greater [argument] than this: Even if there was an actual condition

ישראל ז״ל [זכרונו לברכה] נתן בה שני טעמים ע״ש [עיין שם]. ואני חדשתי בה טעם אחר והוא כי צריך לדקדק בו בכל אותם הדקדוקים שנאמרו בגיטין דאי כתב ליה בעל או דכתב ליה סופר מפומיה ואתי בעל ומערער ואמר אנא הוא דפסילנא בהני דקדוקי ולקלקלה אתכווית ומשום הכי קרעינן ליה כי היכי דלא ליתיה בעל למפסליה באחד מהני דקדוקי דלא מעכבי מן התורה ולא תנשא בו לכתחילה וכ״ש [וכל שכן] לדעת האומרים אפי׳[לו] אם נשאת תצא וכיון שהבעל יודע דמיד קרעי׳[נן] ליה ולא מצי תו לקלקלה הילכ׳[ך] גומר ומגרש לגמרי ואינו מכוין לקלקלה או אינו מגרש כלל כיון שהוא יודע דלא מצי לקלקלי׳[ה] ומנהג יפה הוא אבל הדבר ברור שאם לא נקרע לא בשביל כך הפסדנו. וגדולה מזו אני אומר שאפי׳[לו] שהיה תנאי גמור

Bava Metsiʻa 18a. Even if a woman wants her *get* to prove that she is divorced, it should be torn and on the back it should be written that her marriage settlement was paid, but the *get* is not invalid. See also *Kʻtubbot* 89b. See *SA EH, Seder ha-Get* 86. Isserlein (ibid.) further states that his teacher said that perhaps the reason a *get* is torn was because of a Roman decree forbidding Jews from practicing their religion, as stated in *Gittin* 64a, and even though the reason is no longer relevant, the practice continues.

87 Such as a spelling error. See *MT Hilkhot Gerushin* (The Laws of Divorce) 4,13-14.

88 By making an adulteress of her, should she remarry on the basis of her *get* that is later shown to be invalid. According to some decisors, in such a case, if the woman remarried based on that invalid *get*, she must separate from the new husband, since she was viewed as still married to her first husband. See R. Isaac ben Abba Mari of Marseilles (1120?–1190?), *Sefer Ha-ʻIttur* 7,27b, and *Maggid Mishne, Hilkhot Gerushin* (The Laws of Divorce) 4,14.

on the divorce, but the *get* was lost before the time [the condition took effect], she is divorced. First of all, the language clearly indicates that it [the *get*] was "from now," and according to all opinions, even if the *get* was lost during the time [she had to wait], she was divorced retroactively, because they said to her, "This writ of divorce is for your benefit, because your husband went by sea to distant places, and if he would drown or die, you would be an *'aguna* for all of your days." This would be fine if the divorce were "from now"; then it would be for her benefit, because if he did not come during the [specified] time, she would be divorced retroactively. But if the divorce were neither "from now" nor absolute [i.e., unconditional], what would be her benefit? If he would die or drown at sea, she would not be divorced, because when the divorce would take effect—that is, at the end of the time—he would already not be in the world, and "there is no divorce after death." It would turn out that the divorce would be of no use to her at all, because if we found out that he had died during that time, [then] if he had brothers but no offspring, she [still] would be subject to levirate marriage. And if we found out that he had died after the time [specified] for the divorce, she would be permitted in any event;[89] and if it is because she was not [to be] subject to levirate marriage [that the divorce was intended to take effect only at the end of the specified time], it would not be such a benefit to her.[90] Further, the language that he [the *ḥakham*] spoke, that she

בגט ונאבד הגט קודם הזמן מגורשת חדא שהלשון משמע בהדיא שהיה במעכשיו ולדע״כ [ולדעת כולם] אפילו נאבד הגט בתוך הזמן מגורשת למפרע שהרי אמרו לה כי זה הגט הוא לטובתיך כי בעליך הלך דרך ים למרחקים ואם יטבע או ימות תהיי עגונה כל ימיך ובשלמא אם היה הגט במעכשיו היינו לטובתה שאם לא יבוא תוך הזמן תהיה מגורשת למפרע. אבל לא היה הגט מעכשיו ולא לחלוטין מה היא טובתה אם ימות או יטבע בים לא תהיה מגורשת דהא בשעתא דחייל גטא דהיינו סוף הזמן כבר אינו בעולם ואין גט לאחר מיתה נמצא שאין לה בגט תועלת כלל דאם ידעי׳[נן] שמת בתוך הזמן אם יש לו אחים ואין לו בנים הרי היא זקוקה ליבום ואי ידעי׳[נן] דמית אחר זמן הגט בלאו הכי מותרת ואי משו׳[ם] דלא נפלה קמי יבם אין זו טובה כל כך. ותו דלישנא דקאמרי

---

89 Whether the divorce was "from now" or from a later specified time, but before he died.

90 Abi Zimra aims to dismiss any possibility that the divorce that was sent was anything other than effective immediately or retroactively, either of which is a better option for her than a conditional divorce that would take affect only after a specified time. If it were known that she was not subject to levirate marriage, the benefit of such a conditional divorce is that if the husband did not return within the specified time and there was no testimony that he died,

"would be an *'aguna* for all of your days," means that she would have no remedy. Also, who could tell us [for certain] that he had brothers, but did not have sons, if we did not know what [brothers or sons] he had? Suppose that death is not [so] common, and she would be permitted [to marry another] when the time arrives [for the divorce to take effect]. What do you think?!⁹¹ In any event, if he drowned in [a body of] water without a [visible] end,⁹² [in which] most die, she would not be permitted to marry, because "there is no divorce after death." You should know that if he fell into [a body of] water without a [visible] end, his wife is permitted from the Torah, because, here [in the law] we have that if she married [under such a circumstance] she need not leave [her new husband, in the event that the first husband turns up alive].⁹³ Rather, the Sages decreed that she should not marry, a priori. That means that he is presumed to be dead, and "there is no divorce after death."⁹⁴ Therefore, it is clear to me that the court did not do anything improper, for "it is presumed that a *ḥaver* [does not release anything

תהיי עגונה כל ימיך משמע שאין לה תקנה. ותו דמאן לימא לן דיש לו אחים ואין לו בנים אם לא ידענו מה היה לו נהי דמיתה לא שכיח ומותרת בהגעת זמן ממה נפשך מ"מ [מכל מקום] אם נטבע במים שאין להם סוף דרובם למיתה אינה מותרת לינשא דאין גט לאחר מיתה תדע שאם נפל במים שאין להם סוף אשתו מותרת מן התורה דהא אם נשאת לא תצא אלא דרבנן גזרו שלא תנשא לכתחלה משמע דבחזקת מת מוקמי'[נן] ליה ואין גט לאחר מיתה. הילכך הדבר ברור אצלי שלא עשו ב"ד [בית דין] דבר שאינו מתוקן דחזקה על חבר וכו'[לי] אלא הגט היה לחלוטין או במעכשיו וממה

---

then the divorce would "kick in," and the woman would not be an *'aguna*. But it becomes clear that they don't know whether her husband had brothers or sons or not.

91 Lit., "what is it your desire [to say]"?! In the Talmud, this expression poses the rhetorical question "which position would you adopt?"—in either case the result would be the same!

92 The situation of a woman whose husband has apparently drowned is considered in *Y'vamot* 121a-b. Though the husband's body was not found, the reasoning is that if the body of water has a visible end (such as a lake), and a witness saw the man fall into the water, since the witness did not see him reappear within the time before which he would expire, he is presumed to have drowned. However, if there is no visible end to the body of water, such as an ocean, it is considered feasible that he managed to get ashore or was rescued beyond the sight of the witness, and therefore might not be dead; therefore the woman is not permitted to marry.

93 See, for example, *MT Hilkhot Gerushin* (The Laws of Divorce) 13,20.

94 Therefore, a divorce that would take affect only after a specified time might not be of value to her.

improper from under his hand]."⁹⁵ Rather, the divorce was absolute [and not conditional], or [it was conditional] "from now." What do you think?! The woman is permitted, and, moreover, it is implied by the question, according to what the woman said, that the *hakham* who gave the *get* arranged that these two [characteristics pertain to it]: that it be absolute and "from now." All the more so, from what the permitting *hakham* wrote, since the custom in Ashkenaz is only to give an absolute divorce, so it would be astonishing if the court would have given a divorce that is not "from now" and is conditional. We do not suspect that the court erred, as is [stated] in [chapter] "There are those who inherit" [*Bava Batra* 138b],⁹⁶ even more so because the Ashkenazim are very scrupulous in matters of divorce, and it is obvious that nothing improper would leave their hand. It cannot be said that the husband did not want to give a *get* unless it was conditional but not "from now"; and if you say, "What does he [the husband] care if he dies before the [supposed conditional] time, and she is subject to [levirate marriage] with his brother, and his name would be carried on in Israel"⁹⁷—we cannot say this, first of all, because the custom in Ashkenaz is that *halitsa* is preferred to the commandment of levirate

---

95 "Rabbi Ḥanina Ḥoza'a said, 'It is presumed that a *haver* does not release anything improper from under his hand.'" ('Avoda Zara 41b and other locations in the Talmud) A *haver* [lit., a fellow or associate] is someone who is considered scrupulous in observing the laws of ritual purity, separation of tithes (*ma'asᵉrot*), priestly dues (*tᵉrumot*) and the like. The expression is used by rabbinic authorities in referring to their colleagues in other courts.

96 It is asked there whether a certain precaution is taken out of concern that a court might have erred. The response is that one court does not scrutinize the decision of another court, but it does scrutinize the witnesses who testified previously. See *MT Hilkhot 'Edut* (The Laws of Testimony) 6,5.

97 Deut. 25:5-6.

marriage. Also, we do not presume that people trespass or change the custom of [their] communities, for the custom of our fathers is like Torah,[98] as stated in scripture: *do not forsake your mother's teaching* (Prov. 1:8). Further, the language of the [ḥakham] who arranged the divorce does not imply this [that it was a conditional divorce]. Further, we do not attribute absurd opinions[99] to courts. Also, we ought not to seek out unproven assumptions, or to be concerned about remote suspicions, so as to make the woman an ʿaguna. On the contrary, we should pursue the path of permission, as all the Sages, may their memories be blessed, wrote, and for that reason we do not suspect that he [the husband] might have come and fulfilled his condition [of returning before the specified time], [thereby] canceling the *get*. Even if there were such a suspicion, she is believed that he did not come and did not appease her [i.e., reunite with her], because if she wanted, she could have said "I am single," because there are no witnesses that she was married.[100] This is very clear in my eyes, and therefore I permit her to marry. I wrote what appears right to me, in my humble opinion.

מחזקי[נן] ומנהג אבותינו תורה היא שנאמר ואל תטוש תורת אמך. ותו כי לשון מסדר הגט לא משמע הכי. ותו דלא תלי[נן] בוקי סריקי בבי דינא. ותו דלית לן למיהדר אאומדני דלא מוכחי ולחוש לחששות רחוקות כדי לעגן את האשה אלא אדרבה אית לן למיהדר אאנפי דשריותא כאשר כתבו כל הראשונים ז"ל [זכרונם לברכה] ומהאי טעמא לא חיישי[נן] שמא בא וקיים תנאו ובטל את הגט. ואפי[לו] אם היתה שם חששא היא נאמנת שלא בא ולא פייס מגו דאי בעיא אמרה פנויה אני כיון דליכא סהדי שהיתה נשואה וזה ברור מאד בעיני ולכן אני מתירה לינשא. הנל"ד [הנראה לעניות דעתי] כתבתי.

---

98 *Maḥzor Vitry* 165 and other sources.

99 Lit., "empty vessels." The expression "do not attribute absurd opinions" appears in *Bava Batra* 7a and other locations in the Talmud.

100 See Halakhic Background.

Discussion

Abi Zimra rules that Hanna is a divorced woman who is permitted to marry. He has two main courses of argument:[101]

[1] One can believe Hanna's own testimony that she was married and divorced, relying on established legal reasoning that relates to a woman's testimony about herself in the absence of witnesses, and upon the legal construct of an *amatla*—a reasonable explanation for what might at first seem contradictory. Any discrepancies or inaccuracies in Hanna's testimony are attributed to her not understanding the fine points of divorce law, such as that a lost *get* does not invalidate a divorce and render her an *'aguna*.

[2] The divorce had to be either absolute, or conditional and retroactive to the time when it was given to her. More likely, it was absolute, considering the customs of Ashkenaz. The stipulation made to the woman was that she wait before remarrying, according to Ashkenazi custom in such a case as this. Whether a *get* is torn or not is of no consequence as to the validity of the divorce.

Our exploration of a responsum about a sixteenth-century woman in Jerusalem sheds light on a facet of divorce that is not commonly considered today. Divorce is not only a legal procedure for terminating a marriage mired in discontent, but it was also routinely employed to avoid *'iggun* or widowhood, a status that can be less desirable than divorce, if levirate marriage (or perhaps even worse, a brother-in-law who cannot or will not either marry or perform *ḥalitsa*) might otherwise be on the horizon.

R. Elijah Mizraḥi[102] describes the sending of a *get* under such circumstances as:

> an honorable divorce, because everybody will respect him by saying that the only reason he sent his wife a *get*, which is a *get* with a[n associated] time,[103] is because of a concern that she might be subject to levirate marriage, if he had a brother, or that he might die in a location where there were no witnesses, such as occurs with travelers, and she would remain an *'aguna* for all of her days. There is no honor greater than this.[104]

---

101 See the section numbers in square brackets in the responsum.
102 C. 1450–1526.
103 The time that must elapse for the divorce to go into effect, even if retroactively.
104 *Responsa of R. Elijah Mizraḥi*, 23.

R. Mordecai ben Hillel[105] called a divorce given by a husband who traveled afar and feared leaving his wife as an ʿaguna, a "divorce out of love" (get me-ahava).[106]

The application in such cases of conditional (or, as was preferred within Ashkenazi Jewry, unconditional) divorce makes it clear that the Sages viewed the Jewish legal system as being subject to creative compliance, and so did halakhic decisors for centuries thereafter. That is, they used the letter of the law to construct devices that are perfectly legal and yet undermine the very intent of the law. It would be difficult to claim that the intent of the Torah was to avoid levirate marriage or for men to divorce their wives without any grounds for divorce. The instructions in Deuteronomy 25:9 are for the widowed sister-in-law to spit at the levir who will not marry her; and, according to the Torah, a man divorces his wife on the grounds of ʿervat davar.[107] The Sages expressed multiple opinions about how loosely the grounds for divorce are to be interpreted,[108] but the intent is clearly not for a happily married couple to divorce in order to circumvent an inconvenient aspect of Jewish law. The Sages and later decisors exhibited radical judicial activism in their concern to avoid levirate marriage and ʿiggun, notwithstanding their respect for the divinity of the law.

R. Eliezer Waldenberg[109] has written:

> the basis of the ordinance [stating] that one who goes to war should write a bill of divorce for his wife, unconditionally, was from the outset [to circumvent such cases as that] of a man who had no sons, so that she [his wife] would not be subject to levirate marriage. *This was already practiced in the days of Moses.*[110]

What an amazing statement! The Torah was revealed to Moses at Sinai, and he saw fit to go about circumventing its law! R. Waldenberg bases this fantastic claim on the commentary of R. Jacob ben Asher[111] on the Torah. The Baʿal ha-Turim notes that the word *ḥaluts* appears in two places in the Pentateuch—three times in Numbers 32, where it means "armed" (or "vanguard"), and in the

---

105 1240?–1298.
106 *Sefer Ha-Mordᵉkhai*, Gittin 359, in the name of the Tosafist R. Isaac (the Elder) ben Samuel.
107 Something unseemly (Deut. 24:1).
108 *Gittin* 90a.
109 1912–2006.
110 *Tsits Eliʿezer* 15:57, §5; emphasis is mine.
111 C. 1269–1343; known as Baʿal ha-Turim, author of the *Arbaʿa Turim*, or the *Tur*.

passage on levirate marriage in Deuteronomy 25:10, in the expression *bet ḥaluts ha-na'al*.[112] He sees a connection between these two uses of the word:

> This is the basis for saying that everyone who goes [to fight] the wars of the House of David writes a *get* for his wife, so that she would not be subject to a levir or to perform *ḥalitsa* on the levir [*Shabbat* 56a]. From here [this verse] we learn that Moses also did so, and David learned from him. That is [the meaning of] *v*ᵉ*'avar lakhem kol ḥaluts* [Num. 32:21], meaning, *ḥaluts ha-na'al*.[113]

At this point in the Torah, the Israelites were about to enter the Land of Israel when the tribes of Gad and Reuven and the half-tribe of Menashe made a deal with Moses to take part in the conquest of the Land, even though they preferred to settle east of the Jordan River. According to the interpretation of Ba'al ha-Turim, Moses saw fit to require that every fighting man, or at least every one who was childless but had a brother, give his wife a *get* to avoid any need for levirate marriage or *ḥalitsa*. Can there be any greater attestation that the fluidity of the halakha was built into the system from the outset?

Questions for Further Discussion

What are your thoughts about using conditional divorce (or unconditional divorce) to avoid problems of *'iggun* and levirate marriage? Why did rabbinic law prefer to use divorce rather than annulment to prevent problems of *'iggun* and levirate marriage?[114] Which method is preferable, and why? Is it preferable to find solutions with "creative compliance" or to amend the laws—in this case marriage and divorce laws?

Compare the status and options of an abandoned spouse (or someone whose spouse has disappeared) as reflected in Jewish law (based on what you learned here) with the situation in other legal systems, ancient and modern, in various cultures and locations.[115]

---

112 I.e., "the family of the one whose sandal was removed." See Deut. 25:7-10.

113 R. Jacob b. Asher, *Rimzei Ba'al ha-Turim* (Commentary on the Torah) to Num. 32:21. The JPS version renders the phrase, which refers to the commitment of the tribes of Gad and Reuven to join in the conquest of the Land of Israel, as "every shock fighter among you crosses [the Jordan]," but R. Jacob's comment takes it in the sense of "every *ḥaluts* will pass away from you"—that is, there will be no men who have had their sandals removed for refusing to marry their brothers' widows.

114 See [Westreich].

115 For example, see [Rapoport] and [Rapoport2].

How long is a reasonable minimum to be defined by law for a person to wait for a "missing-in-action" spouse before the person should be permitted to remarry, if they wish? Should it be the same if a nonmilitary spouse disappears? Consider the situation in various times in history, and the available methods for identification of a dead person (fingerprints, DNA, etc.) and communication at each point in time that you consider.[116]

Should this "time to wait" be different if the couple divorces—conditionally or unconditionally—at the time of a spouse's departure?

Why do you think using divorce as a method to avoid problems of 'iggun and levirate marriage has practically fallen out of use during the latter half of the twentieth century?[117]

Nine cases of 'agunot from the 9/11 tragedy were presented to the Beth Din of America and subsequently resolved.[118] All of the cases were resolved by establishing that each of the women's husbands had died, following excruciating deliberation and analysis, using halakhic reasoning and precedents together with modern technologies.[119] How did the circumstances of those women's 'iggun differ from those of a sixteenth-century woman whose husband traveled afar and didn't return? Do you feel it would have been better if each 9/11 declared-widow had had a conditional divorce given to her?[120]

---

116 Consider the case of Tom and Dorothy Gordy, [Carter].

117 [Fixler] points to several halakhic and societal concerns that arose during this period in the State of Israel. Differences in circumstances of modern warfare are also discussed. There does seem to be a dissonance between the common use of divorce for such purposes in previous generations and the halakhic concerns that arose beginning approximately in the middle of the twentieth century.

118 See [Reiss]. Several other cases presented to other religious courts were subsequently referred to the Beth Din of America.

119 By declaring each of the women a widow, any case that would have then required levirate marriage would need to be followed by ḥalitsa, so that the widow would be able to remarry under Jewish law. In fact, a ḥalitsa ceremony was held on May 30, 2002 for each of two widows whose husbands had no biological offspring (see [Reiss], 32). Fortunately, neither of the cases involved a minor levir, which would have rendered the widow, for almost all practical purposes (except that she would observe the mourning customs for her deceased husband), an 'aguna—chained to the minor levir, until the time he could perform ḥalitsa. (Levirate marriage is no longer practiced, with very rare exceptions.) Permitting husbands to remarry in cases of wives who have perished is much less complex, given that it is not forbidden by the Torah for a man to take a second wife, and there is no concern about mamzerut. One such case was presented to the Beth Din of America ([Reiss], 17).

120 This is not a totally impractical idea. One might think that since a conditional divorce is invalid if a man cohabits with his wife after the get is given, it would make no sense for a man to give a conditional divorce to his wife every day that he leaves for the office. However,

Further Reading

[Carter] Carter, Jimmy. *An Hour before Daylight*. New York: Simon & Schuster, 2001. Pages 252-253.

[Fixler] Fixler, Dror, and Amihai Radzyner. "The Granting of a *Get* Prior to Going to War" [Hebrew]. *Teḥumin* 27 (2007): 409-425.

[Goitein] Goitein, S. D. *A Mediterranean Society*. Vol. 3, *The Jewish Communities of the Arab World as Portrayed in the Documents of Cairo Geniza Economic Foundation*. Berkeley: University of California Press, 1978.

[Goitein2] ———. *Letters of Medieval Jewish Traders*. Princeton: Princeton University Press, 1973.

[Goldman] Goldman, Israel M. *The Life and Times of Rabbi David Ibn Abi Zimra*. New York: The Jewish Theological Seminar of America, 1970.

[Lamdan] Lamdan, Ruth. *A Separate People: Jewish Women in Palestine, Syria and Egypt in the Sixteenth Century*. Jewish Studies 26. Leiden: Brill, 2000.

[Lamdan2] ———, ed. *Sefer tikkun sof'rim of Rabbi Itzḥak Tzabah*. Hebrew; Tel Aviv: Tel Aviv University, 2009.

---

because men going to the army might have a leave during which they can visit their wives, such concerns have been addressed by instructing a man who has no children but does have a brother to give his wife a *get* with the condition that she "be divorced from me the first moment after I depart from you, my wife, for the last time, before I travel to the army camp of the government of North America, under condition that I do not return, even due to unusual circumstances of coercion, during the first year following official declaration of peace by our government of North America ... or if you receive official notice from the government that I died or am missing, it too should be [a divorce] from the first moment after I depart from you, my wife, for the last time, before I travel to the army camp of the government of North America, but if I return during the first year following official declaration of peace by our government of North America, in an official manner to the place where you, my wife, reside, to the home where you, my wife, reside at that time, then [this] will not be a *get*. Further, I trust you, my wife, to state [in testimony] that I did not come [following my final departure] and that I did not appease you" (see Pardes, "Ki Tetse La-milḥama," Hapardes 16, no. 2 [May 1942]: 2-3).

Notice the twofold condition ("be divorced from me ... under condition that I do not return ... but if I return ... will not be a *get*"), which we saw in Maimonides's Laws of Personal Status in Halakhic Background. The final statement is required so that there is no suspicion that the *get* was canceled (see Gittin 76b and *MT Hilkhot Gerushin* [The Laws of Divorce] 9,9). Thus, using this approach, one could theoretically deposit a conditional divorce with his wife to take effect, retroactively, in the event that he does not return for a specified amount of time. R. Avraham Y. Karelitz (known as the Ḥazon Ish) opposed this method on certain halakhic grounds, but historically it was considered acceptable by many authorities.

One must also consider the aspect of mourning—a widow has an obligation to mourn her deceased husband according to a defined set of customs; a divorcee clearly does not, but that is not to say that she is prohibited from mourning in some manner.

[Rapoport] Rapoport, Yossef. *Marriage, Money and Divorce in Medieval Islamic Society.* Cambridge: Cambridge University Press, 2005.

[Rapoport2] ———. "Women and Gender in Mamlūk Society: An Overview." *Mamlūk Studies Review* 11, no. 2 (2007): 1-47.

[Reiss] Reiss, Yona. "The Resolution of the World Trade Center Agunot Cases by the Beth Din of America: A Personal Retrospective." In *Contending with Catastrophe: Jewish Perspectives on September 11th*, edited by Michael Broyde, 13-35. New York: Beth Din of America Press & K'hal Publishing, 2011.

[Stein] Stein, Peter. *A Textbook of Roman Law from Augustus to Justinian.* Cambridge: Cambridge University Press, 1963. Chapter 10.

[Westreich] Westreich, Avishalom. "Annulment of Marriage (*Hafka'at Kiddushin*): Re-Examination of an Old Debate." *Working Papers of the Agunah Research Unit*, no. 11 (June 2008). https://static1.1.sqspcdn.com/static/f/784513/11612805/130216 5216787/Avishalom+Westreich+Annulment+of+Marriage+2008.pdf.

2.
The Tax Cut Lobby
Rabbi Joseph ibn Lev Responsum 4:14

Historical Background

The question posed to R. Joseph ibn Lev[1] in the following responsum provides a window into the methods of survival of Jewish communities in the sixteenth century in both the Ottoman Empire and the parts of Europe where Jews were allowed to reside.[2] While taxes of various types and customs duties were imposed on all residents of a domain, additional demands of heavy taxes and higher customs duties on merchants' wares were levied on the Jews[3] in exchange for the privilege of living under the ruler's protection. In the Ottoman Empire Jews were very involved in trade, so that the customs duties had a significant impact on their livelihoods and ability to compete.[4] Offering gifts and other favors so as to reduce these taxes or customs duties was a common phenomenon.

The events referred to in this question took place during the reign of Sultan Murad III (1574 until 1595).[5] The fact that Jews were tolerated and even at times

---

1   Known as Mahari ibn Lev, 1505–1580. Mahari is the Hebrew acronym for Morenu Ha-Rav Yosef.

2   The events in this responsum took place in 1576. The first Portuguese Jews and crypto-Jews in Amsterdam, a city that was relatively tolerant for that era, did not arrive there until approximately 1590, so the tolerance later experienced in Amsterdam was yet unknown to Jewish communities (though even after 1590 the Jews in Amsterdam were not accepted as citizens, nor could they practice trades that were protected by guilds; see the chapter "Excommunication in Amsterdam").

3   In the Ottoman Empire, higher taxes were levied on Christians, as well. For example, in the city of Bodon, north of Belgrade, the customs duty on merchandise imported by Jews or Christians was 5%, while on goods imported by Muslims it was 3%. See [Goodblatt], 51. For a description of other taxes imposed on Jews in the Ottoman Empire, see [Rozen], 26-34.

4   For further reading on the trade activity of Jews of the Ottoman Empire during this period, see [Shmuelevitz], chapter 4. For a description of the variety and levels of taxes that Jews paid to the sultans, see [Shmuelevitz], chapter 3, and [Goodblatt], chapter 6.

5   "The happy relations between the Jews and the Ottoman rulers reached their climax during the reign of Sulaiman and Selim II. The death of the latter in 1574, however, marked the close of this happy period. When his successor, Murad III, ascended the throne, the era of

welcomed to live in the lands ruled by the Ottomans[6] did not absolve them from the additional taxes imposed on minorities. Like anyone who is excessively burdened with taxes (and who is not?), the Jewish community attempted to use its available means to reduce that burden.

The question posed to ibn Lev is of significant interest from a historical perspective. The detailed response also serves as an opportunity to introduce the readers to Jewish contract law, which is a common application of Jewish civil law, even in present times. The reader will be rewarded with some interesting aspects of the Sages' attitudes towards obligatory contracts and breach of agreements. Students and practitioners of contract law can compare the legal systems with which they are familiar to Jewish law. Beyond the contract law, the response offers an interesting collection of resources from which ibn Lev draws his arguments, and some of the challenges facing an adjudicator who wants nothing more than to maintain peace within the community.

Halakhic Background

In his discussion of the question, ibn Lev considers the specifics of a signed agreement and how binding it is.

The very nature of Jewish contract law is enigmatic. While Jewish law is quite explicit about transfer and acquisition of property, whether through a sale or a gift, and about monetary debts, such as loans, the fundamental law does not include contractual obligations to transfer property or to perform an act in the future.

Thus, Jewish law distinguishes between sale of an object and contracting to sell an object. Sale is a current transfer of ownership of something concrete. Such a transfer must be finalized with an "act of acquisition," called a *qinyan*.[7] Among the methods of acquisition for the sale of an object (not all of which are appropriate for all types of property) are transfer of money, transfer of a deed, lifting or

---

peace and freedom that the Jews had enjoyed for eighty years declined sharply" ([Goodblatt], 119).

6   A frequently found narrative says that the Ottomans welcomed expelled Jews to their empire, but for a different version see [Rozen], 37-44.

7   The root is *qnh*, which means "to take possession" or "to acquire."

pulling the object, or an act called *qinyan sudar*,[8] whereby, for example, a scarf or a handkerchief[9] is passed from the buyer to the seller[10] to finalize the acquisition. Generally, unqualified use of the word *qinyan* refers to a *qinyan sudar*.

In contrast to the sale of an object, a contract to sell an object is an agreement to a future transfer of ownership. Actual ownership of an object permits the owner to perform certain legal acts with that object that require ownership of it.[11] However, such legal acts cannot be performed with a contract of obligation to transfer ownership. Even if a *qinyan* is performed, an agreement to a future transfer of ownership is considered a *qinyan d^evarim* (roughly translated as an "acquisition of words"), which is not binding. For a *qinyan* to be binding, it must relate to a concrete object, and words have no substance (even if they are written). Therefore, a *qinyan* performed to finalize an agreement for an act to be performed in the future is not binding.[12]

Even though a *qinyan d^evarim* is not binding, the Sages frowned upon someone who failed to uphold such an agreement: "One who conducts a verbal transaction[13] does not effect an acquisition, yet one who reneges from it—the spirit of the Sages is displeased with him."[14] R. Yoḥanan says that retracting such a transaction is a "breach of trust."[15] However, the displeasure of the Sages cannot enforce a *qinyan d^evarim* in a court of law.

---

8   A *sudar* is a head scarf or turban.
9   In Ruth 4:7-8, which is considered the basis in Jewish law for this type of transaction, a sandal was used for the act of transfer of the deceased Elimelech's estate, including his deceased son's wife Ruth, to Boaz.
10 But is returned to the buyer (*SA ḤM* 195:1-2), as it is a symbolic act.
11 For instance, one of the three methods to betroth a woman is for a man to give her something he owns that is worth at least a *p^eruta* (a small denomination). However, a man cannot betroth a woman by transferring to her ownership the future proceeds of a business contract, even one in which, for example, he is promised payment of a million dollars in exchange for his services next month as the star in a film.
12 A contract between an employer and a worker who will be paid for his services is an exception to this rule. Employment of salaried workers has its own distinct set of regulations.
13 A *qinyan d^evarim* need not be verbal—it is an agreement to perform a future transaction or action. However, this source is more specifically interpreted to be referring to a verbal agreement to purchase (and therefore sell, from the perspective of the other party) something, but there was no actual act of acquisition, such as lifting the object. Therefore, it falls under the category of a *qinyan d^evarim*.
14 *Bava M^etsi'a* 48a.
15 Lit., "lacking in trust" (*m^eḥusrei amana*). *Bava M^etsi'a* 49a. Rav maintains that it does not involve a breach of trust. Maimonides rules (*MT Hilkhot M^ekhira* [The Laws of Sales] 7,8) that one who reneges on a verbal transaction—whether it is the buyer or the seller—are

Be that as it may, a commercial system without an instrument for obligatory contracts would be difficult to maintain, and the nonbinding nature of a *qinyan d'varim* is circumvented in Jewish law by several methods.[16] One of these is called *situmta*, which, according to Rashi,[17] is a seal used on a wine jug.[18] Maimonides ruled that if it is the common practice in a particular land to use such a sign to finalize an agreement to sell, then in that location neither party can renege if that sign was used.[19] In the *Shulḥan 'Arukh* there is a ruling similar to that of Maimonides, and even a handshake, if such is the custom, is binding.[20] Thus, custom that is external to the fundamental Jewish law is permitted so as to permit certain obligatory contracts.

Our first source, from *Bava Batra* 3a, explores the concept of *qinyan d'varim*, for which it is the primary Talmudic source. The excerpt is part of a discussion in the *g'mara* that is only incidental to the point of interest for us.

The discussion is about the first *mishna* in *Bava Batra*, which begins with the following statement: "If two joint owners [or tenants] wish [and agree] to make a division in a courtyard, they must build the wall in the middle." The *g'mara* presents two methods to explain the *mishna*. According to the second method, because the *mishna* states that they are to build a wall, rather than some other simpler mark of division, the *g'mara* deduces that damage is inflicted when a per-

---

among those lacking in trust, and the spirit of the Sages is displeased with him. However, such a person is not subject to the curse *mi she-para* (He who exacted, etc., found in the final source in Halakhic Background). Applying the term *m'ḥusrei amana* might be more severe than it seems at first glance. In the midrashim (e.g., *M'khilta d'Rabbi Yishma'el B'shalaḥ Masekhta d'Vayisa* 4), those who were lacking in faith in Moses and in God—such as those who did not trust that there would be manna every day and therefore saved some that rotted (Exod. 16:20) and those who did not trust that there would be no manna on the Sabbath and went out to collect it (Exod. 16:27)—are called *m'ḥusrei amana*. Applying this term to those who breach trust in their business transactions is equating them to such sinners, deserving of retribution.

16 Each method has its proponents and opponents among Jewish legal authorities, and each one is considered more appropriate for some specific circumstances and less appropriate for others; in this context we can only touch on the fact that there are, indeed, methods to grapple with the inherent limitations of Jewish contract law, so as to render an obligatory contract that is enforceable in a rabbinical court.

17 *Bava M'tsi'a* 74a at *situmta*.

18 The source of this legal expression is *Bava M'tsi'a* 74a. There are several definitions offered for the word, all of which refer to some indication that was commonly used on merchandise to indicate that a sale was final, even if money had not yet exchanged hands.

19 MT Hilkhot M'khira (The Laws of Sales) 7,6.

20 YD 201:1-2

son looks into another's property. The question is raised, then, if that is so, why do the joint owners need to agree to make a division? Either owner has a right to demand it! Rav Asi suggests in the name of R. Yoḥanan that the *mishna* is referring to situations where a partner cannot demand a division (such as when the courtyard is too small to divide, as a division would result in less than four cubits per owner). In such a case, if they agree to make a division, then the *mishna* instructs them to build a wall. The citation begins with a question about this instruction.

Bava Batra 3a	בבא בתרא ג׳ א׳
Under what circumstance did you interpret the *mishna*? [In the situation] that there is no obligatory division. [But] if it is [in the situation] that there is no obligatory division, what does it matter if they agree? They [either party] can retract! R. Asi said in the name of R. Yoḥanan: "[Our case is in the situation] that they performed a *qinyan* [to commit them-	במאי אוקימתא למתני׳ [תנין] בשאין בה דין חלוקה אי בשאין בה דין חלוקה כי רצו מאי הוי נהדרו בהו א״ר [אמר רב] אסי א״ר [אמר רבי] יוחנן שקנו מידן וכי קנו מידן מאי הוי קנין דברים בעלמא הוא בשקנו מידן ברוחות רב אשי אמר כגון שהלך זה בתוך שלו והחזיק וזה בתוך שלו והחזיק

selves, so that they cannot retract]." [The *g^emara* challenges:] But [even] if they performed a *qinyan*, what does it matter? It is [merely] a *qinyan d^evarim* [with no transfer of anything concrete, and therefore it is not binding]! [The response to this challenge is that] they performed a *qinyan* by choosing sides[21] [of the courtyard, which is a *qinyan* of something concrete]. Rav Ashi said: "Such as this one [i.e., party] traversed his [side] and took possession,[22] and this one [the other party traversed] his [side] and took possession."

---

21 Lit., "with winds," i.e., "winds" meaning "directions."
22 Rav Ashi uses the word *heḥeziq*, which refers to an act of *ḥazaqa*, or taking possession. A *ḥazaqa* is one of the methods employed to take possession of land, and there are a variety of ways that a *ḥazaqa* on real property can be established. Rashi (*Bava Batra* 3a at *v^eheḥeziq*) offers the example that each party digs a little in his portion.

Even if the restrictions of *qinyan d'varim* are overcome, the fact that many contracts include conditions or contingencies raises other complexities in Jewish contract law. For example, an aleatory[23] contract—that is, a contract in which the obligation of one or both parties is contingent upon the uncertain occurrence of a particular event—can be problematic. Certain aleatory conditions are termed in Jewish law *asmakhta* (lit., "reliance"). Suppose Reuben makes a promise or undertakes an obligation conditioned upon the occurrence of an event; if Reuben never really expects the event to occur, then he never expects to have to fulfill his obligation.[24] A similar situation is when Reuben guarantees a penalty payment in the event that he cannot make a certain thing happen or a certain condition does not occur within a specified time. In the first situation, the promisor is confident that something will never happen. In the second, he is confident that it will.

The next source, from *Bava Batra* 168a, provides us with a case of *asmakhta* and informs us of the Tannaitic disagreement as to whether *asmakhta* is binding.

Rashbam[25] defines *asmakhta* as a case of one who promises his fellow to pay or forfeit something unless he performs some act in the future.[26] He relies on the assumption, made at the time of agreement to the condition, that he would be able to perform the act, but due to unforeseen and uncontrollable circumstances he is unable to do it.

---

23 The etymology of the word is the Latin *aleator*, "gambler," derived from *alea*, a dice game. Insurance policies are a common type of aleatory contract.
24 Hence, the word *asmakhta*—Reuben was relying on his assumption that the event would not occur.
25 R. Samuel ben Meir (c. 1080–1085–c. 1174), one of Rashi's grandsons. In *Bava Batra*, the commentary where Rashi's commentary usually appears in the printed editions of the Talmud is in fact Rashbam's commentary from page 29b and on.
26 *Bava Batra* 168a at *asmakhta*.

Bava Batra 168a

בבא בתרא קס"ח א'

mishna: If one paid a portion of his debt, and [the creditor] put his bond [of indebtedness] in escrow,[27] and [the borrower] said to him [the third party]: "If I have not given you [the balance of the debt] between now and such-and-such day, give him [the creditor] his bond,"[28] [and] the time arrived, but he did not pay—R. Yose says he [the third party] must give [the bond to the creditor, but] R. Yᵉhuda says he should not give [it].

מתני'[תין] מי שפרע מקצת חובו והשליש את שטרו ואמר לו אם לא נתתי לך מכאן ועד יום פלוני תן לו שטרו הגיע זמן ולא נתן רבי יוסי אומר יתן רבי יהודה אומר לא יתן גמ'[רא] במאי קמיפלגי ר'[בין] יוסי סבר אסמכתא קניא ורבי יהודה סבר אסמכתא לא קניא אמר רב נחמן אמר רבה בר אבוה אמר רב הלכה כרבי יוסי

gᵉmara: About what [issue] do they disagree? R. Yose maintains that *asmakhta* is binding, while R. Yᵉhuda maintains that *asmakhta* is not binding. Rav Naḥman said in the name of Rabbah bar Avuh, who said in the name of Rav: "Halakha is according to R. Yose."[29]

---

27 When a person borrows a sum from a creditor, the creditor holds a bond (an IOU) as proof of the loan. Upon payment of the debt, the creditor should return the bond to the borrower, who should then destroy it. Rashbam (*Bava Batra* 168a at *vᵉhishlish et shᵉtaro*) explains that in the case in this *mishna*, because the payment of the debt is only partial, rather than for the creditor to write a receipt for the portion paid—which was considered a bother—he agreed with the borrower to deposit the bond with a third party, who was trusted to keep track of the balance due.

28 If this would come to be, then the creditor would be able to demand the full amount from the borrower. This is an example of an aleatory condition. The borrower expects to pay the balance by the promised date. In fact, if he had to pay the full amount because he did not pay the balance by the promised date, it would be like paying interest, which was strictly prohibited. For this reason, several Rishonim offer explanations of the intent of this agreement, so that it would not constitute an agreement to pay interest.

29 The Tosafot state (at *amar Rav Naḥman amar Rabbah bar Avuh*) that the text should read "halakha is **not** according to R. Yose" and that this version is consistent with *Nᵉdarim* 27a, where Rav Naḥman states "halakha is not according to R. Yose, who says that *asmakhta* is binding." The Tosafot also state that such is the text in most books (which, of course, were manuscripts at that time). Other Rishonim apparently also had the text as the Tosafot say it should be. Occurrences of each version are found in the extant manuscripts. The conclusion of the *gᵉmara* is the same, either way, but the Tosafot's arguments (not all of which are summarized here), the prevalence of that version in the Rishonim, and the flow of the conversation all point to the Tosafot's version being the correct one, so that Rav Naḥman states that halakha is not according to R. Yose, but R. Ami feels at a loss, as R. Yoḥanan, his teacher, taught him otherwise. However, indeed, the *gᵉmara* states, halakha is not according to R. Yose.

When they [people with a question of *asmakhta*] would come before R. Ami, he would say to them: "Since R. Yoḥanan has taught us time and again that halakha is according to R. Yose, what can I do?"[30] [However, the *gᵉmara* rules:] But halakha is not according to R. Yose, [but according to R. Yᵉhuda].	כי אתו לקמיה דרבי אמי אמר להו וכי מאחר שרבי יוחנן מלמדנו פעם ראשונה ושניה הלכה כרבי יוסי אני מה אעשה ואין הלכה כרבי יוסי

Given the restrictions regarding a *qinyan dᵉvarim* and *asmakhta*, it would appear quite difficult for anyone to form a binding agreement to do something. However, various "workarounds" that are later employed by Rishonim to circumvent these restrictions are already grounded in Talmudic cases.

The following source, from *Bava Batra* 173b, presents a case of what would, at first glance, appear to be a situation of *asmakhta*—the case of a loan guarantee, where the guarantor never really expects the borrower to default. However, as it turns out, even though *asmakhta* is not binding, the guarantor "obligates himself" to pay in the event of default, in exchange for the gratification of being considered trustworthy by the creditor. Thus, the loan guarantee is binding. Such a construct is only one of several constructs grounded in Talmudic law that are employed to overcome the limitations on *qinyanim* and contractual agreements.

Bava Batra 173b	**בבא בתרא קע״ג ב׳**
Amemar said: "There is a dispute between R. Yᵉhuda and R. Yose [as to whether] a guarantor [of a loan] is liable [to pay the debt if the borrower defaults]. According to R. Yose, who said that *asmakhta* is binding, a guarantor is liable. According to R. Yᵉhuda, who said that	אמר אמימר ערב דמשתעבד מחלוקת ר׳[בין] יהודה ור׳[בין] יוסי לרבי יוסי דאמר אסמכתא קניא ערב משתעבד לר׳[בין] יהודה דאמר אסמכתא לא קניא ערב לא משתעבד אמר ליה רב אשי לאמימר הא מעשים בכל יום

asmakhta is not binding, a guarantor is not liable."[31] Rav Ashi said to Amemar:

---

30 So that R. Ami would rule according to R. Yose.

31 The agreement of a guarantor to back someone's loan could be considered a classic case of *asmakhta*. The guarantor agrees to it under the assumption that the borrower will not default. Otherwise, he never would have agreed to guarantee another person's loan.

"But every day there are occurrences [of us ruling] that *asmakhta* is not binding, and [yet] a guarantor is liable! Rather," said Rav Ashi, "on account of the gratification of being trusted [by the creditor, the guarantor] fully accepts liability."

דאסמכתא לא קניא וערב משתעבד
אלא אמר רב אשי בההוא הנאה דקא
מהימן ליה גמר ומשתעבד נפשיה

Two cases in *Bava M'tsi'a*, presented below, are compared to the case in the following *mishna*.

Bava M'tsi'a 104a[32]	בבא מציעא ק״ד א׳

mishna: If one leases a field from his fellow[33] and lets it lie fallow, we assess it for how much it is capable of producing, and he [the sharecropper] pays him [the agreed percentage of the assessed amount], because he writes for him thus: "If I let it lie fallow and do not cultivate it, I will pay according to the [value of] the best [produce]."

מתני׳ [תין] המקבל שדה מחבירו
והובירה שמין אותה כמה ראויה
לעשות ונותן לו שכך כותב לו אם
אוביר ולא אעביד אשלם במיטבא

The Sages fine-tune the definition of *asmakhta* by comparing the following two cases with the case just seen above. In the two following sources, stipulations that are either exaggerated or not within the total control of the person upon whom the stipulation would fall are considered *asmakhta*, and therefore are not binding.

---

32 This is Mishna *Bava M'tsi'a* 9:3. The reference above is to the page in the BT because the following source is part of the discussion in the *g'mara* on that *mishna*.

33 For a percentage of the crops, as a sharecropper.

Bava M'tsi'a 104b — בבא מציעא ק"ד ב'

A certain man who leased a field from his fellow said: "If I should let it lie fallow, I will pay you a thousand *zuz*." He let one third lie fallow. The [Sages of] Nehardea said: The law is that he should pay 333 1/3 [*zuz*]. Rava said: It is [a case of] *asmakhta*, and *asmakhta* is not binding. [The *g'mara* asks:] According to Rava, what is the difference from what we teach [in a *mishna*]: "If I let it lie fallow and do not cultivate it, I will pay according to the [value of] the best [produce]"? There, he is not exaggerating. Here, because he states something excessive, he is exaggerating [making it a case of *asmakhta*].

ההוא גברא דקבל ארעא מחבריה אמר אי מוברנא לה יהיבנא לך אלפא זוזי אוביר תילתא אמרי נהרדעי דינא הוא דיהיב ליה תלת מאה ותלתין ותלתא ותילתא רבא אמר אסמכתא היא ואסמכתא לא קניא ולרבא מאי שנא מהא דתנן אם אוביר ולא אעביד אשלם במיטבא התם לא קא גזים הכא כיון דקאמר מילתא יתירתא גוזמא בעלמא הוא דקגזים

Bava M'tsi'a 73b — בבא מציעא ע"ג ב'

Rav Ḥamma said: If someone gives his fellow *zuzim* to purchase wine for him, but he was negligent and did not buy for him, then he [the fellow must] pay him according to the going [price] in the market of Zolsh'fat.[34] Amemar said: I said this halakha before Rav Z'vid of Nehardea. He said: What Rav Ḥamma says is so only for the case of [a request to purchase] unspecified wine, but not if he [the one requesting the purchase said] "this [specific] wine," because who said they would sell it to him? Rav Ashi said: Not even if he [requested] unspecified wine [would the fellow be required to pay]. What is the reason? Because it is [a case of] *asmakhta*, and *asmakhta* is not binding. So according to Rav Ashi, what is the difference from what we teach:

אמר רב חמא האי מאן דיהיב זוזי לחבריה למיזבן ליה חמרא ופשע ולא זבין ליה משלם ליה כדקא אזיל אפרוותא דזולשפט אמר אמימר אמריתא לשמעתא קמיה דרב זביד מנהרדעא אמר כי קאמר רב חמא הני מילי בייו סתם אבל ביין זה לא מי יימר דמזבני ליה ניהליה רב אשי אמר אפילו יין סתם נמי לא מאי טעמא אסמכתא היא ואסמכתא לא קניא ולרב אשי מאי שנא מהא דתנן

---

34 There are several versions of the spelling of the name.

"If I let it lie fallow and do not cultivate it, I will pay according to the [value of] the best [produce]"? There, it is within his reach.³⁵ Here, it is not within his reach [because it is not even certain he can buy the requested wine].

אם אוביר ולא אעביד אשלם במיטבא
התם בידו הכא לאו בידו

The final source, which presents the attitude of the Sages towards those who renege on their business deals, counterbalances the allowance for claims of *asmakhta*.

Mishna *Bava M'tsi'a* 4:2	משנה בבא מציעא ד,ב
How [is movable property acquired]? If he pulls³⁶ the produce from him [the seller], but did not [yet] pay him the money, he [the buyer] may not renege. If he paid him the money, but did not yet pull the produce, he may renege, but they [the Sages] said: "He who exacted punishment from the people of the generation of the flood³⁷ will also exact punishment from one who does not stand by his word."³⁸ R. Shimon says: "Whoever has the money in his hand has the upper hand."³⁹	כיצד משך ממנו פרות ולא נתן לו מעות אינו יכול לחזור בו נתן לו מעות ולא משך ממנו פירות יכול לחזור בו אבל אמרו מי שפרע מאנשי דור המבול עתיד להיפרע ממי שאינו עומד בדיבורו ר'[בי] שמעון אומ'[ר] כל שהכסף בידו ידו לעליונה

---

35 Lit., "in his hand," referring to the ability of the sharecropper to cultivate the land.

36 Pulling an object (or drawing it towards the purchaser) is one of the methods for an act of acquisition.

37 Gen. 6:11-13.

38 This curse is called *mi she-para* (He who exacted) in the halakhic literature. The curse applies in cases where the money was transferred, but the act of acquisition was not yet performed, which would permit the transfer to be cancelled. It is codified as halakha that such a curse applies in those cases; see MT Hilkhot M'khira (The Laws of Sales) 7,1. It is not applied in cases of either a *qinyan d'varim* or a verbal agreement.

39 That is, he has the right to cancel the transaction (and return the money, if appropriate).

Discussion

In the first source, concerning the division of a courtyard, a *qinyan* (with, for example, a handkerchief) is not effective in the case of *qinyan dᵉvarim*. Rather, there has to be some more substantive act relating to the substance of the agreement, such as digging a little in each party's portion of the property to be divided. Therefore, in Talmudic law an obligation to perform an act can be formalized, so long as the agreement is made according to certain procedural requirements.

Several more sources cited above attempted to clarify the distinction between a valid conditional agreement and one considered *asmakhta*, in which case the agreement would not be binding, as R. Yᵉhuda's opinion that *asmakhta* is not binding prevails. In spite of these attempts to distinguish between *asmakhta* and binding aleatory agreements, consensus among the Rishonim was elusive, and they offered many opinions about exactly what *asmakhta* is.

The Rashba[40] wrote:

> the scholars of earlier and later generations exerted effort in an attempt to solve the matter of the *asmakhta*—what is this thing *asmakhta*, and upon what does it depend—and I have not seen one colleague agree with another. One says that it is something that is beyond his [he who made the condition] reach to uphold, or that it is exaggerated. Another says that *asmakhta* is [defined] only by what is dependent upon himself [he who made the condition,] but not by what depends upon the conscientiousness of others. There are those who say that there is no *asmakhta* [in the case of] one upon his deathbed.[41] And each one brings proof [of his opinion] that is worthy of being relied on. And I grew weary and found questions and arguments with every one of these opinions.[42]

Thus, the Talmudic sources examined here by no means present the last word on which conditional agreements are binding and which ones are considered *asmakhta* and therefore nullified. Likewise, though ibn Lev takes a stand regarding the particular contract under consideration, his ruling is not necessarily consistent with what became prevailing law after many more centuries of debate, analysis of cases that came before rabbinical courts, and attempts to accommodate accepted business practices while remaining (perhaps creatively) within the letter of the law.

---

40   R. Solomon ben Abraham Adret, c. 1235–c. 1310.
41   I.e., no matter how exaggerated his words seem, we accept them as sincere.
42   *Responsa* 1:933.

The limitations of obligatory contracts would be quite restrictive in the business world, even that of the Middle Ages. The Geonim and Rishonim responded to the challenges of these restrictions by broadening the interpretations of the Talmudic law, which were further developed by the Aḥaronim,[43] resulting, over the centuries, in methods whereby halakhic obligatory contracts could be signed, finalized with a *qinyan*, and upheld in religious courts, while meeting the business needs of parties to agree upon future sales, performance of acts, and other matters that are under the rubric of *qinyan d^evarim*. These methods entail using very specific legal language derived from the relevant cases in the Talmud, the details of which, if not met, render the agreement not worth the paper it is written on.

Responsum

Mahari ben Lev Responsum 4,14	שו״ת מהר״י בן לב חלק ד סימן יד

Question: The members of the communities in a certain city had become disgusted[44] with the burden of customs duties that has been renewed for it, and God awakened the spirit of Reuben, among the dwellers of that city, so that he arose and went to the gate of the king,[45] his majesty, time after time to annul the edicts and to cancel his pronouncement and to remove this death from them. When the heads of the said Jewish community,[46] the wise men, the

שאלה בני קהלות עיר א׳[חת] אשר קצה נפשם בעול מכס מחודש עליה והנה העיר ה׳ את רוח איש ראובן מבני העיר ויקם ויבא אל שער המלך יר״ה [ירום הודו] פעם אחר פעם להוציא גזרות ומאמרו לבטל ולסלק מעליהם רק את המות הזה וכאשר ראו ראשי הק״ק [הקהילה הקדושה] הנז׳[כרת] חכמיה פרנסיה ובני המעמד ז׳ טובי

---

43 Lit., "last ones," the name given to Jewish scholars who lived in the period following the Rishonim.

44 Derived from Num. 21:5.

45 Inspired by Esther 4:2.

46 A Jewish community is referred to as a *q^ehilla q^edosha*, "holy community," the term perhaps arising so as to attribute holiness to the communities of Jews in spite of their situation in the Diaspora. (However, the term persists today for some communal synagogues even in the modern State of Israel.) See E. Bareket, "A Holy Community—the Terminology and Its Usage According to Genizah Letters in the 11th Century" [Hebrew], in *Judaica Petropolitana* (St. Petersburg-Jerusalem: Academy of Cultures Research, 2013).

administrators, the people of stature, the seven communal leaders[47] and some of the tradesmen [all] realized the diplomatic efforts that Reuben had made for this matter and the large expenditures that he spent, they came to an agreement with him to give him the sum of one thousand parahs[48] if he brought this matter to a good conclusion. This is the rendering of the document of agreement that was made between them: On the matter of the customs duties that have been customary here in such-and-such city for years and years, and those who went before him *were seized with fear* (Job 18:20) at the gate of the king[49] [when trying] to annul or diminish [the tax], to no avail.[50] When a new king arose,[51] his

העיר וקצת סוחרי העיר השתדלות שעשה ראובן הנז׳[כר] בענין הנז׳[כר] וההוצאה מרובה שפז׳[ר] והוציא נתפשרו עמו והסכימו לתת לו סך אלף פרחים בהביאו העיין לידי גמר טוב וזה נוסח שטר ההסכמה הנעשה ביניהם על דבר המכס הנהוג פה מתא פלוני זה ימים ושנים וקדמונים אחזו שער בשער המלך לבטלו ולגרעו ולא אסתייעא מילתא ועתה כי קם מלך חדש ונתחדשו גזרותיו ותעל צעקת

---

47 A common Jewish communal organization would have seven communal leaders, called the seven *tuvei ha-'ir*, lit., "best of the city." "Although their number was to have been seven, in reality the number varied from three to twelve, and sometimes there were as many as twenty-four." ([Goodblatt], 62) The title *tuvei ha-'ir* carries over from antiquity, and is found in M^egilla 26a-27a.

48 A parah (or para, from the Persian *parah*, "portion" or "piece") was a monetary denomination. According to [Goodblatt], 59, it was approximately equivalent to the (gold) sultani, and they had the approximate value of fifty aspers. Though other sources refer to small silver coins called parahs (for example, [Shmuelevitz], 169-171, and [Pamuk], 96), it is more consistent with this responsum to equate the parah with the gold sultani, because later in the text we find reference to one thousand sultanis in place of the one thousand parahs. The sultani was the standard gold coin of the Ottoman Empire, approximately equivalent to the Venetian ducat. The term *parah* for gold coins or coins of significant value is found in responsa literature as early as the eleventh century, well before the first coins of the Ottoman Empire were minted, and it appears that such is the intent of ibn Lev. To put a perspective on the value of the sum: a person who owned five thousand to ten thousand aspers was considered middle class [Goodblatt], 59). For more on the monetary system and standards of living in the Ottoman Empire, see [Pamuk] and [Inalcik].

49 Aside from repeating a previously used phrase, "the gate of the king," there is a play on words here in that the word *sha'ar* is used for "gate" and *sa'ar* is used for fear (with the letter *sin* rather than the letter *shin*, which look identical without the diacritical marks, which are never used in responsa).

50 The Aramaic phrase *v^elo istay'a milta*, meaning "the thing was not helped" is found in several places in the BT, among them K^etubbot 8a.

51 Derived from Exod. 1:8.

decrees were renewed, [and] the cry of the children of Israel[52] arose before him, and he [Reuben] was tremendously benevolent to uproot it [the tax] from the city. But good deeds are done by good men,[53] [in this case] the faithful envoy, the dear and honorable Reuben, may God protect him and grant him long life, who with the might of his own hand[54] and great efforts with money that *he dispersed freely and gave* (Ps. 112:9) last year, and he went into the storm and tempest,[55] and did not find mercy, and nevertheless he returned and showed great fortitude[56] and dove right in with strength and courage to bring to light what he sought after and desired, because he is great. As is seen, he recently brought to our hands a copy of the writing[57] of the ruling[58] from the gate of the king, his majesty, with great authority to uphold that there will not be any more extortion of taxes heard of in our land. Therefore, we, the signatories below, in the name of the holy community such-and-such, here in the city of so-and-so, in that we recognize that annulment of the taxes as stated is a great and awesome act, to offer us survival in the land and to sustain the children of Israel who come and go by way of our land for a great deliverance,[59]

בני ישראל לפניו והגדיל לעשות חסד לעקור אותו מהעיר ומגלגלין זכות על ידי זכאי ציר אמוני'[ם] היקר הנכבד ראובן יצ"ו [וישמרהו צורו ויחייהו] אשר בעוצ'[ם] ידו והשתדלותו הרב בממון אשר פזר נתן אשתקד והלך בסופה ובסער'[ה] ולא היתה עת רצון ובכל זאת חזר ושם פניו כחלמיש ונכנס בעובי הקורה בכח וגבורה להוציא לאור מבוקשו וחפצו כי רב הוא וכנראה עתה מקרוב הביא בידי פתשגן כתב החקום משער המלך יר"ה [ירום הודו] בכל תוקף וקיום להקימו לא ישמע עוד שוד מכס בארצנו ע"כ [על כן] אנחנו ח"מ [חתומים מטה] בשם ק"ק [קהילה קדושה] פלוני אשר פה מתי'[א] פלו'[ני] בראוותנו כי בטול המכס הנז'[כר] דבר גדול ונורא הוא לתת לנו שארית בארץ ולהחיות בני ישראל העוברים ושבים דרך ארצנו לפליטה גדולה במשאם ובמתנ'[ם]

---

52 Derived from Exod. 3:9.
53 *Shabbat* 32a.
54 Derived from Deut. 8:17.
55 Derived from Isa. 29:6.
56 Lit., set his face like flint, derived from Isa. 50:7.
57 Derived from Esther 4:8.
58 The word in Hebrew characters ḥukum is from the Arabic *hukm*, an Islamic legal term for a judgment or ruling, also used in Turkish.
59 Derived from Gen. 45:7.

[and] in their trade *they will find relief and deliverance* (Esther 4:14), for this [reason] we have convened and assembled and agreed with Reuben [the following], after the said ruling will be shown to the great judge[60] who rules this land, if the said judge decrees[61] according to the aforementioned ruling to set [any] such customs duties other than the seventeen *mithkals*,[62] [or whether the customs] will be totally cancelled, and then the decree of the said judge not to take any customs at all, as they wrote in the aforementioned ruling, will be proclaimed throughout the land—[if it comes to pass] in that manner, then we, all the signatories below, have obligated ourselves as of now a final and complete obligation and also to impose on and force, with all sorts of methods of coercion with *might and power* (Ps. 68:36) of our hands, all those who come through the gate of our city, stranger or citizen of the land,[63] to pay to Reuben without any delay or refusal a customs duty of half a percent of all the wares that we send or [the wares of] those that come and go [by way

יעמוד להם ריוח והצלה אי לזאת
נועדנו ונתקבצנו והסכמנו עם ראובן
הנז'[כר] אשר לאחר שיראה החוקום
הנז'[כר] בפני הדיין הגדול שופט
הארץ הלזו אם יגזור אומר הדיין
הנז'[כר] ע"פ [על פי] החוקום הנז'[כר]
להקים המכס הנז'[כר] מה שהוא חוץ
מהשבעה עשר מאטאכיי"ש ולבטלו
לגמרי ואחר זה ימשך מאמר הדיין
הנז'[כר] בפרסום בקרב הארץ לבל
יקח מכס כלל כמו שכתבו בחוקום
הנז'[כר] באופן זה נתחייבנו מעכשיו
כל החתומים למטה חיוב גמור ושלם
הן לכוף ולהכריח בכל מיני כפיה בעוז
ותעצומות ידינו לכל באי שער עירינו
כגר כאזרח הארץ לפרוע לראובן
הנז'[כר] בלי שום עכוב ומיאון מכס
חצי למאה מכל הסחורות שנשלח
אנחנו ושישלחו העוברים ושבים או
שיבאו לנו או שיביאו הם משלהם
עד כדי שיגבה ראובן הנז'[כר] אלף
שולטניש זהב והם בעד מה שפיזר

---

60 This likely refers to a judge appointed by the sultan to be responsible for relations with the Jews.

61 Derived from Job 22:28.

62 The Hebrew transliteration of this word corrupts the pronunciation and is spelled differently two times in the responsum. A *mithkal* is a Persian and Arabic weight of gold. According to Pamuk, during the period of the end of the fifteenth century and early sixteenth century, "the mints were instructed to strike 129 sultani pieces from one hundred *mithkal* of pure gold." ([Pamuk], 61n13) Ibn Lev is referring to a customs duty that would be paid regardless of any easements that would be made.

63 These words of the contract are derived from Lev. 24:22: "You shall have one manner of law, as well for the stranger, as for one of your own country." However, the "citizenship" is, of course, much more local and refers to citizens or members of the Jewish communities within that city.

Chapter Two	The Tax Cut Lobby

of our city] or [the wares] that arrive for us or that they bring that are theirs, until Reuben collects one thousand gold sultanis, which are in compensation for what Reuben dispersed and expended to annul the customs duty, also remuneration for his pains and efforts, in a manner so that Reuben will be certain and confident about [receiving] the whole sum. [This commitment is] not an *asmakhta*,[64] etc.,[65] with cancellation of any kinds of declarations,[66] etc., sincerely,[67] etc., without any trace of coercion, etc., with all the corroboration of the scribe,[68] etc., and

והוציא ראובן הנזכר לבטל המכס הנזכר גם כשכר טרחו ועמלו באופן יהיה נכון ובטוח ממנו ראובן הנזכר על כל הסך הנז'[כר] כנ"ל [כנזכר לעיל] דלא כאסמכתא וכו'[לי] בבטול כל מיני מודעי וכו' בלב שלם וכו'[לי] בלי שום זכר אונס וכו'[לי] בכל חזוקי סופר וכו'[לי] וחתימת ידינו תעיד על כל א'[חד] ממנו כשני עדים כשרים על החיוב הנ"ל [הנזכר לעיל] כאלו היה בקנין גמור ובשבועה חמורה וכו'[לי] בלי שום חזרה וחרטה וכו'[לי] ועל כל הרשום בכתב אמת תכון לעד חתמנו

our signatures testify as to the stated obligation for each one of us as two proper witnesses,[69] as if it were with a finalized *qinyan*[70] and with a severe oath, etc., without any reneging or regret, etc., and on all that is recorded in writing that is true and will be established forever,[71] we signed our names here on such-and-such day [in the week] so-and-so in [the month of] *Sh^evat* [the year] 5336 of the creation,[72]

---

64 See Halakhic Background. By declaring that the agreement is not an *asmakhta*, the signatories are stating that they cannot later say that they did not really expect to have to pay. However, Rishonim disagree as to the efficacy of such a statement.

65 Each of these phrases intended to state that the contract was signed without any possibility to renege is followed by "etc.," the intent being along the lines of "whatever the usual clauses that are added for this purpose."

66 Such as a declaration that the contract was signed under compulsion. The concept of such a declaration arises in the Talmud in, for example, *Y^evamot* 52a, where it is used relating to a writ of divorce. The Tosafot (*Y^evamot* 52 at *d^emasar moda'a aggitta*) uses the phrase "cancellation of all declarations." This phrase became commonly used in contracts to indicate that there could be no claim that the contract was signed under coercion, and even if there is such a claim, such a claim is nullified.

67 Isa. 38:3 and 1 Chron. 28 and 29. The phrase *b^elev shalem*, meaning "with perfect heart" or "wholeheartedly," is frequently used in contracts, agreements, and the like.

68 This is another phrase that is commonly used in contracts to guarantee their authenticity.

69 In monetary matters, two proper witnesses to an agreement (without a written contract) are sufficient to uphold a claim of one party against another. The statement that a signature is like "two proper witnesses" is another customary expression of the validity of the contract.

70 I.e., an act of obligation. See Halakhic Background.

71 Derived from Prov. 12:19.

72 This would be early 1576.

and we gave it into Reuben's hand as evidence and entitlement, and all is firm and established.[73] The cancellation of the customs duties will be recognized, following proclamation of the decree of the judge throughout the land, [if] for the duration of three contiguous months there is no collection of customs duties at all, as is written in the aforementioned ruling. In this manner have we obligated ourselves to the above obligation, and all is firm and established.

This is the format of the document that was made [in agreement] with Reuben and was signed by the ḥakham[74] of the community, the administrators, the people of stature, and in this manner so did the members of the other community write and sign [it], and it was given into Reuben's hand to be as entitlement and evidence, as above. For this reason, in pursuit of his request [to annul the

שמותינו פה יום פלוני כך לשבט השלי״ו ליצירה ונתננו ביד ראובן הנזכר לראייה ולזכות והכל שריר וקים הבטול של המכס הנ״ל [הנזכר לעיל] יובן אחר שימשך מאמר הדיין בפרסום בקרב הארץ שלשה חדשים רצופים לבל יקחו מכס כלל כמו שכתוב בחוקים הנזכר באופן זה הוא החיוב הנ״ל [הנזכר לעיל] שנתחייבנו והכל שריר וקים

זהו טופס השטר אשר עשו עם ראובן הנזכר וחתמו בו החכם של הקהל והפרנסים ובני המעמד וכן בסגנון הזה כתבו וחתמו בני הקהלה האחרת ונתנו ביד ראובן להיות לו לזכות ולראיי[ה] כנ״ל [כנזכר לעיל] ולסבת זה חזר ראובן ללכת ולהתאמץ בשאלתו זאת ימים רבים ולפזר פזורים והוצאות בשער המלך אנה ואנה והיה מתבטל מעסקיו כי כל ישעו וכל חפצו להשיג מבוקשו

customs duties], Reuben went again and exerted effort for many days and dispersed great expenditures at the gate of the king, to and fro, and was not able to do his own business because all of his satisfaction and desire[75] was to achieve this request. He presented a petition[76] to the king, his majesty, numerous times for

---

73 This is a standard closing to a contract. The term appears in *Bava Batra* 161a.

74 The term ḥakham (scholar) is used, as is common in the Sephardi communities, rather than the term *rav* (rabbi), which is used in the Ashkenazi communities.

75 Derived from 2 Sam. 23:5.

76 The Hebrew text contains a transliteration of the Arabic word *ruqʿah*, which means a piece of paper or note, including a memo, complaint letter, or written petition. See al-Muhassin ibn ʿAli al-Tanukhi, *Stories of Piety and Prayer: Deliverance Follows Adversity*, ed. and trans. Julia Bray (New York: New York University Press, 2019), 291; Werner Diem, "Arabic Letters in Pre-Modern Times: A Survey with Commented Selected Bibliographies," *Asiatische Studien: Zeitschrift der Schweizerischen Asiengesellschaft* 62, no. 3 (2008): 857.

this matter, and they kept the answer from him, but he showed great fortitude[77] and showed how the form of the [written] ruling that was in the hand of the customs officer was forged. As a result, they gave the petition's response that it was the wish of the king, his majesty, that the customs duties should be cancelled and removed. [Reuben] also furnished additional corroboration.

[Considering] that the customs duty of seventeen *mithkals* were [found to be] mixed with other customs duties [from the] recent [collection] in the hand of the customs officer, the residents of the city agreed that Simeon would take it, and they sent [a written authorization] to Simeon to take it and to cancel the new customs duty, and so Simeon came with a few important people to the gate of the king, and they showed Reuben the authorization that they had from the communities, and they took all the authorizations and corroboration that Reuben had in his hands. Then Simeon warned him [Reuben] to go outside of the city, lest he be an obstacle, because they were done and [Simeon and his companions] would take the ruling, and he [Reuben] would not lose his reward for this. And so, Reuben went to another place to do his business, and Simeon and his cohorts, with that same evidence and corroboration, retrieved the ruling and went to their locale and showed it to the judge and the mentioned customs duties were removed. Now Reuben has made a claim to the signatory heads of the communities with the contract of agreement that is in his hand that they should uphold what they have obligated to him, and they claim that it is not he who completed the matter, but

הלז ונתן רוקא למלך יר״ה [ירום הודו] על הדבר פעמים רבו מספר והיו מעלימים ממנו התשובה עד ששם פניו כחלמיש והראה איך החוקים צורתו אשר ביד המוכס היה מזוייף ובכן נתנו לו תשובת הרוקא כי רצון המלך יר״ה [ירום הודו] שיתבטל ויסתלק המכס הנז'[כר] וכן הוציא חזוקים אחרים

ולהיות שמכס הי״ז מתכיי״ש היה מעורב ביד המוכס עם המכס הלז המחודש הסכימו בני העיר לקחת אותו ע״י [על ידי] שמעון ושלחו לשמעון שיקחהו ושיבטל המכס החדש ובכן בא שמעון עם קצת יחידי סגולה אל שער המלך והראו לראובן הכח שבידם מאת הקהלות ולקחו כל הכחות והחזוקים שהיו ביד ראובן והתרה בו שמעון שילך חוץ לעיר פן יהיה להם למוקש כי הם גמרו ויקחו החוקים וכי לא יפסיד שכרו בשביל זה וכן הלך ראובן למקום אחר לעשות מעשהו ושמעון וסיעתו באות'[ם] הכחות והחזוקים הוציאו החוקים והלכו לארצם והראוהו

---

77 Lit., "set his face like flint," derived from Isa. 50:7.

rather the other person. Reuben claims that even if they had not sent Simeon and his cohorts to him he would have completed the matter easily, because when they [Simeon and his group] came, everything was ready and in order like a table set before them. Further, [Reuben claims] that Simeon warned him to no more be seen or found,[78] because they would be impaired in some manner. They claim that he [Reuben] needs to wait until three years have passed to ascertain if the customs duties will be reimposed or not, and he [Reuben] claims that such was not the condition between them, but rather to wait three months and no more. Please guide us, our teacher, as to with whom the justice of the law [concurs], and his [the rabbi's] reward will be doubled from Heaven.

Response: [1][79] Indeed, on the face of it, it appears that the law is on Reuben's side, and that the members of the communities are obligated to act so that the merchants will pay half a percent until payment of the one thousand sultanis [is made] to him [Reuben], and even though there was no *qinyan*[80] for that deal. On what I do I base this? From what the [author of the] *Mordᵉkhai*[81] wrote, in these words: "Our rabbi Meir[82] ruled that [regarding] any monetary condition that one stipulated at the outset, at the time of the act, the condition is valid without a

---

78 The phrase "not to be seen or found" is inspired by the phrase used for the prohibition of leavened food to be seen or found on Passover, based on Exod. 13:7 and Exod. 12:19.

79 Numbers are inserted to facilitate reading the discussion following the responsum.

80 See Halakhic Background.

81 Authored by Mordecai ben Hillel Ha-Kohen, ?1240–1298.

82 R. Meir ben Baruch, known as Maharam of Rothenberg (c. 1215–1293), who taught Mordecai ben Hillel.

qinyan, and he [the one who stipulates] is subject to the law of guarantors[83] ... and for this reason we conclude in this case that an unpaid guardian may stipulate verbally that he be [regarded legally] as a borrower[84] [by virtue] of that gratification from the fact that [the owner] trusts him,[85] etc., and we do not say that it is [a case of] *asmakhta*. Every [claim] that 'if' is not binding[86]—it is different in this case, because he relies on the beginning of his transfer, and he is trusted, and by

ואע״ג [ואף על גב] דלא הוה קנין באותו העסק ומנא אמינא לה ממאי דכתב המרדכי וז״ל [וזה לשונו] פסק רבינו מאיר שכל תנאי ממון שהתנה עליו בתחלתו בשעת מעשה תנאו קיים בלא קנין ומשתעבד מדין ערב וכו׳[לי] עד ומהאי טעמא מסקינן הכא מתנה שומר חנם להיות כשואל בדברים בההוא הנאה דמהימן ליה וכו׳[לי] ולא אמרינן אסמכתא היא וכל דאי לא קני דשאני הכא דבתחלת

virtue of that gratification he fully assumes responsibility.[87] [This is] because every monetary stipulation such as this is a valid stipulation so long as he does

---

83 Ibn Lev does not quote his source entirely, but provides the opening and closing words. The continuation is as follows: "at the time that money is transferred. This is as we find at the end of chapter 'A plain document' [*Bava Batra* 173b; see Halakhic Background] according to [R.] Y^ehuda that one may verbally make himself responsible [without a *qinyan*] even though no benefit comes to him, until it is concluded that even for one who maintains that *asmakhta* is not binding [which is R. Y^ehuda's view], one makes himself responsible by virtue of that gratification from the fact that he is trusted, as if he receives money for this [verbally assuming responsibility]."

84 Jewish law defines four types of guardians, based on Exod. 22:6-14. A large portion of tractate *Bava M^etsi'a* revolves around interpretation of these verses. The four guardians are the unpaid guardian, the paid guardian, the borrower, and the renter. They each have specified rights regarding use of the item and specified responsibility in the event of damages or theft. An unpaid guardian is not allowed to use the item, and in the event of loss or theft, he must take an oath that he did not touch the item and was not negligent, whereby he is not obligated to pay any damages. A borrower is, of course, permitted to use the item; in the event of loss, theft, or death (such as of an animal), even under a situation of coercion, the borrower is responsible for reimbursing the owner (unless the owner was present when the event occurred). If the death was a result of the work for which the animal was borrowed, in which case it is considered normal use, there is no responsibility for reimbursement.

85 The unpaid guardian has gratification from the fact that he is trusted as a borrower. The situation of the unpaid guardian stipulating that he be regarded as a borrower arises in *Bava M^etsi'a* 94a. The standard Vilna text reads: "A **paid** guardian may stipulate verbally that he be [regarded legally] as a borrower." However, all the extant manuscripts read as the version that the *Mord^ekhai* quotes (in the name of Maharam), as does the *Tosefta* (Lieberman) 8:19, as well as several locations in the JT. See Saul Lieberman, *Tosefta Kifshutah Bava M^etsi'a* 268, lines 54-55.

86 Such as "if I do not repay, take such-and-such property."

87 *Bava Batra* 173b. See Halakhic Background.

not exaggerate and it is within his [the promisor's] reach. Proof of this is in chapter 'One who leases' [*Bava M*e*tsi'a* 104a]: 'If I should let it [the land] lie fallow and do not cultivate it, I will pay according to the [value of] the best [produce],' and it is not considered *asmakhta*."[88,89] The Rosh[90] (may his memory be blessed) also agreed to this reasoning in his responsa, principle 1[,5], saying: "On the question about Reuben who hired a lad from Simeon and Simeon said to him [Reuben] to rely on him [Simeon] and he would pay him [Reuben for] everything that the lad might damage in his [Reuben's] house, since he [Simeon] had some of the lad's [property] in his possession. There was no *qinyan* of a [concrete] object, but rather merely of words. Is it fully permitted for Reuben to obtain the full value of his loss from Simeon? Response [of the Rosh]: This is a [matter of] hiring [a worker], and any condition on [an agreement for] hiring does not require a *qinyan*." From what we write, it means

מסירתו עליה סמיך והימניה ובההיא הנאה גמר ומשעבד נפשיה דכל תנאי שבממון כזה תנאו קיים היכא דלא גזים ובידו וראיי[נ]ה) מפרק המקבל אם אוביר ולא אוביר [צריך להיות: "אם אוביר ולא אעביד"] אשלי[ם] במיטבא ולא חשיב אסמכת/[א] עכ"ל [עד כאן לשונו] והרא"ש ז"ל [זכרונו לברכה] ג"כ [גם כן] הסכים לזאת הסברא בכלל הא' מתשובותיו וז"ל [וזה לשונו] בשאלת ראובן ששכר נער משמעון ואמר לו שמעון לסמוך עליו שישלם לו כל מה שיפסיד הנער בביתו יען כי היה לו משל הנער תחת ידו ולא היה קנין בדבר אלא דברים בעלמא אם יכול ראובן ליטול משמעון בהיתר גמור דמי הפסדו. תשובה שכירות הוא וכל תנאי שכירות אין צריך קנין עד כאן ומהך דכתבינן משמע דבנדון דידן אע"ג [אף על גב] דליכא קנין מחוייבים בני הקהלות לפרוע לראובן ולעשות עם הסוחרים שיפרעו לו חצי למאה עד תשלום האלף פרחים איברא

that in our case, even though there is no *qinyan*, the members of the communities are obligated to pay Reuben and ensure that the merchants will pay him one half of a percent up to payment of one thousand parahs. Indeed, that matter regarding [the situations] for which we say in several locations in the *g*e*mara* that a *qinyan* for an agreement is not a [valid] *qinyan* should be examined. The

---

88 In *Bava M*e*tsi'a* 104b (see Halakhic Background), it becomes clear that the case in the *mishna* is an agreement that is not *asmakhta* because it is not exaggerated. In *Bava M*e*tsi'a* 73b (see Halakhic Background) the *g*e*mara* explains that this same case is not *asmakhta* (unlike another example that is) because it is within the reach of the promisor.

89 *Sefer Ha-Mord*e*khai Bava M*e*tsi'a* 370.

90 R. Asher ben Jehiel, c. 1250–1327.

essence of this matter is [found] in *Bava Batra* chapter "Partners" [3a]. We say there: R. Yoḥanan said: "Our *mishna* is [the case of a courtyard] when it is not subject to the law of division," but if it is subject to the law of division, even though they do not want [i.e., agree] to divide [the courtyard], they divide [it] [if one of the neighbors demands a division], because the damage [inflicted] by [someone] looking [into another's property] is truly damage. If so, [even] if they [both] want to, what does it matter? They [either party] can retract! R. Asi said in the name of R. Yoḥanan: "[Our case is in the situation] that they performed [a formal agreement with] a *qinyan* [*sudar* to commit themselves, so that they cannot retract]." But [even] if they performed a *qinyan*, what does it matter? It is a *qinyan* of mere words! They can retract![91] [The response to this challenge is that] they performed a *qinyan* by choosing sides [of the courtyard, which is a *qinyan* for something concrete]. That is to say, so-and-so received the eastern side, and so-and-so received the western side.[92] Rav Ashi said: "Such as this one [i.e., party] traversed his [side] and took possession, and this one [the other party traversed] his [side] and took possession," and because of this they are not able to change their minds. The author of *Nimmuqei Yosef*[93] wrote: "The Geonim stated[94] that it is the law that if one says to his fellow 'I will give you two hundred *zuz*' and they performed a *qin*-

דאיכא לעיוני בהך מילתא במאי דאמרינן בכמה דוכתי בגמרא דקנין דברים לא הוי קנין ועיקרא דהאי מילתא איתא בבבא בתרא פ/[רק] השותפין אמרי/[נן] התם אמר רבי יוחנן משנתינו כשאין בה דין חלוקה אבל אם יש בה דין חלוקה אע״ג [אף על גב] דלא בעי למפלג פלגי דהיזק ראיה שמיה היזק אי הכי כי רצו מאי הוי להדרו בהו א״ר [אמר רבי] אסי א״ר [אמר רבי] יוחנן בשקנו מידו וכי קנו מידו מאי הוי דברים בעלמא הוא ולהדרו בהו שקנו מידו ברוחות כלומר פלו/[ני] קבל רוח מזרחית ופלו/[ני] קבל רוח מערבי/[ת] רב אשי אמר כגון שעלה זה בעצמו והחזיק בחלקו וזה בעצמו והחזיק בחלקו ומשום הכי לא מצו הדרו בהו וכתב בעל נמוקי יוסף וז״ל [וזה לשונו] אמרו הגאונים דהוא הדין האומר לחבירו אתן לך מאתים זוז וקנו מידו דלא מהנו דקנין דברי/[ם] הוא והא דאמרי/[מן] בפרק בתרא דע״ז [עבודה זרה] דההוא גברא דאמר לחבריה כי מזבנינא

---

91 This last phrase appears in some manuscripts.
92 This explanation is apparently based on Rashi's explanation (*Bava Batra* 3a at *bᵉruḥot*).
93 R. Joseph Ḥabiba, beginning of the fifteenth century.
94 See Hai Gaon, *Sefer Meqaḥ U-Mimkar* 37.

yan, it is not effective, because it is a *qinyan d'varim*. What we relate in the last chapter of *'Avoda Zara* [72a] about the one who said to his fellow 'if I sell this piece of land, I will sell it to you for one hundred [*zuzim*],' but he went and sold it to someone else for 120, and we rule [there] according to R. Yose of Nᵉhar Pᵉqod,⁹⁵ who said 'those *zuzim* compelled him [the one who sold it],'⁹⁶ so that the second person acquired it, implies that if he had sold it for one hundred, the first person would have acquired it. But why? It is merely a *qinyan d'varim*! They [the Geonim] explained that he [the seller] said '[if I sell this piece of land, I will sell it to you] from now,'

ליה לההוא ארעא לדידך מזבינא במאה אזל זבניה לאחרינא במאה ועשרים ואסיקנא כרבי יוסי מנהר פקוד דאמר האי זוזי אנסוה וקני בתרא משמע דאי זבנה במאה קנה קמא ואמאי קנין דברים בעלמא הוא ותירצו דההוא כד אמר ליה מעכשיו וקנו מידו דלאו קנין דברי[ם] הוא ע״כ [עד כאן]

והרשב״א ז״ל [זכרונו לברכה] כתב בתשובותיו מי שקנו מידו שיחזיר לראובן כל זכיות שיש לו עליו גם שיעשה לו שטר מחילה הוא ואשתו מי הוי קנין דברים או לא תשובה זו מחלוקת בין הגאונים ז״ל [זכרונם לברכה] יש מהם שאומר דכל בלשון

and they performed a *qinyan*, and so it is not merely a *qinyan d'varim*."⁹⁷,⁹⁸ The Rashba (may his memory be blessed) wrote in his responsa:⁹⁹ "[Question:] If someone performed a *qinyan* [on an agreement] that he would return all the claims that he has against Reuven, and even that he and his wife would provide a bond of remission, is this [merely] a *qinyan d'varim* [and therefore not binding], or not? Response: This is a dispute among the Geonim, of blessed memory. There are among them those who say that any [agreement] using the future tense, [such as] 'I will do such and such' or 'I will give so much and so much' is [merely] a *qinyan d'varim*, until they perform a *qinyan* by choosing sides.¹⁰⁰ And

---

95 The correct name is Rav Yaakov of Nᵉhar Pᵉqod, as appears in *'Avoda Zara* (72a) in the standard (Vilna) edition, as well as in the extant manuscripts.

96 I.e., he was so tempted by the increased amount that he could not control himself and he reneged on his agreement. No one could be expected to resist a better offer, if it came along, before the transfer is complete.

97 Rather, it is a conditional sale: "I am selling this piece of land to you as of now, under the condition that I decide to sell this land." By stating that the sale is "as of now," the ineffectiveness of a *qinyan d'varim* is circumvented.

98 *Bava Batra* 2a in the pages of the Rif (R. Isaac Alfasi, 1013-1103).

99 1,1033.

100 As in *Bava Batra* 3a, but in this case the intent is a *qinyan* for something of substance, rather than a *qinyan d'varim*.

there are those who say that whoever says 'I will give so much and so much' is not merely a *qinyan devarim*. Rather, it is as if he performed a *qinyan* for a debt of that sum, but there is no [valid] *qinyan* if one says 'I will divide with you.' Rather, [that would be] mere words. We do such an act [as a *qinyan* for a debt] every day, when [the value of] a dowry is agreed to with a *qinyan*, that so-and-so will give so-and-so such-and-such [amount of] gold as the dowry of his daughter. This dispute is [discussed in] *Sefer Ha-'Ittur*[101] in [article] *Qinyan*. Therefore, if one performed a *qinyan* with another that he [the latter person] and his wife would provide a bond of remission, it seems [to me] that he did not do anything [i.e., the *qinyan* is not binding]. And [it is] needless to say that if one performed a *qinyan* with another that his [the latter person's] wife would provide a bond of remission, this need not be included that it is not anything [binding], because if one performs a *qinyan* with another that he [himself] would forgive [any loans], he did not do anything, because this is merely a *qinyan d^evarim*. Forgiving [of loans] is nothing but dismissal of obligation, and if one performed a *qinyan* with another that after some time he [the latter] would dismiss an obligation that he has to him [the first person], this is merely [a *qinyan* of] words, and he did nothing."

And I say that even though we might say that our case is similar to a *qinyan d^evarim*, even so, we are able to state that though we say that a *qinyan d^evarim* is not a [binding] *qinyan*, and that the rabbis disagree about which are the matters that are referred to as a *qinyan d^evarim*, [the dispute is about] those matters that

עתיד שאעשה כך וכך או אתן כך וכך הוי קנין דברים עד שקנו מידם ברוחות ויש מי שאומר שכל האו[מר] אתן כך וכך לאו קנין דברים הוא אלא הרי הוא כאלו קנו מידו בחיוב אותו סך ואין קנין באומר אחלוק עמך אלא דברים בעלמא וכך אנו עושי[ם] מעשה בכל יום בפסקי הנדוני[א] שקונין מפלו[ני] שיתן לפלו[ני] כך וכך זהוב בנדונייית בתו ומחלוקת זה בספר העיטור בקנין והילכך כל שקנו מידו שיעשה לו הוא ואשתו שטר מחילה נראה שלא עשה ולא כלום ואין צריך לומר במה שקנו מידו שתעשה אשתו שטר מחילה שזה אין צריך לפנים שאינו כלום שאם קונה מזה שיעשה הוא מחילה לא עשה ולא כלום שזה קנין דברים בעלמא הוא שאין מחילה אלא סילוק שיעבוד ואם קנו מידו שיסלק לאחר זמן שיעבוד שיש עליו אין זה אלא דברים בעלמא ולא עשה לא כלום ע״כ [עד כאן]

ואני אומר דאע״ג [דאף על גב] דנימא דנדון דידן דומ[ה] לקנין דברים אפי״ה [אפילו הכי] מצינא למימר דאי

---

101 By R. Isaac ben Abba Mari (1120?–1190?).

need a *qinyan*. But those matters that do not need a *qinyan*, such as our case, which does not need a *qinyan*, considering that it [the agreement] was [made] at the outset of the act, as we write in all matters, we say that since he relied on words to perform an act, it stands to reason that they are obligated to uphold the condition that they stipulated with him.[102] There is proof for this in what Mahari Colon[103] (may his memory be blessed) wrote [in his responsa] principle 20: "And when he claims that there is nothing of substance in the stipulation that they stipulated not to sell to either this one or that one without the permission of his fellow, because he did not write 'from now,' the revered *ḥakham*[104] (may God protect him) wrote well, that since they performed a *qinyan sudar*,[105] it means 'from now,'" etc. "Further, besides these [reasons],[106] wherever we say that 'from now' is required, it means that a *qinyan* is required [...]. But in a matter such that two [people] stipulate with one another—this does not require a *qinyan*, as the Maharam wrote," see there.[107]

אמרינן דקנין דברים לא הוי קנין ואי פליגי רבוותא לדעת מה הם הדברים שיאמר עליהם דהוו קנין דברים היינו בדברים שצריכין קנין אבל בדברים שאינם צריכים קנין כעין נ״ד [נידון דידן] דלא בעי קנין כיון שהיה בתחלת המעשה כדכתבינ[ן] בכל מילי אמרי[נן] דכיון דעל דברים סמך לעשות מעשה מסתברא דחייבים לקיים לו התנאי שהתנו עמו ויש ראייה לדבר זה ממאי דכתב מהר״י [מורינו הרב יוסף] קולון ז״ל זכרונו לברכה] בסי[מן] כ׳ וז״ל [וזה לשונו] ואשר טוען שאין ממש בתנאי שהתנו שלא למכור לא זה ולא זה בלתי רשות חבירו מאחר שלא כתבוהו מעכשיו הלא יפה כתב מעלת החכם יצ״ו [ישמרהו צורו וגואלו] דמאחר שעשו קנין שובר היינו מעכשיו וכו׳[לי] ועוד בר מדין ובר מדין היכא אמרינן דבעי מעכשיו היינו דבעי קנין אבל בענין שנים שמתנים זה עם זה דלא בעי קנין כמ״ש [כמו שכתב] מהרי״ם [מורינו הרב מאיר] יעויין שם

---

102 The important distinction is that this agreement does not require a *qinyan*, so that there is not a question of a *qinyan d'varim* at all.

103 The Italian halakhist, R. Joseph ben Solomon Colon, c. 1420–1480, often referred to by the acronym Maharik.

104 R. Colon is referring to the author of the question.

105 Though the Hebrew text reads "*qinyan shovar*," i.e., a *qinyan* with a voucher (or receipt), this is not a type of *qinyan* found in the literature. Further, printed editions of Colon's responsa have *qinyan sudar*.

106 The phrase in Aramaic *bar min den u-var min den* (as it appears in Colon's response), which means "aside from this and aside from this," is borrowed from tractate B'rakhot 38b.

107 Ibn Lev is referring the reader to Colon's response. R. Colon's citation of the Maharam is not through a primary source, but refers to the *Sefer Ha-Mordekhai Bava Qamma* 176.

[2] What [remains] to hesitate [about] and to examine in our case is what he wrote in his question: "[If it comes to pass] in that manner, then we, all the signatories below, have obligated ourselves as of now a final and complete obligation and also to impose on and force, with all sorts of methods of coercion with might and power of our hands, all those who come through the gate of our city, to pay to Reuben without any delay or refusal a customs duty of half a percent of all the wares that we send or [the wares of] those that come and go [by way of our city] or [the wares] that will be brought to us or that they bring of theirs, until Reuben collects one thousand gold sultanis, which are in compensation for what Reuben dispersed and expended to annul the customs duty, also remuneration for his pains and efforts, in a manner so that Reuben will be certain and confident about [receiving] the whole sum." On the face of it, it appears that in such matters it has been said "the more you say, the worse you make it,"[108] as it appears that they did not want to obligate themselves to give the money, and they did not want to obligate themselves other than to coerce those merchants who will pay the customs duty of half a percent, with all sorts of coercive methods, and they would say that they would do everything in their power to coerce with shunning and excommunication,[109] and bringing them [the merchants] to their [the Gentiles'] courts.[110] But if they do not suc-

ומה שיש לפקפק ולעיין בנדון זה הוא במה שכתב בשאלה וז״ל [וזה לשונו] באופן זה נתחייבנו מעכשיו כל החתומים למטה חיוב גמור ושלם הן לכוף להכריח בכל מיני כפיה בכל עוז ותעצומות ידינו לכל באי שער עירנו לפרוע לראובן הנזכר בלי שום עיכוב ומיאון מכס חצי למאה מכל הסחורות שנשלח אנחנו וששלחו העוברים ושבים או שיביאו לנו או שיביאו הם משלהם עד כדי שיגבה ראובן הנזכר אלף סולטני זהב והם בעד מה שפזר והוציא ראובן הנזכ׳[ר] לבטל המכס הנזכר גם בשכר טרחו ועמלו באופן שיהיה נכון ובטוח ממנו ראובן הנז׳[כר] על כל הסך הנז׳[כר] ולכאורה נראה דבכיוצא בזה נאמר כל המוסיף גורע דנראה שלא רצו לחייב עצמם בנתינת המעות ושלא רצו להתחייב כי אם לכוף לאותם הסוחרים שיפרעו אותו המכס מחצי למאה בכל מיני הכפיות והם יאמרו שיעשו כל הבא מידם לכוף בנדויים וחרמות ובהביאם בערכאו׳[ת] שלהם

---

108 *Sanhedrin* 29a.
109 See the chapter "On Excommunication." The text of the agreement, presented in the question to Ibn Lev, does not mention any method of enforcement. However, the only methods of enforcement available to Jewish courts or communities were shunning and excommunication.
110 The agreement, as quoted in the question, said nothing about using Gentile courts for enforcement. That ibn Lev includes such action as one of the methods of enforcement is

ceed after all these coercive methods, they [would say they] are not obligated to pay the money. Truthfully, it is incumbent to plead in Reuben's favor, according to the superfluous language that is written at the end of this obligation that they wrote: "in a manner so that Reuben will be certain and confident," as every superfluous text is intended to add something,[111] so that it is possible to say that the result of this text is to obligate the members of the communities not just with coercing [the merchants] but with monetary obligation. One must examine this, as the Rashba [wrote] two responsa that contradict one another. In one responsum he wrote that it is incumbent upon us to consider superfluous language,[112] and

אבל אם לא יעלה בידם אחר אלו הכפיות שהם אינם מחוייבי[ם] לפרוע הממון הנזכר איברא שיש ללמד על זה הראובן זכות ממאי דכתיב בשטר לישנא יתירא בסוף זה החיוב שכתבו וז״ל [וזה לשונו] באופן יהיה נכון ובטוח ממנו ראובן הנזכר וכל לישנא יתיר[א] לטפויי אתא דאפשר לומר דמהני האי לישנא לחייב על בני הקהלות לא כפיה לבד אלא חיוב ממון וצריך לעיין בה שיש ב׳ תשובות להרשב״א סותרות זו לזו בתשובה אחת כתב שיש לנו לדון בלישנא יתירא ובתשובה אחרת כתב וסגר לנו הדלת ואין לנו לדון בלישנא יתירא באומדן דעתינו כי אם בהנהו לישני יתירי דאיתנהו בגמרא.

in another responsum he wrote and closed the door for us, and we are not to consider superfluous language in our assumptions, other than those superfluous texts that are in the g'mara.[113]

---

quite extreme, considering the proscriptions against using the Gentile courts: "Whoever has a judgment adjudicated according to Gentile laws, or in their courts, even if their laws are like Jewish law, is considered wicked" (Maimonides, *MT Hilkhot Sanhedrin* [The Laws of the Sanhedrin] 26,7). It is the following law in Maimonides's code that explains ibn Lev's extreme recommendation: "[However,] if the authority is in the hands of the Gentiles, and one's disputant is violent [or powerful], and one cannot expropriate property through the Jewish system of law [which has no power of enforcement], he should first sue him before Jewish judges. If he [the disputant] is not willing to appear, he [the plaintiff may] obtain permission from a [Jewish] religious court and salvage [his property] from his disputant by [appealing to] Gentile judges" (ibid. 26,8).

111 The concept of superfluous language, *lishana y'teira*, refers to additional conditions or phrases in a document when the document could have been understood without those phrases. The halakhic presumption, based on the view of R. Akiva (*Nazir* 7b, *Bava Batra* 138b, *'Arakhin* 19a), is that such superfluous language has a purpose to be more specific or limiting in the contract. The dictum is: "Every phrase that is not necessary is stated to add something."

112 It cannot be certain which responsum ibn Lev is referring to. Rashba's responsum 4:85 is one possibility.

113 Rashba was asked (responsum 2:270): "In what matter is it appropriate to apply the dictum "every phrase that is not necessary is stated to add something"? In his response he stated: "we

Therefore, I say that one must examine, for our case, what is [found] in *Gittin* chapter "Any writ of divorce" [30a]. We relate there [the case of] someone who told them [people with whom he deposited a writ of divorce]: "If I do not appease her [my wife] within thirty days, let this be a writ of divorce." He went and [attempted to] reconcile with her, but she was not appeased. Rav Yosef said: "Did he give her a basketful[114] of dinars, and [yet] she was not appeased?!"[115] The Ran wrote:[116] "If I do not appease her within thirty days, let this be her writ of divorce from now," and he gave her	ולכן אני אומר שצריך לעיין בנדון דידן בההיא דפרק כל הגט דאמרי[נן] התם ההו[א] דא[מר] להו אי לא מפייסנ[א] עד תלתין יומין ליהוי גיטא אזל פייסה ולא אפייסה אמר רב יוסף מי יהיב לה תרקבא דדינרי ולא איפייסה וכתב הר"ן אם לא מפייס[ה] עד תלתין יומין להוי גיטה מעכשיו ומסר לה גט על תנאי זה אזל פייסה בדברים והרבה עליה רעים ולא נתרצית להשלים אטו מי יהב לה תרקב[א] דדינרי ולא איפייסה וכיון שלא עשה כן נמצא שלא פייסה ואע"פ [ואף על פי] שאין

a divorce under this condition. He went and [attempted to] reconcile with her with words and sent her many friends,[117] and she was not satisfied to make peace. So did he give her a basketful of dinars, but [yet] she was not appeased?! And since he did not do so, we find that he did not appease her, and even though he

---

are not sufficiently expert in the matter, and we do not do such a deed, other than those that were interpreted in the *g'mara*." He further explains: "Every superfluous phrase is not [necessarily] required for the matter [under consideration], because at times it is to add something and at times it is to detract."

114 Lit. "a tarkavful." Though *tarkav* referred to a dry measure of three kavs, there is an assumption that etymologically it was two (prefix "two" + kav) and evolved to mean three (see Mishna *Tamid* 5:4; Rashi, *Shabbat* 59a at *tarkav*, explains that it means "two and one kav"); A. Steinsaltz (*Gittin* 30a) suggests that the word is derived from the Greek word for three kavs (τρίκαβος).

115 Rav Yosef's point is that he did not make an adequate effort to appease her, and therefore he did not fulfill the condition, so that the divorce is valid. Refer to the chapter "Divorce out of Love" for discussion of conditional divorce and its appropriate language.

116 *Gittin* 15a on the pages of the Rif. Ibn Lev quotes from the Ran for each phrase, the source text and the commentary as one running text. The first lines of the Ran's commentary on the Rif, until he cites the Tosafot, is almost a verbatim quote of Rashi's commentary on the corresponding page in *Gittin*, proper, *Gittin* 30a.

117 In *Yoma* 87a there is a discussion about how one person should appease his fellow so that the latter will forgive the former's transgressions against his fellow. R. Yitsḥak offers a midrashic play on Prov. 6:3, interpreting *u-rhav re'ekha* (and urge your fellow) to mean send him many friends (to ask him to forgive). Therefore, the intent of the Ran's explanation is to suggest that he attempted to appease his wife in the manner that one would appease a fellow to gain forgiveness.

does not have [such wealth], we do not say that he was compelled [to divorce her, against his will], because a person cannot claim that he was forced in the stipulation of a divorce, and it is a [valid] divorce. The Tosafot questioned [Rav Yosef's statement]:[118] 'Even if he [did] give her a basketful of dinars, the divorce would be valid, because in any event he did not appease her!' Ri [the Elder] (may his memory be blessed) explained the difficulty [as follows]:[119] '"If I do not appease her" means "if I do not take pains to appease her with something substantial," and if he gave her [the basketful of dinars], then he did take pains to appease her, and he upheld his condition, even though she was not appeased.' But if he did not give her [anything], he did not fulfill his condition, and even though he was coerced, there is no [allowance to claim] coercion in [matters of] divorce. It was necessary to teach us that there is no [allowance to claim] coercion [in matters of divorce]; [from this] we learn that in monetary law there is [an allowance to claim] coercion, [such as] if one says 'my field is given to you if I do not appease so-and-so,' and he [attempted to] appease him with everything that was within his ability to do, but he was not appeased, [then] he [the one who set the condition] is exempt [from giving the field], because he was coerced."[120]

[3] And since this is so, it is a simple matter that in our case under consideration, the [signatory] members of the communities must and are obligated to enforce upon the merchants with whatever means they have, whether by shunning and excommunication, and by bringing them to [the Gentile] court. We also wrote,

---

118 Tosafot Gittin 30a at *mi yaheiv lah tark*eva d*edinarei v*ela ipaisa*.
119 R. Isaac (the Elder) ben Samuel of Dampierre, d. c. 1185; ibid.
120 See *Ḥiddushei ha-Ramban Gittin* 30a at *ha paisah v*ela ipayas*.

above, that because of the superfluous language we might even obligate the [signatory] members of the communities for payment of one thousand sultanis.

[4] Regarding that the [signatory] members of the communities claim that the matter was not completed by him [Reuben] and Reuben claims what is written in the question, I see what he says and I'm surprised at what is written in the question, that they claim that "he should wait until the conclusion of these first three years until it becomes clarified whether the customs duties will be reimposed or not." But I see that above in the question [quoting the document] it is written that "the cancellation of the customs duties will be recognized, following proclamation of the decree of the judge throughout the land, [if] for the duration of three contiguous months there is no collection of customs duties at all, as is written in the aforementioned ruling. In this manner have we obligated ourselves to the above obligation, and all is firm and established." [Therefore] it appears that the words of the question are self-contradictory,[121] but at this time I am not fit to write more than what I have written. As a matter of fact, I must, if God will decree that he heals me and grants me life, reexamine what I wrote to see if it is good and straightforward.[122] [But] it is good and determined by God[123] for people who fear God and respect His name to compromise among themselves, and each would return to his place

יתירא יש להסתפק אי מחייבינן להו לבני הקהלות אפילו על חיוב נתינת המעות אלף שולטני

במה שטוענים בני הקהלות שלא נגמר הדבר על ידו וראובן טוען מה שכתוב בשאלה רואה אני את דבריו ואני תמה מה שכתוב בזאת השאלה שהם טוענין שימתין עד כלות ג' שנים ראשונים אלו עד שיתברר אם יחזור המכס לסורו הראשון אם לאו עד כאן ואני רואה שכתוב למעלה בזאת השאלה הביטול של המכס הנזכר לעיל יובן אחר שימשך מאמר הדיין בפרסום בקרב הארץ ג' חדשים רצופי'[ם] לבל יקחו מכס כלל כמ"ש [כמו שכתוב] בחקוק[ים] הנזכ'[ר] באופן זה היה החיוב הנזכר לעיל שנתחייבנו והכל שריר וקים ע"כ [עד כאן] ונראה דדברי השאלה סותרות זו לזו וכעת אין לי שעת הכושר לכתוב יותר ממה שכתבתי אדרבא שאני צריך אם יגזור הש"יי [השם יתברך] להחלימני ולהחייני לשוב לעיין במה שכתבתי לראו[ת] אם הם דברי[ם] טובי[ם] ונכוחי[ם] וטוב ונכון הדב'[ר] מעם האלהי'[ם]

---

121 Presumably, Reuben has the copy of the document that was put in his hands, which raises the question as to why this cannot be verified one way or the other.

122 Derived from Prov. 24:26.

123 Derived from Gen. 41:32.

in peace.[124] Signed by the bitter and lamenting Joseph ibn Lev.

שאנשי[ם] יראי ה׳ וחושבי שמו יפשרו ביניהם ואיש על מקומו יבא בשלו[ם] נאם המר ונאנח יוסף ן׳ לב.

Discussion

Following a lengthy and detailed question, ibn Lev addresses the following points:[125]

[1] The largest portion of the response is dedicated to explaining why the agreement that the community leaders signed and gave to Reuben is not a *qinyan d'varim*, but a binding document, even though there was not an actual *qinyan* at all; nor is it a case of *asmakhta*.

[2] Ibn Lev then considers whether the signatories are obligated themselves to pay one thousand sultanis to Reuben, if they are unable to raise the one thousand sultanis by forcing the merchants, with every means possible, to pay a percentage of the value of their trade. Ibn Lev would like to derive this conclusion from the superfluous language in the agreement, but such a conclusion is not definite.

[3] Ibn Lev reiterates that the signatories must use every means possible to compel the merchants to pay the promised percentage, but remains noncommittal as to whether if they do not, the signatories themselves must pay the one thousand sultanis. Ibn Lev's language would suggest that he thinks they ought to, but cannot prove it for certain.

[4] Lastly, and only briefly, does ibn Lev address the claim of the signatories, that Reuben did not complete the goal, and that they claim that in any event three years of reduced taxes must elapse before any payment would be made. As is often the conclusion of such disputes, the parties are encouraged to reach a compromise. After all, the means of enforcement of the rabbi's decision are limited.

Ibn Lev expends most of his effort on proving that the agreement signed by the community leaders was neither a situation of *qinyan d'varim*, nor a case of *asmakhta*, even though, according to the question, the respondents did not make either of these claims. Rather, they claimed that the complainant did not actually complete the goal. Further, the respondents are changing the "rules of the game."

---

124 Derived from Exod. 18:23.
125 See the section numbers in square brackets in the responsum.

They now say that the complainant must wait three years to see if to see if the adjustment in taxes is long term, and only then can he collect the money owed him.

So which is it? Are they attempting to breach the agreement because the complainant did not actually fulfill his side of the agreement? If that is so, then why would he ever be entitled to the payment, even after three years? Or, are they withholding payment because they deny the text of the agreement? The text of the agreement, contained in the question, clearly states "three months." Ibn Lev points this out, close to the very end of the responsum, stating that the text of the question is self-contradictory.

Ibn Lev does not address the matter of Simeon arriving on the scene and preempting Reuben's conclusion of the matter. Apparently, he does not regard this as a serious reason to absolve the signatories of any responsibility. If that is so, then a detailed discussion of the theoretical possible claims—*asmakhta* or *qinyan d'varim*—to dismiss the contract is, in a sense, like setting up a straw man, to be dispelled. Never mind the claim that Reuben did not complete the task. That already appears to be an attempt to evade responsibility. But, perhaps the respondents will then claim that they never intended to force the merchants to pay—after all, this is a difficult task, is it not? Is it within their reach? (Well, yes, it is, because the community leadership signed the agreement, and they can, for example, direct community members not to deal with merchants unless they pay.) So, just in case the respondents would even think of claiming *asmakhta* or *qinyan d'varim*, ibn Lev puts these out of the realm of possible arguments. He also provides proof that force can be applied in the case of monetary judgments.

Yet, perhaps their claim that they really meant three years is in a sense a claim that the agreement was not to be taken literally, within the realm of claiming *asmakhta*. Again, ibn Lev's ruling out claims of *asmakhta* would eliminate such an angle.

Though it is quite convincing that the complainant is justified, and ibn Lev rules that all the methods of enforcement of the merchants are in order, at the very end of the responsum ibn Lev exhorts the parties to come to a compromise. What could be the motivation for this, rather than to expect the respondents to pay, thus exacting absolute justice? It must be kept in mind that the actual agreement did not state that the signatories guarantee payment of one thousand sultanis to Reuben, but rather that they would use every method to force the merchants to pay one half of a percent of the value of their wares until the total was one thousand sultanis, thus absolving the signatories of responsibility if for some reason collection was not successful. They did not elaborate on the methods that could be used to enforce the ruling, but ibn Lev did, and he suggested that they even resort to excommunication and going to the Gentile courts—neither of which are easy matters, nor are they at all desirable, the latter being a most extreme measure. It is reasonable to think that for these reasons ibn Lev encouraged compromise. Compromise is considered a peaceful path to justice: "R. Yehoshua ben Korḥa said: 'It is an imperative [in a judgment, for the judges] to [bring about] compromise, as it states *Execute the judgment of truth and peace in your gates* (Zechariah 8:16). But in a place where there is [absolute] justice, there is no peace, and in a place where there is peace, there is no [strict] justice! Rather, what kind of justice contains peace? You must say: 'Compromise.'"[126] Ibn Lev truly wished nothing more than that "each would return to his place in peace.

Questions for Further Discussion

SHYLOCK: This kindness will I show.
Go with me to a notary, seal me there
Your single bond; and, in a merry sport,
If you repay me not on such a day,
In such a place, such sum or sums as are
Express'd in the condition, let the forfeit
Be nominated for an equal pound
Of your fair flesh, to be cut off and taken
In what part of your body pleaseth me.

ANTONIO: Content, i' faith: I'll seal to such a bond
And say there is much kindness in the Jew.

BASSANIO: You shall not seal to such a bond for me:
I'll rather dwell in my necessity.

---

126 *Sanhedrin* 6b. This midrash also appears in several locations in the Tannaitic literature and the JT.

ANTONIO: Why, fear not, man; I will not forfeit it:
Within these two months, that's a month before
This bond expires, I do expect return
Of thrice three times the value of this bond.[127]

But Antonio's ships are lost at sea. He writes to Bassanio: "Sweet Bassanio, my ships have all miscarried, my creditors grow cruel, my estate is very low, my bond to the Jew is forfeit."[128]

SALARINO: I am sure the duke
Will never grant this forfeiture to hold.

ANTONIO: The duke cannot deny the course of law:
For the commodity that strangers have
With us in Venice, if it be denied,
Will much impeach the justice of his state;
Since that the trade and profit of the city
Consisteth of all nations.[129]

Indeed, Antonio is correct—the duke will not set a legal precedent and nullify the contract. The duke refers the case to a lawyer, who is actually Portia in disguise. She could not agree with Antonio more:

BASSANIO: [...]And, I beseech you,
Wrest once the law to your authority:
To do a great right, do a little wrong,
And curb this cruel devil of his will.

PORTIA: It must not be. There is no power in Venice
Can alter a decree established:
'T will be recorded for a precedent,
And many an error by the same example
Will rush into the state. It cannot be.[130]

---

127 Shakespeare, *The Merchant of Venice*, act 1, sc. 3.
128 Ibid., act 3, sc. 2.
129 Ibid., act 3, sc. 3.
130 Ibid., act 4, sc.1

If this case were to come before a Jewish religious court rather than the duke of Venice and Venetian law, this surely would be a case of *asmakhta*. Antonio had every confidence that he would be able to pay the bond. In no way did he seriously consider that his flesh would be cut out. However, the duke (and Venetian law) abided by the principle of *pacta sunt servanda* (agreements must be kept). [131]

Discuss the conflict between the principles of *pacta sunt servanda* and *asmakhta*, which renders an agreement void in certain situations. Can you think of examples of agreements or contracts that perhaps should be subject to the rule of *asmakhta*? (Some health insurance contracts and their "fine print" come to mind as an example.) Does allowing for a claim of *asmakhta* show compassion for human weakness, desperation, or gullibility? Do you think "the spirit of the Sages" is pleased or displeased with someone who does not uphold an agreement on account of a claim of *asmakhta*?

[Wehberg] primarily relates to international agreements in his discussion of *pacta sunt servanda*. Read the article. Is there a reason to maintain different standards for international agreements and for personal contracts regarding the principles of *pacta sunt servanda* and *asmakhta*?

The curse *mi she-para* (He who exacted [punishment from the people of the generation of the Flood will also exact punishment from one who does not stand by his word]) indicates that the Sages have a severe view of someone who breaches an agreement,[132] and yet, a religious court might nullify certain agreements that contain *asmakhta*. How do you explain this seeming contradiction? Consider a theoretical case of an agreement that you could not uphold. Use your most analytical, sharpest legal mind to explain why it is a case of *asmakhta* and that you are not subject to *mi she-para*.

Does the curse *mi she-para* counter the legal principle of *asmakhta* or calm any concerns you have about *asmakhta*? Why or why not?

---

131 See [Wehberg].

132 However, as noted in Halakhic Background, the curse does not apply to someone who reneges on a verbal transaction or *qinyan d'varim*.

Further Reading

[Epstein] Epstein, Mark Alan. *The Ottoman Jewish Communities and their role in the 15th and 16th centuries.* Freiberg: Klaus Schwarz Verlag, 1980.

[Goodblatt] Goodblatt, Morris. *Jewish Life in Turkey in the XVIth Century as Reflected in the Legal Writings of Samuel De Medina.* New York: Jewish Theological Seminary of America, 1952.

[Inalcik] Inalcik, Halil, and Donald Quataert, eds. *An Economic and Social History of the Ottoman Empire: 1300–1914.* Cambridge: Cambridge University Press, 1994. (For further reading on the monetary system and standards of living in the Ottoman Empire.)

[Levy] Levy, Avigdor, ed. *The Sephardim in the Ottoman Empire.* Princeton: Darwin Press, 1992.

[Levy2] ———, ed. *The Jews of the Ottoman Empire.* Princeton: Darwin Press, 1994.

[Levy3] ———, ed. *Jews, Turks, Ottomans: A Shared History, Fifteenth Through the Twentieth Century.* Syracuse: Syracuse University Press, 2002.

[Pamuk] Pamuk, Sevket. *A Monetary History of the Ottoman Empire.* Cambridge: Cambridge University Press, 2000.

[Rozen] Rozen, Minna. *A History of the Jewish Community in Istanbul: The Formative Years, 1453–1566.* Leiden: Brill, 2010.

[Shmuelevitz] Shmuelevitz, Aryeh. *The Jews of the Ottoman Empire in the Late Fifteenth and the Sixteenth Centuries: Administrative, Economic, Legal and Social Relations as Reflected in the Responsa.* Leiden: E. J. Brill, 1984.

[Wehberg] Wehberg, Hans. "Pacta Sunt Servanda." *American Journal of International Law* 53, no. 4 (October 1959): 775-786.

3.
Are You Calling Me a Heretic?!
Z^eqan Aharon 25

Historical Background

When Spanish and Portuguese Jewish exiles began to arrive in Constantinople (Istanbul) following the expulsions from Spain and Portugal,[1] they found an established, thriving and intellectual community of Romaniot Jews, Greek-speaking Jews who lived under Byzantine rule for a millennium.

There is no explicit indication that the case discussed in the responsum in this chapter took place in Constantinople, but the responding rabbi, R. Elijah ben Benjamin Ha-Levi (1481–after 1540),[2] was a member of the Romaniot community in Constantinople, a member of the highest rabbinical court in the city, and, following the death of R. Elijah Mizraḥi in c.1526, the head of that rabbini-

---

1   See introduction, note 1.
2   A practically identical version of this responsum was first identified by Simha Assaf as written and signed by R. David ben Solomon ibn Abi Zimra, a Spanish-born rabbi known as Radbaz (1479–1573), based on a manuscript now called JER NLI MS Heb. 6549; see Simha Assaf, "Miginzei Bet Ha-S^efarim BiYrushalayim," *Minḥa L^eDavid, Sefer Ha-Yovel L^eDavid Yellin* (Jerusalem: Rubin Mass, 1935), 221-236. However, David Tamar published a convincing argument, including comparisons of linguistic style and of Radbaz's signature on several other manuscripts, that the signature was not authentic and the responsum was actually penned by R. Elijah ben Benjamin Ha-Levi; see David Tamar, "'Al T^eshuva B^e'Iny^enei Filosofia Ha-M^eyuḥeset B^eTa'ut La-Radbaz," *Sinai* 78 (1976): 66-71. Though Assaf was aware that the responsum appeared in the printed collection of responsa by Ha-Levi (*Z^eqan Aharon*, Constantinople, 1734), he maintained that it was written by Radbaz on the basis of his signature; see Simha Assaf, *M^eqorot L^eTol^edot Ha-Ḥinnukh B^eYisrael*, vol. 3, *Addenda and Corrigenda* (Tel Aviv: Dvir, 1936), 120. Tamar admits that it is a mystery why the manuscript is signed with Radbaz's name (70n25). The consensus among those who are aware of the duplication of the responsum is that Ha-Levi is the author; see Shmuel Glick, *Quntres ha-T^eshuvot he-Ḥadash* (Jerusalem: Schechter Institute for Jewish Studies, 2006), 3:1037 entry 3546 and 1:334 entry 1347. However, Yosef Shevaḥ states that it has not yet been clarified who the author is; see *Z^eqan Aharon*, ed. Y. Shevaḥ (Jerusalem: Mekhon Ha-Ketav, 2017) 139.

cal court.[3] There is also no indication of whether the plaintiff and defendant in the case were of Iberian origins or Romaniot (or one of each, possibly playing out some cultural conflict), but we shall see that the tragedy of the expulsion was in his mind when Ha-Levi wrote his response. This responsum, which addresses an issue that was controversial in both the Romaniot and Spanish-Portuguese communities at the time,[4] provides a fascinating view of the cultural life of Jews in the Ottoman Empire, where so many of the exiles found refuge.

The controversial issue is the study of external (non-Jewish) wisdom, frequently referred to as "Greek wisdom," which included philosophy,[5] commentaries and translations of Greek philosophy, mathematics, logic, and perhaps rhetoric.[6] In fact, the dispute between those who opposed Jewish engagement with general culture and those who embraced such culture was already a millennia-old debate. Ha-Levi was among those scholars for whom study of philosophy was common.[7] It is no surprise, then, that when asked about a man who is derided because of his study of philosophy, Ha-Levi comes not only to the defense of this man, but to the defense of those Jewish scholars before him who also engaged in external wisdom, maintaining that such study was a part of Jewish tradition from Talmudic times. Although it is conceivable that the question was posed hypothetically by the rabbi himself, in order to write a polemical response to anyone (or to someone specific but unnamed) who might have challenged this outlook,[8] the very end of this responsum, in which Ha-Levi addresses the communal rabbis who might have brought the question, suggests that it was actually in response to a question posed.

---

3   Joseph Hacker, "The 'Chief Rabbinate' in the Ottoman Empire in the 15th and 16th Century" [Hebrew], *Zion* 49 (1984): 225-263, 252.

4   See Joseph Hacker, "Polemics in Opposition to Philosophy in Istanbul in the 16th Century" [Hebrew], in *Studies in Jewish Mysticism, Philosophy and Ethical Literature: Presented to Isaiah Tishby on his Seventy-Fifth Birthday* [Hebrew], ed. Joseph Dan and Joseph Hacker (Jerusalem: Magnes Press, 1986), 507-536.

5   In ancient times, natural philosophy was the study of phenomena in nature. Therefore, throughout this chapter, reference to philosophy might also include scientific endeavor.

6   See [Hacker], 116-120.

7   See [Rozen], 246-250.

8   As Shmuel Glick states: "responsa literature … includes everything that an experienced scholar may actually have answered, as well as answers to questions he felt should have been asked" ("The Contribution of Responsa Literature to the Study of Halakha, Jewish Culture and History," https://schechter.edu/the-contribution-of-responsa-literature-to-the-study-of-halakha-jewish-culture-and-history).

Ha-Levi's responsum reiterates the viewpoints expressed in defenses of studying philosophy and science, of Maimonides's *The Guide for the Perplexed* and of rationalist interpretations of the Bible and the Talmud, against those who opposed such study and literature, even to the point of burning Maimonides's *Guide* and excommunicating those who studied what was considered forbidden literature.

As Jacob Schacter points out:

> ...the attitude of Jews throughout history to Gentile learning and culture is not monolithic and unidimensional and cannot be reduced to any simplistic, facile generalization. On the contrary, it is complex, changing, and nuanced, very much reflecting "conditions of time, place, circumstance, and environment."[9] Affirmation and acceptance in one part of the world or during a specific century was countered by rejection and denial or simple benign disinterest in other times and places. Often differences existed even within the same cultural milieu and identical chronological time frame. All sorts of factors directly influenced how Jews in any given place or time throughout their history reacted to non-Jewish culture.[10]

We should consider Ha-Levi's responsum below in light of this ongoing debate.

Halakhic Background

This responsum does not involve complex legalistic analysis or discussion. Two major halakhic issues are at the core of this somewhat polemic discourse: one issue is how a Jew should relate to Gentile, or non-Judaic, knowledge, and the other is the extent of a Jew's obligation to study Torah.[11] The two issues are not independent, for if a Jew is obligated to study Torah *day and night* (Josh. 1:8), then the question of whether or not Gentile knowledge is considered taboo is moot.

---

9 This quote is from a 1934 responsum written by R. Abraham Isaac Bloch, first printed by L. Levi, "An Unpublished Responsum on Secular Studies," *Proceedings of the Association of Orthodox Jewish Scientists* 1 (1966): 106-112.

10 [Schacter], x.

11 The study of Torah is always understood to mean both the written and oral Torah, i.e., Talmud. Though the word "Torah" literally refers to the Pentateuch, rabbinic Judaism presumes that it is impossible to understand the Pentateuch without the Sages' interpretation and elaboration, contained in the Talmud.

In every generation from Talmudic times until the present, there have been those who opposed Jews studying Gentile knowledge. And it is reasonable to ask, are they opposed because such studies are "intrinsically worthless, deficient, or dangerous (potentially undermining the absolute superiority or centrality of Torah study) or simply because they are superfluous and irrelevant for someone whose religious obligations require him to study Torah all day long"?[12] Is undermining the centrality of Torah study the only danger, or is there a perceived danger of inciting heretical thoughts? When studying the responsum by Ha-Levi, readers can take note of how these different concerns are manifested in the question and in the response.

In his responsum, Ha-Levi cites the two Talmudic sources presented here, and he uses interpretations of them to advance his arguments. The first, from *Sota*, focuses on defining which Gentile knowledge is taboo and which benign. The second source, from *Mʿnaḥot*, presents midrashic rhetoric about the time demands of the commandment to study Torah.

Sota 49b[13]	סוטה מ"ט ב'
[Concerning] "and that one should not teach his son Greek":[14] Our rabbis taught: When the kings of the house of the Hasmoneans fought one another, Hyrcanus was outside [the walls of the city,] and Aristobulus was within. Every single day they would let down dinars in a basket and bring up for them [sacrifi-	ושלא ילמד את בנו יוונית ת"ר [תנו רבנן] כשצרו מלכי בית חשמונאי זה על זה היה הורקנוס מבחוץ ואריסטובלוס מבפנים בכל יום ויום היו משלשלין דינרים בקופה ומעלין להן תמידים היה שם זקן אחד שהיה מכיר בחכמת יוונית לעז להם בחכמת

cial animals for the] daily offering. An elderly man was there who was knowl-

---

12 [Schacter], xi.
13 Parallel versions of this text are found in *Bava Qamma* 82b (where the positions of Hyrcanus and Aristobulus are reversed) and *Mʿnaḥot* 64b.
14 From Mishna *Sota* 9:14, which appears in *Sota* 49a: "During the war of Titus, they [the Sages] decreed against [the use of crowns] worn by brides and that no man should teach his son Greek." (A few manuscripts of the Mishna and the Talmud have "Qitus [Lucius Quietus]" rather than "Titus," which is probably the correct text; see, for example, the *Soncino Babylonian Talmud, Sotah* 49a, note 29, trans. A. Cohen, and Lieberman, *Tosefta Kifshutah, Sota*, p. 767.)

edgeable in the wisdom of Greek.[15] He spoke to them in a foreign tongue, in the wisdom of Greek, and told them: "So long as they are performing the Temple-service, they will not be delivered to your hands [in surrender]." The next day they let down dinars in a basket, and they sent up a pig. When it reached half the [height of the] wall, it dug in its claws, and there was a tremor in the Land of Israel for four hundred parasangs. At that moment they [the Sages] said: "Cursed be the person who raises pigs, and cursed be the person who teaches his son the wisdom of Greek." ... Really?! [Is the wisdom of Greek forbidden?] But is it not so that Rabbi [Judah Ha-Nasi] said: "Why [use] Syriac in the Land of Israel? Rather, [use] either the holy tongue [Hebrew] or Greek." And Rav Yosef said: "Why Aramaic in Babylon? Rather, either the holy tongue or Persian." [But] Greek language is one thing, and the wisdom of Greek is another. Is the wisdom of Greek forbidden? But Rav Yehuda said that Shmuel said, in the name of Rabban Shimon ben Gamliel:

"What [is the meaning of that] which is written, *My eye affects my soul because of all the daughters of my city* (Lam. 3:51)? There were one thousand youngsters in Father's house. Five hundred learned Torah, and five hundred learned the wis-

יוונית אמר להן כל זמן שעוסקים בעבודה אין נמסרין בידכם למחר שלשלו להם דינרים בקופה והעלו להם חזיר כיון שהגיע לחצי חומה נעץ צפרניו נזדעזעה א״י [ארץ ישראל] ארבע מאות פרסה אותה שעה אמרו ארור אדם שיגדל חזירים וארור אדם שילמד לבנו חכמת יוונית. ... איני והאמר רבי בא״י [בארץ ישראל] לשון סורסי למה אלא אי לשון הקודש אי לשון יוונית ואמר רב יוסף בבבל לשון ארמי למה אלא או לשון הקודש או לשון פרסי לשון יוונית לחוד וחכמת יוונית לחוד וחכמת יוונית מי אסירא והאמר רב יהודה אמר שמואל משום רשב״ג [רבן שמעון בן גמליאל] מאי דכתיב עיני עוללה לנפשי מכל בנות עירי אלף ילדים היו בבית אבא חמש מאות למדו תורה וחמש

---

15 Various interpretations have been offered as to what *ḥokhmat yᵉvanit*, "the wisdom of Greek," actually meant to the Sages in the Talmudic sources. The phrase is sometimes translated as "Greek wisdom" and explained as some form of Greek philosophy, and perhaps also rhetoric or another field of study in Greek culture (see, for example, [Blidstein], 8-9). However, the grammatical construction "the wisdom of Greek" (*ḥokhmat yᵉvanit*), rather than a straightforward noun modified by an adjective (*ḥokhma yᵉvanit*), and the fact that the elderly man used this knowledge to communicate to the enemy, suggest that this denotes something different. This context supports Rashi's explanation (*Sota* 49b at *ḥokhmat yᵉvanit*) that it was a language spoken by courtiers, but not known by the common people, and Maimonides's interpretation of it as a language of allusions and riddles used by the ancient Greeks for such purposes as espionage (Commentary on the Mishna *Sota* 9:15; see also [Kellner]: 110-113).

dom of Greek, and none of them remain other than myself here and my nephew in 'Asia!"[16] Those in the house of Rabban Gamliel are different, because they had close associations with the [Roman] government, as is taught: Though cutting a Greek-styled haircut (*qomi*)[17] is considered one of "the ways of the Amorite,"[18] Avtolos ben Reuven was permitted to cut his hair in the *qomi* [style], because he had close associations with the government. Those in the house of Rabban Gamliel were permitted the wisdom of Greek[19] because they had close associations with the government.

מאות למדו חכמת יוונית ולא נשתייר מהן אלא אני כאן ובן אחי אבא בעסיא שאני של בית ר״ג [ורבן גמליאל] דקרובין למלכות הוו דתניא מספר קומי הרי זה מדרכי האמורי אבטולוס בן ראובן התירו לספר קומי שהוא קרוב למלכות של בית רבן גמליאל התירו להן חכמת יוונית מפני שקרובין למלכות

M^enaḥot 99b

מנחות צ״ט ב׳

R. Yose said: "[If he] even removed the old [shewbread] in the morning and arranged the new in the evening, there is no problem.[20] Rather, how do I uphold *before me always* (Exod. 25:30)? [It means] that the table should not remain overnight without bread." R. Ami said: "We learn from R. Yose's words that even if a person studies merely a chapter in the morning and a chapter in the evening, he has fulfilled the commandment of *This book of the Torah shall not depart from your mouth* (Josh. 1:8)." R. Yoḥanan said in

רבי יוסי אומר אפי׳[לו] סילק את הישנה שחרית וסידר את החדשה ערבית אין בכך כלום אלא מה אני מקיים לפני תמיד שלא ילין שלחן בלא לחם א״ר [אמר רבי] אמי מדבריו של ר׳ יוסי נלמוד אפילו לא שנה אדם אלא פרק אחד שחרית ופרק אחד ערבית קיים מצות לא ימוש ספר התורה הזה

---

16 Several explanations have been suggested for the location of 'Asia. I find most convincing the one that explains 'Asia as most likely the town 'Azia, situated between the ancient cities of Keziv and Tyre (Tsor); see Ben-Zion Segal, *Geography in the Mishna* s.v. *Asia, 'Asia* [Hebrew] (Jerusalem: Ha-Makhon LeḤeqer Ha-Mishna,1979).

17 *Qomi* is the Greek word for hair style.

18 These practices are not idolatrous, per se, but are prohibited in accordance with Lev. 18:3 or Exod. 23:24.

19 The parallel passage in *Bava Qamma* has "was permitted to speak in the wisdom of Greek."

20 The context is Mishna M^enaḥot 11:7, which contains laws about the placement of the shewbread in the Temple.

the name of R. Shimon ben Yoḥai: "Even if he only recited *qᵉriat shᵉma'*²¹ morning and evening, he has fulfilled *It shall not depart*; but it is forbidden to say this in the presence of *'amei ha-arets*."²² [However,] Rava said: "It is meritorious to say it in the presence of *'amei ha-arets*."²³

The son of Dama, R. Yishmael's sister's son, asked R. Yishmael: "What is [the law] for [someone like] me, who has studied the whole Torah, to study the wisdom of Greek?" He [R. Yishmael] read this verse to him: *This book of the Torah shall not depart from your mouth, but study it day and night* (Josh. 1:8) [and said:] "Go and find a time when it is neither day nor night, and study then the wisdom of Greek."²⁴ But [this] disagrees with that of R. Shmuel bar Naḥmani, because R. Shmuel bar Naḥmani said in the name of R. Yonatan: "This verse is neither an obligation nor a commandment,²⁵ but rather a blessing. The Holy One, blessed be He, saw that the words of the Torah were most precious to Joshua, as it states, *But his attendant, Joshua, the son of*

מפיך אמר רבי יוחנן משום ר"יש [רבי שמעון] בן יוחי אפי'[לו] לא קרא אדם אלא קרית שמע שחרית וערבית קיים לא ימוש ודבר זה אסור לאומרו בפני עמי הארץ ורבא אמר מצוה לאומרו בפני עמי הארץ

שאל בן דמה בן אחותו של ר' ישמעאל את ר' ישמעאל כגון אני שלמדתי כל התורה כולה מהו ללמוד חכמת יונית קרא עליו המקרא הזה לא ימוש ספר התורה הזה מפיך והגית בו יומם ולילה צא ובדוק שעה שאינה לא מן היום ולא מן הלילה ולמוד בה חכמת יונית ופליגא דר' שמואל בר נחמני דאמר ר' שמואל בר נחמני א"ר [אמר רבי] יונתן פסוק זה אינו לא חובה ולא מצוה אלא ברכה ראה הקדוש ברוך הוא את יהושע שדברי תורה חביבים עליו ביותר שנאמר ומשרתו יהושע בן

---

21 "Hear, O Israel," referring to the paragraphs in Deut. 6:4-9, 11:13-21, and Num. 15:37-41, which are read twice daily, morning and evening.

22 *'Amei ha-arets*, pl. (*'am ha-arets*, s.), literally means "the people of the land." The term can refer to a peasant, an ignoramus, or one who is not careful in matters of tithes. Here it denotes ignoramuses.

23 Rashi gives rationales for both conclusions (at *asur lᵉomro* and *mitsva lᵉomro*): R. Shimon bar Yoḥai reasons that an *'am ha-arets* might conclude that, since reciting *qᵉriat shᵉma'* suffices, he need not accustom his sons to study Torah; Rava, on the other hand, reasons that an *'am ha-arets* might conclude that if one's reward for merely reciting *qᵉriat shᵉma'* is great (as promised in the latter portion of Josh. 1:8, "for then your way will prosper"), then the reward for someone who devotes all his time to studying Torah would be even greater, so he would accustom his sons to study.

24 Compare JT *Pe'a* 1:1 (15c) and JT *Sota* 9:15 (24c).

25 Because the verse is not in the Pentateuch, it is not actually a commandment.

Nun, would not stir out of the tent (Exod. 33:11).²⁶ The Holy One, blessed be He, said to him: 'Joshua, the words of Torah are so precious to you! May the book of the Torah never depart your mouth!'"

נון נער לא ימיש מתוך האהל אמר לו הקדוש ברוך הוא יהושע כל כך חביבין עליך דברי תורה לא מוש ספר התורה הזה מפיך

Discussion

In *Sota* 49b, a distinction is made between Greek, the language, and "the wisdom of Greek," an obscure type of knowledge. Its obscurity will serve Ha-Levi in his aim to distinguish between forbidden study and permissible access to Gentile scholarship.

Mᵉnaḥot 99b demonstrates the interdependence between the quantification of the commandment to study Torah and the permissibility of studying Gentile knowledge. Though the commandment to study Torah is based on the command "you shall teach them [the words of the Torah] to your sons" (Deut. 11:19), and a midrash on the verse teaches that "whoever is commanded to teach is commanded to learn" (*Qiddushin* 29b),²⁷ there is no specification of how much time a person is commanded to devote to this obligation. For this, the Talmud brings Joshua 1:8 ("study it day and night") and offers several interpretations. Clearly, if one is to accept R. Yishmael's opinion, even assuming he was referring to the time in a day and night when a person is not working to earn a living, not eating, not sleeping, and not praying or performing other commandments, there could not be justification for using the remaining time to study Greek philosophy or the "wisdom of Greek," or for that matter, anything else! Perhaps, however, R. Yishmael did not truly require that someone study day and night (barring the necessities mentioned), but that it was specifically the "wisdom of Greek," that obscure, perhaps threatening, realm of knowledge from which he wished to dis-

---

26 There are many midrashic explanations of why Joshua remained in the tent. One is that he was studying Torah there.

27 The Hebrew for "you shall teach" is *vᵉlimadtem*, while the Hebrew for "you shall learn" is *ulmadtem*—without vowels, they are spelled the same way. The midrash uses both vocalizations to derive two imperatives—to teach and to learn—from the same verse. These imperatives constitute the commandment of *talmud Torah* (study of Torah). Other verses in the Torah also command to teach one's son Torah (Deut. 4:9 and 6:7) and to study Torah (Deut. 5:1).

suade his nephew, that motivated him to interpret Joshua 1:8 in such a literal manner in response to his nephew's question.

Responsum

Z'qan Aharon 25	זקן אהרן כ״ה

[I write here regarding] what you have asked in the matter of Reuben who said to Simeon[28] in the presence of a large audience: "It is forbidden to pray with you because you are an apostate and heretic. Others say in their prayers 'the God of Abraham, the God of Isaac,'[29] but you pray and say 'the god of Aristotle.'" Reuben said other such things in a congregation and quorum, *with great force and with overflowing fury* (Ezek. 20:33, 34), in public, he shrieked like a crane[30] in a large gathering, *he opened his mouth and cursed* (Job 3:1), and did not concern [himself] about embarrassing his fellow,[31] but has not *borne reproach for [his behavior to] his neighbor* (Ps. 15:3).[32]

מה ששאלתם על ענין ראובן שאמר בקהל רב לשמעון אסור להתפלל עמך כי אתה מין אפיקורוס. ואחרים בהתפללם יאמרו אלקי אברהם ואלקי יצחק. ואמנם אתה תתפלל ותאמר אלקי ארסטו כזאת וכזאת אמר ראובן בתוך קהל ועדה בכח גדול ובחימה שפוכה בפרהסי[א] ובכנופיא צווח ככרוכיא פתח את פיהו ויקלל ולא חשש למלבין פני חבירו וחרפה לא נשא על קרובו.

התשובה: אמרינן בפ׳[רק] במה בהמה יוצאה אמר ר׳ שמואל בר נחמני

Response: We say in chapter "In what way does an animal go out" [*Shabbat* 55b]: R. Shmuel bar Naḥmani said: "Whoever says Reuben sinned is mistaken"—

---

28 These are pseudonyms; it is usual for pseudonyms to be used in naming the protagonists in responsa literature.

29 The opening benediction of the Jewish silent devotion, said thrice daily, addresses "the God of Abraham, the God of Isaac, and the God of Jacob."

30 *Qiddushin* 44a.

31 See Mishna *Avot* 3:11: "R. Elazar of Modi'in said: One who desecrates the sacred things, or who scorns the festivals, or who embarrasses his fellow publicly ... has no share in the world to come"; and *B'rakhot* 43b and *K'tubbot* 67b: Rather, a person should throw himself into a fiery furnace than embarrass his fellow publicly.

32 Though the psalmist used this phrase as a positive description of a person who never did anything to his fellow that would warrant reproach, the term is used here to indicate that Reuben has not been the recipient of reproach he deserves.

[this refers to] Reuben the son of Jacob,[33] but this Reuben [in the question above] is a sinner and a dimwit, and *a defamer is a fool* (Prov. 10:18). We should shun him.[34] [1][35] Even though we say in the first chapter of *Qiddushin* [28a]: If one says to his fellow, "slave!"[36] [when he is not], he should be shunned;[37] [if] "mamzer!,"[38] he should be given 40 lashes;[39] [if] "wicked!," he [the one who was insulted] may torment him,[40] which implies that the rabbinical court is not required [to enforce the penalty] on one who calls his fellow wicked, [in our case the rabbinical court has the authority to impose a punishment on the defendant for the following reasons]. This [in *Qiddushin*] is the type of an ordinary wicked person, such as one who has transgressed a mere prohibition,[41] such as we state

האומר ראובן חטא אינו אלא טועה ודוקא ראובן בן יעקב אבל ראובן זה חוטא ושוטה ומוציא דיבה הוא כסיל ומחינן ליה אמוחא בסילוא דלא מבע דמא. ואע״ג [ואף על גב] דאמרינן בקדושין פ״ק [פרק קמא] האומר לחברו עבד יהא בנדוי ממזר סופג את הארבעים רשע יורד עמו לחייו משמי[ע] דהקורא לחבירו רשע אין ב״ד [בית דין] נזקקין לו היינו רשע בעלמא כגון שעובר בלאו גרידא כדאמרינן בפרק זה בורר לאביי רשע דחמס בעינן והיינו לאו גרידא. וכן גבי

---

33 This citation from the Talmud (which refers to Jacob's son Reuben in Gen. 35) is not brought for any legal purpose, but simply as a homiletical device.

34 Lit., "We should hit him in the head with a thorn that does not cause blood to flow." This expression is from *Bava Batra* 151b (also *K^etubbot* 91a). According to R. Samuel ben Meir (Rashbam) (*Bava Batra* 151b) and Rashi (*K^etubbot* 91a) the expression is a sobriquet for shunning and excommunication. See the chapter "On Excommunication."

35 Numbers are inserted to facilitate reading the discussion following the responsum.

36 Ha-Levi's text here ("one who says to his fellow") is in a Spanish print edition of the Talmud (ca. 1480), but the extant manuscripts and the Vilna edition have "one who calls his fellow," as Ha-Levi writes towards the end of this responsum, where he refers to this text again.

37 Refer to the chapter "On Excommunication."

38 A *mamzer* is someone born of most (though not all) forbidden sexual relationships.

39 The Sages limited such corporal punishment to a maximum of thirty-nine lashes (though it is called forty), so as to be certain to not exceed the maximum, as iterated in Deut. 25:3 (Mishna *Makkot* 3:10-11). See the chapter "On Excommunication," note 17.

40 There are several explanations of what the victim is permitted to do to torment the perpetrator, such as being allowed to hate him (usually a person is forbidden to hate his fellow, in accordance with Lev. 19:17) and to trespass on his occupation or livelihood, even causing him to lose income (Rashi on *Qiddushin* 28a); to hit him (Meiri on *Qiddushin* 28a); and even to burn one third of his wheat (Rav Tsadok Gaon as cited in *Tosafot Bava M^etsi'a* 71a, but the Tosafot express surprise and wonder about his basis for this).

41 "Mere prohibition" refers to a prohibition that does not incur a punishment more severe than lashes.

in chapter "One [litigant] chooses" [Sanhedrin 27a] [regarding disqualified witnesses] that, according to Abaye, it must be someone wicked with the intent to gain by it.[42] That is what we call a mere prohibition. Likewise with lending [money] for interest,[43] as it states [Sanhedrin 25a] that such is a wicked person. But to call someone an apostate and heretic[44] [is such a severe defamation] that it requires [a case before a rabbinical court, to sue] for damages, and he [the offender] should be punished [by the court]. [There is] proof in what [is found] in chapter "The gold" [Bava M^etsi'a 58b]: *Do not defraud one another* (Lev. 25:17)—the text refers to [defrauding] by insulting words.[45] [... How?][46] Do not say [to a penitent] "remember your previous deeds,"[47] [...] and one who calls his fellow person by a nasty name [...] even if he [the victim] is used to it, is among those who go down to the netherworld[48] and without [being able] to come up,[49] and one who insults his fellow is not called a friend. If one who states the truth [such as about a penitent's past] has such a severe punishment, even more so [regarding] one who tells a lie and slanders, as is [found]

לוה ברבית דקאמר האי רשע הוא וכו'[לי] אבל לקרותו מין ואפיקורוס נזקקין לנזיקין ומענישין אותו. וראיה מההיא דפרק הזהב ולא תונו איש את עמיתו באונאת דברי[ם] הכתוב מדבר אל יאמר לו זכור מעשיך הראשונים והמכנה שם לחברו ואע״ג [ואף על גב] דדש ביה הוא מיורדי שאול בלי יעל והמאנה את עמיתו לא מקרי עמיתו. ואם האומר אמת עונשו כל כך גדול

---

42 Such as a thief or robber. *Sanhedrin* 27a includes a statement that someone who eats carrion in order to satisfy his greed (because it is less expensive than properly slaughtered meat) is disqualified from being a witness, and there is no dispute about that. But if someone eats carrion to be provocative, then Abaye maintains that he too should be disqualified, but Rava maintains that he is a valid witness, because to be disqualified, he must be wicked with the intent to gain. Thus it is actually Rava who required that the wicked person have intent to gain to be disqualified, but the law is in accordance with Abaye. Perhaps Ha-Levi intended to write "even with no intent to gain by it."

43 One who lends money to a fellow Jew with interest is also disqualified as a witness.

44 In Jewish law such a person is considered a much greater sinner than the previously mentioned wrongdoers, and can be subject to vigilante punishment. See *MT Hilkhot Rotse'ah* (The Laws of the Murderer) 4,10.

45 The text there explains that since Lev. 25:14 refers to monetary fraud, Lev. 25:17 must refer to another kind of fraud, i.e., fraud by words, or insulting or painful words.

46 Ha-Levi omits portions of the text in his quotation.

47 Other examples given in this text but not quoted by Ha-Levi include not reminding a convert of his past, or rebuking someone who is suffering illness or death in the family, as Job's friends rebuked him.

48 Sheol.

49 This is a paraphrase from the continuation of *Bava M^etsi'a* 58b.

in chapter "In the [laws of] dedications and valuations there are" ['Arakhin 15a]: R. Elazar ben Perata said: "[Come and see][50] how great the strength of slander is from [the case of] the spies.[51] If the spies who only spoke about trees and stones in this manner [were punished], so much more so [should be] one who slanders his fellow. [This is so] even if it [the insult] is not in front of him [but behind his back; and] how much more so [if] to his face, "because [after] he turns red [from embarrassment,] the white returns."[52] All this is when there is some element [of truth] to what was said, but one who states a falsehood—there is no one who bears false witness against his fellow[53] more than he; and one who embarrasses his fellow in public is deserving of a great punishment, and [the court] is required [to enforce the punishment] in any place and in any time, and "all [awards of damages are] according to the offender and the one who is embarrassed."[54] If the one who is embarrassed is a scholar whose [study of] Torah is his vocation, or even if [it is] not [his vocation] but he sets aside regular times for Torah, it is a circumstance of one who humiliates a scholar, and [the court] determines to excommunicate [the offender], even if [offender and offended] are equals. This is understood from chapter "One whose dead" [B‎ʿrakhot 19a], where it is taught that [R. Yehoshua ben Levi said:] "There are twenty-four situations in which

---

50 "Come and see" appears in all manuscripts.
51 See Num. 13-14.
52 *Bava Mʿtsiʿa* 58b. This is an explanation of the statement that one who embarrasses (lit., "whitens") his fellow in public is as if he spilled blood, i.e., commits murder.
53 Derived from Exod. 20:12 in the Ten Commandments. (In some editions of the Pentateuch it is verse 13 due to different numbering of the verses in the Ten Commandments.)
54 *Bava Qamma* 83b. The payment of damages for shaming someone varies according to the status of the people involved—for example, a very important person who is shamed in public might be embarrassed more.

[the religious court]⁵⁵ shuns because of [an insult to the] honor of a rabbi, and we have taught them all in the Mishna." [R. Elazar said to him: "Where?" He replied: "See if you find them!"] He went out and checked and found three: [one who scorns hand-washing, one who makes remarks about scholars after their death, and one who acts irreverently towards Heaven.] One who makes [derogatory] remarks about scholars after their death—what is that?

מקומות מנדין על כבוד הרב וכלן שנינו במשנתינו עד נפק דק ואשכח תלת המספר אחר מטתו של תלמיד חכם מאי היא דתנן הוא היה אומר אין משקין לא את הגיורת ולא את המשוחררת אמרו לו מעשה בכרכמית שפחה משוחררת והשקוה שמעיה ואבטליון ואמר להם דוגמא השקוה ונדוהו ומת בנדוי מפני רמז בעלמא. ופשיטא שבחייהם חמור. וכן כתב הרמב״ם המבזה ת״ח [תלמיד חכם]

What we teach in a *mishna*:⁵⁶ "He [Akavya ben Mahalalel] would say: 'They do not give a woman convert or an emancipated [formerly Gentile] bondwoman [the bitter water]⁵⁷ to drink.' [But the Sages say they do.] They [the Sages] said to him: 'There is the case of Karkᵉmit, a freed bondwoman, and Shemaya and Avtalyon gave her [the bitter water] to drink.' He [Akavya] said to them: 'They gave her, [who was] like [themselves],⁵⁸ to drink.' They then excommunicated him [Akavya], and he died in excommunication."⁵⁹ [This was] because of a mere innuendo. So it is obvious that [an insult] in their [the scholars'] lifetime is more severe. Thus wrote Maimonides: "[A person is shunned for twenty-four offenses ... and they are: [1.] humiliation of a Torah scholar, even after his

---

55 "Religious court" appears in all manuscripts.
56 ʿEduyyot 5:6.
57 See Num. 5:11-31.
58 Shemaya and Avtalyon are said to be descendants of Sanḥeriv (the Babylonian king Sennacherib) (*Gittin* 57b), and therefore descendants of converts. This is how Rashi explains the obscure intent of the word *dugma* (Bᵉrakhot 19a at *dugma hishquha*). The Tosafot (at *dugma hishquha*) point out that Rashi's explanation is also consistent with JT *Moʿed Qatan* 3:1 (81d), and then cite *Sefer Ha-ʿArukh* (Nathan ben Jehiel of Rome), where the word *dugma* is explained to mean that she was given colored water like the bitter water, but not the actual bitter water, and they did it to alarm her.
59 Such a severe reaction to Akavya's statement would be consistent with Rashi's explanation of the intent of *dugma*, but not with the interpretation in *Sefer Ha-ʿArukh*, which would be consistent with R. Yehuda's opinion that Akavya was not excommunicated. This is related in the continuation of ʿEduyyot 5:6 (cited on Bᵉrakhot 19a): "R. Yehuda said: 'Perish the thought that Akavya ben Mahalalel was excommunicated! The [gates] of the Temple court never closed for anyone in Israel who was his equal in wisdom, purity, or fear of sin.'"

death."[60] Even more so and a fortiori if the offender is an ignoramus, because [then] there is desecration of the Torah. [We know this from the midrash] "ever since the small said to the great, 'I am greater than you,' human longevity was cut short,"[61] [so that] the Torah is made a fraud,[62] and it is the manner of ignoramuses to be very insolent towards scholars. And as is stated in chapter "[There is a greater] stringency with hallowed things" [Ḥagiga 22b]: The vessels[63] of an ignoramus [... are] impure. But if you tell him [it is] impure, will he pay any attention to you at all? [No!] Not only that, but if you tell him [it is] impure, he will say to you "mine is pure, and yours is impure"[64]—just the reverse!

אפי'[לו] אחר מותו וכ"ש [וכל שכן] וק"ו [וקל וחומר] אם המבזה הוי עם הארץ שיש שם חילול התורה דמדאמר זעיר'[א] לרבה אנא רב מינך אקטעו שניהון דבני נשא ונעשית התור'[ה] פלסתר ודרכם של עמי הארץ דחציפי טובא לגבי תלמידי חכמים. וכדאמרינן פ'[רק] חומר בקדש כליו של עם הארץ טמא ואם אתה אומר לו טמא כלום משגיח עליך ולא עוד אלא שאם אתה אומר לו טמא אומר לך שלי טהור ושלך טמא כלפי לייא. ועוד אני אומר שזה המגדף לא על שמעון לבד תלונתו אלא על קדושים אשר בארץ שהרי הוציא לעז על הגאונים ועל החכמים הראשונים שנתעסקו בחכמ'[ה] כרבינו סעדיא

[2] I also say about this offender: his complaint is not only about Simeon, but about *the saints that are on the earth* (Ps. 16:3).[65] Clearly he slandered the Geonim and the Rishonim who engaged themselves with [worldly] wisdom, such as our rabbi Saadiah Gaon and our rabbi Hai Gaon and those sages after them—such

---

60 MT Hilkhot Talmud Torah (The Laws of Torah Study) 6,14.

61 The citation is from either *Sifrei dᵉAggadᵉta 'al Esther Midrash Abba Gurion* 1 or *Yalqut Shim'oni* Esther 1044 or Job 920.

62 The expression "to make the Torah a fraud (*plaster*, derived from Greek)" is common in rabbinic literature.

63 The Vilna printing and some manuscripts have this as singular, while the Venice printing and some manuscripts have plural, as does the text of the responsum.

64 This is an excerpt of a debate between R. Yehoshua and a follower of the school of Shammai on the subject of the ritual impurity of vessels that belong to *'amei arets*, i.e., those who were not considered reliable in matters of ritual purity and tithes.

65 This expression is commonly used in responsa literature to refer to rabbinic scholars.

as ibn Gabirol[66] and R. Judah Halevi,[67] R. ibn Ezra[68] and Maimonides, and scholars of every generation who built a magnificent tower,[69] a fortress to stop up the mouth of those who speak[70] arrogance against our holy Torah. Maimonides wrote therein [the fortress] propositions[71] to prove the existence of God, and the wise men of the [other] nations copied them and interpreted them and were praised for them;[72] he brought proofs about the secrets of the Torah and its foundations, and removed from people's hearts much perplexity that had troubled earlier and later scholars about the way to study Torah [and] "how to answer the skeptic,"[73] etc. The Sages have already written that it is known that our holy Rabbi [R. Judah Ha-Nasi] was expert in

גאון ורבי'[נו] האיי גאון והחכמי'[ם] אחריהם כאבן גבירול ור'[בי] יהודה הלוי ורבי אברהם בן עזרא והרמב"ם וחכמי כל דור ודור שבנו מגדל לתלפיות תל פיות לסכור פי דוברי עתק כנגד תורתנו הקדושה. והרמב"ם כתב בהם הקדמות לאמת מציאות השי"ת [השם יתברך] וחכמי האומות העתיקום ופרשו אותם ונשתבחו בהם והביא מופתים על סתרי התורה ושרשיה והסיר מבוכות רבות מלב האנשים נבוכו בם ראשונים ואחרונים ע"י [על דרך] למוד תורה מה שתשיב לאפיקורס

---

66   Solomon ben Judah ibn Gabirol (c. 1021–c. 1057) was a Spanish poet and philosopher. His poetry includes liturgical, religious, and secular compositions. His philosophical works reflect his knowledge of non-Jewish philosophers and their works.

67   R. Judah Halevi (c. 1075–1141) was a Spanish physician, poet, and philosopher. His poetry includes liturgical, religious, and secular compositions, including love poems, and reflects his familiarity with Arabic poetry of his contemporaries. His philosophical work reflects familiarity with non-Jewish philosophy.

68   R. Abraham ibn Ezra (1089–1164) was a Spanish commentator on the Bible, a grammarian, poet, astronomer, mathematician, and philosopher.

69   Derived from the Song of Sol. 4:4, the word *talpiyyot* (turrets) is expounded upon in various midrashim, such as found in B*e*rakhot 30a. In these homiletic interpretations, the word is frequently broken into two parts: *tel piyyot* (a mound of mouths), and Ha-Levi uses this interpretation in his metaphor that describes a fortress of wisdom built to protect the Torah.

70   Derived from Ps. 63:12.

71   Ha-Levi refers to the twenty-five propositions that Maimonides enumerates in his introduction to part two of *The Guide for the Perplexed*. Maimonides attributes them to "Aristotle and the Peripatetics after him."

72   Maimonides influenced several Christian theologians, the most well-known being Thomas Aquinas, to whom Ha-Levi most likely refers here. Much has been written about the influence of Maimonides on Aquinas; see, for example, Alexander Broadie, "Maimonides and Aquinas," in *History of Jewish Philosophy*, ed. Daniel H. Frank and Oliver Leaman (London: Routledge, 1997), 293.

73   Mishna *Avot* 2:14.

all [manner] of wisdom, and he determined and stated that the words of the wise people of the [other] nations of the world make more sense than the words of the wise people of Israel in the matter of the sun that moves below the sky in the daytime and at night below the earth, as is found in *P'saḥim*, chapter "Whoever was impure" [94b].[74] Shmuel the astronomer[75] said: "The paths of the sky are clear to me like the paths of Nehardea, except a comet, [about which] I do not know," as is found in [chapter] "He who beholds" [*B'rakhot* 58b]. Should it not be said that their expertise was in

וכו'/לין]. וכבר כתבו החכמים מקובל
אצלי/ןם] שרבינו הקדוש היה בקי בכל
חכמה והוא הכריע ואמר שנראים
דברי חכמי אומות העולם מדברי
חכמי ישראל בעניין חמה שמהלכת
ביום למטה מהרקיע ובלילה למטה
מהקרקע כדאיתא בפסחים פרק מי
שהיה טמא ושמואל ירחינאה אמר
נהירין לי שבילי דשמיא כשבילי
דנהרדעא בר מכוכבא דשביט דלא
ידענ/[א] כדאית[/א] בהרואה וליכא
למימר דבקיאותם היה בתכונת
הגלגלים והיינו תקופות ומזלות
דאמר בשבת פרק כלל גדול כל מי

the characteristics of the spheres,[76] that is, the seasons and constellations, [as] said in *Shabbat*, chapter "An important principle" [75a],[77] that whoever does not calculate the seasons and the constellations—it is said of him *they regard not the*

---

74 *P'saḥim* 94b: The wise men of Israel say the sun moves under the heavens in the day and over the heavens at night; the wise men of the [other] nations of the world say the sun moves under the heavens in the day and under the earth at night. Rabbi said: "What they say makes more sense than what we say, for in the daytime the springs are cool, and in the nighttime they are hot [because of the sun heating them from under the earth]."

75 Shmuel was from Nehardea and a contemporary of Judah Ha-Nasi. In *B'rakhot* 58b he is not referred to as "the astronomer" (*Yarḥina'a*, derived from the word *yare'aḥ*, moon), but there is a Shmuel Yarḥina'a mentioned in *Bava M'tsi'a* 85b, and most presume it is the same person (see A. Steinsaltz, *Bava M'tsi'a*, Hebrew edition, 371n).

76 Ha-Levi refers to the Aristotelian and Ptolemaic concepts of spherical rotations. Copernicus's revolutionary (pun not intended, but nice, anyway) work on astronomy was published in 1543 in Nuremberg, just around the time of Ha-Levi's death, and it took a generation for astronomers to accept his cosmology.

77 *Shabbat* 75a: Rav Zutra bar Tuvia said in the name of Rav: "One who knows to calculate the seasons and planetary courses and does not calculate—it is forbidden to repeat his teachings." ... R. Shimon ben Pazi said in the name of R. Yehoshua ben Levi, [who said] in the name of Bar Kappara: "Whoever knows how to calculate the seasons and the planetary courses and does not calculate—Scripture says of him, *they regard not the work of the Lord, neither consider the operation of His hands* (Isa. 5:12)." R. Shmuel bar Naḥmani said in the name of R. Yoḥanan: "From where [do we know that] it is a commandment for a person to calculate the seasons and the planetary courses? As is said *Keep them therefore and do them; for this is your wisdom and your understanding in the sight of the nations* (Deut. 4:6). What wisdom and understanding is in sight of the nations?—that refers to the calculation of the seasons and planetary courses."

work of the Lord, neither have they considered the operation of His hands (Isa. 5:12). [Knowledge of] a comet is [a matter] of the science of nature, and they are called stars with tails and leaping stars, as is elucidated in *Otot Ha-Shamayim*.[78] Further, he [Shmuel] was also a scientific physician, as is told in chapter "One who hires" [*Bava Mᵉtsiʿa* 85b]:[79] Shmuel the astronomer was Rabbi's physician. Rabbi's eye ailed him. He [Shmuel] said to him: "I'll apply a medication." "I cannot bear [it," replied Rabbi]. "I'll apply an ointment." "I cannot bear [it]," etc.[80] ... [Shmuel comforted him and] said to him: "I saw in Adam's book[81] that it is written that Shmuel the astronomer will be called a scholar,[82] but he will not be called a rabbi, and he will provide Rabbi [Judah Ha-Nasi]'s medical treatment." Therefore, perforce, he [Shmuel] had to learn natural science, because it was not possible to become a physician had he not known [this] wisdom. Rav Pappa was also an expert physician, as is stated in the first chapter of *Rosh Ha-Shana* [17a]: Rav Huna, Rav Yehoshua's son, became ill. Rav Pappa went to

שאינו מחשב בתקופות ומזלות עליו נאמר ואת פועל ה׳ לא יביטו ומעשה ידיו לא ראו דהא כוכבא דשביט מחכמ׳[ת] התולדת הוא והם הנקראי׳[ם] כוכבים בעלי הזנבות וכוכבים מדלגים כמו שמבואר באותות השמים. וגם כן היה רופא טבעי כמו שבא פרק השוכר שמואל ירחינאה אסיא דר׳[בי] היה חש ליה ר׳[בי] בעיניה א׳׳ל [אמר ליה] אמלי לך סמא לא יכילנא אשטר לך משטר לא יכילנא וכו׳[לי] עד אמר ליה אנא חזינא בספריה דאדם הראשון וכתוב ביה שמואל ירחינא חכים ליקרי ר׳[בי] לא ליקרי ואסותיה דר׳[בי] על ידיה תהא וע׳׳כ [ועל כרחך] למד חכמת הטבע שאי אפשר להיות רופא אם לא ידע החכמה ורב פפא גם כן רופא מובהק הוה כדאמר בר׳׳ה

---

78   *Otot Ha-Shamayim* (Signs of Heaven) is Samuel ibn Tibbon's Hebrew translation and commentary of the Arabic version of Aristotle's *Meteorology*, completed in 1210. The book contains a chapter on comets, which are referred to as "stars with tails." I thank Joseph Sadan for assisting me in identifying the correct reference.

79   See note 75.

80   The continuation of this episode is that Shmuel was such a great physician he cured Rabbi by placing a vial with medication under Rabbi's pillow. Though Rabbi wanted to bestow the title rabbi on Shmuel, he did not succeed, and Rabbi was distressed about this. Ha-Levi continues with Shmuel's consolation of Rabbi.

81   Rashi and other commentators explain that the Holy One, blessed be He, showed Adam the future generations and its wise men.

82   Ḥakim in the Aramaic. In Arabic, the title Ḥakim is used as a title for a wise man, an honorific like "doctor," for physicians, and as a title for polymath scientists and philosophers in medieval Islam.

[inquire about][83] him. He [Rav Pappa] saw that he was very ill.[84] He said to them [those with Rav Huna]: "Prepare shrouds for him," [However,] eventually he recovered, etc.[85] R. Ḥanina was also an expert physician, as is told in the first chapter of *Ḥullin* [7b]: R. Ḥanina said, "No one ever consulted with me about an injury from a white mule and survived."[86] Several scholars were physicians and experts in the natural sciences. Would it come to anyone's mind to think [ill] of them? There is no doubt that one who scorns [such] wisdom also scorns those who study it, and *yet they* [*who study it*] *are the wisest of the wise* (Prov. 30:24) [but] who *dwell in the dust* (Isa. 26:19).[87] Even though the teachings of

[בראש השנה] פ״ק [פרק קמא] רב הונא בריה דרב יהושע חלש על לגביה רב פפא חזא דחליש ליה עלמ׳[א] א״ל [אמר להו] לצבתו ליה זודיתא לסוף איתפח וכו׳[לי] ור׳[בי] חנינא רופא מובהק הוה כדאמר פ״ק [פרק קמא] דחולין אמר ר׳[בי] חנינא מעולם לא שאלני אדם על מכת פרדה לבנה וחיה וכמה חכמים היו רופאים ובקיאים בחכמת הטבע היעלה על הדעת להרהר אחריהם. ואין ספק מי שמבזה החכמה בכלל מבזה לומדיה והמה חכמים מחוכמי׳[ם] שוכני עפר ואעפ״י [ואף על פי] שיש בדברי הפלוסופים דבור סרה בעניני ההשגחה וקצת מהם יגיעו בשרשי התורה לא מפני זה יגונה מי שלמד דבריהם כי אין

the philosophers contain *rebellious speech* (Deut. 13:6) in the matter of Divine Providence, and some of them even reach the foundations of the Torah [with their challenges],[88] one who studied their teachings should not be censured because of this, because their [the philosophers'] concerns are not dependent upon faith, but rather upon proof, and their proofs are proofs based on evidence, [and] one who has filled his belly with the nourishment of Torah,[89] who *ate the bread of noblemen* (Ps. 78:25), could most swiftly refute them and would not be led astray by them. Further, many of them [the philosophers] disagree with each

---

83   The text here is slightly different from available manuscripts and printed editions of the BT.
84   Lit., "the world was getting weak for him."
85   The BT does not state here that Rav Pappa was a physician, nor does it relate that Rav Pappa offered any treatment, but it does indicate that he was consulted as a physician.
86   R. Ḥanina clarifies that a wound specifically from a white mule does not heal. Though it is not so evident from this citation that R. Ḥanina was a physician, the same anecdote is told in *Yoma* 49a, as proof that he was an "expert in medical treatments."
87   I.e., who are in the earth, no longer alive, and cannot defend themselves.
88   See Maimonides, *The Guide for the Perplexed*, trans. M. Friedlander (New York: Dover, 1956), 3:17.
89   Lit., "bread of the Torah."

other's teachings, and anyone to whom God has given eyes to see and a portion of intelligence will be able to see with his eyes and understand with his heart that the intellect of man is not adequate to understand what is above him [God], and there is no path to proof about this, and the authentic tradition will transcend and invalidate poor reasoning that may arise in the words of the philosophers. On such matters it is said, "Should not our perfect Torah be [as convincing] as their idle chatter?"[90] Whoever trembles at the word of God will choose from their [the philosophers'] words what is useful and agrees with our beliefs, in the manner that R. Meir ate the inside and threw away the rind,[91] and will use them for [useful] perfumery and cookery.[92]

To conclude, my meat is prepared, and my wine is mixed.[93] It has been *decided once and for all* (Isa.10:23)[94] *to finish the transgression and to make an end to sins* (Dan. 9:24) of those who *speak arrogantly* (Ps. 94:4) about those who engage in wisdom, to call one who has read such [literature] an apostate and a heretic, *that the righteous should be as the wicked* (Gen. 18:25) to discredit the pious of the world, and there is no greater

---

90 Derived from *Bava Batra* 116a, where R. Yoḥanan ben Zakkai debates with a Sadducee about proofs of the laws of inheritance and says, "Fool, should not our perfect Torah be [as convincing] as your idle chatter?!"

91 In *Ḥagiga* 15b R. Meir continued to learn from Elisha ben Avuya (known as Aḥer, "Other") even after ben Avuya adopted views that were heretical in the eyes of the Sages. A parable is told to explain how he could do this: R. Meir found a pomegranate, ate out the inside, and threw away the rind.

92 Derived from 1 Sam. 8:13.

93 Derived from Prov. 9:2. (Wine was customarily mixed with water for serving.)

94 Lit., "determined and decreed."

[case of] one who makes derogatory remarks about scholars after their death than this.⁹⁵

[3] [Regarding] what the Sages said in chapter "More often" [*Bava Qamma* 82b] and at the end of *Sota* [49b]—At that moment they said "Cursed be the one who teaches his son the wisdom of Greek"⁹⁶—Rashi and Maimonides have already explained that it is "a language of wisdom that courtiers speak, but not known by the common people,"⁹⁷ and so it appears from the related incident. Regarding what they [the Sages] said in chapter "Portion" [*Sanhedrin* 100b]— And R. Akiva says "even one who reads the noncanonical books"⁹⁸ [has no portion in the world to come]⁹⁹—the *gᵉmara* explained: What are noncanonical [books]?¹⁰⁰ [It is taught:] Books of the *minim*.¹⁰¹ Rashi explained that they are the books of Christian priests,¹⁰² which is consistent with his opinion in that he refers to a *min* as a student of Jesus¹⁰³ in some places.¹⁰⁴

על חסידי עולם ואין לך מספר אחר מטתם של תלמידי חכמים יותר מזה. ומה שאמרו פרק מרובה וסוף סוטה באותה שעה אמרו ארור המלמד את בנו חכמה יונית כבר פי'[רשו] רש"י והרמב"ם שהוא לשון חכמה שמדברים בו בני פלטין ואין שאר העם מכירים בו וכן נראה מאותו מעשה. ומה שאמרו פ'[רק] חלק ורע"א [ורבי עקיבא אומר] אף הקורא בספרים החצוניים ופר'[ש] בגמ'[רא] מאי חצוניים ספרי המיני'[ם] ופירש"י [ופירש רש"י] ספרי גלחי'[ם] הולך לשטתו שקורא בכ"מ [בכמה מקומות] מין תלמידי ישו' וכן פירש הרמב"ם אבל ספרי הפלוסופים נקראי'[ם] אצל החכמים חכמי אומות העולם

---

95 B‘rakhot 19a.
96 Almost all textual witnesses of the tractates cited have *ḥokhmat yᵉvanit* (the wisdom of Greek), rather than *ḥokhma yᵉvanit* (Greek wisdom), as Ha-Levi has.
97 Rashi *Sota* 49b at *ḥokhmat yᵉvanit*. See note 15.
98 Lit., "external books." This statement by R. Akiva is a quote from the Mishna *Sanhedrin* 10:1.
99 *Sanhedrin* 90a (Mishna *Sanhedrin* 11:1) that states that all of Israel have a portion in the world to come, with specified exceptions.
100 The question does not appear in the text of the *gᵉmara*—just an answer.
101 It is not certain what these books are. For elaboration, see Daniel Sperber, "Sifrei Ha-Minim," in EJ, 18:564-565. Sperber translates *min* as "sectarian" under "Min," in ibid. 14:263-264. The Vilna edition of the BT has Sadducees, but Ha-Levi's text is in accordance with the uncensored versions of the BT; see William Popper, *The Censorship of Hebrew Books* (New York: Franklin, 1969 [1899]).
102 Lit., "tonsured," a commonly used sobriquet for Christian priests in rabbinic literature in Christian Europe. This, too, is censored from Rashi's commentary in the Vilna edition of the BT.
103 The Hebrew spelling for Jesus here is as it appears in MS JER NLI 28°6549.
104 These have been censored from Rashi's commentary in the Vilna edition of the BT.

Maimonides interprets likewise.[105] But the books of the philosophers are called by the Sages [the books of] "the wise men of the nations of the world," like that [citation, above] in P*saḥim* [94b], and it is explicitly stated in the first chapter of M*egilla* [16a]: R. Yoḥanan said: "Whoever says something wise, even from among the [Gentile] nations of the world, is called wise," as is stated, *His wise men said to him* (Esther 6:13).[106] I also found in the homiletic literature[107] a story about four elders who went to attend a private counsel [with Roman authorities],[108] and they had a wise philosopher [there]. They were Rabban Gamliel, [R. Yehoshua], R. Akiva and R. Elazar ben Azarya. R. Yehoshua said to Rabban Gamliel: ...[109] "Do you want us to pay a visit to our colleague, Aristotle[110] the philosopher?" He replied to him: "Yes." They went, and R. Yehoshua knocked on the door. The philosopher thought: "This can only be the good manners of a sage." ... He went out to meet them and saw the sages of Israel... . He [the philosopher] considered and thought: "How shall I greet the sages of Israel? If I say 'Peace to you, Rabban Gamliel,' I insult his

כההיא דפסחים ובפירוש אמר מגילה פ״ק [פרק קמא] א״ר [אמר רבי] יוחנן כל האומר דבר חכמה אפי׳[לו] מאומות העולם נקרא חכם שנאמר ויאמרו לו חכמיו ומצאתי באגדה מעשה בד׳ זקנים שהלכו להקביל למלכות פנימית והיה להם פלוסוף א׳[חד] חכם ואלו הם רבן גמליאל ור׳ עקיבא ור׳[בי] אלעזר בן עזריא א״ר [אמר רבי] יהושע לרבן גמליאל רצונך שנלך ונקבל פני ארסטו הפילוסוף חברנו א״ל [אמר לו] הן הלכו וטפח לו ר׳ יהושע על הדלת וחשב הפלוסוף שאין אלו אלא דרך ארץ של חכם יצא לקראתו וראה חכמי ישראל והיה מחשב בדעתו היאך אתן שלום לחכמי ישראל אם אומר שלום עליך רבן גמליאל הריני מבזה את חבירו

---

105 For example, Maimonides's Commentary on the Mishna *Ḥullin* 1:2.

106 Only in MS Goettingen 3 do we find the quote from Esther in the *g*emara*, and it precedes the statement by R. Yoḥanan there.

107 *Pirqei ben Azzai* 3:2 (Michael Higger, *The Treatises Derek Erez* [New York: Moinester Publishing, 1935]), with some textual differences. (A similar narrative appears in *Kalla Rabati* 7:4, Higger edition.)

108 Lit., "inner kingdom"; trans. Marcus van Loopik, *The Way of the Sages and the Way of the World: The Minor Tractates of the Babylonian Talmud: Derekh 'Eretz Rabbah, Derekh 'Eretz Zuta, Pereq ha-Shalom* (Tübingen: J. C. B. Mohr, 1991), 100.

109 Ellipses indicate portions of the source text omitted by Ha-Levi.

110 The philosopher is not referred to by this name in any of the variants of *Pirqei ben Azzai*, the source Ha-Levi is referring to.

companions."[111] He said to them: "Peace to you sages of Israel, headed by Rabban Gamliel." Notice well that they [the visiting elders] referred to the philosopher, who was one of the wise people of the [Gentile] nations, as their colleague, because of his wisdom, because one is not a colleague other than through wisdom. We find thus in *Sukka*, chapter "A *lulav*[112] that was stolen" [39a] [regarding] one who purchases a *lulav* from his fellow [during the Sabbatical year], Rashi comments: "We [should] read the text as 'one who purchases from an *'am ha-arets*,'[113] because [this text] refers to an *'am ha-arets* [as the seller], as we state in the *gᵉmara*,[114] and in [a relationship] between an *'am ha-arets* and a *ḥaver*, [the former] is not called his colleague."[115]

א״ל [אמר להם] שלום עליכם חכמי ישראל ורבן גמליאל בראש. ראה גם ראה איך קראו לפלוסוף מחכמי האומות חבירם מצד החכמה שאין חבר אלא בחכמה. שכן מצינו בסוכה פרק לולב הגזול הלוקח לולב מחבירו ופרש״י [ופירש רש״י] דהלוקח מעם הארץ גרסינן דהא בעם הארץ קא מיירי כדאמרי׳[נן] בגמר׳[א] ועם הארץ לגבי חבר לא קרי ליה חבירו. ועוד אני אומר שהאומ׳[ר] שכל מי שלמד חכמה אחת או ספר מספרי האומו׳[ת] יקרא מאמין בהם אין לך אפקירותא גדולה הימנה שהרי

I further say that one who says that anyone who has learned an [aspect] of wisdom or one book from the literature of the [Gentile] nations should be dubbed a believer in those [works]—there is no greater insolence than that! Consider the Great Sanhedrin, who sat in the Chamber of Hewn Stone,[116] from whom

---

111 By ignoring them. The passage continues: "but if I say 'Peace to you, sages of Israel,' I insult Rabban Gamliel," by not acknowledging Rabban Gamliel's position as head of the Sanhedrin. Ha-Levi omitted this portion from his quotation.

112 This is the palm branch that is used in the ritual of the four species on Sukkot (Lev. 23:40).

113 Here *'am ha-arets* denotes one who is not careful in such rituals as tithes, nor does he observe unrequired stringencies in matters of purity.

114 The *gᵉmara* presumes that this text from the *mishna* is referring to a seller who is an *'am ha-arets*, because giving money to an *'am ha-arets* in exchange for fruit is prohibited in the Sabbatical year. An *'am ha-arets*, who is not careful about the laws of the Sabbatical year, may not nullify such money, as is obligatory, and thus must receive an additional gift, which is not subject to the same requirement. Rashi is stating that in relation to the *'am ha-arets* in this situation, the buyer (presumably not an *'am ha-arets*) would not refer to the *'am ha-arets* as a *ḥaver* (one who is stringent in matters of purity and careful in all ritual matters such as tithes) either in the ritual sense or as an equal intellectual colleague. In fact, the *mishna* is using *ḥavero*—his fellow—in the very simple sense, making Rashi's alternative reading superfluous.

115 Ha-Levi uses this citation from Rashi to make a rhetorical point that the Gentile philosopher was a wise man and an intellectual colleague of the four Sages.

116 *Lishkat ha-gazit*, the seat of the Great Sanhedrin at the Temple.

Torah emanated to all of Israel, [and the members] were expert in every language and in every form of pagan worship in the world, so that they would know if one who worshipped did so in the usual manner of [idolatrous] worship, to find him deserving of death [or not].[117] [This is] as stated in *Mᵉnaḥot*, chapter "R. Yishmael" [65a]: Only those who are wise, of [good] appearance, etc., with [a knowledge of] sorcery and who know seventy languages, etc. are appointed to the Sanhedrin. [These requirements are] because, as it says, "The one who exposes himself to Mercury and the one who casts [a stone] to Peʻor[118] is exempt,"[119] because that is not the manner of their worship. It is further stated that "our forefather Abraham's [tractate] *ʻAvoda Zara* had four hundred chapters,"[120] and if we say that a person believes whatever he learns, then "you would not let anyone live!"[121] Heaven forbid that a person should be doubted due to this. They [the Sages] explicitly said, in [interpreting] the verse *Do not learn to do in the manner of the abominations of those nations* (Deut. 18:9), "you may not

---

117 One who commits idolatry is deserving of the death penalty only if the manner in which he worships another god is the usual manner by which that god is worshipped; see *MT Hilkhot ʻAvoda Zara* (The Laws of Pagan Worship) 3,2.

118 The text presupposes that the usual manner of these types of worship was the opposite of the examples given. Though there is much historical evidence consistent with the Sages' perception of the worship of Mercury (see Barbara C. Bowen, "Mercury at the Crossroads in Renaissance Emblems," *Journal of the Warburg and Courtauld Institutes* 48 (1985): 222-229), there is no such evidence about the worship of Peʻor.

119 *MT Hilkhot ʻAvoda Zara* (The Laws of Pagan Worship) 3,2. This ruling and Ha-Levi's paraphrased continuation of the sentence are based on *Sanhedrin* 60b–61a.

120 *ʻAvoda Zara* 14b.

121 *Bava Qamma* 91b. That is, if everyone believed everything he learned, no one would be innocent.

learn [in order] to do, but you may learn [in order] to understand and instruct."[122] And we have not found anywhere that the Sages forbade studying philosophical inquiry.[123] [Regarding] what is in M^enaḥot, chapter "The two loaves" [99b]: ben Dama, R. Yishmael's sister's son, asked R. Yishmael "What is [the law] for [someone like] me, who studied the whole Torah, to study the wisdom of Greek?" he [R. Yishmael] read this verse to him: [*This*] *book of the Torah shall not depart ...* (Josh. 1:8) [and said]: "It is written: *but study it day and night ...*—find a time when it is neither day nor night, and study then the wisdom of Greek"[124]—we have already explained the matter of the wisdom of Greek, but to engage in philosophical inquiry is not prohibited, as we wrote. [Regarding]

אבל למד אתה להבין ולהורות. ולא מצינו בשום מקום שאסרו חכמים ללמוד חכמת המחקר. ומה שבא במנחות פ׳[רק] שתי הלחם שאל בן דמא בן אחותו של ר׳ ישמעאל אני שלמדתי כל התורה כולה מהו ללמוד חכמה יונית קרא עליה המקרא הזה לא ימוש ספר התורה וכו׳[לין] והגית בו יומם ולילה כתיב ראה שעה שאינה לא מן היום ולא מן הלילה ולמוד בה חכמה יונית. כבר פירשנו עניני חכמה יונית אבל לעסוק בחכמת המחקר אינו אסור כמו שכתבנו. ומה שכתב רש״י בפרש׳[ת] אחרי מות ללכת בהם שלא הפטר מתוכם שלא תאמר למדתי חכמת התורה אלך ואלמוד חכמת האומות ר״ל [רוצה לומר] שלא יפרוש מלמוד התורה אחר שכבר למד כל חכמתה אבל ללמוד

what Rashi wrote in [the Torah Portion] "After the Death" (Lev. 16-18) *to walk therein* (Lev. 18:4)—"Do not exempt yourself from them, that is, do not say 'I have studied the wisdom of the Torah, I will (now) go study the wisdom of the (other) nations.'"[125] He means to say that one should not depart from the study of the Torah even though he already learned all its wisdom; do not do that, but

---

122 *Sanhedrin* 68a.

123 In 1305, R. Solomon ben Abraham Adret (known as Rashba) was the major signatory on three bans against the study of secular wisdom (such as philosophy and natural sciences other than medicine and astronomy) before age twenty-five. In response, R. Yedaiah Bedershi wrote the *K^etav Hitnatslut* (Letter of Apology), a defense of the study of philosophy and other secular wisdom; see *Responsa of the Rashba*, vol. 1, 418 (Bnei Braq, 1958). Ha-Levi apparently draws from this letter, in particular in his use of the phrase *ḥokhmat ha-meḥqar* (philosophical inquiry), which is used by Bedershi, to refer to this type of study. For an analysis of the intellectual atmosphere in which the letter was written, see [Halkin] and [Berger], 85-108.

124 Though Ha-Levi's text here and in the next clause has *ḥokhma y^evanit* (Greek wisdom), internal consistency and extant versions of the Talmud indicate that it should read *ḥokhmat y^evanit* (the wisdom of Greek).

125 Rashi's source is *Sifra* 13,11.

study [other] wisdom and set times for Torah. However, the truth is that in our times I have always restricted students from learning this wisdom, because hearts [devoted to piety and scholarship] are fewer[126] and the "springs of wisdom have been stopped up."[127] [Restriction is out of concern] lest a person be led astray to nonsense, as our Sages taught: There are four characteristics of those who sit [to learn] before the Sages: a sponge, a funnel, a strainer and a sieve.[128] And the Sages said: Be careful in what you say, lest you be liable for the penalty of exile, and you will be exiled to a place with bad water [that is, inadequate Torah],[129] and there is no greater exile than in our time, when Torah [study] has become lessened, and *there is no one to search and no one to seek* (Ezek. 34:6). We find that they [the Sages] did not even permit a person to enter [the realm

החכמה ויקבע עתים לתורה אל תעשה כך. אעפ״י [אף על פי] שהאמת שאני מנעתי התלמידים בזמננו זה תמיד מללמוד החכמה הזאת מפני שנתמעטו הלבבו׳[ת] ונסתתמו מעייני החכמה ושמא יטה האדם לדברי הבאי כמו ששנו חכמי׳[ם] ד׳ מדות ביושבי לפני חכמים ספוג ומשפך משמרת ונפה ואמרו חכמים הזהרו בדבריכ׳[ם] שמא תחובו חובת גלות ותגלו למקו׳[ם] מים הרעי׳[ם] ואין לך גלות גדולה מזמננו זה שנתמעטה התורה ואין דורש ואין מבקש והנה מצינו שאפי׳[לו] לחכמה המופלאה לא התירו להכנס האדם שמא יטה

---

126 This expression is commonly used throughout rabbinic and responsa literature to describe a decline of the generations in piety and scholarship, so as to justify different rulings from those made by predecessors. See, for instance, Rashi *Bava Mᵉtsi'a* 33a at *vᵉena mida*; R. Asher ben Jehiel (Rosh) *Responsa*, principle 55,9; and R. Simeon ben Zemaḥ Duran *Responsa* 1,146 and 1,160.

127 *Sota* 49b describes the tragedy that befell the Jewish people during the war with Vespasian and after the deaths and executions of the great Sages, saying that when Akiva died, the "springs of the Torah were stopped up." It is fitting for Ha-Levi to choose these words, in light of the devastation to Jewish communities and centers of learning that resulted from the Spanish inquisition and expulsions from Spain and Portugal. The great Jewish communities in Spain were thought of as Jerusalem in the West. However, in reality, the expelled scholars who settled in the Ottoman Empire enriched Torah scholarship in their new locales. See [Hacker].

128 Mishna *Avot* 5:15; it continues, "A sponge absorbs everything, a funnel takes in on this [end] and lets out on that [end], a strainer takes out the wine and saves the lees, and a sieve takes out the chaff and keeps the fine flour." Ha-Levi means that to safely study non-Jewish wisdom, one must be able to separate the good from the bad, but not all students can do this.

129 Mishna *Avot* 1:11; it continues "and [lest] the students who follow you there drink and die, and the name of Heaven is thus desecrated." Here Ha-Levi alludes again to the devastating consequences of the exile from Spain and Portugal.

of] wondrous knowledge, lest he be led astray,[130] as we find with the four who entered the orchard [of mystical study], and only R. Akiva came out unharmed.[131] How much more so [would be the result] with irreligious matters!

[4] Nonetheless, [it is] not because of these [concerns] that we would permit someone to give free rein to his tongue and humiliate one who studied wisdom, while his deeds are in accordance with the Torah and the commandments, [and he is] *wholehearted with the Lord, his God* (Deut. 18:13). On the contrary! It is befitting to praise him, since his actions demonstrate that [his study] is for the sake of Heaven. As they [the Sages] expounded on the verse *Do not defraud one another* (Lev. 25:17)—the nation that is with you [in observing] the Torah and the commandments.[132] I will be even more precise, based on the statement in *Qiddushin* [28a], that if one calls his fellow a slave [when he is not], he should be shunned. Rashi explained[133] that a court is required to shun him, because one who humiliates is obliged to be shunned. Rashi explained the reason—since "he disparaged a Jew so much, they will disparage him too." Even more so, in our case, where there is no greater disparagement than this, to call him a *min* and heretic, who are worse than the wicked of the Gentile[s], because he [the *min* or heretic]

---

130 Lit., "lest his heart be diverted."

131 Ḥagiga 14b.

132 *Bava M'tsi'a* 59a, where Rav Ḥinnana, the son of Rav Idi, interprets the use of the word *'amito* (his fellow man) in Lev. 25:17, breaking it into *'am ito* (the nation with him).

133 Our editions of the Talmud do not include this explanation by Rashi. It is likely that Ha-Levi deduced it from the quote that follows, where Rashi states, at *y'he b'niddui*, "they would shun him." "They" must mean a rabbinic court, as the procedure for shunning requires a rabbinic court. See the chapter "On Excommunication."

is among those who are lowered.[134] This is in accordance with what Maimonides wrote in chapter three of The Laws of Testimony:[135] "The Sages did not need to list [...] the *minim* and the apostates[136] in the list of those who are invalid witnesses, because they specified only those who are evil, but these heretics are even lowlier than Gentiles, etc.,[137] and they have no portion in the world to come." According to the other reason that we said—that the reason for shunning is [that it is] measure-for-measure, [just as] he [who called his fellow a slave] places his fellow in the category of those who are cursed, as it is written, *cursed is Canaan; [the lowest of slaves]* (Gen. 9:25), so we place him [who insulted his fellow] in the category of those who are cursed, as we say in *Sh‘vu‘ot* [36a]: "cursed" may imply shunning or cursing [or taking an oath].[138] Even more so in this case, since he [who called his fellow a heretic] put him in the category of cursed [*arur*], as it is written, *cursed be he who*

וכמו שכתב הרמב"ם פי"ג [פרק ג'] מהל'[כות] עדות המינים והמשומדים לא הצריכו חכמים למנותם בכלל פסולי עדות שלא מנו אלא הרשעים אבל אלו הכופרים הם פחותים מהגוים וכו'[לי] ואין להם חלק לעה"ב [לעולם הבא]. לפי הטעם האחר שאמרנו שטעם הנדוי הוא מדה כנגד מדה הוא מוקי ליה בארור דכתי'[ב] ארור כנען מוקמינן ליה אנן בארור כדאמרינן בשבועות ארור בו נדוי בו קללה כל שכן הכא דמוקי ליה בארור דכתיב ארור אשר לא יקים דדין הוא דנוקמיה בארור. זה הוא הנראה לי

---

134 *‘Avoda Zara* 26a–b and other locations in the Talmud. "Lowering" and "raising" people refers to causing their death indirectly, for example, by putting ("lowering") them into a pit (or a river), perhaps by a ruse, and not assisting ("raising") them to get out. In *‘Avoda Zara* 26a–b R. Abahu teaches: "Gentiles ... are neither raised nor lowered, but *minim* ... are lowered and not raised." In other words, whereas Gentiles (the Vilna BT has "pagans") who fall into a pit should be ignored (neither induced to fall nor rescued), *minim* deserve to be actively "lowered" and not rescued.

135 Sic. This is in *MT Hilkhot ‘Edut* (The Laws of Testimony) 11,10.

136 Ha-Levi uses *m‘shummadim* to refer to apostates, in accordance with uncensored editions of the *MT*. Although the common printed editions (such as those based on the Warsaw 1881 edition) have replaced "*minim* and *meshummadim*" with *mumarim*, for our purposes there is no difference; see Popper, *Censorship*, and S. Zeitlin, "Mumar and Meshumad," *Jewish Quarterly Review* 54 (1963): 84.

137 The continuation is: "because the Gentiles are neither raised nor lowered, and the righteous among them have a portion in the world to come, while these [Jewish heretics] are lowered and not raised, and they have no portion in the world to come."

138 In the context of which words imply that someone is taking an oath, a *baraita* is cited that teaches that the word *arur*, which is typically translated as "cursed," can be a term used by a rabbinic court to shun or excommunicate someone, or it may be intended as a curse, or it may be construed to invoke an oath.

will not uphold [the words of this Torah] (Deut. 27:26), by law he should be put in the category of shunned [*arur*].[139] That is what seems to me to be the law in this matter. I now hand this matter over to those *ḥakhamim*[140] who instruct the law, [requesting that they] emphatically close breaches and devise [ways that are] appropriate to the times, as they see fit, so that not everyone will build [himself] an altar[141] and sacrifice upon it while in an impure state, *like an* [*impure*] *altar* (Isa. 2:22).[142] [May the offender] ... *repent and be healed* (Isa. 6:10) with *the words of the wise* [*that*] *heal* (Prov.12:18).[143] I have written to them what is in accordance with my humble opinion. Elijah Ha-Levi.

מדינא בזה. ואני מוסר הדבר ביד החכמי׳[ם] מורי התורה כפי ראות עיניהם לגדור פרצו׳[ת] נמרצות ולהביא עצות לעשות כפי הזמן, שלא יהא כל אחד בונ׳[ה] במה ומקריב עליה קרבן בטומאה כי במה נחשב ושב ורפא לו בלשון חכמים מרפא. הנראה לע״ד [לעניות דעתי] כתבתי להם אליא הלוי.

Discussion

Ha-Levi has several stages in his response.[144]

[1] In the first stage, his aim is to prove that Reuben's offense is so severe that he can be judged and punished by a rabbinic court. It is as if Reuben had a lawyer who might claim that it was not within the jurisdiction of a rabbinic court

---

139 Using the word *arur* to shun or excommunicate.

140 The term *ḥakham* (pl. *ḥakhamim*) is the common term for rabbinical authorities, rather than the term *rav*, as used in the Ashkenazi communities. Most often, rabbinical authorities at the level of Ha-Levi wrote their responsa to communal rabbis, in response to questions that they posed for or regarding their community members.

141 *Ḥagiga* 22a. We are taught there that everyone is trusted throughout the year in the matter of the ritual purity of wine (for libations) and of oil (for meal offerings), so that "not each and every one would go build his own altar" (which would cause divisiveness). The expression is frequently used as a metaphor to mean that not everyone is permitted to establish one's own faction.

142 Ha-Levi is quoting the end of Isa. 2:22, with a play on words. See *Sota* 4b, where a string of Sages offer metaphors to describe someone who is haughty. Ula offers: "It is as if he built an [idolatrous] altar, as it states: *Oh, cease to glorify man, who has only a breath in his nostrils, for by what does he merit esteem (ki va-me neḥshav)?* (Isa. 2:22) [The midrash explains]: 'Do not read it *va-me* (by what), but rather *bama* (altar).'"

143 The Hebrew word for "wise" in the proverb is *ḥakhamim*, and Ha-Levi quotes these words to refer to the *ḥakhamim* to whom he is addressing this responsum.

144 See the section numbers in square brackets in the responsum.

to punish Reuben, considering the *baraita* from *Qiddushin* 28a, so Ha-Levi proceeds to demonstrate why that *baraita* does not apply in this case, but rather, a rabbinic court does have the authority to punish Reuben.

[2] In the next stage, Ha-Levi makes the case that the transgression, being very severe, is deserving of shunning. Further, he points out that, by insulting Simeon, Reuben also criticizes the many great sages and scholars throughout the generations who were versed in various fields of study and literature beyond the narrow field of religious Jewish studies, and even participated in those endeavors. In making this point, Ha-Levi rewards the reader with a survey of some of the greatest Jewish scholars and thinkers, some of the most colorful Talmudic persona, and some delightful Talmudic stories. Concluding this survey, he asserts that one who is steeped in the knowledge of Torah is impervious to whatever potential harm lies in the Gentile philosophy, but can retain what is of value.

[3] Only at this point does Ha-Levi address the question of what type of study, if any, is prohibited by certain passages in the Talmud. He defines the prohibited sphere, "the wisdom of Greek" in the narrowest of senses, thus virtually not restricting the pursuit of knowledge, nor does he take Joshua 1:8 literally. Nevertheless, he does demur over permitting students in his time to pursue external knowledge, given the state of piety and religious study in his generation.

[4] Ha-Levi reiterates the seriousness of the offense and his opinion that such an offender is deserving of shunning, but the concluding sentences suggest that what he really is hoping for is repentance on the part of the offender and reconciliation, as can be facilitated by those *ḥakhamim* who are the communal leaders.

Questions for Further Discussion

Considering the halakhic sources in this chapter, the responsum and perhaps some of the additional readings, do the halakhic sources support those who oppose the study of Gentile philosophy and knowledge, or is there no inherent halakhic objection to such study?

For those who oppose the study of Gentile philosophy and knowledge, is it a) because these fields of study are Gentile, b) because they are not "Torah," or is it c) because they conflict with or present challenges to religious belief?

According to the halakhic sources, is a Jew obligated to study Torah "day and night," literally? What is the intent of the verse?

What was Ha-Levi's personal view on these questions? Did his defense of Simeon (and condemnation of Reuben) reflect his personal view, or did it reflect a respect for a view that was not his own? How do you reconcile his unwillingness to permit students in his day to pursue study that he so adamantly defended?

Can Ha-Levi's explanation for his restriction on his own students and its historical context be compared to the attitudes of the ultra-Orthodox community and their single-minded devotion to yeshiva study in the post-Holocaust era, until the present time? What similarities and differences are there between the two historical situations and between the respective attitudes?

Read [Berger] 85-108, the section entitled "The Second Climax: 1230–1235 in Europe" in [Ben-Sasson et al.] and [Grant]. Does putting the Maimonidean Controversy into the historical context of the Condemnations in Paris, and into the context of the general social and cultural climate in Provence during that period, change your perspective? What insights have you gained?

Read [Galileo]. Discuss the similarities and differences between the objections raised against Galileo's scientific publications, as described by Galileo, and the objections in the Jewish world to the study of Gentile philosophy and knowledge. Do you think that the opposition that was often found in the Christian world to new scientific theories influenced attitudes among Jews? Do you think such is the situation today with, for example, opposition to Darwinism among some Christians and other religious groups? Does that opposition have a "ripple affect" among some Jews?

The tension between religion and science—or religion and reason—is ages old. Just a small sampling of quotations gives evidence to this tension:

> The history of Science is not a mere record of isolated discoveries; it is a narrative of the conflict of two contending powers, the expansive force of the human intellect on one side, and the compression arising from traditionary faith and human interests on the other.[145]

> But faith is in its nature unchangeable, stationary; Science is in its nature progressive; and eventually a divergence between them, impossible to conceal, must take place.[146]

---

145 John William Draper, *History of the Conflict Between Religion and Science* (New York: D. Appleton and Co., 1875), vi.

146 Ibid., vii.

In all modern history, interference with science in the supposed interest of religion, no matter how conscientious such interference may have been, has resulted in the direst evils both to religion and science, and invariably; and, on the other hand, all untrammeled scientific investigation, no matter how dangerous to religion some of its stages may have seemed for the time to be, has invariably resulted in the highest good both of religion and science.[147]

Let there be no doubt that as they are currently practiced, there is no common ground between science and religion. As was thoroughly documented in the nineteenth-century tome, A History of the Warfare of Science with Theology in Christendom, by the historian and one time president of Cornell University Andrew D. White, history reveals a long and combative relationship between religion and science, depending on who was in control of society at the time. The claims of science rely on experimental verification, while the claims of religions rely on faith. These are irreconcilable approaches to knowing, which ensures an eternity of debate wherever and whenever the two camps meet.[148]

There is thus no reason for competition of any kind between reason and faith: each contains the other, and each has its own scope for action. Again the Book of Proverbs points in this direction when it exclaims: "It is the glory of God to conceal things, but the glory of kings is to search things out" (Prov. 25:2). In their respective worlds, God and the human being are set within a unique relationship. In God there lies the origin of all things, in him is found the fullness of the mystery, and in this his glory consists; to men and women there falls the task of exploring truth with their reason, and in this their nobility consists.[149]

This rapid survey of the history of philosophy, then, reveals a growing separation between faith and philosophical reason. Yet closer scrutiny shows that even in the philosophical thinking of those who helped drive faith and reason further apart there are found at times precious and seminal insights which, if pursued and developed with mind and heart rightly tuned, can lead to the discovery of truth's way. ... This is why I make this strong and insistent appeal—not, I trust, untimely—that faith and philosophy recover the profound unity which allows them to stand in har-

---

147 Andrew Dickson White, quoting himself from his address at Cooper Union, New York City, December 18, 1869, in his introduction to *A History of the Warfare of Science with Theology in Christendom* (New York: D. Appleton and Company, 1896).
148 Neil deGrasse Tyson, "Holy Wars," *Natural History Magazine*, October 1999.
149 John Paul II, *Fides et Ratio*, Vatican website, Sep. 14, 1998, www.vatican.va/content/john-paul-ii/en/encyclicals/documents/hf_jp-ii_enc_14091998_fides-et-ratio.html.

mony with their nature without compromising their mutual autonomy. The *parrhesia* of faith must be matched by the boldness of reason.[150]

Discuss Ha-Levi's responsum in the context of this tension. Do you find relevance to any of the current or historically recent controversies, such as *Kitzmiller et al. v. Dover Area School District*, in which case the court ruled for the plaintiffs and against the school board (and against intelligent design)? In the conclusion of the court's ruling it states:

> The proper application of both the endorsement and Lemon tests to the facts of this case makes it abundantly clear that the Board's ID [Intelligent Design] Policy violates the Establishment Clause. In making this determination, we have addressed the seminal question of whether ID is science. We have concluded that it is not, and moreover that ID cannot uncouple itself from its creationist, and thus religious, antecedents.
>
> Both Defendants and many of the leading proponents of ID make a bedrock assumption which is utterly false. Their presupposition is that evolutionary theory is antithetical to a belief in the existence of a supreme being and to religion in general. Repeatedly in this trial, Plaintiffs' scientific experts testified that the theory of evolution represents good science, is overwhelmingly accepted by the scientific community, and that it in no way conflicts with, nor does it deny, the existence of a divine creator.
>
> To be sure, Darwin's theory of evolution is imperfect. However, the fact that a scientific theory cannot yet render an explanation on every point should not be used as a pretext to thrust an untestable alternative hypothesis grounded in religion into the science classroom or to misrepresent well-established scientific propositions.
>
> The citizens of the Dover area were poorly served by the members of the Board who voted for the ID Policy. It is ironic that several of these individuals, who so staunchly and proudly touted their religious convictions in public, would time and again lie to cover their tracks and disguise the real purpose behind the ID Policy.[151]

Use this example, or any other that in your opinion derives from similar conflict of approaches to science, rationalism, or the acquisition of knowledge, for your discussion.

It is fitting to end this chapter with a brief selection from Maimonides's *Guide*:

---

150 Ibid.
151 Kitzmiller et al. v. Dover Area School District, Dec. 20, 2005, 04cv2688 (U.S. District Court for the Middle District of Pennsylvania).

> I will begin the subject of this chapter with a simile. A king is in his palace, and all his subjects are partly in the country, and partly abroad. ... Of those that desire to go to the palace, some reach it, and go round about in search of the entrance gate; others have passed through the gate, and walk about in the ante-chamber; and others have succeeded in entering into the inner part of the palace, and being in the same room with the king in the royal palace. ...
>
> My son, so long as you are engaged in studying the Mathematical Sciences and Logic, you belong to those who go round about the palace in search of the gate. ... When you understand Physics, you have entered the hall; and when, after completing the study of Natural Philosophy, you master Metaphysics, you have entered the innermost court, and are with the king in the same palace.[152]

Further Reading

[Ben-Sasson et al.] Ben-Sasson, Haim Hillel, Raphael Jospe, and Dov Schwartz. "Maimonidean Controversy." In EJ, 13:371-381.

[Berger] Berger, David. "Judaism and General Culture in Medieval and Early Modern Times." In *Judaism's Encounter with Other Culture: Rejection or Integration?*, edited by Jacob Schacter. Jerusalem: Maggid Books, 2018.

[Blidstein] Blidstein, Gerald J. "Rabbinic Judaism and General Culture: Normative Discussion and Attitudes." In *Judaism's Encounter with Other Culture: Rejection or Integration?*, edited by Jacob Schacter, 1-69. Jerusalem: Maggid Books, 2018.

[Galileo] Galilei, Galileo. "Letter to Madame Christina of Lorraine, Grand Duchess of Tuscany," 1615.

[Grant] "The Reactions of the Universities and Theological Authorities to Aristotelian Science and Natural Philosophy." In *A Sourcebook in Medieval Science*, edited by Edward Grant, 42-52. Cambridge, MA: Harvard University Press, 1974.

[Hacker] Hacker, Joseph. "The Intellectual Activity of the Jews of the Ottoman Empire during the Sixteenth and Seventeenth Centuries." In *Jewish Thought in the Seventeenth Century*, edited by Isadore Twersky and Bernard Septimus, 95-135. Cambridge: Harvard University Press, 1987.

[Halkin] Halkin, A. S. "Yedaiah Bedershi's Apology." In *Jewish Medieval and Renaissance Studies*, edited by Alexander Altmann, 165-184. Cambridge, MA: Harvard University Press, 1967.

---

152 Maimonides, *The Guide for the Perplexed*, 3:51, 384-385.

[Kellner] Kellner, Menachem Marc. "Rabbi Isaac Bar Sheshet's Responsum Concerning the Study of Greek Philosophy." *Tradition* 15, no. 3 (Fall 1975): 110-118.

[Rozen] Rozen, Minna. *A History of the Jewish Community in Istanbul: The Formative Years, 1453–1566.* Leiden: Brill, 2010.

[Schacter] Schacter, Jacob J., ed. *Judaism's Encounter with Other Cultures: Rejection or Integration?* Jerusalem: Maggid Books, 2018.

4.
Families Torn Apart
Rabbi Moses ben Joseph di Trani Responsum 1,142

Historical Background

In the many historical accounts and published research about the expulsions from Spain and Portugal,[1] there is a range of estimated numbers of refugees, migrations, and forced conversions.[2] There are descriptions of the hardships of travel and of finding places of refuge, and the difficulties of moving to different countries with different languages. There is information about the vast amounts of property that the expelled Jews had to leave behind, selling it at a great loss, if they were able to sell it at all.[3] Anyone can imagine that there were families destroyed—whether by children being forcibly removed to be converted, or due to the stresses of travel, or because of the starvation and disease that are the companions of refugees at all times and in all places. But history books tend to focus on the masses, the "refugees," the "conversos," the "crypto-Jews," and rarely tell us of the struggles and divided loyalties of individual families that were torn apart as a result of these relocations.

Before 1492 families that contained both conversos and Jews could maintain strong family ties and celebrate important occasions and holidays together, even to some extent after the Inquisition made it more dangerous to do so. But, as David Gitlitz notes, such "interactions ceased altogether when the last legal Jews left Spain in the summer of 1492. ... [Then] a religious split within a family spelled trouble. Divided families were frequently unhappy families, and the unhappiness spilled into the public record in diverse ways. ... In many divided families there

---

1   See introduction, note 1.
2   See Further Reading for the introduction: [Beinart], 284-290; [Marx]; [Pérez], ch. 5.
3   [Beinart], ch. 3 and 6.

came a time when the Judaizing member chose to emigrate from the Iberian Peninsula rather than to continue to face the dangers of existence there."[4]

The responsum in this chapter tells of such a family. Some members chose to stay in Spain or return to Spain and live as Christians; some returned to their Jewish faith in the Ottoman Empire.[5] The question to the author of the responsum, R. Moses ben Joseph di Trani,[6] relates to the rights of inheritance of such a mixed family.

Halakhic Background

As background for the responsum, a selection of inheritance laws and laws about a last will and testament, and a look at some legal loopholes in these laws, will clarify di Trani's discussion. The first sources consist of some verses from Numbers and Deuteronomy, which can then be compared with the rabbinic law, the foundation of normative Jewish religious legal practice, which often does not interpret the Torah literally.

Numbers 27:8-11	במדבר כ״ז ח׳-י״א
Further, speak to the children of Israel as follows: "If a man dies without leaving a son, you shall transfer his property to his daughter. If he has no daughter, you shall assign his property to his brothers. If he has no brothers, you shall assign his property to his nearest relative in his own clan, and he shall inherit	וְאֶל־בְּנֵי יִשְׂרָאֵל תְּדַבֵּר לֵאמֹר אִישׁ כִּי־יָמוּת וּבֵן אֵין לוֹ וְהַעֲבַרְתֶּם אֶת־נַחֲלָתוֹ לְבִתּוֹ: וְאִם־אֵין לוֹ בַּת וּנְתַתֶּם אֶת־נַחֲלָתוֹ לְאֶחָיו: וְאִם־אֵין לוֹ אַחִים וּנְתַתֶּם אֶת־נַחֲלָתוֹ לַאֲחֵי אָבִיו: וְאִם־אֵין אַחִים לְאָבִיו וּנְתַתֶּם אֶת־נַחֲלָתוֹ לִשְׁאֵרוֹ הַקָּרֹב אֵלָיו מִמִּשְׁפַּחְתּוֹ וְיָרַשׁ

---

4 [Gitlitz]: 1, 8, 18.

5 Because the author of the responsum lived in the Ottoman Empire, it is almost certain that the questioner did as well.

6 Known by the acronym Mabit, 1500–1580. In 1492 many Jewish exiles from Spain and Sicily settled in Trani, where there was a Jewish community at least as far back as the twelfth century, though the conditions afforded the Jews in Trani during this period were far from consistently good. Along with the rest of the Jews in southern Italy, the Jews in Trani were expelled in 1510–1511. Di Trani came from a family of Spanish origin who clung to their faith, moving from Italy to find refuge in Salonica in the Ottoman Empire, where di Trani was born. He eventually moved to Safed, where he served as rabbi and rabbinical judge.

it." It shall be to the children of Israel a statute of judgment, in accordance with the Lord's command to Moses.

אֹתָהּ וְהָיְתָה לִבְנֵי יִשְׂרָאֵל לְחֻקַּת מִשְׁפָּט כַּאֲשֶׁר צִוָּה יְהֹוָה אֶת־מֹשֶׁה:

| **Deuteronomy 21:15-17** | **דברים כ"א ט"ו-י"ז** |

If a man has two wives, one loved and the other hated, and both the loved and the hated have borne him sons, but the firstborn son is the son of the hated one—when he wills his property to his sons, he may not treat as firstborn the son of the loved one in disregard of the son of the hated one who is older. Instead, he must accept the first born, the son of the hated one, and allot to him a double portion of all that he possesses; since he is the first fruit of his vigor, the birthright is his due.

כִּי־תִהְיֶיןָ לְאִישׁ שְׁתֵּי נָשִׁים הָאַחַת אֲהוּבָה וְהָאַחַת שְׂנוּאָה וְיָלְדוּ־לוֹ בָנִים הָאֲהוּבָה וְהַשְּׂנוּאָה וְהָיָה הַבֵּן הַבְּכוֹר לַשְּׂנִיאָה: וְהָיָה בְּיוֹם הַנְחִילוֹ אֶת־בָּנָיו אֵת אֲשֶׁר־יִהְיֶה לוֹ לֹא יוּכַל לְבַכֵּר אֶת־בֶּן־הָאֲהוּבָה עַל־פְּנֵי בֶן־הַשְּׂנוּאָה הַבְּכֹר: כִּי אֶת־הַבְּכֹר בֶּן־הַשְּׂנוּאָה יַכִּיר לָתֶת לוֹ פִּי שְׁנַיִם בְּכֹל אֲשֶׁר־יִמָּצֵא לוֹ כִּי־הוּא רֵאשִׁית אֹנוֹ לוֹ מִשְׁפַּט הַבְּכֹרָה:

| **Mishna Bava Batra 8:5** | **משנה מסכת בבא בתרא ח,ה** |

One who says: "So-and-so, my firstborn son, shall not take a double portion," [or] "so-and-so my son shall not inherit with his brothers"—[it is as if] he[7] has not said anything, for he has made a condition against what is written in the Torah.[8] One who divided his assets [among his sons] orally, and gave more to one and less to another, or made the firstborn equal to them—his words are valid. But if he said, "as an inheritance"—he has not said anything [effective]. If he wrote either at the beginning or in the middle or at the end [of a will] "as a gift"—his words are valid. One who says "so-and-so [who is not a child] shall

האומ[ר] איש פלוני בני בכור לא יטול פי שנים איש פלוני בני לא יירש עם אחיו לא אמ[ר] כלום שהיתנה על הכתוב שבתורה המחלק נכסיו על פיו ריבה לאחד ומיעט לאחד הישווה להן את הבכור דבריו קיימין ואם אמ[ר] משם ירושה לא אמ[ר]

---

7   Though the *mishna* uses masculine pronouns, there are situations in which the same would be true of a mother.

8   "If someone makes a condition [that is contrary] to what is written in the Torah, his condition is null and void." (*Kᵉtubbot* 83b)

inherit me" in a situation where there is a daughter, [or] "my daughter shall inherit me" in a situation where there is a son—he has not said anything, for he has made a condition against what is written in the Torah. R. Yoḥanan ben Bᵉroqa says: "If he spoke concerning one who is qualified to inherit him, his words are valid, and if about one who is not qualified to inherit him, his words are not valid." One who assigns his assets in writing to others and omitted his children—what he did is done, but the Sages find no pleasure in him. [On the other hand,] Rabban Shimon ben Gamliel says: "If his sons did not conduct themselves with propriety, it is remembered to his credit."

כלום כתב בין בתחילה ובין באמצע ובין בסוף משם מתנה דבריו קיימין האו'[מר] איש פלו'[ני] יירשני במקום שיש בת בתי תירשני במקום שיש בן לא אמ'[ר] כלום שהיתנה על הכתוב שבתורה רבי יוחנן בן ברוקא או'[מר] אם אמ'[ר] על מי שהוא ראוי לו לירושה דבריו קיימין ועל מי שאין ראוי לו לירושה אין דבריו קיימין הכותב את נכסיו לאחרים והניח את בניו מה שעשה עשוי אבל אין רוח חכמ'[ים] נוחה ממנו רבן שמעון בן גמליאל או'[מר] אם לא היו בניו נוהגין כשורה זכור לטוב:

Bava Batra 130a-130b בבא בתרא ק״ל א׳—ב׳

mishna: One who says "So-and-so shall inherit me" in a situation where there is a daughter, [or] "My daughter shall inherit me" in a situation where there is a son—he has said nothing, for he has made a condition against what is written in the Torah. R. Yoḥanan ben Bᵉroqa says: "If he spoke concerning one who is qualified to inherit him, his words are valid, and if about one who is not qualified to inherit him, his words are not valid."

מתני'[תין] האומר איש פלוני יירשני במקום שיש בת בתי תירשני במקום שיש בן לא אמר כלום שהתנה על מה שכתוב בתורה ר'[בי] יוחנן בן ברוקה אומר אם אמר על מי שראוי ליורשו דבריו קיימין ועל מי שאין ראוי ליורשו אין דבריו קיימין גמ'[רא] טעמא דאחר במקום בת ובת במקום בן הא בן בין הבנים ובת בין הבנות דבריו קיימין אימא סיפא רבי יוחנן בן ברוקה אומר אם אמר על מי

gᵉmara: [According to the first *tanna* in the *mishna*,] the reason [the testator's instructions are invalid is] because [he appointed] another [legal heir, but of lower priority than a daughter] where there was a daughter, or a daughter where there was a son. Therefore, [had he appointed] a son among the [other] sons or a daughter among the [other] daughters, his instructions would have been valid. [The g'mara challenges:] Tell [me, then, what you understand by] the latter clause, "R. Yoḥanan ben B'roqa says: 'If [someone] said [it] concerning one who is entitled to be his heir, his instructions are valid.'" This [represents] the same [view as] the first *tanna*! And if you would say R. Yoḥanan ben B'roqa maintains [that] even another [legal heir of lower priority may be appointed] where there is a daughter, and [that] a daughter [may be appointed as heir] where there is a son, [it may be retorted]: but it is taught in a *baraita*: R. Yishmael, son of R. Yoḥanan ben B'roqa, says, "There was no dispute between [my] Father and the Sages concerning [the law] that one's instructions are invalid when another [legal heir of lower priority is appointed] when there was a daughter, or [where] a daughter [was appointed heir] when there was a son. What was their dispute about? [Only the case of the appointment] of a son [as sole heir] among the [other] sons or a daughter among the [other] daughters, [in] which [case my] Father says [the one appointed] inherits, and the Sages say [that] he does not inherit." [The g'mara offers a response:] If you want, say: Since he [R. Yishmael] said that they [his father and the Sages] did not dispute, it may be inferred that the first *tanna* is of the opinion that they did dispute. [The g'mara offers another response:] If you want, say: All [the *mishna*] is according to [the views of] R. Yoḥanan ben B'roqa, but some [words are] missing [from the text,] and thus it teaches: If someone said "so-and-so shall be my heir" where there is a daughter, [or] "my daughter shall be my heir" when there is a son, his instructions are to be disregarded, but [in the case of the appointment of] a daughter among [other] daughters or a son among [other] sons, if [the father] said [one of them] should inherit all his estate, his instruction is legally valid, for R. Yoḥanan [ben Bᵉroqa]⁹ said: "if [someone] said [it] concerning one who is entitled to be his [immediate] heir, his instructions are legally valid." [The *gᵉmara* continues:] Rav Yᵉhuda said in the name of Shmuel: The halakha is in agreement with R. Yoḥanan ben Bᵉroqa. And so said Rava: the halakha is in agreement with R. Yoḥanan ben Bᵉroqa. Rava said: What is the reason [for the opinion] of R. Yoḥanan ben Bᵉroqa? Scripture said: *And on the day that he bequeaths to his sons* (Deut. 21:16), [from which it can be inferred that] the Torah gave authority to a father to bequeath [his estate] to anyone whom he desires.

ברוקה אמר רבא מאי טעמיה דרבי יוחנן בן ברוקה אמר קרא והיה ביום הנחילו את בניו התורה נתנה רשות לאב להנחיל לכל מי שירצה

| Maimonides *MT Hilkhot Nᵉḥalot* (The Laws of Inheritance) 6 | רמב״ם משנה תורה הלכות נחלות ו |

1 A person is not permitted to bequeath [his property] to someone who is not deserving to be an heir, and he may not uproot the inheritance from an heir, even though this is a monetary [matter],¹⁰ as it states in the portion on inheritance ... *it shall be to the children of Israel a statute of judgment* ... (Num. 27:11), to tell [us] that this statute does not change and a condition on it is not effective, whether he instructed when he was healthy or whether he was on his deathbed,¹¹ whether orally or whether in writing—it is not effective.

א אין אדם יכול להוריש מי שאינו ראוי ליורשו, ולא לעקור הירושה מן היורש, אף על פי שזה ממון הוא, לפי שנאמר בפרשת נחלות "והיתה לבני ישראל לחוקת משפט״, לומר שחוקה זו לא תשתנה ואין התנאי מועיל בה, בין שציוה והוא בריא בין שהיה שכיב מרע, בין על פה בין בכתב, אינו מועיל:

---

9   MS Vatican 115b includes this.

10   There is accepted halakha that "in monetary matters [even Toraitic], a stipulation is valid." (See *Kᵉtubbot* 56a; halakha is according to R. Yᵉhuda.) The laws of inheritance, though they are monetary matters, are an exception.

11   The translation of *shᵉkhiv mᵉra'* reads "on his deathbed," throughout this chapter, because this is the scenario that is typically envisioned; but the term *shᵉkhiv mᵉra'* actually refers to a critically ill person, who is likely to die, but does have a chance of recovering, in which case his request might not be binding, dependent upon several factors.

2 Therefore, one who says "so-and-so my firstborn son will not receive a double portion" [or] "so-and-so my son will not inherit together with his brothers"—[it is as if] he did not say a thing. [If he said,] "so-and-so will inherit me" in the case that there is a daughter, or he said "my daughter will inherit me" in the case that there is a son—he did not say a thing. Likewise for any [statement] of the sort. But if he had many heirs, such as many sons or daughters or brothers, and he said when he was on his deathbed, "so-and-so my brother, out of all my brothers, will inherit me" or "so-and-so my daughter, out of all my daughters, will inherit me"—his words are valid, whether he said it orally or wrote it in writing. But if he said, "so-and-so my son alone will inherit me"—if he stated it orally, his words are valid, but if he wrote that all of his property [was bequeathed] to his son, he only appointed him as executor, as we explained.[12]

ב לפיכך האומר, איש פלוני בני בכורי לא יטול פי שנים, איש פלוני בני לא יירש עם אחיו, לא אמר כלום. איש פלוני יירשני, במקום שיש לו בת, או שאמר, בתי תירשני, במקום שיש לו בן, לא אמר כלום. וכן כל כיוצא בזה: אבל אם היו לו יורשין רבים, כגון בנים רבים או בנות או אחים, ואמר כשהוא שכיב מרע, פלוני אחי יירשני מכלל אחי, או בתי פלונית בתי תירשני מכלל בנותי, דבריו קיימין, בין שאמר על פה בין שכתב בכתב: אבל אם אמר, פלוני בני יירשני לבדו, אם אמר על פה דבריו קיימין, אבל אם כתב כל נכסיו לבנו, לא עשהו אלא אפטרופא כמו שביארנו:

ה במה דברים אמורים, בשאמר בלשון ירושה, אבל אם נתן מתנה, דבריו קיימין. לפיכך המחלק נכסיו על פיו לבניו כשהוא שכיב מרע, ריבה לאחד, ומיעט לאחד, והשוה להן הבכור, דבריו קיימין, ואם אמר משום ירושה, לא אמר כלום:

5[13] What do these words refer to? When he said [these things] in terms of inheritance. But if he gave a gift, his words are valid. Therefore, one who divides his property orally to his sons when he is on his deathbed—if he gave more to one and less to another or if he equalized with them the amount given to the firstborn, his words are valid, but if he said it [in terms] of inheritance, he did not say a thing.

---

12   *MT Hilkhot Zᵉkhiyya U-Matana* (The Laws of Acquisition and Gifts) 6,2-3.
13   Halakhot 3 and 4 are less relevant to this chapter.

| *Maggid Mishne*[14] *Hilkhot N^eḥalot* (The Laws of Inheritance) 6,2 | מגיד משנה הלכות נחלות ו:ב |

[Regarding] "Therefore, one who says 'so-and-so …'" etc.—This is verbatim from the *mishna*, and it means, for example, he did not say anything more. But if he said specifically, "but I give all the rest of my property to his brothers," they are entitled [to it], and if he states it in terms of a gift, as explained adjacently,[15] and it is clear [that] if he said, "he will not inherit with his brothers, but the rest of his brothers inherit all," they are entitled, and it is not even necessary to say that if he stated [it] in terms of a gift, such as will be clarified, [and] so wrote the Rashba[16] (may his memory be blessed).

לפיכך האומר איש פלוני וכו׳[לין]. משנה כלשונה ופירוש כגון שלא אמר יותר אבל אם אמר בברור אבל אני נותן כל שאר נכסי לאחיו זכו אלו וכשאמר בלשון מתנה וכמו שיתבאר בסמוך ופשוט אם אמר לא יירש עם אחיו ושאר אחיו יירשו הכל זכו ואין צ״ל [צריך לומר] אם אמר בלשון מתנה כמו שיתבאר כך כתב הרשב״א ז״ל [זכרונו לברכה]:

Discussion

The *mishna* and the *g^emara* presented above consider situations in which a parent wishes to override the basic inheritance law.[17]

The *mishna* begins with two theoretical situations: one in which a father specifically does not want his firstborn son to inherit a double portion, the other in which a father wants to cut one of his sons out of his will altogether. The *mishna* teaches that the specific language used will render a father's statement either null and void, or valid. If the father refers to his transfer as a gift, whether it occurs before or after his demise, verbally or in writing, then he can assign his assets to his children in any way that he desires, including completely eliminating a child from the receiving end. By designating his assets as a "gift," a father may distribute his assets among his children as he wishes.

---

14 R. Vidal Yom Tov of Tolosa (second half of the fourteenth century).
15 Halakha 5.
16 R. Solomon ben Abraham Adret, c. 1235–c. 1310.
17 The derivation of the law for a first-born son is discussed in *B^ekhorot* 51b and *Bava Batra* 122b.

R. Yoḥanan ben Bᵉroqa takes this flexibility one step further. Even if the father uses the word "inherit," so long as the recipients are somewhere in the chain of heirs, his statement is valid. And with a written document, a father may cut all his children (or other heirs) out of his will, perhaps provoking the displeasure of the Sages. But when emotional factors are at play, as they always are in such matters, human nature might be to ignore that or to rationalize one's actions.

Following the *mishna*, elaborating on the words of the first *tanna*, the *gᵉmara* immediately expands the possibilities of bequeathing property, even using the language of inheritance, to include choosing one heir out of several heirs with the same level of precedence. However, the *gᵉmara* challenges: is it not so that R. Yoḥanan ben Bᵉroqa's view is the same as the first *tanna*? The *gᵉmara* offers two possibilities, and tells us that the halakha is according to R. Yoḥanan ben Bᵉroqa, offering a verse as the basis for R. Yoḥanan ben Bᵉroqa's approach.[18]

This conclusion, that "the Torah gave authority to a father to bequeath [his estate] to anyone whom he desires," is certainly a far cry from the "law of the first born" and the precedence order for inheritance as articulated in the Torah.[19] Maimonides's codification serves as a succinct summary of his conclusions from the *gᵉmara*, while the *Maggid Mishne*'s gloss on Maimonides's second halakha, citing the Rashba, goes even further to demonstrate how flexible the law is in permitting someone to designate his heirs.

In the case of inheritance laws, the rabbinic law is far more flexible than what one might conclude from the actual verses in the Torah. In fact, in examining the Mishna, the Talmud, and Maimonides's codification of rabbinic law, it becomes obvious that the Sages were quite comfortable with creative compliance. Apparently, the Sages recognized that human emotion and circumstance, family dynamics, and other factors could at times—perhaps quite often—render strict interpretation of the Torah to be unpalatable at best, or totally ignored, at the worst.

---

18   This is followed by a discussion, not presented here, about reliance on this verse rather than another.

19   Therefore, the specified precedence order in the Torah is a default, which may be overridden with an appropriate statement or document.

Responsum

Mabit Responsum 1,142	שו"ת מבי"ט חלק א סימן קמב

Question: [Concerning] Reuben, who was among the forced conversos[20] of these times and [who] came to a place that is safe to worship God, and he worshipped Him, and he had three sons. One [now] conducts himself according to the laws of Moses and Israel in lands where they permit them [Jews] to worship God, and the [other] two [remain] Gentiles in the land of their birth, where they [all Jews] are forced [to abandon their faith]. The time of Reuben's demise was approaching, and he gave his last will and testament to his family. He left a known sum to the [son] who was a Jew, and another sum to one of the conversos, and stipulated and said, "If so-and-so my son comes to any of those places where they [Jews] worship

שאלה ראובן שהיה מאנוסי הזמן ובא למקום בטוח לעבוד את ה' ויעבדהו ולו שלשה בנים האחד מתנהג כדת משה וישראל בארצות אשר יניחום לעבוד בהם את ה' והשנים בגיות בארץ מולדתם אשר אנוסים שמה והגיע זמן ראובן ליפטר ויצו את ביתו והניח סך ידוע לאשר הוא יהודי וסך אחר לא[ו]חד[חד] מן האנוסים והתנה ואמר אם פלוני בני יבא באלו המקומות אשר יעבדו בם את ה' וישא אשה הגונה וישתקע כאן או בשאר מקומות העובדים בהם את ה' תנו לו מנכסי סך פלוני ואם לא יקיים תנאים אלו יתן הסך ההוא ליורשי והניח גם את השני סך ידוע בתנאי שיבא במקומות אלו ושאשר הוא יהודי עתה יאכל פירות

God [according to Jewish law] and marries a proper [Jewish] woman and dwells here or in any of the other places where they worship God, give him such-and-such sum of my property, but if he does not uphold these conditions then said sum should be given to my heirs." And he also left a known sum for the second [converso] brother, under the condition that he come to [any of] these places, while the one who is presently a Jew would receive the earnings of said sum until the second [converso] brother arrived, while the principal of the bequest to him would be held in escrow. Afterwards, the first [converso brother] arrived,

---

20 Two Hebrew terms for converts are used in the responsum. Reuben is described as one of the *anusim* (forced converts), which is a term used in Jewish law for someone compelled to transgress, while one of the brothers is referred to as a *mumar* (apostate). *Anus* is generally considered to reflect a forgiving attitude towards the *converso*; *mumar* is derogatory.

and he and the Jewish brother twisted [the arrangement] so that the property was transferred from the escrow agent to the control of their mother, Reuben's wife. But when this first [converso brother] came to these locations, he did not circumcise [himself,] nor did he behave according to the laws of Israel, and he was still a Gentile; on the contrary, he transgressed profusely and violated the covenant and returned to his [former] land, the land of the Gentiles. But his mother gave him a portion of the sum that was designated for him, or perhaps all of it. Presently, his Jewish brother is suing his mother, because she transgressed by giving him [the first converso brother said sum], as he did not uphold the said conditions. The Jew claims that he is the one who should inherit his brother's portion, since he [the first converso brother] did not uphold the conditions. Please, our Teacher, instruct us if his mother is obligated to give him [the Jewish brother], out of her property, the entire sum [that she gave to the converso brother], or [should she give it] to a religious court? Also, regarding the words of the one who gave the command [i.e., the deceased], when he said that if the first [converso brother] did not uphold the conditions, then the sum should be given to his heirs—is the third [brother], who still remains a Gentile, included [in the heirs]?

הסך ההוא עד בוא אחיו השני והיו נכסי עזבונו ביד שליש ואחר כך בא הראשון והוא והאח היהודי סבבו שיצאו הנכסים מיד השליש ויונחו ביד אמם אשת ראובן וכשבא הראשון למקומות אלו ולא מל ולא התנהג כדת ישראל ועודנו בגיות ואדרבה הרבה לפשוע והפר ברית וחזר לארצו לארצות הגוי[ים] ותתן לו אמו קצת דמי הסך המגיע לו או כולו ועכשיו תובע אחיו היהודי את אמו שפשעה באשר נתנה לו כי הוא לא קיים התנאים הנז[כרים] וטוען היהודי כי הוא הראוי לירש חלק אחיו אחר שלא קיים התנאים יורונו המורה אם חייבת אמו לתת בידו מנכסיה כל הסך ההוא או ביד ב"ד [בית דין] וגם אם בכלל דברי המצוה באמרו שאם לא יקיים הא[חד] התנאים ינתן ליורשיו יכנס גם השלישי הנשאר בגיות עודנו בגיותו.

תשובה דברי ש"מ [שכיב מרע] ככתובין וכמסורין דמו וכל מה שהוא מתנה אם יתקיים התנאי יתקיים המתנה ואם לא יתקיים התנאי לא

Response: [1][21] The [spoken] words of someone who is on his deathbed are just as if they were written and transmitted,[22] and everything that he stipulates—if the condition is upheld, then the gift is upheld, and if the condition is not upheld,

---

21 Numbers are inserted to facilitate reading the discussion following the responsum.
22 *Gittin* 13a.

then the gift is not upheld. Therefore, in our case, if the first [converso] already came and did not conduct himself according to the laws of Israel, as is presented in the question, the condition for the gift, that he come and marry a proper woman and dwell in a place where they worship God, etc., has thereby been abrogated, because he did not do so, but came and returned to his bad habits. One does not even have to say [i.e., emphasize] here [in this case], that [the deceased] used the term "gift," which he only gave on condition, and the conditions were not upheld. But even if he had used the term "inheritance" and said, "if he comes, he inherits, but if he does not come and does not uphold these conditions, then he will not inherit," it would be requisite that the conditions be upheld, and if they were not upheld, he would not inherit. This [even if he used the term "inheritance"] is not a case of making a condition [that is contrary] to what is written

יתקיים המתנה ואם כן בנ״ד [בנידון דידן] אם בא כבר הא[חד] ולא התנהג כדת ישראל כמו שבא בשאלה הרי בטל תנאי המתנה שיבוא וישא אשה הגונה וישתקע במקום אשר יעבוד ה׳ כו[ליה] והוא לא כן עשה אלא שבא וחזר לסורו וא״צ [ואין צריך] לומר הכא דהזכיר לשון מתנה דלא נתן אלא ע״מ [על מנת] כן ולא נתקיים התנאי אלא אפילו היו בלשון ירוש[ה] שהיה אומר אם יבא יירש ואם לא יבא ולא יקיים תנאים אלו לא יירש היה התנאי צריך להתקיים ואם לא נתקיים לא יירש ולא הוי מתנה על מה שכתוב בתורה משום דאיפסיק[א] הלכת[א] פי[רק] י"נ [יש נוחלין] ברבי״ב [ברבי יוחנן בן ברוקה] דלבן בין הבנים דבריו קיימי[ם] אפילו בלשון ירושה כשריבה לזה ומיעט לזה והא דתנן לא יירש פלוני בני עם אחיו לא אמר כלום היינו דלא סיים ששאר אחיו יירשו או יזכו בכל או בשאר אבל אם אמר לא יירש פלוני בני אלא אחיו

in the Torah, because it was ruled in chapter "There are those who inherit" [*Bava Batra* 130a] according to R. Yoḥanan ben Beroqa that for a son among sons, his [the one on his deathbed] words are upheld, even if using the language of "inheritance," when he increased the amount for one and decreased the amount for another. What we have learned [in a *mishna*]²³—"[if one says] 'my son so-and-so shall not inherit with his brothers,' he did not say anything,"—that is in the case that he did not conclude [his statement] that the rest of his brothers would inherit or would be entitled to everything, or to the remainder. But if he said, "my son so-and-so will not inherit, but his brothers will inherit everything," his words are valid. [This is] as the *Maggid Mishne* wrote at the beginning of chapter

---

23 Mishna *Bava Batra* 8:5; see Halakhic Background.

six of The Laws of Inheritance[24] in the name of the Rashba (may his memory be blessed). Also, [according to] the *Nimmuqei Yosef*[25] on our *mishna*, [this applies] even more so in the case of language of a "gift," as in our case, and [as is] written in the question, "if he does not uphold these conditions, the sum should be given[26] to my heirs."

[2] It seems [to me] that this [the valid heir] is the son who presently conducts himself according to the laws of Moses and Israel, because the other son [the second converso] is still a Gentile, [and] even the known sum that he [the deceased] left for him was left for him so that he would come here, and so long as he does not come, he does not attain what he left for him; all the more so, he should not now gain the portion that his brother [the first converso] did not receive because of abrogation of the condition. What he [the deceased] commanded to be given to his heirs is [given] in the event that the condition is not upheld, and at the time of the abrogation of the condition, his heir obtains [it].[27] Since the other [second converso] was not present at the time of the abrogation of the condition by his brother, he is not included in the category of "his [father's] heirs," because clearly his father did not want him to inherit his property unless he was here. And since he did not come and his brother abrogated the condition, he does not obtain that inheritance, just as he does not obtain the sum

ירשו הכל דבריו קיימים כמו שכתב הרב מי״מ [מגיד משנה] ראש פי״ו [פרק ו'] מהלכות נחלות בשם הרשבי״א ז״ל [זכרונו לברכה] ונמוקי יוסף עלה דמתניתין וכל שכן היכא דהוי בלשון מתנה כי הכא בני״ד [בנידון דידן] וכתוב בשאלה ואם לא יקיים תנאים אלו יינתן הסך ההוא ליורשי

ונראה דהיינו הבן שהוא מתנהג עתה כדת משה וישראל שהבן האחר שהוא עדיין בגיות אפילו מה שהניח לו סך ידוע לא הניחו אלא ע״מ [על מנת] שיבוא פה וכל שלא בא לא זכה במה שהניח לו וכ״ש [וכל שכן] שלא זכה מעתה בחלק שלא זכה אחיו שבטל התנאי שמה שצוה הוא שינתן ליורשיו הוא כשלא יתקיי[ם] התנאי ובשעת ביטול התנאי זוכה היורש שלו וכיון שלא נמצא זה האח[ר] פה בשעת ביטול תנאי אחיו לא נכלל בכלל יורשיו שהרי לא רצה אביו שירש מנכסיו אלא כשיהיה פה ואחר שהוא לא בא ואחיו בטל התנאי לא זכה הוא בירושה זו כמו שלא זכה

---

24 *Hilkhot N^ehalot* (The Laws of Inheritance) 6,2; see Halakhic Background.
25 R. Joseph Ḥabiba, beginning of the fifteenth century; *Bava Batra* 55b in the pages of the Rif (R. Isaac Alfasi, 1013–1103).
26 Rather than "bequeathed."
27 The only heir at this point is the son who is a practicing Jew.

that his father left for him until he came. And if he [the second converso] dies there and his heirs come afterwards, they will not inherit said sum, because if their father did not ever deserve what his father left for him when or if he came, but he did not come, how could they [the grandchildren] deserve it? Even if he [the second converso brother] did come etc., and receive the amount that his father left him, he would not have a portion of what was left for his brother who abrogated the conditions, because at the time of the abrogation the heir who was here gained [the inheritance], but he [who was not here] did not inherit, even his own portion, and the only one who is called an heir is the one who was upholding the laws of Moses and Israel at the time of the abrogation of the condition by his brother. See here, it is written that if he does not uphold these conditions, said sum would be given to his [father's] heirs, and only

בסך שהניח לו אביו עד שיבוא ואם מת שם ויבואו יורשיו אחר כך לא ירשו הסך הנז'[כר] שאם אביהם לא זכה עדיין במה שהניח לו אביו לכשיבוא ולא בא איך יזכו הם ואפילו היה בא וכו'[לי] והיה זוכה בסך שהניח לו אביו לא היה לו חלק במה שהניח לאחיו שביטל התנאי כיון שבשעת ביטולו זכה היורש שהוא כאן והוא אינו יורש אז אפי'[לו] חלק שלו ואינו נקרא יורש אלא זה שהוא עומד בדת משה וישראל בשעת ביטול תנאי אחיו שהרי כתו'[ב] שאם לא יקיים תנאים אלו ינתן הסך ההוא ליורשיו ולא קרא הוא יורשיו כי אם העומדים שם בשעת ביטול התנאי וכיון שאין כאן אלא הא'[חד] שהיה מקודם בדת משה אליו ראוי ואליו רצה שינתן כי האחר אפילו מה שהניח לו אינו זוכה בו עדיין עד בואו כמו שכתב כי מה שאמר ינתן ליורשיו שהוא לשון רבי'[ם] הוא אם בזמן ביטול התנאי של הא'[חד] היה

those who were present at the time of abrogation of the condition did he call "heirs." Since only the one [brother] was already [conducting himself] according to the laws of Moses, he was worthy, and to him he [Reuben] wanted [the inheritance] to be given. The other does not yet deserve even what he [Reuben] set aside for him, until he comes, as he [Reuben] wrote. What he said "will be given to his heirs," which is in the plural, means that if, at the time of the abrogation of the condition by the one [brother], the other [brother] was already here, then the two of them would inherit what the one who abrogated the condition left for them. But, since at the time of abrogation of the condition the other was not here, the stipulation that [the inheritance] be given immediately could not be upheld, since they could not even give him what was set aside for him until he came. And, therefore, he [Reuben] used the term "giving" only regarding the one who would be present at the time of the abrogation of the condition. If he had written "would be for my heirs," then it would be possible to say that it [the portion of the first converso] would be for the two of them, and the portion of the other [the second converso] would be in the hand of this one [who was already conducting himself as a Jew] to benefit from the profits, so long as [the other] does not come, like the sum that his father bequeathed and wrote "he should have the profits until his brother comes." But because he wrote "give"— that is, the term of "gift"—[it is given] to whoever is here.

[3] It appears, too, that they should give [the gift] immediately to the one who is here, worshipping God, because this was the original intent of the testator. We follow an assumption,[28] like that of R. Shimon ben Mᵉnasya [who said] that if his [a person's] son went overseas and he [the parent] heard that he [the son] died, etc.[29] Maimonides (may his memory be blessed) cited [this] extensively in The Laws of Gifts.[30] Even though the Ribash[31] (may his memory be blessed) wrote in Responsum 207 that we

האחר כבר פה היו שניהם יורשים מה שהניח להם שבטל התנאי אבל כיון שבזמן ביטול התנאי לא היה כאן האחר לא יתקיי[ם] בו לשון נתינה מיד שהרי אינם יכולים לתת לו אפילו מה שהניח לו עד שיבוא ואם כן לא כתב לשון נתינה אלא על אותו שימצא בשעת ביטול התנאי ואם היה כות[ב] יהיה ליורשי היה איפש[ר] לומר שיהיה לשניהם והחלק של האחר יהיה ביד זה לאכיל[ת] פירות כל זמן שלא יבוא כמו הסך שהניח לו אביו שכתב שיהיו לו הפירות עד בוא אחיו וכיון שכתב תנו הוי לשון מתנה למי שהוא כאן.

ונראה נמי שיתנו מיד לזה שהו[א] עומ[ד] פה לעבוד[ת] ה' דכך היתה כוונת המצוה מקודם ואזלי[נן] בתר אומדנא כי הך דר[בי] שמעון בן מנסיא הרי שהלך בנו למדינת הים ושמע שמת כו[לי] וטובא דמייתי הרמב״ם ז״ל [זכרונו לברכה]

---

28   The term used in the responsum is *umdana*, which means an estimation or assumption, and refers to an assumed motive in a specific legal situation.

29   *Bava Batra* 132a. A *baraita* cited there states: [Regarding] someone whose son went overseas and he [the parent] heard that he [the son] died, and he [the parent] went and assigned in writing all his [the son's] property to others, but subsequently his son reappeared: the gift is a [legally valid] gift. [But] R. Shimon ben Mᵉnasya says: "His gift is not a [legally valid] gift, because had he known that his son was alive, he would not have assigned it [to someone else]." The assumption in this case is that the parent only intended to give away his son's property because he thought his son was dead, and R. Shimon ben Mᵉnasya takes this intention into account. Di Trani rules in accordance with that view, which is the accepted halakha (*MT Hilkhot Zᵉkhiyya U-Matana* [The Laws of Acquisition and Gifts] 6,1, in accordance with *Bava Batra* cited above in this footnote and *Bava Batra* 146b–147a).

30   *MT Hilkhot Zᵉkhiyya U-Matana* (The Laws of Acquisition and Gifts) 6,1.

31   R. Isaac ben Sheshet Perfet, 1326–1408.

do not make an assumption about the wishes of someone who is on his deathbed, this is in the situation that legally his words have no substance, such as "so-and-so should live in this house" or "eat the fruits of this date palm."[32] But when the language has legal substance if we go according to the assumed intent of his wishes, then we do so, as the Rosh[33] (may his memory be blessed) wrote [in] principle 83[,3] in a responsum about Reuben's will,[34] in which he ordered to bequeath to his brother Simeon a *ma-ne*[35] out of the claims that were due from a certain Gentile nobleman. [Reuben further instructed that] if [these claims] did not suffice, then the money should be paid [by his heirs] with [the proceeds of] such-and-such mortgage,[36] etc.[37] They [the heirs] did not collect anything from the nobleman, and he [the Rosh] wrote that Reuben's wishes and intent should be adhered to, which was to bequeath to him [Simeon] a full

בהלכו[ת] מתני[ה] ואע"פ [ואף על פי] שכתב הריב"ש ז"ל [זכרונו לברכה] תשובת ר"ז דלא אמדי[נן] לדעתי[ה] דש"מ [דשכיב מרע] היינו היכא שמן הדין אין ממש בדבריו כמו ידור פלו[ני] בבית זה או יאכל פירות דקל זה אבל כשיש בלשון משמעות שיהיה בדין אם נלך אחר כוונתו באומדן דעתיה כי הכא אזלי[נן] כדכתב הרא"ש ז"ל [זכרונו לברכה] כלל פ"ג בתשובת צוואת ראובן שצוה לתת לשמעון אחיו מנה מן התביעות שיצאו לו מישר אחד גוי

---

32 The Ribash's ruling is in accordance with the following from *Bava Batra* 147b: Rav said in the name of Rav Naḥman: "One who is on his deathbed who said 'so-and-so shall live in this house' or 'so-and-so shall eat the fruit of this date palm' has said nothing, until he says 'give this house to so-and-so, so that he may live in it' or 'give this date palm to so-and-so, so that he may eat its fruit.'" This is understood by the *g'mara* to mean that Rav Naḥman maintained that a matter of substance for a healthy person is also of substance for someone on his deathbed, while a matter that has no substance for a healthy person is considered of no substance for someone on his deathbed. Thus, according to that view, even though the wishes of a person on his deathbed are generally considered binding, they are not binding if the wish expressed is of no legal substance. "Living" and "eating" are considered to have no legal substance, much like "speech" or "sleep," and thus ruled Maimonides (*MT Hilkhot Z'khiyya U-Matana* [The Laws of Acquisition and Gifts] 10,15).

33 R. Asher ben Jehiel, c. 1250–1327.

34 A different "Reuben."

35 A *ma-ne* is a Talmudic monetary denomination equal to one hundred silver dinars and commonly used in rabbinic literature. Just as the names of the claimant and the plaintiff, Simeon and Reuben, are pseudonyms, it is very likely that the actual amount of money that Reuben bequeathed to Simeon is not specified in the responsum, but rather the intent of the word *ma-ne* is "X amount."

36 For which Reuben was the creditor.

37 The question in the responsum continues with "or with a certain plot of land."

ma-ne. In our case, as well, we say that it was in his mind that it [the inheritance] should be given to the son who worships God, because we saw that it was in his [father's] mind and his intent that he would want [to bequeath] to him over the others, because he would not give them anything unless they came and converted.[38] Similarly, the Rashba (may his memory be blessed) wrote in responsum 704 that one does not add or detract from the expressed wishes of one on his deathbed, even though he previously revealed his intent.[39] But when it is not necessary to detract or add to his words—in such a case, one follows his [presumed] intent.

Even more so, if we approach this [question] from the perspective that, since the one who was there was an apostate, and we rule that he does not inherit [from] his father, as a penalty,[40] it is obvious that he is not called an "heir" to this portion. Rather, the one who was here, as a Jew [is the heir]. After all, he [the father] said, "give to my heirs." Even though the father made him [the second converso brother] an heir, [he did this] precisely in the portion that he gifted to him [conditionally]; but in the portion of the other [first converso], which he

ואם לא יספיק שיפרע במשכונה פלוני וכו'[לי] ולא גבו שום דבר מן השר וכתב שהולכים אחר דעתו וכוונתו של ראובן שהיי[ה] שיתנו לו מנה שלם וה"נ [והכא נמי] אמרי[נן] דדעתו היה שינתן לבנו אשר הוא עובד ה' כי ראינו בדעתו וכוונתו שהיה רוצה בו יותר מהאחרי[ם] שלא היה מזכה להם שום דבר אלא כשיבואו בגירות וכן הרשב"א ז"ל [זכרונו לברכה] תשובת תשי"ד כתב שאין מוסיפי[ם] או גורעים דברי ש"מ [שכיב מרע] אף על פי שגלה כוונתו שנראה דהיכא דאין צריך לגרוע ולא להוסיף על דברו כי הכא הולכין אחר הכוונה:

וכל שכן אם נכנס בזה מצד היות העומד שם מומר ונפסוק שאינו יורש את אביו דרך קנס דפשיטא שלא יקרא יורש בחלק זה אלא זה העומד ביהדות כאן והרי אמר תנו ליורשי שאף על פי שהאב עשהו יורש דוקא בחלק שהניח לו דרך מתנה אבל

---

38 Back to Judaism. Though di Trani uses the term *gerut* in the response, the question never suggested a need to "convert," but rather to begin to worship as a Jew. For a spectrum of views from different times and places about the obligations of a returning apostate, see David Golinkin, "Ketsad Ḥozᵉrim Mumarim La-yahadut?," in *Zehut Yᵉhudit*, ed. Asher Maoz and Aviad Ha-Kohen (Tel Aviv: Tel Aviv University Faculty of Law, 2014), 49-62.

39 At the outset in this responsum, the Rashba explains a general rule that "one may not add or detract from his [someone on his deathbed] words in order to carry them out, even though he previously revealed his intent." Therefore, if he said "such-and-such son shall have the fruits of this date palm," this wish cannot be carried out, even though his intent is clear, because the wording would have to be altered to carry it out.

40 MT Hilkhot Nᵉḥalot (The Laws of Inheritance) 6,12 and *Maggid Mishne Hilkhot Nᵉḥalot* 6,12.

[the father] said should be given "to my heirs," he [the second converso] should not be included in the heirs. In actuality, we rely on two reasons as one to clarify the halakha:[41] the reason that [he is] an apostate and the reason of well-grounded intent. Signed by the Mabit.

בחלק של האחר שאמר ינתן ליורשי לא יהיה נכלל הוא ביורשים ולענין מעשה סמכי[נן] אתרי טעמי כחדא ומטעמא דמומר וטעמ[א] דאומדנא דמוכח תסתיים שמעתתא. נאם המבי"ט.

Discussion

The question states that Reuben gave his "last will and testament," with no indication that it was written rather than spoken. In his response, di Trani makes the following points:[42]

[1] Reuben had the right to give his property to whichever heirs he chose, and to include stipulations, for several reasons: an oral direction, including any stipulations, from someone on their deathbed is as good as written; Reuben "gifted" his property rather than "bequeathed" it, which makes the law even more flexible.

[2] There is only one heir—the son who is a faithful Jew—who is entitled to receive the portion of his brother who, though he came to the country where Reuben was living, did not return to Judaism and later returned to the Christian country where he was living before. That son thus abrogated the conditions and lost his portion. Neither he, nor the brother who never came to his father's locale, is entitled to a portion of his father's property, given that neither returned to Judaism. If the son who did not come repents later, he would be entitled to his own portion (presumably in escrow), but not to any of the portion of his brother who abrogated the conditions of his inheritance, because at the time of abrogation he was not yet a valid heir.

[3] It is accepted law to rely on a reasonable assumption about the intent of the deceased, and in this case it was the intent of the deceased to give his property to whichever sons were practicing Jews.

---

41   The expression *tistayyem shʿmaʿatata* is from Pʿsaḥim 88a, where Rav Naḥman says to Rav Eyna that "from me and from you the halakha will be clarified." Based on that citation, the expression is used to evoke the idea of a resolution based on a synthesis of opinions or reasons.

42   See the section numbers in square brackets in the responsum.

Given di Trani's own family history, and his position as a rabbinic leader, it is no surprise that he ruled to cut the apostate son out of any inheritance and to consider only the one who was a Jew to be an "heir" for the purpose of receiving the apostate's portion. Though di Trani did not state in so many words that Reuben's widow now owes the Jewish son the sum that she paid out to the first converso son, this is the reasonable conclusion from the response and, specifically, his words: "It appears, too, that they should give [the gift] immediately to the one who is here, worshipping God."[43] The converso son to whom she gave the money abrogated the condition; the son who is a practicing Jew—and only he—is entitled to be compensated for what is rightfully his.

What is not addressed is what is to be done with the sum that was set aside for the third son, the converso who remains in the land of his birth. It appears that Reuben did not specify a timeframe within which the converso sons must return to Judaism in order to inherit their portions. Di Trani clearly makes a distinction between the son who came to his mother's location (and took his portion of the estate from her) but remained a converso, and the son who did not ever present himself. The former is referred to as having abrogated the conditions of inheritance. His portion should be reassigned to the Jewish brother—or brothers. But the second converso brother has not yet upheld the conditions. Di Trani writes that "so long as he does not come," he does not obtain his own portion, much less the portion of his brother who abrogated the conditions. However, he adds, "if he dies there and his heirs come afterwards, they will not inherit said sum," which suggests that the converso has until he dies to return to Judaism.[44]

Apparently, Reuben's request is taken to mean that the conversos would have until their death to return to Judaism, and, until they did, the sums set aside for each one were to remain in escrow, with the one righteous, Jewish son receiving the any profits from those sums (such as if the money was loaned out at interest).

Upon the death of a converso who never returned to Judaism, the living Jewish brother(s) or their heirs would inherit the principal. The converso brother who appeared, took his portion and then returned to his former country demon-

---

43 At [3] in the response.
44 This is consistent with the Jewish attitude to repentance. Maimonides states in *MT Hilkhot T*shuva* (The Laws of Repentance) 2,1 that though it is not the ultimate form of repentance "even if he transgressed all his days and repented on the day of his death, and died a penitent, all his sins are forgiven, as it states: *before the sun, or the light, or the moon, or the stars are darkened, and the clouds return after the rain* (Eccl. 12:2), which is the day of death."

strated that he had no intent to become a practicing Jew, thereby abrogating the conditions of the inheritance and forfeiting any future claim.

According to the responsum, this brother did not have the right to his portion, but he managed to get it through his mother. One might think that she believed he meant to return to Jewish practice, but if he did not even get circumcised, it is not clear why she would think this. Perhaps she hoped that by giving him his portion, she might win him over. And, in spite of everything, he was still her son. Indeed, a quandary for any parent.

Questions for Further Discussion

Discuss the place of "creative compliance" in a religious legal system.

Were the Sages justified in expanding the options available to a person when bequeathing their assets, to the point of overriding the literal interpretation of the biblical verses? (Does the resulting law, in fact, contradict the literal meaning of the biblical verses?)

Compare the approach of the Sages in bringing flexibility to inheritance law with other legal "loopholes" that you are familiar with in present-day law.

How consistent is the Sages' adjudication in inheritance law with the concept that religious law is an expression of the will of God? Based on the example of inheritance law, is religious law (or Jewish law, in particular) an expression of God's will? In discussing these questions, consider the following verses from Micah:

> He has told you, O man, what is good,
> And what the Lord requires of you:
> Only to do justice
> And to love goodness,
> And to walk modestly with your God;
> Then will your name achieve wisdom.[45]

Further Reading

[Gitlitz] Gitlitz, David. "Divided Families in *Converso* Spain." *Shofar* 11, no. 3 (1993): 1-19.

---

45   Mic. 6:8-9.

5.
What's in a Name?
Rabbi Samuel de Medina *Yo-re De'a* 199

Historical Background

One of the processes that the conversos in Spain and Portugal underwent was receiving a Christian name,[1] and the historical records are replete with details of conversos and their Christian names, whether they were sincere converts or Crypto-Jews.[2] For those Crypto-Jews who returned openly to Judaism, use of a Jewish name, perhaps the one they had before converting, perhaps one their parents had secretly given them, or perhaps one they adopted upon their return to Judaism, was clearly an important aspect of their renewed identity.

Thus, in post-expulsion, openly Jewish Spanish-Portuguese communities, Hebrew names, or their equivalent in the local language, dominate. For example, Swetschinski states that though "the dominant and persistent Portuguese tone appears as the most striking feature of Amsterdam's Portuguese Jewish culture" in the seventeenth century and "in almost every form of expression the Portuguese Jews remained consciously and distinctly Iberian,"

> The first conspicuous change came in their adoption of Hebrew (that is, biblical) forenames. At first mainly the Jewish equivalent of more commonly used Iberian names, the Hebrew names eventually replaced their Christian counterparts completely.[3]

---

1 [Zsom]: 193-194.
2 See, for example, Richard L. Kagan, *Inquisitorial Inquiries: Brief Lives of Secret Jews and Other Heretics* (Baltimore: Johns Hopkins University, 2011).
3 Daniel M. Swetschinski, *Reluctant Cosmopolitans: The Portuguese Jews of Seventeenth Century Amsterdam* (London: Littman Library of Jewish Civilization, 2000), 285.

The chapter "Families Torn Apart" focuses on a family divided by religious loyalty, an example of the dysfunction in families in which not all members made the same decisions when faced with conversion or emigration and return to Judaism, as described by Gitlitz.[4] In this chapter, a different phenomenon is viewed through the lens of a responsum: that of conversos who emigrated rather than remain Christian in Iberia, but maintained contact with family, friends, or business associates in Iberia.[5]

The Midrash teaches in the name of Bar Kappara that one of the reasons the Israelites were redeemed in Egypt was that they did not change their names.[6] Neither does the protagonist in this chapter's responsum, written by R. Samuel de Medina,[7] lightly consider using a Christian name.

Halakhic Background

In de Medina's response, a halakha cited from the *Tur*,[8] which is based on *Sanhedrin* 74a, is set up as a "straw man," so that de Medina then offers a number of qualifications and exceptions to that halakha, and arguments as to why the case presented in the question is different, to prove his ruling.

Tur Yo-re De'a 157[9]	טור יורה דעה סימן קנז
[For] all transgressions, with the exception of pagan worship, forbidden sexual relationships and murder, if they [Gentiles] say to a [Jewish] person to transgress them or he will be killed, if he is in private, if he wants, he can transgress and	כל העבירות חוץ מע״ז [מעבודה זרה] וגילוי עריות ושפיכות דמים שאומרים לו לאדם שיעבור עליהם או יהרג אם הוא בצנעא אם ירצ[ה] יעבור ואל יהרג ואם ירצה להחמי[ר]

not be killed, and if he wants to be stringent with himself and be killed, he is per-

---

4 David Gitlitz, "Divided Families in Converso Spain," *Shofar* 11, no. 3 (1993): 1-19.
5 [Zsom]: 195-196; Zsom discusses the responsum in this chapter on pages 210-212.
6 *Vayiqra Rabba* 32:5 (M. Margaliot edition).
7 Known by the acronym Maharashdam, 1506–1589.
8 *Arba'a Turim*, written by R. Jacob ben Asher (c. 1269–1343).
9 The Hebrew text here is from the Hanau, 1610 printing, so as to present an uncensored version, as the most common editions were censored. On censorship, see William Popper, *The Censorship of Hebrew Books* [1899] (New York: Franklin, 1969).

mitted. But if he is in public, he is obligated to be killed rather than transgress. In what [situation] are these things said? When the Gentile intends to cause him to transgress his religion. But if he [the Gentile] only intends [it] for his own benefit, he should transgress and not be killed. But in a time of persecution, even for merely a custom that they [Jews] practice, if they [Gentiles] come to demand of him to transgress it, he should be killed and not transgress. However, for pagan worship, forbidden sexual relationships and murder, even in private he should be killed and not transgress, and even if the Gentile does not intend to cause him to transgress his religion, but only for his own benefit. A person is prohibited to say that he is a Gentile so that they will not kill him, because by saying he is a Gentile, he thereby admits to their faith and denies the fundamental principle [of God]. But [regarding] one who is obligated [to accept] death and saves himself by fleeing to a pagan house of worship, my master and father, the Rosh[10] (may his memory be blessed) wrote that he could flee into it and there is no aspect of admission to pagan worship.[11]

על עצמו וליהרג רשאי ואם הוא בפרהסיא חייב ליהרג ולא יעבור. בד״א [במה דברים אמורים] שהגוי מכוון להעבירו על דת. אבל אם אינו מכוין אלא להנאתו יעבור ואל יהרג. ובשעת השמד אפילו על מנהג בעלמ׳[א] שנהגו אם באין להעביר עליו יהרג ואל יעבור ובע״ז [ובעבודה זרה] ובגילוי עריות ושפיכות דמ׳[ים] אפי׳[לו] בצינעא יהרג ואל יעבור ואפילו אין הגוי מכוין להעבירו על דת אלא להנאתו אסור לאדם לומ׳[ר] שהוא גוי כדי שלא יהרגוהו דכיון שאומ׳[ר] שהוא גוי הרי מודה לדתם וכופר בעיקר אבל מי שנתחייב מית׳[ה] ומציל עצמו במה שבורח לבית ע״ז [עבודה זרה] כתב א״א [אדוני אבי] הרא״ש ז״ל [זכרונו לברכה] שיכול לברוח לתוכה ואין בזה משום מודה בע״ז [בעבודה זרה].

---

10 R. Asher ben Jehiel, c. 1250–1327.
11 Compare the *Tur*'s ruling here with that of Maimonides, *MT Hilkhot Y^esodei Ha-Torah* (The Laws of the Foundations of the Torah) 5,1-4, presented in the chapter "Is Your Blood Any Redder?," Halakhic Background.

Responsum

Maharashdam *Yo-re De'a* 199	שו״ת מהרשד״ם חלק יורה דעה סימן קצט

Question: [Regarding] those forced conversos who came from Portugal, and they had names like the Gentile names, but after they came to seek God and his Torah, they would change their names to *names of the Children of Israel* (Exod. 1:1), and they have a need to write [correspondence] from the place where they dwell as Jews to the place where they had names like the Gentile names, whether to their relatives or to those who conduct business with their money, are they permitted to write and change their names to the names that they had when they were Gentiles, or is there a concern of a prohibition in this matter, because it appears that he is still a Gentile and does not acknowledge God's Torah?

Response: Truthfully, I do not speak of [exceptionally] pious conduct,[12] because certainly it is an attribute of piety for a person to distance himself with all sorts of precautionary measures that are possible, particularly someone who was baptized.[13] However, according to the law, it appears to me that it is a clear matter that there is no concern of a prohibition at all, and even though, at first sight, it could have seemed [appropriate] to bring evidence to prohibit, based on what the *Tur* wrote in *YD* section 157, as follows: "It is forbidden for a person to say that he is a Gentile, so that they will not kill him, because by say-

שאלה אלו האנוסים שבאו מפורטוגאל והיו להם שמות כשמות הגויים ואחר שבאו לבקש את ה' ואת תורתו משנים שמם לשמות בני ישראל ויש להם צורך לכתוב ממקום אשי[נר] הם יושבי[ם] ביהדותם אל המקום אשר היה להם שמות כשמות הגויים אם לקרוביהם ואם למי שנושא ונותן ממונם אם יכולים לכתוב ולשנות שמם כשמות אשר היו להם בגיותם או אם יש חשש איסור בדבר מפני שנראה מקיים היותו עדין גוי ובלתי מודה בתורת ה':

תשובה אמת כי מדת חסידות לא קאמינ[א] דודאי מדת חסידו[ת] הוא להרחיק האדם עצמו בכל מיני הרחקה שאיפשר ובפרט למי שעברו על ראשו המים הזדוני[ם] אכן מן הדין נראה בעיני דבר ברור שאין בזה חשש איסור כלל ואף על גב דלכאורה היה נראה להביא קצת ראיה לאסור ממה שכתב הטור יי״ד

---

12 As a requirement.
13 Lit., "over whose head the wicked waters passed."

ing he is a Gentile, he thereby admits to their faith and denies the existence of God." One might say that here, too, because he calls himself a Gentile name it is as if he says he is a Gentile, and it is prohibited. Even if you could say that it is different in that case [in the *Tur*], in any event in that case [there] is stronger [justification], because it is to save himself from death, and even so it is prohibited. Here, when it is only for monetary needs or some other matter, it would be proper to prohibit. However, it appears without doubt that after any amount of inspection, one would find that the law is that it is permitted, [1][14] and proof of the matter [is found] in what they [the Sages] said in *Nᵉdarim* chapter "*Qonam*"[15] [62b]: Rava said: "It is permitted for a rabbinical disciple to say 'I am a servant of the fire [worship],[16] [therefore] I will not pay the poll tax.'"[17] What is the reason [he is permitted]? He is saying it to chase a lion away from him.[18] Rashi's interpretation that a servant of fire is "a servant of

[יורה דעה] סימן קנ״ז וז״ל [וזה לשונו] אסור לאדם לומר שהוא גוי כדי שלא יהרגוהו דכיון שאומר שהוא גוי הרי מודה לדתם וכופר בעיקר ע״כ [עד כאן] ויאמר האומר דהכא נמי כיון שקורא עצמו בשם גוי הוה ליה כאומ׳[ר] שהוא גוי ואסור ואפי׳[לו] אם תמצא לומר דשאני התם מ״מ [מכל מקום] גם יש בנדון ההוא יתר שאת שהוא להציל עצמו מן המות ואפילו הכי אסור הכא דלא הוי אלא לצורך ממון או דבר אחר היה ראוי לאסור אלא שנראה בלי ספק שאחר עיון כל דהו ימצא האדם שהדין הוא שהוא מותר וראיה לדב׳[ר] ממה שאמרו בנדרי׳[ם] פרק קונם אמר רבא שרי לצורבא מרבנן למימר עבדא דנורא אנא לא יהיבנא אכרגא מאי טעמא לאברוחי אריא מיניה הוא דאמר ולא מבעיא לפרש״י [לפירוש רש״י] דעבדא דנורא היינו

---

14 Numbers are inserted to facilitate reading the discussion following the responsum.

15 A word used for expressing a vow.

16 This refers to the Zoroastrian religious practice prevalent where the Babylonian Sages resided. See Mary Boyce, "On the Zoroastrian Temple Cult of Fire," *Journal of the American Oriental Society* 95, no. 3 (1975): 454-465.

17 For a detailed discussion of the poll tax, see David M. Goodblatt, "The Poll Tax in Sasanian Babylonia: The Talmudic Evidence," *Journal of the Economic and Social History of the Orient* 22, no. 3 (1979): 233-295. See 281-287 for Goodblatt's discussion of Rava's statements on *Nᵉdarim* 62b.

18 I.e., to avoid the harm of losing money. This questionably ethical method of attempting to evade the tax is discussed in Jacob Neusner, *A History of the Jews in Babylonia IV: The Age of Shapur II* (Leiden: Brill, 1969), 85-91. Neusner concludes that the Sages received no exemption and did, in fact, pay the tax, as does Beer (Moshe Beer, "Were the Babylonian Amoraim Exempt from Taxes and Customs?" [Hebrew], *Tarbiz* 33, no. 3 [1964]: 247-258), whom Neusner cites (90n4). Both Neusner and Beer say that this claim of exemption would have

such-and-such pagan worship"[19] is not needed,[20] because the matter [can be derived] a fortiori, and [even] the grandson of a fortiori,[21] because there [in N^edarim] he presents himself clearly as a servant of pagan worship because they are then exempt from the tax, [and it is] permitted, because the context is clear that he said this only to be exempt from the poll tax, and in our case, such that he is a Jew who worships God and is himself not situated in the place that the letter is destined so that the Gentiles would regard him as a Gentile, but rather so that in case the letter falls into the hands of a Gentile, he will not lose his property on account with a Gentile. [And this,] even though they cannot know *who is he and where is he* (Esther 7:5) who is named thus. Further, the

עבד של ע״ז [עבודה זרה] פלונית שהדברים ק״ו [קל וחומר] ובן בנו של ק״י [קל וחומר] דהשתא התם שמראה את עצמו בפי׳[רוש] עבד הע״ז [העבודה זרה] כי מפני זה פטורים מהמס מותר משום דמוכח מלתא דלא אמר הכי אלא לאפטורי מכרגא הכא בנדון דידן שהוא יהודי ועובד ה׳ ואינו עומ׳[ד] הוא עצמו במקו[ם] שהולך שם הכתב לשנאמר שיחזיקו אותו הגוים לגוי אלא כדי שאם יבא הכתב ביד גוי לא יפסידו נכסיו בחשב[ון] מגוי הם אעפ״יי [אף על פי] שהם אינם יכולים לידע מי הוא זה ואי זה הוא הנקרא בשם זה וגם אל מי שנשתלח אליו הכתב כבר יודע כונה זו וברור[ר] לו שהכותב יהודי פשיט[א] ודאי דמותר אלא אפי[לו] לדעת שאר המפרשי[ם]

addressee of the letter already knows this intent, and it is clear to him that the author is a Jew. [Based on this interpretation] it is obvious: certainly it is permitted [in our case, to use a Gentile name]. Rather, even according to the opinion of the

---

been made to the Jewish community's own tax collector, in vain, but Goodblatt states that there is no evidence to support this ("Poll Tax": 269-270).

19 N^edarim 62b at *'avda d^enura*. The commentary ascribed to Rashi on N^edarim was not written by him, and modern scholars often refer to it as "Pseudo-Rashi." (See Rothkoff, Aaron, et al. "Rashi," in EJ, 18:101-106.) Goodblatt concludes that "servant of fire" "means 'worshipper of the fire', or Zoroastrian" ("Poll Tax": 284-285). However, Maria Macuch is more convincing in her argument, based on Sasanian legal texts, that "a rabbinical disciple could well have claimed to have been an *'ebd' dnwr'* [*'avda d^enura*] without saying that he was an apostate, since this would only mean that he worked on the estate of a fire foundation, hence belonged to the personnel of a fire-temple, and was consequently exempt from paying the poll tax" (Maria Macuch, "The Talmudic Expression 'Servant of the Fire' in the Light of Pahlavi Legal Sources," *Jerusalem Studies in Arabic and Islam* 26 [2002]: 109-129).

20 A less extreme interpretation will serve de Medina for his argument.

21 Z^evahim 50b.

other commentators,[22] who interpreted that "I am a servant of fire" [means] "a servant to a man who is a priest of the fire-worshippers," which means that he specifically presents himself as a servant to a priest. If so, it is possible to say that he is a Jew and even as such he can serve that priest, as the Torah said,[23] *and your brother being in straits, comes under his authority ... [and sells himself to a stranger who lives among you] or to the offshoot of a stranger's family* (Lev. 25:47), and because of this,[24] it is permitted; therefore [one might conclude that] if they regard him as a Gentile, it is forbidden. [But] this is not so! *Nimmuqei [Yosef]*[25] (may his memory be blessed) already explained in chapter "One who robs and feeds" [*Bava Qamma*] that even according to this interpretation it is deduced that "there is no doubt that they do not regard him as a Jew, considering that he serves priests of pagan worship."[26] So it also clearly seems from the Ran's words (may his memory be blessed) in chapter "*Qonam*" [*Nᵉdarim* 62b], which he explained and said "'servant of the fire' [is] a servant to a man who is a priest for the fire worshippers, because his servants are exempt from the tax, and it is not as if he accepts pagan worship, because the context is clear that he ... would

שפירשו עבדא דנורא אנא עבד לאיש שהוא כומר לעובדי האש דמשמע דדוקא שמראה עצמו עבד לכומר ואם כן כבר אפשר לומר שהוא יהודי ואפי'[לו] הכי עובד לאותו כומר וכמו שאמר הכתוב ומך אחיך עמו וכו'[לי] עד לעקר משפחת גר ומשום הכי מותר הא אם מחזיקים אותו לגוי אסור לא היא דכבר פירש הנמקי ז"ל [זכרונו לברכה] בפרק הגוזל ומאכיל דאפילו לפי פירוש זה נמשך שאין ספק שאין מחשבין אותו ליהודי אחר שעובד כומרי ע"ז [עבודה זרה] וכן נראה בפירוש מדברי הר"ן ז"ל [זכרונו לברכה] בפרק קונם שהוא פירש ואמר עבדא דנורא עבד לאיש שהוא כומר לעובדי האש שעבדיו פטורים ממס ולא הוי כמודה בע"ז [בעבודה זרה] דמוכח[נא] מלתא דלא אמי[נר] הכי אלא לאפטורי מכרגא הרי שהוא ז"ל [זכרונו לברכה] פירש

---

22 Such as the Ran (R. Nissim Gerondi, 1310?–1375?), *Nᵉdarim* 62b (found in the Vilna edition alongside the text) at *'avda dᵉnura ana* and Rashba (R. Solomon ben Abraham Adret, c. 1235–c. 1310) *Nᵉdarim* 62b.

23 Lit., "as the written [law] said."

24 That he is known as a Jew.

25 R. Joseph Ḥabiba, beginning of the fifteenth century.

26 *Bava Qamma* 40b in the pages of the Rif (R. Isaac Alfasi, 1013–1103). See Macuch, "The Talmudic Expression," for an explanation of why a servant of a priest could be regarded as a Jew. However, what is important in de Medina's argument is not the academic analysis of the Talmudic text, but rather its traditional interpretation.

say this only to be exempt from the poll tax." So he (may his memory be blessed) interpreted as the [other] commentators [did],[27] and even here [in Ran's commentary] he said, "and it is not as if" etc., and if they would consider him a Jew who is even so a servant of a priest, it is obvious that it was not as if he accepts [pagan worship]. And [for] what does he have to say "the context is clear" etc., and did he not certainly know all this? For it is certainly as the *Nimmuqei [Yosef]* (may his memory be blessed) explained that one who says such is not assumed to be a Jew, and with all this, because he says so to exempt himself, and it is they [to whom he says this who] are the ones themselves who err by thinking he is a Gentile, it is permitted. All the more so in our case, that they only see the letter and do not know the person, but only his correspondence, as mentioned, so it is obvious that it is permitted. Further, even though there are those commentators who explain [on the matter in *Nᵉdarim*] that [what Rava permitted] is permitted specifically for rabbinical disciples, as the Rosh (may his memory be blessed) wrote, that "we are not concerned that he [a rabbinical disciple] would take license and further disregard [the commandments]," while the *Nimmuqei [Yosef]* (may his memory be blessed) gave a different reason, which is that the rabbinical disciple knows how to direct his heart to the Holy One, blessed be He, who is a *devouring fire* (Deut. 4:24). Therefore [according to these opinions], for another person it is prohibited. In any case, in our case there should not be a distinction between a rabbinical disciple and another person. In fact, there [in *Nᵉdarim*] there is [reason] to be concerned that one who is not a rabbinical disciple might take license and dis-

---

27 Rashba and *Nimmuqei Yosef*.

regard [the commandments], because perhaps they will interrogate him in the matter and he would feel compelled to say other various prohibited things to reinforce his first statement, which a rabbinical disciple would not do, for if [that situation] presents itself to him,[28] that is how he would lose [the sum] of the tax. Further, he would not utter any forbidden words. This is not relevant in our case at all, since merely a letter is sent to another realm—it is obvious that there is no reason to prohibit, and so it is accepted by us. Even more so according to the reasoning of the *Nimmuqei [Yosef]* that in our case there is no distinction between a rabbinical disciple and another person at all, and there is no need to prolong this at all. Even more so, and a fortiori according to the opinion of the Ran (may his memory be blessed) who explained that the one who maintained that [it is permitted] for a rabbinical disciple, maintained [that] for inclusivity—even for him it is permitted.[29] All the more so for another person.

דידן ליכא לפלוגי בין צורבא דרבנן לאיניש אחרינ'[א] דדוקא התם איכא למיחש שמא יתפקר ויזלזל יותר אם אינו צורבא מדרבנן דשמא יחקרו אותו בדברים ויצטרך לומר דברים אחרים מגונים ואסורים כדי להחזיק דבריו הראשוני'[ם] מה שלא יעשה הצורבא מרבנן שאם יבא לידו כך יפסיד המס ויותר ולא יוציא דבר איסור מפיו מה שבנדון דידן לא שייך זה כלל כיון שאינו אלא כתב א'[ןחד] בעלמא שלוח אל מלכות אחר פשיטא דליכא למיגזר וק"ל [וקיימא לן] וכ"ש [וכל שכן] לטעמו של הנמקי שבנדון דידן אין חלוק בין צורבא דרבנן לאיש אחר כלל ואין צורך להאריך כלל בזה וכ"ש [וכל שכן] וק"ו [וקל וחומר] לדעת הר"ן ז"ל [זכרונו לברכה] שפירש דהאי דנקט צורבא דרבנן לרבותא נקט דאפילו לדידיה שרי כ"ש [כל שכן] לאד'[ם] אחר

ועוד יש להביא ראיות אחרות וכתבם מהררי"ק [מורנו הרב רבי יוסף קולון]

[2] Further, other evidence should be brought, written by our teacher the Maharik[30] (may his memory be blessed) in principle 88,[31] in order to prove [the response] to a different question,[32] as follows: "It also seems to me that evi-

---

28 Lit., "would come to his hand."
29 Ran N^edarim 62b at 'avda d^enura ana. I.e., you might think that a rabbinical disciple would be held to a more stringent standard, and Rava's statement means that "not only are common people permitted, but even a rabbinical disciple is permitted."
30 The Italian halakhist, R. Joseph Colon, c. 1420–1480.
31 *Responsa of the Maharik*, principle 88 (Venice, 1519).
32 The question there is whether a certain medieval garment is prohibited to Jews because it is a Gentile garment, and wearing it might transgress the commandment *nor shall you follow their*

dence should be brought from what is taught in a *baraita* [in] chapter 'One who robs [and feeds]' [*Bava Qamma* 113a] regarding a garment of *kil'ayim*:³³ It is prohibited to elude the customs [tax] with it,³⁴ etc. [...] And I saw in a gloss on *Smaq*,³⁵ 'There are those who interpret [the text to mean] that whoever allows eluding the customs with it, that is to manifest oneself as a non-Jew, such as with a customs duty that is only demanded of Jews'" etc. "... and from the words of the one who permits we can derive a fortiori regarding the matter that we are considering"³⁶ etc. "... And even for whoever disagrees and explains that eluding the customs is such as [the case] that customs are not charged on garments that a person wears, but to manifest oneself as a non-Jew is prohibited, it is very obvious³⁷ that perforce it is not prohibited except in that case that his garment would attest that he is not a Jew, considering that he is wearing something forbidden to Jews, and also he intends such that he would

---

laws (Lev. 18:3).

33 A garment made of linen and wool, which is prohibited in Lev. 19:19.

34 By wearing it, even on top of allowable garments. The Vilna edition does not have the word *bo* (with it), but the text here agrees with the most reliable manuscripts (such as MS Munich 95). The Talmud continues with R. Akiva's opinion that it is permitted to wear a garment of *kil'ayim* to elude the customs (under a situation such as, for example, that it is a duty charged only to Jews), because the wearer is not doing it to derive the usual benefit from the garment, such as to keep warm.

35 *Sefer Mitsvot Qatan*. The original name of this book, written by R. Isaac ben Joseph of Corbeil (d. 1280), was *Shiv'at 'Amudei Gola*. Due to the popularity of the book, many different annotations were added in numerous manuscripts, with certain popular ones appearing in the printed editions. The gloss that Maharik refers to would be on §32, where it states that it is permitted to wear *kil'ayim* to elude customs (but the cited gloss is not found in the ubiquitous editions).

36 Lit., "that we are standing upon."

37 Lit., "obvious and obvious."

not be recognized as a Jew. In that case, he should be likened to that in chapter 'A rebellious and disobedient son' [Sanhedrin 74b] that even [changing] a sandal strap is prohibited.[38] But in such a case [as we are dealing with], it is obvious that it is permitted in all opinions, because this garment is not prohibited to Jews at all." He [Maharik] further brought another proof from a gloss on the *Smaq* that states "'What we say—that a sandal strap is prohibited—is specifically when the Gentiles say to do such in order to profane God; then it is prohibited. But so that he should not be recognized as a Jew, such as to wear Gentile garments or to behave in a way that he would not be recognized—[this is] permitted. Or, [it would be permitted] to elude the customs, because it states, do not wear a garment of *kil'ayim* [even on top of ten [permitted] garments,] to elude the customs,[39] but some other item is permitted [for this purpose]' [...] and there are those who dispute [this]."[40] In any event, I say that also in our case we can say in the words of Maharik (may his memory be blessed) from his first proof, we will say "and according to whoever permits [wearing *kil'ayim* to elude the customs] [...] a fortiori" for our current case, because in that

יהודי מאחר שהוא לבוש האסור ליהודי'[ם] וגם מתכוין הוא בכך שלא יכירוהו שהוא יהודי התם הוא דיש לדמותו להההיא דפרק בן סורר ומורה דאפילו לשנויי ערקתא דמסאנא אסור אבל בכה"ג [בכהאי גוונא] פשיטא דשרי לכולי עלמא שהרי אין הלבוש הזה הוא אסור ליהודים כלל ע"כ [עד כאן]. עוד הביא ראיה אחרת מהגהת הסמ"ק [ספר מצוות קטן] שכתב וז"ל [וזה לשונו] הא דאמרי'[נן] דערקת'[א] דמסאנא אסור היינו דוקא כשהגוים אומרים עשה כך כדי לחלל ה' אז הוא דאסו'[ר] אבל כדי שלא יהיה ניכר שהוא יהודי כגון ללבוש בגדי נכרי או להתנהג בדבר שלא יהא ניכר מותר או כדי לעבור המכס דהכי קאמר לא ילבש אדם כלאים כדי לעבור בו המכ'[ס] אבל דבר אחר מותר ואיכ'[א] מאן דפליג מכל מקו'[ם] אומר אני שגם בנידון דידן נוכל לומר בדברי מהרר"יק ז"ל [זכרונו לברכה] מן הראיה הראשונה

---

38 That is, to change even the slightest detail of a practice that distinguishes a Jew from a Gentile (see Rashi *Sanhedrin* 74b at *arqʿta dimsana*). The discussion on *Sanhedrin* 74 is regarding those commandments that a Jew must let himself be killed rather than transgress, specifically in a time of persecution or in public. See Halakhic Background, above, and in the chapter "Is Your Blood Any Redder?"

39 *Bava Qamma* 113a.

40 *Responsa of the Maharik*, principle 88. R. Joseph Caro (*Bet Yosef YD* 157:2) also cites this gloss on *Smaq* (most likely on §3, but it is not found in the ubiquitous editions) from Maharik's responsum (rather than directly from an edition of *Smaq*).

case such that he personally committed an act[41] and wearing [the prohibited garment] itself is a matter of the prohibition of *kil'ayim*, we permit him so that they would not recognize him as a Jew, in our case, where the purpose is only so they would not be able to determine if the author [of the letter] is a Jew or a Gentile, but not that they should consider this about the man who is before their eyes, because *they have eyes but cannot see* (Ps. 115:5);[42] even more so and a fortiori that it is permitted.

[3] Also, the distinction that Maharik (may his memory be blessed) made regarding the opinion of those who forbid [wearing *kil'ayim* to elude the customs] should be made in our case, and we will say that there [in that case] they did not prohibit except when his garment testifies about him that he is not Jewish, since it is a garment prohibited to Jews. But Gentile names are not prohibited to Jews! Proof of this [is found in] what we say in *Gittin* chapter one [11b]: Writs of divorce that come from overseas [and are signed by witnesses], even though the names on them are like Gentile names, are valid, because the names of the majority of Jews outside of the Land [of Israel] are like Gentile names, and also in the Land of Israel their names were like the names of Gentiles, because there is no [difference] between the Land of Israel and outside of

נאמר דלדברי המתיר ק״ו [קל וחומר] לנ״ד [לנידון דידן] דהשתא התם דעביד מעשה בידים והלבישה בעצמה הוא דבר איסור כלאים אנו מתירים לו כדי שלא יכירוהו שהוא יהודי נדון שלנו שאין הכונה אלא כדי שלא יכירו הכותב אם הוא יהודי אם גוי לא שיחשבו על זה האיש הנראה לעיניהם כי עינים להם ולא יראו כל שכן וקל וחומר שהוא מותר

גם החלוק שחלק מהררי״ק ז״ל [זכרונו לברכה] לדעת האוסרים יש לחלק בנדון דידן ונאמר דעד כאן לא קאסרי התם אלא דוקא התם שלבושו מוכיח עליו שאינו יהודי מאחר שהוא לבוש האסור ליהודים אבל שמות הגוים אינם אסורים ליהודים וראיה לדבר דאמרינן בגיטין פרק א׳ גיטין הבאים ממדינת הים אעפ״י [אף על פי] ששמותיהם כשמו[ת] גוים כשרים מפני שרוב ישראל שבחוצה לארץ שמותיהם כשמות גוים וגם בארץ ישראל היו שמותיהם כשמות גוים דלא איכא

---

41 Lit., "committed an act with his hands."

42 Other than the fact that by association de Medina thought to cite these words, the relevance is weak. The intent of using a Gentile name in the letter might very well be to protect the recipient, and the suggestion that the Gentile authorities would not consider whether he is Jewish or not is not convincing. However, it is not the recipient that committed this act of using a Gentile name to disguise himself. The letter's sender is providing a secondhand potential benefit.

the Land [of Israel] other than "majority," as is seen there in Rashi's commentary.[43] Do not say that [Jews use] only names that are common to both Jews and Gentiles, but not names that are indubitably Gentile, because here from the words of the Rosh (may his memory be blessed) it can be clearly learned that Jews were called names that are indubitably Gentile, as he wrote: "He said to him,[44] we received no writ of divorce other than one that was signed by Lucius and Gaius,[45] and we declared it valid, ... because Jews with those names are not common.[46] Certainly the messenger [who brought the writ to the woman] did not err in having people like this sign, whose names are like those of Gentiles, until he investigated and scrutinized them and he knew that they are Jews, and [then] he had them sign."[47] Here, [we see] explicitly that a Jew who calls himself by an indubitably Gentile name is a proper Jew who can validly sign a writ of divorce, and if so, we can say according to this in our case also, even according to those who prohibit there [in the matter of kil'ayim],

בין ארץ ישראל לחוצה לארץ אלא רוב וכמו שנראה שם מפרש״י ולא תימא דוקא שמות הרגילים ישראל וגוים יחד אבל שמות מובהקים לגוים לא שהרי מתוך דברי הרא״ש ז״ל [זכרונו לברכה] משמע בפירוש שהיו ישראלים נקראים כשמות מובהקים של גוים שכתב וז״ל [וזה לשונו] א״ל [אמר ליה] לא בא לידנו אלא גט שהיו חתומים עליו לוקוס ולוס והכשרנוהו דכיון דלא שכיחי ישראל בשמות הללו ודאי לא טעה השליח להחתים אנשים כאלה שהם דומים בשמותם לגוים עד שחקר ופשפש אחריהם ונודע לו שישראלים הם והחתימם. הרי בפירוש שישראל שקורא עצמו בשם שמות גוים מובהקים ישראל כשר הוי וכשר לחתום בגט ואם כן נוכל לומר כפי זה דבנדון דידן נמי אפילו לדברי

---

43 Rashi Gittin 11b at 'edim ha-ḥatumim 'al ha-get comments on the case posed before the one cited by de Medina, which asks whether a writ of divorce is valid if it is signed by witnesses with names that are like Gentile names. Rashi explains, "it comes from the Land of Israel, because it does not say 'from overseas.'" Regarding the writ from the Land of Israel, at u-shmoteihen kishmot 'ovdei kokhavim, Rashi explains "we do not know if it is a Gentile or a Jew [who signed]." These comments imply what de Medina states, that Jews in the Land of Israel also sometimes have names like those of Gentiles.

44 R. Yoḥanan to Resh Laqish (Shimon ben Laqish). In the case posed before the one cited by de Medina, Resh Laqish asked R. Yoḥanan what the ruling is about a writ of divorce such that the signed witnesses have Gentile names, and this was the response from Resh Laqish, implying that these names are indubitably Gentile names.

45 See Marcus Jastrow, *A Dictionary of the Targumim, the Talmud Bavli and Yerushalmi, and the Midrashic Literature* s.v. *gayus* (New York: Putnam's Sons, 1903).

46 Gittin 11b.

47 Rosh, Gittin 1:11

here [in our case] it is certainly permitted. All this seems, in my humble opinion, to be unnecessary, other than for the comfort of the matter,[48] to appease the questioner's mind, but the truth is that everything that the authorities, of blessed memory, prohibit and are stringent [about] is only that a person should not change himself in the presence of Gentiles, so that they would not think he is a Gentile and point to him and say,[49] "so-and-so is a Gentile," and there is [in such behavior] profanation of God's name. But regarding [the case that] he writes what he needs to and then signs his name with a Gentile name, and he who is the recipient of the letter knows certainly that he is a Jew, and others who see the letter think that this property is not from a Jew but a Gentile, and they do not know the man himself—all this, and also it is not a public matter that one could say there is profanation of God's name, God forbid—it is permitted. I wrote what seems [to me,] in my humble opinion.

האוסרים התם הכא מותר בודאי כל זה נרא[ה] לע״ד [לעניות דעתי] שאינו צריך אלא לרווחא דמלת[א] להפיס דעת השואל אבל כפי האמת כל מה שאוסרים ומחמירים הפוסקים ז״ל [זכרונם לברכה] אינו אלא שלא ישנה האדם עצמו וגופו בפני הגוים שלא יחשבוהו לגוי ויאמרו ויראו באצבע פלוני זה גוי הוא ואיכא חלול השם אבל במה שכותב צרכיו ואחר כך חותם שמו כשם גוי ומי שנשתל[ח] אליו הכתב יודע בודאי שהוא יהודי ואחרים הרואים הכתב חושבים שנכסים אלו אינם מיהודי אלא מגוי ואינם יודעים האיש בעצמו וכל זה גם כן אינו דבר של פרהסיא דלימא דאיכא חלול השם חלילה ומותר הנרא[ה] לעניות דעתי כתבתי:

Discussion

De Medina begins by stating that what he is about to say is the law, rather than exceptionally pious conduct. Following citation from the *Tur* of a halakha, in accordance with which one might think it would be prohibited for a Jew to use a Gentile name so as to pass as a Gentile, de Medina presents several cases from the Talmud that qualify this prohibition.[50]

---

48 I.e., as an extra precaution (*Bava Qamma* 116a; Rashi explains there at *lirvaḥa demilta*: so that there would not be any objection).
49 Lit., "say and show with their finger."
50 See the section numbers in square brackets in the responsum.

[1] In N^edarim 62b, it is taught that Rava said it is permitted for a rabbinical disciple to claim that he is a "servant of the fire," which might suggest that he pretends to be a Gentile. De Medina offers several interpretations, all of which, he argues, would prove that if that is permitted, it certainly would be permitted to use a Gentile name in the case of the question posed to him.

[2] De Medina cites a responsum written by Maharik in which Maharik concludes that it is permitted for a Jew to wear a garment that is commonly worn by Gentiles. The Maharik presented arguments to justify permission based on *Bava Qamma* 113a, where there is a discussion of whether it is prohibited to elude certain taxes by wearing a garment of *kil'ayim*. Since *kil'ayim* is prohibited to Jews, this suggests pretending to be a Gentile. De Medina argues that the logic Maharik employed for his case of a Gentile garment would certainly apply to the case in the question posed to him, and therefore it would be permitted to use a Gentile name.

[3] Unlike *kil'ayim*, which is prohibited by the Torah, Gentile names are not prohibited to Jews, as is learned from *Gittin* 11b; this strengthens his case further.

Questions for Further Discussion

What makes a (given) name Jewish? Does a given name have to be a Hebrew name to be considered Jewish?[51]

In a responsum, R. Yitzchok Zilberstein[52] tells about a Holocaust survivor who gave his son a Gentile name, to honor a righteous Gentile who saved the father from the Nazis. The son asks if there is some blemish in having this Gentile name.[53] Among many sources, Zilberstein cites the responsum presented in this chapter. How would you respond to this son, and with what arguments?

Jews have used Gentile names throughout their history. In modern times,

> name changing was an important and widely-practiced phenomenon among New York Jews in the 20th century. Between 1917 and 1967, thousands of American-born New York Jews submitted name-change

---

51   The discussion can include modern times; see Jason H. Greenberg, "From Rochel to Rose and Mendel to Max: First Name Americanization Patterns among Twentieth-Century Jewish Immigrants to the United States" (master's thesis, City University of New York, 2017). The discussion can be expanded to surnames; see [Fermaglich] and [Fermaglich2].

52   B. 1934.

53   Yitzchok Zilberstein, *Ḥashuqei Ḥemed*, K^etubbot 104b.

petitions as families in order to combat antisemitism, find jobs, and receive an education. ... The New York Jews who changed their names ... had a powerful impact on American Jewish communal life. For one thing, their neighbors, friends, and relatives in the city, and indeed all over the country, had to confront the practice and its implications: ... Would a new, less ethnic name improve their lives? Did changing their names mean that they were deserting their religion or their family?[54]

What do you think? Consider, as well, twentieth- to twenty-first-century Jewish experience outside of Israel.[55]

Both Rava's permission to rabbinical disciples to declare that they are "servants of fire" and the possibility of wearing *kil'ayim* to elude customs raise ethical questions about Jews misleading Gentiles in order to avoid paying certain taxes. In the case of *kil'ayim*, can a stronger case be made if, as suggested in one of the statements about such a ruse, the tax was one levied only from Jews? Read [Dratch] and then discuss the ethical issues raised by the texts seen in this chapter.

Further Reading

[Dratch] Dratch, Mark. "Nothing but the Truth." *Judaism* 37, no. 2 (1988): 218-228.
[Fermaglich] Fermaglich, Kirsten. "'Too Long, Too Foreign ... Too Jewish': Jews, Name Changing, and Family Mobility in New York City, 1917–1942." *Journal of American Ethnic History* 34, no. 3 (2015): 34-57.
[Fermaglich2] ———. *A Rosenberg by Any Other Name: A History of Jewish Name Changing in America*. New York: New York University Press, 2018.
[Zsom] Zsom, Dora. "'But the Name of the Wicked will Rot' (Prov. 10:7). Names Used by Conversos in the Responsa Literature." *Hispania Judaica Bulletin* 8 (2011): 193-213.

---

54 [Fermaglich2], 3.
55 Read the epilogue in [Fermaglich2] and [Fermaglich] to enrich the discussion.

6.
Is Your Blood Any Redder?
The Case of an Informer in the Venetian Inquisition
Rabbi Solomon ben Abraham Ha-Kohen Responsum 4,31

Historical Background

Based on the historical sources available, including Inquisition records and responsa, historians have attempted to characterize baptized Jews who seemed to waver between Christianity and Judaism or accommodated themselves to some sort of blending of the two. Jews who left Iberia at the time of the expulsion from Spain or perhaps later from Portugal,[1] so that they could practice their faith, are relatively easy to define. So are those who converted to Christianity and, as far as anyone knew, became good Christians and raised their descendants as such.

But then there are those who fit neither of those simple categories. Whether they are referred to as Crypto-Jews, Marranos, conversos, New Christians, or Judaizing Christians, these are baptized Jews or their descendants who remained in Iberia, or perhaps traveled to other Christian countries where Judaism could not be practiced openly, and yet evidence reveals that they maintained some Jewish practices or reverted to Jewish practices, even several generations after their parents were baptized. These were the "cultural commuters,"[2] New Christians who really were not so "new," who emerged in Jewish communities in the Ottoman Empire, or perhaps Amsterdam or London, sometimes following much

---

1   See introduction, note 1.
2   [Melammed], viii, used the term "cultural commuter" to describe someone who changes, perhaps several times, in cultural and religious guise. [Pullan], 221-228, too, describes the restless journey of some New Christians wavering between two worlds "in search of one's true religious identity."

migration through the Low Countries, Germany, and Italy. Venice was a frequent last stop in Christendom before a final stop in areas under Ottoman rule.

The responsum in this chapter—which relates to events that took place in Venice—is fascinating from a historical perspective because it corroborates one of the trial records, or *processi*, from the Venetian Inquisition.[3] The details of the case presented in a question to R. Solomon ben Abraham Ha-Kohen[4] of Salonica are so consistent with the Inquisition records for the case of someone by the name of Filippo de Nis (aka Salomon Marcus) that there can be little doubt that this responsum is in fact an epilogue to the de Nis case that took place in the Ottoman Empire, where Ha-Kohen was widely respected[5]—perhaps in Salonica, where he resided and where Filippo had friends and contacts.[6]

The transcript of the trial and ordeal of de Nis, a Portuguese New Christian accused of Judaizing by the Venetian Inquisition in the late sixteenth century, would lead a reader to believe that after extended imprisonment, fines, and house arrest, Filippo became a good Catholic.[7] But the lawsuit presented in Ha-Kohen's responsum disproves this conclusion. Ha-Kohen concluded that the defendant (de Nis) had left Venice and was living in a place where he could practice Judaism openly and had returned to the Jewish faith.

The Venetian Inquisition differed from the more familiar Spanish and Portuguese Inquisitions, and the situation in Venice was very different from the situation in Spain or Portugal after the expulsions from those two countries— foremost, because it was not forbidden to be a Jew in Venice in the sixteenth century. Generally, "putting the needs of the state first, even if they clashed with the prerogatives and freedom of action of the Catholic Church,"[8] the Venetian

---

3   Pier Cesare Ioly Zorattini, ed., *Processi del S. Uffizio di Venezia contra Ebrei e Giudaizzanti*, vol. 7, *(1585–89)* (Florence: L. S. Olschki, 1989), 77-171.

4   Known by the acronym Maharshakh, c. 1520–c. 1601.

5   Ha-Kohen's responsa addressed cases throughout the Ottoman domain. See Mordecai Margaliyot, ed., *Encyclopedia lᵉTolᵉdot Gᵉdolei Yisra'el* (Tel Aviv: Chechik, 1946), 1293.

6   For a full presentation of the de Nis Inquisition trial and its correlation to Ha-Kohen's responsum, see [Koren].

7   As do the historians Renée Melammed (see [Melammed], 123) and Zorattini, bolstered by a 1594 document (see Zorattini, *Processi*, vol. 7, 15). Though the conclusion of the Inquisition record is dated 1589, Zorattini also refers to a deed drawn up in Venice on 27 July, 1594. This deed, transcribed in W. Brulez, *Marchands Flamands à Venise*, vol. 1, *(1568–1605)* (Brussels: Institut Historique Belge de Rome, 1965), 179n522, refers to "Filippo Denis, [a] Portuguese merchant living in the parish of Santa Marina."

8   P. C. Ioly Zorattini, "Jews, Crypto-Jews, and the Inquisition," in *Jews of Early Modern Venice*, ed. Robert C. Davis and Benjamin Ravid (Baltimore: Johns Hopkins University Press,

Holy Office showed an attitude of leniency towards the Jews.[9] Nevertheless, it was prohibited for a Jew to live outside of the ghetto, and it was prohibited for any Christian to behave as a Jew. De Nis, who apparently was baptized as a child, but whose identity as a Christian or Jew was rather fluid, probably would not have called attention to himself at all had he remained inside the ghetto.

According to the records of the Venetian Inquisition,[10] the authorities learned of the de Nis family and its questionable practices from the testimony of Maria Lopes, who denounced her father and step-mother to the Holy Office in 1585 for the crime of Judaizing.[11] In this testimony she mentioned meeting a family of Portuguese New Christians named de Nis while traveling through Cologne on her way to Italy, and she complained that her father wanted to force her to practice as the de Nis family did. She specified some practices, such as Sabbath observance, that are commonly mentioned in accusations against Judaizers.

A few months after Lopes's complaint, the pastor of St. Leonardo Church appeared before the Venetian Inquisition to reveal Crypto-Jewish practices of the de Nis family: eating meat on days prohibited by the Church; the absence of sacred images of God, the Madonna and the saints in their home; preparing meals on Friday for Saturday; and going to the synagogue on Saturday. He also testified that they lived outside the ghetto, which was forbidden to Jews. The pastor's testimony was buttressed by other witnesses whose testimony contained similar reports of the family's behavior. This information led to the arrest of de Nis, his nephew Iacob, and two servants, who were all ordered to the Prison of the Sant'Offitio in San Marco.

On the day of his arrest, Filippo claimed he was a Jew, born a Jew, who had left Portugal to practice as a Jew in Antwerp, where he lived for many years as a Jew before moving to Venice two years earlier. He said that both he and his nephew Iacob (also a circumcised Jew) took a Christian name and wore the black hat of Christians[12] in order not to be recognized as Jews, as they did not wish to jeop-

---

2001), 104.

9   In addition to Zorattini, "Jews, Crypto-Jews," see [Pullan], 117-142, for a discussion of the different nature of the Venetian Inquisition.

10   See Zorattini, *Processi*.

11   Zorattini, "Jews, Crypto-Jews," 104.

12   The black hat was the designated headgear for Christians, the yellow head-covering for Jews (or red at a later time). See Benjamin Ravid, "From Yellow to Red: On the Distinguishing Head-Covering of the Jews of Venice," *Jewish History* 6 (1992): 179-210.

ardize his business. Nevertheless, Filippo said he had lived as a Jew, and, pressed by the accusers, he stated that it was not his intention to pass as a Christian.

However, during the course of his imprisonment and trial, de Nis changed his story several times, in particular about his circumcision, which was examined by a surgeon and a former Jew, who both testified that scar tissue would indicate that de Nis was not circumcised as an infant, as he first claimed, but as an adult. Other details in his story were problematic, causing the Inquisitors to challenge his story. Given the time and location of his birth, they believed he would have been baptized, which would make him a Judaizing Christian rather than a Jew, as he claimed. If he was a Jew, his only offense would be living outside the ghetto and wearing the Christian hat; if he was a Judaizing Christian, his offense was much more serious. And he was not able to prove that he never was baptized.

At some point in his imprisonment, two converts to Christianity were permitted to see de Nis in prison to try to convince him to repent. One testified that though he had spoken with Filippo in prison, Filippo was stubborn and wanted to die as a Jew. And yet, two days later he told the court that he had been enlightened by God and was ready to return to Christianity. He said he had done penance in prison and requested mercy. In the trial record there is no indication of what caused Filippo to change his mind.[13] Of course, given that we are to learn that he left Venice and appeared in the Ottoman Empire in a Jewish community, it is feasible that he realized that it was his best tactic to get out of prison and be able to resume his business, whether in Venice, or elsewhere.

In his final testimony, de Nis declared that about a year earlier he had been sick and called a Jewish physician, Benarogios, who circumcised him. He said that prior to that, he had found in his home a man named Iosè Naar,[14] who was there to circumcise his nephew Iacob. He claimed he had strongly protested, but

---

13 It is not likely this was torture, which was a rare occurrence in Venice. Zorattini notes very few cases of torture in the years 1541-1600; see P. C. Ioly Zorattini, "The Inquisition and the Jews in Sixteenth Century Venice," *Proceedings of the World Congress of Jewish Studies*, vol. 4 (Jerusalem: World Union of Jewish Studies, 1977), 86. According to [Pullan], 134, "the three examples of torture found among the trials for Judaizing were all concentrated in the 1580s, the decade in which the Inquisition was most aggressive towards Jews, and all three concerned young men of low standing." Although Filippo's servant Francesco was one of those examples (in November 1585), Filippo is not, nor does he fit the profile: he was a prosperous older man.

14 Zorattini, *Processi*, vol 7, 136n110, cites a reference to Cecil Roth, "I Marrani in Italia," *La Rassegna Mensile di Israel*, 2nd ser., 8, no. 9 (Winter 1934): 436-437, where we find testimony from the Lisbon Inquisition (process 5817), recorded on 4 March 1581, about a Portuguese Jew by the name of Giuseppe Naar and his relative, the doctor, Isacco Naar.

his nephew insisted, stating that he wished to join his brother.[15] The Inquisition has already made a search for Iacob, who had been released from prison some time before, but were unable to locate him.

Filippo was found guilty of being a Christian apostate who had converted to Judaism and was circumcised by Benarogios. The court also found that Filippo's nephew had been circumcised by Naar. Filippo was condemned to a term in prison and then perpetual residence in Venice at an address where he could be summoned. He was obligated to abjure Judaism, to make confession and take Communion four times a year, to recite on his knees seven penitential psalms twice a week for a year, to fast every Friday for a year, to recite the Pater Noster three times every day, and other such religious rites.

The officials of the Inquisition posted a notice requiring the doctors Benarogios and Naar to appear in court. However, they failed to appear and were held guilty of having circumcised Christians. The court perpetually banished them from Venice and from the duchy. If they returned to Venice, they would be condemned as apostates and either be burned or drowned in public.[16]

Filippo de Nis was freed from prison in 1587, but not permitted to leave Venice or the duchy. Three years later,[17] a Jesuit priest attested that Filippo was a good Christian, deserving of praise and consolation.

However, as it turns out, this was not the conclusion of the saga of Filippo de Nis, as becomes clear from the responsum presented below, which was written by Ha-Kohen at an indeterminate date after July 1594.[18]

---

15   This was an indication that he planned on leaving for the Ottoman domain, where his brother resided, and returning to practice the Jewish faith openly.
16   According to Zorattini, this was among the harsher punishments meted out by the Venetian Inquisition; see "Inquisition, Sixteenth Century," 86 and P. C. Ioly Zorattini, "The Inquisition and the Jews in 17th and 18th Century Venice," *Proceedings of the World Congress of Jewish Studies, Div. B*, vol. 2 (Jerusalem: World Union of Jewish Studies, 1989), 191.
17   January 3, 1589, following a series of events related in [Koren].
18   In 1594 Filippo was still in Venice (see Brulez, *Marchands Flamands*, 179n522), but by the time of the responsum he had left there.

Halakhic Background

The texts upon which Ha-Kohen relies in his halakhic discussion include some of the most foundational and classic texts in Jewish ethics,[19] texts that address moral questions frequently raised and debated in courses on the philosophy of law, political philosophy, and similar fields.[20]

Other texts that Ha-Kohen might have used but did not—texts that relate to the laws of an "informer" or "betrayer"—are also included here.

The first text is Maimonides's codification of the laws that relate to *qiddush ha-Shem*—sanctification of the name of God.[21] Understanding these laws is essential when considering a forced convert or a Jew who transgresses under duress, and they are an important thread in Ha-Kohen's responsum.

Maimonides *MT Hilkhot Yᵉsodei Ha-Torah* (The Laws of the Foundations of the Torah) 5	רמב״ם משנה תורה הלכות יסודי התורה ה

1 All Jews[22] are commanded to [act for] the sanctification of the great name [of God], as is stated, *I will be sanctified in the midst of the children of Israel* (Lev. 22:32), and admonished not to profane it [His name], as is stated [there], *do not profane My holy name*. How [is this enacted]? When a Gentile arises and forces a Jew to transgress any one of all the commandments that are commanded in the Torah, else he will kill him[23]—he should transgress and not be killed, as is stated regarding commandments *that a person should do them and live by them* (Lev.

א כל בית ישראל מצווין על קדוש השם הגדול הזה, שנאמר ״ונקדשתי בתוך בני ישראל״, ומוזהרין שלא לחללו, שנאמר ״ולא תחללו את שם קדשי״. כיצד, בשעה שיעמוד

---

19 In the field of medical ethics, halakhic discussions of triage frequently refer to some of these texts. See, for example, Elliot N. Dorff, *Matters of Life and Death: A Jewish Approach to Modern Medical Ethics* (Philadelphia: Jewish Publication Society, 1998), 291-299.

20 For example, in chapter 1 of [Sandel2] (as well as the author's renowned course at Harvard University and its companion book [Sandel]) some similar questions are raised, though in different contexts. The halakhic sources in this chapter can serve as a resource to widen the scope of the discussion to include the perspective of the Sages on these moral issues. The questions for further discussion ask the reader to utilize the halakhic texts to consider some of the questions on which Professor Sandel deliberates.

21 These laws as codified by Maimonides are primarily based on *Sanhedrin* 74.

22 Lit., "the entire House of Israel."

23 All the laws of sanctification of the name of God apply to men and women alike.

18:5), and not that he should die by them. If he [chooses to] die rather than to transgress, then he is responsible for his own death.[24]

2 In what [situation] are these things said? In all the commandments, with the exception of pagan worship, forbidden sexual relationships and murder. For any of these three sins, if he [the Gentile] should tell him to transgress one of them or else be killed, he should be killed rather than transgress.

In what [situation] are these things said? When a Gentile intends [this] for his own benefit, such as if he forced him to build his house on Shabbat or to cook his dish [on Shabbat], or if he raped a woman, and the like. But if his intent is solely to cause him to transgress the commandments, then if he is by himself, and there are not ten Jews present, he should transgress and not be killed, while if he forces him to transgress with ten Jews [present], he should [allow himself to] be killed rather than transgress, even if he [the Gentile] intended for him to transgress merely one of the other commandments [i.e., not those three mentioned above].

3 All these statements [apply] when it is not a time of persecution; but in a time of persecution, such as when a wicked king like Nebuchadnezzar and his cohorts arises and decrees persecution of the Jews, to nullify their religion or [even] one

גוי ויאנוס את ישראל לעבור על אחת מכל מצות האמורות בתורה או יהרגנו, יעבור ולא ייהרג שנאמר במצות, "אשר יעשה אותם האדם וחי בהם", ולא שימות בהם. ואם מת ולא עבר, הרי זה מתחייב בנפשו:

ב במה דברים אמורים, בשאר מצוות חוץ מעבודה זרה וגילוי עריות ושפיכת דמים, אבל שלש עבירות אלו, אם יאמר לו, עבור על אחת מהן או תיהרג, ייהרג ואל יעבור:

במה דברים אמורים, בזמן שהגוי מתכוון להנאת עצמו, כגון שאנסו לבנות לו ביתו בשבת, או לבשל לו תבשילו, או אנס אשה לבועלה, וכיוצא בזה, אבל אם נתכוון להעבירו על המצוות בלבד, אם היה בינו לבין עצמו ואין שם עשרה מישראל, יעבור ואל ייהרג, ואם אנסו להעבירו בעשרה מישראל, ייהרג ואל יעבור, ואפילו לא נתכוון להעבירו אלא על מצוה משאר מצוות בלבד:

ג וכל הדברים האלו שלא בשעת השמד, אבל בשעת השמד, והוא

---

24 The phrase *mithayev b'nafsho* actually means he is obligated with his own life, i.e., obligated in the death penalty, clearly not practical in this case. The expression here indicates the gravity of the transgression and is understood to mean that in the World to Come the transgressor will be duly punished. Not all authorities maintain the same opinion on this matter. For example, the Tosafot (*'Avoda Zara* 27b at *yakhol afilu b'farhesya*) state that a person is permitted, if he wishes, to be more stringent with himself (and be killed rather than transgress). See Halakhic Background in the chapter "What's in a Name?"

commandment of the commandments, he should [let himself] be killed and not transgress, even for one of the other commandments [other than the three], whether he was forced in the midst of ten [Jews] or whether he was forced when he was alone among Gentiles.

4 Whoever it is said of him that he should transgress and not [allow himself to] be killed, but [allowed himself to be] killed and did not transgress, is responsible for his own death. And whoever it is said of him that he should be killed rather than transgress and is killed, he has sanctified the name [of God], and if he was among ten Jews, then he sanctified the name in public, like Daniel, Ḥananya, Mishael, and Azarya,[25] and Rabbi Akiva and his colleagues,[26] and these are the [Ten] Martyrs, for whom there is no level higher than theirs, about whom it is said, *For Your sake, we are slain all day, we are considered like sheep for the slaughter* (Ps. 44:23) and about whom it is said, *Gather my devoted ones to me, who have made the covenant with me over sacrifice* (Ps. 50:5).

But whoever it is said of him that he should be killed and not transgress, but transgressed and was not killed—he profanes the name [of God], and if it was in [the presence of] ten Jews, then he profaned the name in public and nullified a positive commandment, which is sanctification of the name, and violated a negative commandment, which is profaning the name. Even so, because he

---

25 Dan. 3.

26 Who were executed by the ancient Romans. For a historical perspective, see Yair Furstenberg, "Was There a 'Period of Persecution (*Shemad*)'? Images of Religious Persecution in Rabbinic Literature" [Hebrew], *Zion* 85 (2020): 129-149.

transgressed under coercion, he is not given lashes [by the religious court], and it is not [even] necessary to say that he is not put to death by a religious court, even if he killed under coercion, because	מלקין אותו, ואין צריך לומר שאין ממיתין אותו בית דין, אפילו הרג באונס, שאין מלקין וממיתין אלא לעובר ברצונו ובעדים והתראה

only one who transgresses of his own will and with witnesses and a warning is given lashes or put to death.[27]

Ha-Kohen cites the following two sources, which are in a similar vein.

Mishna T^erumot 8:12	**משנה תרומות ח,יב**
Similarly, women to whom Gentiles said, "Give us one of you to be defiled; otherwise we will defile all of you"—all of them should be defiled, rather than that they should hand over to them even one Jewish soul.	וכן נשים שאמרו להן גוים תנו לנו אחת מכם תיטמא ואם לאו הרי אנו מטמאין את כולכם יטמאו את כולם ואל ימסרו להם נפש אחת מישרא׳[ל]

JT T^erumot 8:10 (46b)	**תלמוד ירושלמי תרומות ח,י (מו, ב)**
[Suppose] a group of people are walking on their way, and they were encountered by some Gentiles who said, "Surrender one of you and we will kill him, and if [you] do not, then we will kill all of you"—even if all would be killed, they should not hand over even one Jewish soul. [But if] they were to specify one [among them,] like Sheva,	סיעות בני אדם שהיו מהלכין בדרך ופגעו להן גוים ואמרו תנו לנו אחד מכם ונהרוג אותו ואם לאו הרי אנו הורגין את כולכם אפילו כולן נהרגין לא ימסרו נפש אחת מיש׳[ראל] ייחדו להן אחד כגון שבע בן בכרי ימסרו אותו ולא ייהרגו אמ׳[ר] ר׳[בי] שמעון בן לקיש והוא שיהא חייב מיתה

the son of Bikhri,[28] they should hand him over and not be killed. R. Simeon ben

---

27 The fourth halakha in this selection is truncated here, the remaining portion being less relevant (and the last portion that begins *aval im yakhol* as is found in most common printed editions was not in Maimonides's original text but was anonymously inserted later).

28 Who revolted against King David (2 Sam. 20).

Laqish said, "[That is so, provided that] he is deserving of [the penalty of] death, as was Sheva, the son of Bikhri," but R. Yoḥanan said, "Even though he is not deserving of death like Sheva, the son of Bikhri, [if he is singled out, he should be surrendered]."

כשבע בן בכרי ור'[בי] יוחנן אמ[ר] אע"פ [=אף על פי] שאינו חייב מיתה כשבע בן בכרי

The two sources above present cases of groups of people. An argument can be made that surrendering one singled-out person to avoid the deaths of several people is the least of the evils. Ha-Kohen compares such a situation to a one-on-one situation, found in the following source, which follows a statement in the gᵉmara that the obligation that one must submit to death rather than to commit murder is based on reason.

Pᵉsaḥim 25b[29]   פסחים כ"ה ב'

Like him who came before Rava and said, "The governor of my village told me, go kill so-and-so, and if [you] do not, I shall kill you." He [Rava] said to him, "[Let him kill you, but do not kill.] Why would you think[30] that your blood is redder? Perhaps that man's blood is redder!"

כי ההוא דאתא לקמיה דרבא א"ל [אמר ליה] מרי דוראי אמר לי זיל קטליה לפלני[א] ואי לא קטלינא לך א"ל [אמר ליה] ליקטלוך ולא תיקטול מאי חזית דדמא דידך סומק טפי דילמא דמא דההוא גברא סומק טפי

The following law relates to the "informer" or "betrayer" (moser), a term that Ha-Kohen frequently used to refer to de Nis. Though Ha-Kohen did not cite this law, it is implicit in the dialectic.

---

29 This same incident is told in Sanhedrin 74a and in Yoma 82b (though in Sanhedrin it is told of Raba rather than Rava, whose names are often confused in the texts; in this case, examining the manuscripts does not provide a definitive name). Sanhedrin might be the more natural source, but given that Ha-Kohen cites this from Pᵉsaḥim, it was selected here.

30 Lit., "what did you see [to make you think] ..."

Maimonides *MT Hilkhot T^eshuva* (The Laws of Repentance) 3,12[31]	רמב"ם הלכות תשובה ג:יב

... there are two types of betrayers: the one who delivers his fellow to the hands of a Gentile to be killed or beaten, and the one who turns over his fellow's money to a Gentile or a brute, who [though he might technically be Jewish] is regarded as a Gentile. Neither of the two has a portion in the World to Come.

שנים הם המוסרין המוסר חבירו ביד גוים להרגו או להכותו והמוסר ממון חבירו ביד גוים או ביד אנס שהוא כגוי שניהן אין להם חלק לעולם הבא.

Discussion

There are three commandments for which a Jew is obligated to submit his life, rather than transgress. One of them is murder;[32] another is the prohibition against pagan worship.

Ha-Kohen addresses the case of de Nis in light of each of these weighty and grave questions: According to Jewish law, was de Nis guilty of murder by informing on the two circumcisers (since, Ha-Kohen thought, they would be subject to the death penalty according to Venetian law)? Should he have allowed himself even to be killed rather than inform on them? If the answer to those questions is in the affirmative, did he inform on them under coercion, so that he could not be held accountable? And regarding de Nis's conversion to Christianity, was he in a situation of being obligated in the commandment to sanctify the name of God, and guilty of not doing so?

According to *MT Hilkhot T^eshuva* 3,12, de Nis might be considered a *moser*. Following study of the responsum, it would be reasonable to consider whether Ha-Kohen absolved de Nis of guilt under the specifications of this law.

---

31 See also *MT Hilkhot Ḥovel U-Mazziq* (The Laws of Injury and Damages) 8,9.

32 Yet, according to some authorities the halakha is that it is not considered murder if a Gentile specifies the person to be surrendered and killed, while other authorities maintain that even if a person is singled out, it is considered like murder to surrender him, unless he is deserving of a death penalty for some other reason. See note 40.

Responsum

Maharshakh Responsum 4,31	שו״ת מהרש״ך חלק ד סימן לא

Question: Instruct us, our rabbi, [on the following matter]: A Portuguese forced convert (*anus*)[33] was in Venice and was caught by the Inquisition, and they found that he was circumcised. He saved himself by apostasy. The interrogators demanded that he tell them who circumcised him, and this apostate could have saved himself by saying that a passerby from Ashkenaz or Turkey circumcised him, but this apostate wickedly said that Reuben[34] circumcised him. Not only this did he do, but to demonstrate how sincerely he had apostatized, he [also] informed on Simon and told that he circumcised his [the apostate's] nephew, which was not requested of him. [The result] was such that Reuben had to flee for his life to another land, and the members of his family and the[ir] children had to follow him, and they sold all of their possessions for whatever they could get at that moment of urgency, and there were many expenses until they reached the Turkish Empire.

שאלה ילמדנו רבינו אנוס א[י]/[חד] מאנוסי פורטוגאל היה בויניציא ונתפש ביד החוקרי[ן]ם ומצאוהו מהול והציל עצמו כשנשתמד ובקשו ממנו החוקרים שיגיד להם מי מל אותו והיה יכול המשומד ההוא להציל עצמו כשהיה אומר שאיש אחד מאשכנז או מתוגרמה עבר אצלו ומל אותו אבל המשומד ההוא הרשיע ואמ[ו]/[ר] כי ראובן מל אותו ולא זו בלבד עשה אלא כדי להראות את עצמו שהיה משתמד בלב שלם הלשין את שמעון ואמר עליו שהוא מל לבן אחיו מה שלא נדרש על ככה באופן שהוצרך ראובן לברוח להמלט על נפשו אל ארץ אחרת וגם אנשי ביתו והטף הוצרכו ללכת אחריו ומכרו כל כלי הבית ותקוניה כאשר מצאו בשעת הדחק ועשו הוצאות רבות עד בואם למלכות תוגרמה:

---

33 A discussion of the Hebrew terms used in both question and response is in order. Various terms are used to refer to the defendant, so that at one moment he is called *anus* (forced convert), which is a term used in Jewish law for someone compelled to transgress, and at another he is called *mᵉshummad* or *mumar*. Both of these can be translated as "apostate," but I use "apostate" for one and "renegade" for the other, to maintain a distinction in the translation. *Anus* is generally considered to reflect a forgiving attitude towards the *converso*; *mᵉshummad* or *mumar* are generally derogatory.

34 A pseudonym; it is usual for pseudonyms to be used in naming the protagonists in responsa literature.

Please instruct us, our rabbi, if the betrayer [*moser*] is obligated to pay Reuben for all the damages that he incurred as a result of this betrayal, considering that they [the interrogators] did not specify that he betray Reuben, and also considering that he could have saved himself without betraying anyone; further, because according to the [Jewish] law he [the apostate] should have [allowed himself] to be killed rather than transgress. Further, [damages should be paid because] as a result of this betrayal Reuben lost his livelihood, as if he were admitted to a room that was locked in his face. [The apostate] has even further culpability because he instigated and misled in what he wrote and influenced the Inquisitors to send after his [Reuben's] wife and sons, who were in a city of refuge for the community of Israel, and they took them, and they apostatized. Therefore, it becomes clear that all he [the apostate] did, he did with malfeasance, treachery and to *commit a trespass against the Lord* (Num. 5:6) and against Reuben.

ילמדנו רבינו אם חייב המוסר לשלם לראובן כל הנזק הנמשך לו מחמת המסירה הנז'/כרת] בהיות שלא יחדו לו שימסור לראובן ומה גם כי היה יכול להציל עצמו מבלי מסירת שום אדם ומה גם כי מן הדין היה שיהרג ולא יעבור וגם מחמת המסירה הנז'/כרת] נתבטל ראובן ממלאכתו והוי כאילו הכניסו לחדר ונעל בפניו ואף גם זאת הרבה אשמה כי אשתו ובניו של ראובן שהיו בערי המקלט בתוך מחנה ישראל הסית והדיח בכתביו והשתדל עם החוקרים שישלחו אחריהם ולקחום ונשתמדו א״כ [אם כן] מכל זה נתברר שכל מה שעשה בפשע ובמעל עשה למעול מעל בה' ובראובן הנז'/כר]:

תשובה תחילת כל דבר ראיתי לכתוב על מה שבא בשאלה לתת טעם לחייב למומר המוסר לשלם לראובן כל מה שהזיקו מכח מסירותו לפי שעבר על דבר שהדין נותן כי מן הדין היה שיהרג ואל יעבור ומפשט הדברים יראה דהכוונה היא על מה שנשתמד והמיר דתו כי אעפ״י [אף על פי] שאם לא היה משתמד היו ממיתים אותו

Response: I thought it fit[35] to write first of all about what is expressed in the question—that, considering that he [the betrayer] transgressed the law, because according to the law he should have [allowed himself] to be killed rather than transgress, the renegade betrayer should therefore be obligated to pay to Reuben all the damages that resulted from his being betrayed. It seems that the plain meaning of what is said is that this refers to the informer apostatizing and converting, for even though, had he not apostatized they would have put him

---

35 Lit., "I saw."

to death,[36] in any event he should have given his life and be killed, rather than transgress. [1][37] However, that betrayal of his—to inform and say that Reuben circumcised him—he did not say this under duress, [but] rather out of total free will, as is stated in the question, that had he said "a passerby from Ashkenaz or Turkey circumcised me," he could have [also] saved his life. So what is stated in the question—that he transgressed the law—because according to the law he should have [allowed himself] to be killed rather than transgress—only relates to the fact that he apostatized, since the apostasy was under duress [not the betrayal].

[2] [Even] if we say that the betrayal by which he informed that Reuben was the *mohel* was also under duress—because it is not reasonable to think they would

מ״מ [מכל מקום] היה לו למסור נפשו ליהרג ולא יעבור אמנם המסירות שעשה להלשין ואמר שראובן מלו לא אמר כן מחמת אונס שאנסוהו אלא ברצון מוחלט וכמו שבא בשאלה שאם היה אומר אדם א׳[חד] מאשכנז או מתוגרמה עבר עליו ומלני היה מציל נפשו באופן שמה שבא בשאלה שעבר על מה שהדין נותן שיהרג ואל יעבור אינו אלא על מה שנשתמד שהמשומדות היה באונס:

ואם באנו לומר שגם המסירות שהלשין על ראובן שהוא היה המוהל היה באונס כי אינו עולה על הדעת שאם היה אומר אדם א׳[חד] מאשכנז או מתוגרמה עבר עלי ומלני שהיו מאמינים אותו שכיון שהיה במקום שיש מוהלים מוחזקי׳[ם] שהמתין לימול עד שיעבור איש נכרי מארץ אחרת אשר לא הוחזק אצלו

have believed him had he said that "a passerby from Ashkenaz or Turkey circumcised me," that he waited for a stranger from another land with no known reputation for expertise in circumcising adults like him, since there were local reputable

---

36   In fact, a death sentence was not a likely consequence in the Venetian Inquisition. There were no capital sentences issued by the Venetian Inquisition during that period (Zorattini, "Inquisition, Sixteenth Century," 86). In the eyes of the Inquisition, Filippo de Nis was a baptized Christian, guilty of Judaizing. Had he refused to "repent and return" to being a devout Christian, the worst sentence he was likely to have received was either banishment or condemnation to the galleys (though certainly this might well have resulted in death for a man his age). However, neither the defendant, the plaintiff, nor the rabbi would have known this, and they certainly were familiar with Inquisitions whose punishments were death. In addition, Cardinal Savello had sent a letter requesting the extradition of de Nis to Rome to be interrogated, hoping to be able to expose other Judaizing Portuguese New Christians ([Pullan], 46-50). Though this did not occur, the threat and fear of the worst cannot be ignored. But for the point of the responsum, one could say that if Jewish law states that the defendant should have allowed himself to be killed rather than transgress, then certainly he should have endured a lesser, noncapital punishment rather than transgress.

37   Numbers are inserted to facilitate reading the discussion following the responsum.

mohalim, so that they certainly would not have released him until he told who among those in the city circumcised him, and if he did not tell, they would put him to death—nevertheless, it seems appropriate to examine whether the law would be that he should submit his life rather than betray. To comprehend this law, it must be clarified from what is explained in the Jerusalem Talmud about the *mishna* taught in chapter eight of *T^erumot*: Women to whom Gentiles said, "Give us one of you to be defiled," etc.[38] This is what is found there: It is taught: [Suppose] a group of people were walking on their way, and they were encountered by some Gentiles who said: "Surrender one of you, and we will kill him, and if [you] do not, then we will kill all of you"—even if all would be killed, they should not hand over even one Jewish soul. [But if] they were to specify one like Sheva, the son of Bikhri, they should hand him over and not be killed. R. Simeon ben Laqish said: [Provided] he is deserving of the penalty of death, as was Sheva, the son of Bikhri. But R. Yoḥanan said: Even though he is not deserving of death like Sheva, the son of Bikhri [if he is singled out, he should be surrendered].[39] The esteemed rabbi, our teacher R. Joseph Caro, wrote:[40] "This means that the law is according to R. Yoḥanan, and so we see

לבקי ומומחה למול אנשים גדולים כמוהו ובודאי לא היו פוטרין אותו עד שיאמ[ר] להם מי מאנשי העיר מלו ואם לא יגיד ימיתוהו יש מקום לכאורה לדקדק אם הדין נותן שיהרג ואל ימסור ולעמוד על דין זה יתבאר ממה שבא בירושלמי עלה דמתני[תין] דתנן בפ"ח [פרק ח'] דתרומות נשים שאמרו להן גוים תנו לנו אחת מכם ונטמאה כו'[לי] והכי איתא התם תניא סיעת בני אדם מהלכים בדרך ופגעו בהם גוים ואמרו תנו לנו א'[חד] מכם ונהרוג אותו ואם לאו הרי אנו הורגים את כולכם אפי'[לו] כולם נהרגים לא ימסרו נפש א'[חת] מישראל יחדו להם א' כגון שבע בן בכרי ימסרו אותו ואל יהרגו א"ר [אמר רבי] שמעון בן לקיש והוא שיהיה חייב מיתה כשבע בן בכרי ור'[בי] יוחנן אמר אע"פ [אף על פי] שאינו חייב מיתה כשבע בן בכרי וכתב ה"ה [הרב הגאון] מהרי"קא [מורנו הרב יוסף קארו] דמשמע דהלכה כר"יי [כרבי יוחנן] וכן נר[אה]

---

38 Mishna *T^erumot* 8:12; see Halakhic Background.
39 JT *T^erumot* 8:10 (46b); see Halakhic Background.
40 *Bet Yosef* YD 157:1. R. Caro explains there that in a dispute between R. Yoḥanan and R. Simeon ben Laqish, the law is according to R. Yoḥanan, and noted that several authorities ruled according to R. Yoḥanan. Caro provides the reasoning for the ruling in this situation: once someone is singled out to be surrendered to the Gentile to be killed, whether or not he is deserving of a death penalty, it is not considered murder on the part of the Jews who hand him over. Caro also provides a possible explanation for why Maimonides ruled according to

from the words of Rabbenu Samson in [his] commentary on the Mishna[41] and from the words of the Ran in tractate *Yoma*."[42]

Thus, it can be seen that since the interrogation of the betrayer by the Gentiles was such that [they demanded] he tell them and inform them who of the *mohalim* in the city circumcised him, and it would not satisfy [them] otherwise—as I wrote, it is as if they specified a person, and in any case he would have had to inform on one of the *mohalim*, so it is certainly more appropriate that he should inform on Reuben, who circumcised him, and not some other *mohel* who did not circumcise him. This cannot be disputed by saying that the ruling according to R. Yoḥanan (that when one person is specified, even though he is not deserving of death, they can surrender him rather than be killed) is the case when there is a group of people who are ordered to "hand over a specific person and we will kill him"—because then it is the law that they should turn

מדברי רבי׳[נו] שמשון בפי׳[רוש] המשנה ומדברי הר״ן [הרב ניסים] במסכת יומא

והנה יראה דכיון דחקירת הגוים על המוסר היתה שיגיד להם וימסור להם מי ממוהלי העיר מלהו דלא סגי בלאו הכי כמו שכתבתי הוי כאילו יחדו לו איש א׳ ועכ״פ [ועל כל פנים] צריך למסור איש מהמוהלים ובודאי שיותר ראוי שימסור לראובן שמל אותו ולא למוהל אחר שלא מל אותו ואין לחלק ולומר דמה שפסקו כר׳[בי] יוחנן כשיחדו להם איש מיוחד אעפ״יי [אף על פי] שלא יהא חייב מיתה שיכולין למסור אותו ואל יהרגו היינו כשהם סיעת בני אדם שאומרים להם תנו לנו א׳ מיוחד מכם ונהרגהו דאז דין הוא שימסרוהו ואל יהרגו כולם בעבורו אמנם כשאינו אלא א׳ שאונסים אותו שיראה להם לפלוני כדי להורגו ואם לא יהרגו אותו דין הוא שיהרג ואל יראה אותו מטעם מאי חזית דדמא דידך סומק טפי דלמא דמא דחברך סומק טפי וכההיא עובדא

him over rather than for everyone to be killed to save him, but that when there is only one who is being compelled to inform on so-and-so (who is to be killed), and if he does not then they will kill him, it is the law that he should [allow himself to] be killed, rather than to inform, because "why would you think your blood is redder? Perhaps your fellow's blood is redder?" [That reasoning] is like

---

R. Simeon ben Laqish (*MT Hilkhot Y*sodei Ha-Torah* 5,5; this is the halakha that follows the first citation from *MT* in Halakhic Background).

41 R. Samson ben Abraham of Sens, twelfth-century Tosafist, Mishna *T*rumot* 8:12.

42 R. Nissim Gerondi (1310?–1375?), *Yoma* 4a on the pages of the Rif (R. Isaac Alfasi, 1013–1103) at *u-mihu*.

the case cited in the Talmud, in *P*sahim, chapter "The whole time" [25b]: Like him who came before Rava and said, "The governor of my village told me, go kill so-and-so, and if [you] do not, I shall kill you." He [Rava] said to him: "Why would you think that your blood is redder? Perhaps your fellow's[43] blood is redder!" Thus, [one would think] specifically when [the case is] one in relation to one, it is relevant to say "why would you think your blood is redder, etc." However, when there are many who are being forced and they are told to surrender so-and-so, certainly they should hand over that person, because many [lives] take precedence over one, and it is not relevant to say "why do you think, etc." And we accept this. And if so, in our case of the betrayer who was told to betray the *mohel* who circumcised him and if he did not they would kill him, considering that it is one in relation to one, it would seem that it would be

דמייתי תלמודא בפסחי'[ם] פרק כל שעה דההוא דאתא לקמיה דרבא א״ל [אמר ליה] מארי דוראי אמר לי זיל קטליה לפלניה ואי לא קטילנא לך א״ל [אמר ליה] מאי חזית דדמא דידך סומק טפי דלמא דמא דחברך סומק טפי דהיינו דוקא חד לגבי חד שייך לומר מאי חזית דדמא דידך סומק טפי כו'[לי] אמנם כשהם רבים הנאנסים שאומרי'[ם] להם שימסרו את פ'[לוני] ודאי שיתנו להם אותו פ'[לוני] דרבים עדיפי מיחיד ולא שייך לומר מאי חזי'[ת] כו'[לי] וק״ל [וקיימא לן] וא״כ [ואם כן] בנ״ד [בנדון דידן] דאותו המוסר שאמרו לו שיראה להם המוהל שמל אותו ואם לא יראה להם שיהרגוהו כיון דהוי חד לגבי חד נר'[אה] דהיה מקום לומ'[ר] מאי חזית דדמא דידך סומק טפי כו'[לי] כך היה נר'[אה] לומר לכאורה אמנם כד מעיינן נר'[אה] דיש לחלק מההיא דמאי דאמרי'[נן] ברוצח יהרג ואל יעבור מטעמא דמאי חזית

appropriate to say "why would you think your blood is redder, etc." Such it would seem should be said, at the outset. However, when we examine [further], we see that this should be disputed. Because what we say regarding a murderer—that he should be killed rather than transgress based on the reasoning of "why would you think, etc."—applies to the situation in which they tell him that he himself should kill him [so-and-so], and in such [a case] we certainly would say "why would you think, etc." But in our case—where they did not say to him that he himself should kill him, but rather that he should point him out to them and betray him to them—in such a case certainly we do not say that he should be killed rather

---

43 The printed editions (both Vilna and Venice) and most manuscripts have "that man's"; however, JTS Rab. 1623/2 (EMC 271) is in agreement with Ha-Kohen's citation "your fellow's."

than transgress.[44] It should be ruled thus, according to what we say, that a murderer is killed by a court of law only if he himself kills. If he commands or manipulates to kill someone, such as by setting a dog on him or causing a snake to bite him, he is not executed by the court, but rather his death is in the hands of Heaven.[45] This shows that in such cases it is not identified as murder, such that we say he should be killed rather than transgress. Rather, [we say this] only when he himself kills him. Therefore, in our case, [we say] that what they were compelling him to tell and show them who the *mohel* was who circumcised him, and they would do with him [the *mohel*] as they wished—in such [a case] we do not say that he should be killed rather than transgress. So the reasoning that appears in the question—that the renegade should have let himself be killed rather than transgress on account of informing—is not appropriate, but rather [can only be said] on account of the apostasy.

[3] The words of the questioner are to be criticized.[46] For what [justification] does he have to give that the reason the renegade should be obligated [to pay damages is] because he transgressed and sinned when the law states that he should have [allowed] himself to be killed rather than transgress—when in fact what the law states is that he should be killed rather than transgress for his apostasy,

וכו׳[לי] היינו כשאומרים לו שיהרגהו הוא בעצמו בהאי ודאי נאמר מאי חזית וכו׳[לי] אמנם בנ״ד [בנדון דידן] שלא היו אומרים לו שיהרגהו הוא בעצמו אלא שיראה אותו להם וימסרהו לידם בהא ודאי לא אמרי׳[נן] יהרג ואל יעבור ויש לדון כן ממאי דאמרי׳[נן] שאין הרוצח נהרג בב״ד [בבית דין] אלא כשהורג הוא בעצמו אמנם כשמצוי׳[ה] או מסבב להורגו כגון ששה בו כלב או השיך בו את הנחש אינו נהרג בב״ד [בבית דין] אלא מיתתו בידי שמים דיר׳[אה] דבכה״ג [דבכהאי גוונא] לא מקרי רוצח דאמרי׳[נן] ביה יהרג ולא יעבור אלא דוקא כשהורגו הוא בעצמו א״כ [אם כן] בנ״ד [בנדון דידן] שמה שהיו אונסי׳[ם] אותו שיגיד ויראה להם מי היה מוהל שמל אותו והם יעשו אותו כרצונם בהא לא אמרינן יהרג ואל יעבור באופן שאין מקום לטעם הבא בשאלה שיהיה לו לומר ליהרג ואל יעבור מטעם המסירות כי אם מטעם השמדות

ויש לתפוש על דברי השואל דמה לו לתת טעם לחייב למומר מטעם שעבר על עבירה שהדין נותן דיהרג ואל יעבור כי הנה מה שהדין נותן

---

44 Compare to *Tosafot Sanhedrin* 74b at *v*ʿha Esther*.
45 *Sanhedrin* 76b. See also MT *Hilkhot Rotseʾaḥ* (The Laws of the Murderer) 3,10.
46 This translation of *litpos* is in accordance with Bʿrakhot 50a, *en tofsin oto* (one does not criticize him).

while the obligation that the questioner comes to obligate the betrayer is for [damages] that resulted from him betraying Reuben. If the betrayal of Reuben was under duress—because if he did not say that Reuben circumcised him they would have killed him—then, granted that on the matter of apostasy the law is that he should be killed rather than transgress. [But] on what basis can he be obligated [to pay damages] because he transgressed in a matter where the law states that he should [in fact] transgress rather than be killed?[47] And if his informing on Reuben was without duress, but rather totally out of choice, as appears initially from the language in the question, then even if the law allowed him to transgress and apostatize rather than be killed, what would be the grounds to absolve him [from punishment] for informing without duress?

I will further inform the questioner, who justified obligating the cited informer[48] [to pay damages] for the reason that he transgressed in a matter where the law rules he should have [allowed himself] to be killed and not transgress—it seems that he maintains and thinks that someone who does transgress in a matter where the law rules that he should [allow himself] to be killed rather than transgress is wholly sinful, and therefore it is appropriate to obligate him. This is not so! See here what Ribash[49] wrote

---

47 I.e., turning over someone, perhaps to be killed, but by another force.

48 Here the word for informer is *malshin*. For the connotations of this term in the Hebrew liturgy, see Uri Ehrlich and Ruth Langer, "Earliest Texts of the *Birkat Haminim*," *Hebrew Union College Annual* 76 (2005): 63-112.

49 R. Isaac ben Sheshet Perfet, 1326–1408.

in section 11:⁵⁰ "You should know that one who transgresses all the commandments in the Torah under compulsion, and has even committed acts of idolatry such that the law is that he should [allow himself to] be killed rather than transgress—if he [nevertheless] transgressed and was [thus] not killed, he is not disqualified from being a witness,⁵¹ because he did so under force and due to the fear of death that fell upon him. In those countries⁵² where the law is that one should [allow himself to] be killed rather than transgress, if someone transgressed and [thus] was not killed, then he did not fulfill the commandment *you shall love the Lord, your God* (Deut. 6:5);⁵³ and if he did so in public before ten Jews, then he did not fulfill the commandment *I will be sanctified in the midst of the children of Israel* (Lev. 22:32) and transgressed the commandment *do not profane My holy name* (Lev. 22:32).⁵⁴ Nevertheless, because he only profaned Him under compulsion, he is not disqualified from being a witness, because a court of law does not punish him [but rather it is in the hands of Heaven]." The cited rabbi [Ribash continued there] and wrote: "The Rashba⁵⁵ also wrote in a responsum: 'A Jew who has apostatized out of fear, even though he has sinned, is [still] a Jew. And even though he should have [allowed himself] to be killed

ע״ז [עבודה זרה] שהדין הוא שיהרג ואל יעבור אם עבר ולא נהרג ולא נפסל לעדות כיון שעשה כן באונס ומפני אימת מות דנפלו עליו ואעפ״י [ואף על פי] שבאותם מדינות שדינים שיהרג ואל יעבור אם עבר ולא נהרג לא קיים מצות ואהבת את ה׳ אלדיך כו[לו] ואם עשה כן בפרהסייא בפני י׳ מישראל לא קיים מצות ונקדשתי בתוך בני ישראל ועבר על לא תחללו את שם קדשי מ״מ [מכל מקום] כיון שלא חללו אלא מתוך האונס לא נפסל לעדות כיון שאין ב״ד [בית דין] עונשי[ם] אותו וכתב הרב הנז׳[כר] וז״ל [וזה לשונו] גם הרשב״א כתב בתשובה ישראל דנשתמד מחמת יראה אעפ״י [אף על פי] שחטא

---

50   *Responsa of R. Isaac ben Sheshet*, 11. According to the Valencia court records, Ribash was himself baptized under coercion on 4 July 1391 (9th of Av) and a year and a half later managed to leave Valencia and return to living openly as a Jew (Hirsch Jacob Zimmels and David Derovan, "Isaac ben Sheshet Perfet," in EJ, 10:49).

51   Wholly sinful people are disqualified from being a witness in court.

52   Those countries where there is forced conversion. See MT Hilkhot Yᵉsodei Ha-Torah 5,1-3.

53   The verse continues *with all your heart and with all your soul and with all your might*. In Bᵉrakhot 61b, the Sages teach that *with all your soul* means "even if He takes your life."

54   In *Sanhedrin* 74b, this verse is interpreted to derive the ruling that in the presence of ten Jews a Jew must allow himself to be killed rather than transgress any commandment under duress. See also MT Hilkhot Yᵉsodei Ha-Torah, 5,1-2 in Halakhic Background.

55   R. Solomon ben Abraham Adret, c. 1235–c. 1310.

rather than transgress—as is written *I will be sanctified in the midst of the children of Israel*—nevertheless, because he does this out of fear—that is to say, fear lest they kill him—because he is not guilty of an offense convicted in a court of law and it is written *he shall live by them* (Lev. 18:5), and not die by them,[56] they are Jews, and [an animal they ritually] slaughter is permitted [to be eaten], and wine they touch is not prohibited.'"[57, 58] Therefore, we see that the reasoning presented in the question—to obligate the informer because he transgressed a commandment when the law demands that he [allow himself to] be killed rather than transgress—is not a reason at all to obligate him.

[4] Now I come to what Reuben complained about the said betrayer—and this is the main point of his question: that because of his betrayal, he [Reuben] had to spend large quantities [of money], as was related in the question, and he asks if the law would obligate the informer to pay him his expenditures, due to his betrayal. Let us assume that his betrayal, as mentioned, was done willingly, without duress.

I say that the essence of this matter is [found] in chapter "One who brings" [*Bava Qamma* 62a] regarding one who is betrayed.[59] It is asked if they [the

ישראל הוא ואעפ״י [ואף על פי] שהיה לו ליהרג ואל יעבור מדכתי׳[ב] ונקדשתי בתוך בני ישראל מ״מ [מכל מקום] כיון שמחמת יראה הוא עושה ר״ל [רוצה לומר] מפחד שלא יהרגוהו כיון שאין עליו חיוב ב״ד [בית דין] בשביל כך וכתי׳[ב] וחי בהם ולא שימות בהם ישראל הם ושחיטתן מותרת ואין אוסרין יין מגעם עכ״ל [עד כאן לשונו] א״כ [אם כן] יר׳[אה] שהטעם שבא בשאלה לחייב למלשין משום שעבר על עביר׳[ה] שהדי׳[ן] היה נותן שיהרג ולא יעבור אין לו טעם כלל לחייבו

ועתה אבא על מה שנתרעם ראובן על המוסר הנז׳[כר] וזהו עיקר שאלתו שמחמת הלשנתו הוכרח לפזר פזורים גדולים כמו שבא בשאלה ושואל אם הדי׳[ן] נותן לחייב למלשין שישלם לו מה שהוציא ופזר לסבת הלשנתו ונניח שההלשנה הנז׳[כרת] היה ברצון בלי שום אונס

ואומר דעיקרא דהך מלתא איתא בפרק הכונס דבמסור מבעיא אם עשו בו תקנת נגזל להיותו נשבע ונוטל וכתב בעל הטור ח״מ [חושן משפט]

---

56 Sanhedrin 74a. According to the midrashic reasoning cited there, the interpretation "not die by them" does not apply to transgressions committed in public; see *MT Hilkhot Y'sodei Ha-Torah*, 5,1-3 in Halakhic Background.

57 As is wine touched by a Gentile or a Jew who is an apostate by choice.

58 *Responsa of R. Solomon ben Abraham Adret* 7:41.

59 By an informer who gave information to Gentiles about the plaintiff's property, which was then confiscated or taken by force.

Sages] ordained for him the ordinance of one who is robbed,[60] so that he [the betrayed] could take an oath and take [what he claims he lost].[61] Ba'al Ha-Tur[62] wrote in Ḥoshen Mishpat, section 90[63] and also in section 388,[64] the respective rationales of those who rule on this law. Thus he wrote in section 90:[65] "Rav Hai Gaon wrote[66] that this question was not solved in the gᵉmara but was indeterminate, and [for] every unsolved [question] on monetary matters the [disputants] divide [the disputed property, if the plaintiff takes an oath]. But my master and father the Rosh[67] (may his memory be blessed) wrote that in the case of doubt, we do not take money [from a defendant].[68] Rabbenu Tam[69] explained[70] that that question is about [a case] such as when the betrayer denies [the claim of] the betrayed [which is like a thief denying the claim of the one who was robbed];[71]

בסיי[מן] ץ׳ גם בסיי[מן] שפ״ח סברות הפוסקים בדין זה וז״ל [וזה לשונו] בסיי[מן] ץ׳ רב האיי גאון כתב כיון דההיא בעיא לא אפשיטא בגמ׳[רא] וסלקא בתיקו דכל תיקו דממונא חולקין וא״א [ואדוני אבי] הרא״ש ז״ל [זכרונו לברכה] כתב דמספקא לא מפקינן ממונא ופיי[רש] ר״ת [רבינו תם] הך בעיא כגון שהמסור מכחיש את הנמסר אבל אם מסור עצמו אינו יודע כמה הפסיד ישבע הנמסר ויטול

---

60 Mishna Shᵉvu'ot 7:1-2.
61 Rabbinic scholars disagree about the situation of a betrayer and the betrayed, and also about the similarities to and differences from the case of a robber and the one who is robbed. They ask a number of questions, including: Does the betrayer totally deny the act? Are there witnesses, but they do not know the amount of money involved? Does the betrayer claim he paid the damages, but has no witnesses? Ha-Kohen cites a few of these approaches.
62 R. Jacob ben Asher, c. 1269–1343.
63 Tur ḤM 90:14.
64 Tur ḤM 388:4.
65 Ha-Kohen's quotation has some slight differences from the extant printed text. The printed text is more consistent with what we find in Hai Gaon's writings (The Laws of Oaths 2.5), where we do not find specific reference to the question in Bava Qamma that Ha-Kohen cites. However, it is not certain how Rav Hai understood the question.
66 In The Laws of Oaths 2.5, Hai Gaon states that in an unsolved monetary dispute, the disputed amount is divided. See, also, Sefer Ha-Meqaḥ Vᵉha-Mimkar 20:43
67 R. Asher ben Jehiel, c. 1250–1327.
68 Rosh, Bava Qamma 6:15.
69 R. Jacob ben Meir Tam, c. 1100–1171.
70 Tosafot Bava Qamma 62a at 'asu taqqanat.
71 This continuation of the text appears in Rosh Bava Qamma 6:15, and its meaning is as follows. The question is about the case of a betrayer who denies betraying. Can the betrayed take an oath and take what he claims he is owed (or keep what he has taken), just as one who was robbed takes an oath and takes from the robber what he maintains he is owed, even if

but if the betrayer himself does not know how much money he lost [but does not deny the act], the betrayed should take an oath and take [what he claims he lost]."[72] He [Ba'al Ha-Turim] also wrote what Ri[73] explained,[74] which is in accordance with the opinion of the Rosh (may his memory be blessed). And in this manner he wrote what he wrote in section 388. And it is not necessary to go into this at length.

I say further that it is necessary to be precise, so as to recognize that this betrayal that the renegade did—whether under duress or by will—is betrayal in a matter that is life-endangering, because it is possible that those Gentiles would have put Reuben to death for circumcising the forced convert [now a Christian according to the Christians]. Therefore since the betrayer did not commit a monetary betrayal, but rather [a betrayal that was] life endangering, it is not appropriate to obligate him monetarily, because everything that those Sages discussed about the law of a betrayer—whether he is or is not obligated to pay what was lost—is specifically regarding a betrayer who has caused monetary loss by the hands of Gentiles. But in a case such as our case, what they [the Sages] discussed is not relevant. The betrayer did not commit a monetary betrayal, but rather a life-endangering betrayal, and Reuben was compelled to escape for his life and had many expendi-

ועוד כתב מה שפי׳[רש] ר״י [רבינו יצחק] והוא מסכים לסברת הרא״ש ז״ל [זכרונו לברכה] ועל דרך זה כתב מ״ש [מה שכתב] בסי׳[מן] שפי״ח אין צריך להאריך בזה

ואומר דיש לדקדק דיר׳[אה] שזה המסירות שעשה זה המומר או באונס או ברצון הוי מסירות בדבר שיש בו סכנת נפש שאפשר שהגוים ההם היו ממיתים לראובן על שמל את האנוס וא״כ [ואם כן] כיון שהמוסר לא עשה מסירות של ממון אלא של סכנת נפש אין מקום לחייבו ממון דכל מאי דשקלי וטרו הנהו רבותא דשקלי וטרו בדינא דמסור אי חייב לשלם מה שהפסיד או לא לא הוי אלא דוקא במוסר וגורם להפסיד ממון ע״י [על ידי] גוים אבל כה״ג [כהאי גוונא] דנ״ד [דנדון דידן] לא שייך למאי דשקלו וטרו וא״כ [ואם כן] כיון שהמוסר לא עשה מסירות של ממון כי אם מסירות של סכנת נפשות וראובן הוכרח לברוח להנצל מהסכנה

---

the robber denies the crime? It is this question that is left unresolved, according to Rabbenu Tam.

72 This approach is a variation on the general principle in Jewish law that when one party pleads with certainty and the other party admits that he is uncertain, the party who is certain prevails.

73 R. Isaac (the Elder) ben Samuel of Dampierre, d. c. 1185.

74 Tosafot Bava Qamma 62a at 'asu taqqanat.

tures to save his life—because without a doubt it was imperative that Reuben flee from the place where he was, because it became known that he was a *mohel* for a forced convert. Therefore, it should be understood that regarding those expenditures Reuben spent, the betrayer cannot be considered fully responsible for the damages, but rather is to be [considered an] indirect causation of damages—and it is the widespread law that one is exempt [from payment for] indirect causation of damages.⁷⁵

[5] Further, even if we were to say that the damage incurred by Reuben due to his need to flee—that is, the expenses he incurred, such as is reported in the question—is considered damage that the betrayer would be obligated [to pay]—in any event, so long as Reuben is not able to verify his loss with testimony from witnesses, the betrayer cannot be obligated to pay. Even if there is evidence to prove what he lost, we do

ופזר הוצאות להנצל מסכנת נפש כי בלי ספק ראובן היה מוכרח לברוח מהמקום אשר היה שם מחמת שיצא עליו קול מוהל אנוס. וא״כ [ואם כן] יר׳[אה] דהנך הוצאות שהוציא ראובן אין למוסנ[ר] עליהם שם מזיק גמור רק שיהיה גרמה בנזיקי[ן] והלכה רווחת דגרמה בנזיקי[ן] פטור ואפי[לו] נא[מר] שהזק הבא לראובן מחמת שהוכרח לברוח שפזר והוציא מה שפזר כמו שבא בשאלה חשיב כהזק לחייב למוסר מ״מ [מכל מקום] כל שאינו יכול ראובן לברר בעדים ההפסד שהפסיד אין לחייב למוסר לשלם ואעפ״י [ואף על פי] שיש הוכחות להוכיח מה שהפסיד בהוכחות לא מפקינן ממונא כמו שכתב הרא״ש בתשובת שאלה כלל י״ז סי[מן] ה' והביאה הטור ח״מ [חושן משפט] סי[מן] צ' וז״ל [וזה לשונו] ששאלת על לאה שטוענת על ראובן שמסרה בידי גוים ובזה הפסידה הרבה וקצת בררה בעדים וקצת בהוכחות כל

not extract money [from a defendant] based on evidence [alone], as the Rosh wrote in the response to the question in principle 17,5 [of his responsa], and which the *Tur* cited in *Ḥoshen Mishpat* section 90,⁷⁶ as follows: "You asked about Leah who claims that Reuben⁷⁷ betrayed her to Gentiles, and as a result she lost a lot [of money], and a portion of it she verified with witnesses and a portion with evidence. [Response:] Whatever she is able to verify with witnesses that she lost, he must reimburse her, and Reuben must take an oath that he does not

---

75 Bava Qamma 60a.

76 Tur ḤM 90:15.

77 In the question posed to the Rosh, Leah is the pseudonym of the plaintiff, the betrayed, while Reuben is the pseudonym of the defendant, the betrayer. Thus, here Leah corresponds to the person previously called Reuben (i.e., Benarogios), while Reuben corresponds to the betrayer (i.e., de Nis).

know she lost any more; but [based] on evidence [without witnesses], we do not extract money." His [the Rosh's] words (may his memory be blessed) are in accordance with the opinion of Ri (may his memory be blessed), who wrote regarding that question posed in chapter "One who brings," of which I wrote above, that the law is that even if the betrayer cannot make his claim [denying the loss] with certainty, the betrayed is not [entitled] to take an oath and take [what he claims he lost]. As such, I do not see that it is straightforwardly proper to obligate the cited betrayer to pay the damages that Reuben[78] incurred as a result of his betrayal. And this [is my conclusion] even if we assume that the betrayal was by choice without any duress whatsoever.

Nevertheless, after I saw what was in the question, what the betrayer wickedly did, I would say that apparently, from the question, the cited betrayer is now located beyond the place where his forced [conversion] occurred, and he has returned to the true and just faith—because if this were not so, what would be the sense to this question? For if he were still an apostate, for what purpose would it serve to know whether the [Jewish] law requires that he pay damages? And if it is so [that he has now recanted his conversion to Christianity], since he wants to return to the true and just faith, it is necessary to request an atonement for his soul for everything that he sinned and transgressed, if he wishes to remain true to the faith of Moses (peace be upon him). Because without doubt he is in need of a great atonement

---

78 Now, as earlier, Reuben denotes the plaintiff (i.e., Benarogios).

and [should] accept great afflictions,⁷⁹ if what is stated in the question is true. If it is so, then as part of his atonement it is incumbent upon him to placate and appease the cited Reuben with pieces of silver⁸⁰ for what he caused him to lose, because according to what is told in the question, he caused him to lose a substantial amount, even though it was only by indirect cause, even if the informing was under duress. By this [act of appeasement], perhaps he will find forgiveness and atonement, to repent for his soul, considering that he sinned against another.

יסורים גדולים אם האמת הוא כמו שבא בשאלה וא״כ [ואם כן] צריך שבכלל כפרותיו שירצה ויפייס לראובן הנז'[נכר] ברצי כסף על מה שגרם לו להפסידו כי כפי הבא בשאלה הפסידו הזק מרובה אעפ״י [אף על פי] שלא היה כי אם גרמא ואפי'[ואפילו] שהההלשנה היה באונס ובזה אולי ימצא סליחה וכפרה לכפר על נפשו מאשר חטא לנפש

Discussion

Ha-Kohen understands the questioner to claim that, because the defendant should have martyred himself rather than betray the *mohel*, the defendant is obligated to pay damages. In his response, the main thrust of Ha-Kohen's argument and conclusion is that if the defendant was obligated to allow himself to be killed rather than transgress, the transgression that merited martyrdom was his original apostasy, not the revealing of the name of his *mohel*. According to the letter of the law, he is thus not obligated to pay the plaintiff damages. Ha-Kohen's argument consists of several points:⁸¹

[1] The betrayal of the *mohel* was out of free will, so the principle that "he should have allowed himself to be killed rather than transgress" is not relevant to the betrayal.

---

79 It is not clear whether, if he were asked to address acceptance of the defendant to the Jewish community, Ha-Kohen would require that the defendant suffer physical penance or, at the very least, ritual immersion (not as a proselyte, for he is a transgressing Jew, but as a form of penance). For a spectrum of views from different times and places about the obligations of a returning apostate, see David Golinkin, "Ketsad Ḥozᵉrim Mumarim La-yahadut?" in *Zehut Yᵉhudit*, ed. Asher Maoz and Aviad Ha-Kohen (Tel Aviv: Tel Aviv University Faculty of Law, 2014), 49-62.

80 Ps. 68:31. Ha-Kohen employed a frequently used play on words: the Hebrew *ratsei khesef* (pieces of silver) sounds like a phrase related to *ratse*, "placate."

81 See the section numbers in square brackets in the responsum.

[2] Even if the defendant did reveal the name of the *mohel* under duress, rather than out of free will, it is not a case of "be killed rather than kill," because the defendant would not have actually murdered the *mohel*.
[3] The defendant's transgression of apostasy has no bearing on whether he owes damages on account of his betrayal of the *mohel*.
[4] The defendant did not commit a monetary betrayal, and therefore the laws of monetary compensation by a betrayer are not applicable. Because the monetary damages were caused indirectly, the defendant is exempt from repayment.
[5] In any event, the plaintiff does not have witnesses, and without witnesses, the betrayed cannot receive compensation.

In spite of Ha-Kohen's clear conclusion that it is not "straightforwardly proper to obligate the cited betrayer to pay the damages that Reuben incurred as a result of his betrayal," he goes beyond the letter of the law, declaring what the defendant did was wicked, and he is in need of atonement, which should include paying the plaintiff some unquantified amount to appease him.

Ha-Kohen's ruling enlightens us about his attitude towards returning conversos. Given the various interpretations of the available sources and the subtle differences among the precedents, he could have found grounds to obligate the betrayer (Filippo) to pay damages to the betrayed (Benarogios). However, if he had ruled that Filippo was obligated to pay and he failed to comply, Ha-Kohen would have had no choice but to excommunicate[82] him—which he may not have wanted to do to someone he was trying to rehabilitate into the community.

Further, if the rabbi had ruled that Filippo was obligated to pay, it would have been difficult to assess the damages and could have bankrupted Filippo, who had probably already lost much of his wealth and incurred significant expenditures in moving himself and his family from Venice. In addition, it could have planted the idea for others in similar circumstances to sue, thus causing much dissent and feuding in the community. In Jewish communities under Ottoman rule there was much contention between Jews who left Spain and Portugal at the time of the expulsions rather than convert to Christianity, typically sacrificing everything, and those who came a century later, perhaps with some worldly goods and with the taint of having lived as Christians. Ha-Kohen made it clear that acceptance

---

82 The Jewish court had little means to enforce its decisions if both parties did not abide by them. See the chapter "On Excommunication."

and forgiveness within the community would require some appeasement, by financial means, on Filippo's part. But it is reasonable to suggest that, rather than to try to seek the elusive absolute justice, Ha-Kohen considered it more vital to ask the defendant to make amends in good conscience, with compromise and a spirit of forgiveness on the part of the plaintiff, so as to bring lost souls back into the community.

Though at times Ha-Kohen's language in reference to de Nis ("apostate," "betrayer") seems condemning, Ha-Kohen clearly did not wish to reject him from the Jewish community. He did not quote Maimonides and state that de Nis "has no portion in the World to Come,"[83] in spite of the fact that he had delivered "his fellow to the hands of a Gentile to be killed or beaten."[84] Ha-Kohen pointed to sources that proved that even though de Nis had sinned, he was not the same as an apostate by choice. The rabbi's harsh language may have served as rhetoric, to placate the plaintiff and inspire the defendant to feel remorse and guilt and thus choose to make amends, paving his path back into the Jewish fold. Ha-Kohen seems to have followed the approach of R. Jacob ibn Ḥabib,[85] a predecessor in Salonica, who wrote regarding conversos: "Who knows what is in their hearts? It would be better to judge them favorably,[86] like those who were forced (*anusim*) completely, for tomorrow they may come to us, and would we now disgrace them by judging them as though they are complete apostates?"[87]

Questions for Further Discussion

In Ha-Kohen's responsum, the defendant was judged for disregarding the safety of the two *mohalim* whose names he betrayed to the Inquisition. The questions suggested here for further discussion revolve around the difficult ethical quandaries that challenge a person who is faced with conflicting values. The phrase *he shall live by them* (Lev. 18:5) is used to teach the principle of *piku'aḥ nefesh*

---

83 *MT Hilkhot T^eshuva* (The Laws of Repentance) 3,12. See Halakhic Background.
84 Though one might argue that merely providing a name is not sufficient for someone to fall under that category.
85 R. Jacob ibn Ḥabib (1445?–1515/16) was Spanish-born, and in 1492 he went to Portugal before migrating to Salonica some time before 1501.
86 Lit., "in the scale of merit," Mishna *Avot* 1:6.
87 See R. Elijah Mizraḥi (c. 1450–1526), *Responsa*, 47 (Jerusalem, 1938).

(saving a life):⁸⁸ life takes precedence over commandments, so that, for example, saving a life overrides the laws of the Sabbath. On the other hand, the commandment *do not murder* (Exod. 20:13) is an exception to this rule,⁸⁹ so that faced with a choice to kill or be killed, a person must choose the latter, in spite of the verse *guard yourselves well* (Deut. 4:15).

Consider the case presented in the Talmud, *Bava M^etsi'a* 62a, of two people who were traveling, and only one of them had a canteen of water. If they shared the water, they both would nevertheless die of thirst, but if only one would drink the water, he, and he alone, would be able to reach an inhabited area and survive. Ben P^etora taught that it is better for both to drink—and die—rather than for one to see the death of his fellow, perhaps considering the verse *do not stand idly by the blood of your fellow* (Lev. 19:16).⁹⁰ But Rabbi Akiva taught, *your brother should live with you* (Lev. 25:36)—your life takes precedence over your fellow's life.⁹¹ Halakhic consensus is according to Rabbi Akiva.⁹²

Now compare that situation to the case of "Why would you think that your blood is redder?" Why didn't Rava tell the person who asked the question that his own life takes precedence? Is it possible that there is no difference between the two cases, but that Rava agrees with Ben P^etora, and that Rabbi Akiva would disagree with Rava in the case brought before the latter?⁹³

Consider the point raised by Ha-Kohen that one might distinguish between being ordered to kill to save yourself and being ordered to kill to save several

---

88 *Yoma* 85b.

89 *Yoma* 82a.

90 Ben P^etora's opinion can be understood to mean that since each one is obligated to act to save his fellow, each one would have to give the water to the other; thus the water must be shared. See *Minḥat Ḥinnukh* 296 at *ha-sh^elishit* (written as *heh gimel*). In the Jerusalem: Machon Yerushalayim, 1997 edition it can be found in vol. 2, p. 426 §22–p. 427 §23.

91 Compare to *Sifra* (*B^eHar parasha* 5, halakha 3 at *v^ehei aḥikha 'imakh* [109c in Isaac Hirsch Weiss ed., Vienna 1862]).

92 Maimonides did not codify this law, nor did R. Joseph Caro. Rif rules in accordance with R. Akiva (*Bava M^etsi'a* 34a on the on the pages of the Rif at *tanu rabbanan sh^enayim m^ehalkhin*, as does R. Asher ben Jehiel (Rosh) (*Bava M^etsi'a* 5,6). On the other hand, R. Avraham Yitzḥak Ha-Kohen Kook expresses some doubt about the halakhic conclusion of that passage (*Mishpat Kohen* 144,16).

93 Those who wish to discuss this important ethical question in greater depth can refer to *Tosafot Sanhedrin* 74b at *v^eha Esther*, which distinguishes between killing another actively or passively, as does Ha-Kohen in the responsum.

people. Do you see justification for killing one to save many?[94] Consider the situation of scarce medical resources during a pandemic.[95] Are the halakhic texts you saw relevant to the matter of triage?

Ha-Kohen distinguished between the situation of someone being commanded to kill by his own act versus indirectly causing the death of another. He pointed out that in Jewish law, the religious court can punish a murderer who commits murder directly, but if someone indirectly (even though purposely) causes someone to be killed, then the punishment is in the hands of Heaven.[96] Discuss this distinction.

Consider the following cases:

1) "The Queen vs Dudley and Stephens (1884)," about four men stranded in a lifeboat without food or water.[97] The defendants (two of the men) killed one person on the lifeboat to save the lives of the others.

2) The Runaway Trolley.[98]

Discuss those cases in light of the Jewish legal sources presented in this chapter.[99] Are the Jewish legal sources in this chapter relevant to those cases? Why or why not?

---

94 A relevant source for this discussion is *Bet Ha-Bʿhira La-Mʿiri Sanhedrin* 72b at *ze she-beʾarnu she-kol she-en sham rodef*.

95 See Amy Solnica, Leonid Barski, Alan Jotkowitz, "Allocation of Scarce Resources during the COVID-19 Pandemic: A Jewish Ethical Perspective," *Journal of Medical Ethics* 46, no. 7 (2020): 444-446.

96 To put this in a modern perspective, if someone put a car bomb into the victim's car, such that when the victim starts his engine he will be blown up, Jewish law would not penalize the perpetrator in a religious court. This is based on a concept of *gʿrama* (causation). Murder by *gʿrama* is discussed in several passages in the *gʿmara*; see *Sanhedrin* 76b-78a and *Ḥullin* 16a.

97 [Sandel], 3-7. See discussion in [Sandel2], 31-33.

98 Ibid., 21-24.

99 A comparison of the Jewish legal sources with the various views of the political philosophers in ibid. and [Sandel] would certainly make an interesting discussion.

Further Reading

[Koren] Koren, Debby. "Portuguese Jew or New Christian? An Epilogue to the Case of Filippo de Nis" *Jewish Studies Quarterly* 23, no. 2 (2016): 142-167.

[Melammed] Melammed, Renée Levine. *A Question of Identity: Iberian Conversos in Historical Perspective*. Oxford: Oxford University Press, 2004.

[Pullan] Pullan, Brian. *The Jews of Europe and the Inquisition of Venice: 1550–1620*. London: I. B. Tauris, 1997.

[Ray] Ray, Jonathan. *After Expulsion: 1492 and the Making of Sephardic Jewry*. New York: New York University Press, 2012.

[Sandel] Sandel, Michael J., ed. *Justice: A Reader*. Oxford: Oxford University Press, 2007.

[Sandel2] ———. *Justice, What's the Right Thing to Do?* New York: Farrar, Straus and Giroux, 2010.

7.

Excommunication in Amsterdam

Baḥ *(Ha-Y^eshanot)* 5

Historical Background

Tolerance, in the context of the historical Jewish experience, is a relative term, and lacks the connotation of mutual respect and "freedom from bigotry"[1] that we think of as tolerance in our time. Rather, tolerance, in the Jewish experience, is "endurance,"[2] as in "my tolerance of noise is limited."[3] Though intolerance was the norm in other countries in which Calvinism was the dominant religion, Holland of the early seventeenth century is sometimes regarded as the birthplace of a modern state. However, the Union of Utrecht of 1579, which guaranteed all Dutch burghers freedom of conscience, was not truly a model of acceptance of people whose beliefs might differ, and it did not have Jews in mind when it was written. Nevertheless, it contributed to an atmosphere of relative tolerance. Other contributing factors often suggested include the humanism of the Dutchman Erasmus[4] and the Reformation.[5]

Due to this relatively tolerant atmosphere and economic opportunity, Holland became a haven for descendants of Jews who were expelled from Spain and

---

1 *The Random House College Dictionary*, rev. ed. s.v. "Tolerance," definition 1.
2 Ibid., definition 4.
3 Ibid.
4 Erasmus's toleration, however, did not extend to Jews. In his eyes, Judaism was "the most pernicious plague and the bitterest enemy of the doctrine of Christ." (See 26 and 26n63 in [Swetsch].) Swetschinski concludes: "All things considered, therefore, and despite its exalted ideals, humanism had few positive effects on the life of contemporary Jewry" ([Swetsch2], 56). The sources listed in his book contain much background information on the religious atmosphere, the Reformation and Calvinism, humanism and tolerance in the Netherlands in the relevant time period.
5 However, for some Protestants, the Reformation brought hope that Jews would be more likely to convert to Protestantism than Catholicism.

Portugal or who became conversos,[6] and to Crypto-Jews from Portugal who wished to return to their Judaism in a society that would tolerate them.[7] The first Portuguese[8] conversos arrived in Holland in the last decade of the sixteenth century. These "Portuguese merchants," as they were referred to by the burgomasters, did not become citizens when they arrived. "They were to be allowed to acquire citizenship[9] if they so desired; but the authorities assumed that they were Christians. When some doubt about their religious affiliation seems to have arisen, the burgomasters decided that the Portuguese immigrants would be warned in advance—before taking their oath of citizenship—that no public worship outside the recognized churches would be permitted in Amsterdam."[10]

Nevertheless, by the year in which the events we are about to examine took place,[11] there were already two small, cooperating congregations in two synagogues in Amsterdam,[12] Bet Jacob (House of Jacob) and Neve Salom (Dwelling of Peace). Very shortly after the timing of the events described in the responsum in this chapter—perhaps as a direct result—a schism in the Bet Jacob congrega-

---

6   Frequently referred to as "New Christians." Many of these New Christians were forcibly baptized in the century between 1391 and 1497. Thus, these immigrants and their ancestors did not practice Judaism openly, if at all, for one hundred to two hundred years.

7   Historians disagree as to whether these immigrants went to Amsterdam with the intent to return to Judaism, but significant numbers of them clearly succeeded in doing so and in establishing a stable and successful community, with full community services, in a remarkably short amount of time.

8   The Portuguese Synagogue in Amsterdam explains on their website: "At the time, the Netherlands were fighting to get out from under Spanish control, most likely the reason why the Sefardim dropped the 'Spanish' designation" ("History of the Community," www.esnoga.com/en/history-of-the-community/#).

9   Swetschinski points out that "the word 'citizen' is an anachronism. At that time the most any Dutch person could be, if he or she chose to file the application and pay the fee, was a burgher of her or his place of residence" ([Swetsch], 5n6). The oath that they took was not an oath of citizenship, but an oath that allowed them to purchase burgher rights. However, acquisition of these rights did not entitle Jews to the same privileges as Christians; for instance, they could not engage in all professions, nor could they transmit their burghership to their children ([Swetsch], 20).

10 [Huussen], 20-21; "Freedom of worship was never formally granted to the Jews of Amsterdam" ([Swetsch], 11).

11 Depending upon which historian's view is correct, these events took place either in 1618 or otherwise sometime between 1616 and 1618.

12 For discussions of this development and more background on the history of the Portuguese Jews in Amsterdam, see Further Reading.

tion[13] led to the establishment in 1618 of a third synagogue, Bet Israel (House of Israel, first called Es Haim [Tree of Life]).

The squabbles documented in the historical record and in the responsa pique our interest, and we learn from them how the community functioned, governed itself, and interacted with the majority population. But it is not the squabbles that actually characterized the community of Portuguese conversos who settled in Amsterdam. "... almost as soon as these *kehilot* were founded, the elders began discussing plans to bring them together, and from 1639 the unified Amsterdam Portuguese community was known as the Kahal Kados de Talmud Tora."[14] "... the generally smooth re-integration of the New Christians into a traditional Jewish community more than the quarrelsomeness of a few individuals"[15] should be recognized as the accomplishment that it was.

Halakhic Background

The question in this chapter's responsum was sent to R. Joel Sirkes.[16] The following two halakhic sources will shed light on his response.

Sanhedrin 31b	סנהדרין ל"א ב'
A message was once sent [by the religious court in the Land of Israel] to Mar Ukva: "To him whose luster is like that of the son of Bitya,[17] peace be with you! Ukvan the Babylonian has complained to us, saying: 'My brother Jeremiah	שלחו ליה למר עוקבא לדזיו ליה כבר בתיה שלם עוקבן הבבלי קבל קדמנא ירמיה אחי העביר עלי את

---

13   A dispute in the Bet Jacob synagogue surrounding David Farrar was brought to R. Leon de Modena in Venice in 1618 ([Bodian]: 54-55).
14   [Swetsch], 4.
15   [Swetsch], 6.
16   1561–1640. His most famous work by which name he is often referred (using its acronym, the Baḥ) is *Bayit Ḥadash*, a commentary on the *Tur*.
17   An honorific title, perhaps referring to Moses, who was raised by Pharaoh's daughter, Bitya (whose name is mentioned in 1 Chron. 4:18). Another possible explanation of this greeting is that "Bitya" is a corruption of a Persian honorific title. See Richard N. Frye, "Some Early Iranian Titles," *Oriens* 15 (December 1962): 353-354.

has obstructed my path.'[18] [Therefore], speak to him, and make sure that he meets us in Tiberias." [The g'mara asks:] But is this not self-contradictory? First you say, "Speak to him," that is, judge him [in Babylonia]; [and then] "Make sure he meets us in Tiberias," which means "Send him here!" [The g'mara responds:] What they meant was: "Speak to him," [that is,] judge him; if he accepts your decision, well and good; if not, "make sure he appears before us in Tiberias."[19] Rav Ashi says: This was a case of punitive payments,[20] and in Babylonia they do not try cases of punitive payments. And as for their sending him a message in such terms, that was only to show respect to Mar Ukva.[21]

Shabbat 10a — מסכת שבת י' א'

It is taught in the name of Rav Ḥiyya bar Rav from Difti: *and the people stood by Moses from the morning to the evening* (Exod. 18:13). Could you conceive of Moses sitting and judging the entire day? When would his [study of] Torah be done? Rather, it is to tell you that any judge who judges in absolute truth, even for a moment, the Torah regards him as if he is a partner in creation with the Holy One, blessed be He. It states here *the people stood by Moses from the*

---

18 I.e., has committed a grave injustice against me.
19 Hence it can be seen that even where the plaintiff desired the defendant to appear in another religious court, at the outset preference was given to the defendant's local religious court.
20 Such as the double payment for stealing (Exod. 22:3).
21 Who was the Exilarch, but he really had to send the case to the Land of Israel.

morning to the evening and it states there   הבקר עד הערב וכתיב התם ויהי ערב
There was evening, there was morning—   ויהי בקר יום אחד
one day (Gen. 1:5).[22]

Discussion

The excerpt from *Sanhedrin* 31b teaches us that if the defendant's local religious court can settle a complaint, it should. Otherwise, the defendant can be summoned to another court. Though this passage offers Rav Ashi's explanation for the case of Mar Ukva, in his responsum Sirkes relies upon the interpretation of the Tosafot and the Rosh[23] to explain the incident related in *Sanhedrin* 31b. According to this interpretation, the instruction to Mar Ukva ("if he does not [accept your decision]") does not suggest that Mar Ukva, the exilarch, could not force the defendant to accept the court's judgment.[24] Rather, if the defendant wants to "go to the Supreme Court" (i.e., the Great Sanhedrin in the Land of Israel), then he should be sent to Tiberias.

Until the modern era, Jewish communities had religious autonomy and had their own religious courts to maintain order within their communities, including for civil matters, though the types of punishment were usually quite limited (by the ruling authorities who granted the Jewish courts autonomy), as was the power granted to enforce judgments. (However, capital offenses were, with very few exceptions, handled by the Gentile courts.)

The second excerpt, from *Shabbat* 10a, is alluded to in the last paragraph of the responsum. It evokes the Talmud's high regard for judges who judge fairly and in truth.

---

22   Thus equating Moses's service as judge to the creation.
23   R. Asher ben Jehiel, c. 1250–1327.
24   In fact, according to *Sanhedrin* 5a, the Exilarch has the highest authority, as will be explained below.

Responsum

Baḥ (*Ha-Yᵉshanot*) 5	שו"ת ב"ח (הישנות) סימן ה

Question: We have heard the vigorous shouting[25] [from] the city of Amsterdam in a distant land. A rebel has risen, he is the unnamed physician,[26] who purifies the [impure] insect and defiles the land, and who has committed two evil [offenses] in one blow. One is a great evil that has provoked the stout-hearted to be astonished and appalled, that he has boastfully scorned the homiletic passages of the Sages, of blessed memory, and the wisdom of

שאלה קול ענות שמענו במרץ מארץ רחוקה עיר אמשטרדם כי עלה הפורץ הוא פלוני הרופא מטהר השרץ ומטמא את הארץ ושתים רעות עשה בקרץ אחת הוא רעה גדולה התגוללה ועלה שמים עליה ישתוממו ישומו כל אבירי לב והוא כי זה כמה נשא לבבו וכפיו מלא מלעיג על דרז"ל [דברי רבינו זכרונם לברכה] באגדותיהם גם בחכמת הקבלה שולח יד לשונו ומתלוצץ על החכמה חכמת האמת

the Qabbala,[27] and with the power of the tongue[28] he mocks the true wisdom and has spoken slander[29] of it, and says that in his eyes it is not worthy, but rather

---

25 Derived from Exod. 32:18.

26 Historians disagree as to whether the unnamed physician is Abraham Farrar (who died in 1618; see [Bodian], 53n29) or his son-in-law David Farrar. One reading is that the physician is David Farrar, and the events described in this responsum are all related to the 1618 dispute that led to the schism of the Bet Jacob congregation; see [Swetsch], 172-173 and [Swetsch2], 68-69. If the case in Sirkes's responsum involves David Farrar, then the case brought to R. Leon de Modena might be this very case. In this responsum, Sirkes recommends bringing the case to a court that is not in Amsterdam. Given the Venetian influence on the Amsterdam Jews in that period (see [Bodian]), Venice would have been a logical place to hold such a hearing. Other documentation, such as a letter from Modena in Venice (*Ziqnei Yᵉhuda*, Shlomo Simonsohn, ed., Jerusalem, 1956, 48-49 [responsum 33]), provides information about the complaints against David Farrar in 1618. Swetschinski ([Swetsch], 176) suggests that the conflict might really have resulted from "family clusters or circles of friends or associates vying for supremacy in the community" or from "some kind of economic tension." Another position is that the physician in this case is Abraham Farrar and the dispute took place sometime between 1616 and 1618, while it was another dispute in 1618, involving David Farrar, that led to the schism; see [Bodian], 52-56, and other historians cited there.

27 Among the complaints against David Farrar in the letter from R. Leon Modena were that he differed with the classical interpretation of the Bible and that he was skeptical about Qabbala.

28 Derived from Prov. 18:21.

29 Sirkes used an expression from the Jewish acrostic confession recited on the Day of Atonement and other fast days, and, according to some rites, daily.

only philosophy[30] is, which [he believes] everyone should be drawn to alone, and in his insistence in his impurity he [causes] upstanding people to join him and entices them to follow his evil view. Second, in his position as one of the community leaders, he gave permission to a particular man to [ritually] slaughter animals for the community,[31] and the members of the *ma'amad*[32] who are in each of the two synagogues instructed two knowledgeable men among them to question that [newly appointed] slaughterer in the laws of ritual slaughter, but when they asked him, he did not know a thing, and said that what is forbidden is permitted.

ודיבר עליה דופי ואומר כי לא נחשב בעיניו כי אם רק הפלוסופיא ואחריה יהא נמשך כל אדם לא זולת ועוד מחזיק בטומאתו לצרף אליו אנשים הגונים ומפתה אותם לדעתם זאת הרעה. שנית כי לאשר הוא אחד מהפרנסים נתן לאיש אחד רשות לשחוט בהמות לצורך הקהל ואנשי המעמד אשר לשתי בתי כנסיות צוו לשני חכמים שביניהם לשאול אותו פי האיש השוחט ההוא בדיני שחיטה וכאשר שאלוהו לא ידע מאומה ואמר על האסור מותר ומיד בהסכמות המעמדות והחכמים הוכרז בבה״כ [בבית הכנסת] בשתי הק״ק

Immediately, according to a decision[33] of the *ma'amadot* and the *ḥakhamim*,[34] it was decreed in the synagogue in each of the holy congregations[35] that all meat that was slaughtered by this man has not been properly slaughtered,[36] and the

---

30   I.e., scientific thought.
31   This complaint does not appear in the letter from Leon Modena or other documentation enumerating complaints against David, which is one reason why Bodian concludes that the unnamed physician in the responsum is not David, but rather Abraham. However, it is feasible that the set of complaints sent to Sirkes is not identical to the complaints recorded elsewhere for other reasons, and yet it is the same individual involved. Both Abraham and David were among the leaders of the community.
32   The *ma'amad* (often spelled *mahamad*, as the Portuguese did) is a Hebrew term for the body of leadership, or regents, of a Spanish-Portuguese Jewish community.
33   In the Hebrew, the word used is *haskamot* (often spelled *ascamot*, as the Portuguese did), which means "agreements," and refers to the laws, regulations, and decisions of the *ma'amad*.
34   The term *ḥakham* (pl. *ḥakhamim*) is the common term for rabbinical authorities, rather than the term *rav*, as used in the Ashkenazi communities.
35   This term, *qᵉhilla qᵉdosha*, refers to a Jewish community, perhaps so as to attribute holiness to the communities in spite of their situation in the Diaspora. (However, the term persists today for some communal synagogues even in the modern State of Israel.) Here the word "congregation" is more appropriate, because there were two congregations in the one community. See E. Bareket, "A Holy Community—the Terminology and Its Usage According to Genizah Letters in the 11th Century" [Hebrew], in *Judaica Petropolitana* (St. Petersburg-Jerusalem: Academy of Cultures Research, 2013).
36   Lit., "carrion," which is forbidden to be eaten according to Jewish law.

pots that it was cooked in are forbidden, because he did not even learn the laws of [kosher] slaughtering. The mentioned unnamed physician then went up to the pulpit at that time and said in a loud voice to ignore the announcement [that disqualified the slaughterer] and that they [the congregants] can eat the meat, and he takes responsibility [for any transgression],[37] and a few of the people were not concerned about themselves and ate this nonkosher meat. All this has reached us[38] in writing from three distinguished rabbis[39] from the city of Amsterdam, and their signature was verified in the presence of the rabbi who is head of the Jewish court in the holy community of Lublin. Now [I have before me] the writ of the question of the wise rabbis, [who are] impassioned with the *zeal of the Lord of hosts*[40] and [wish] to rid[41] the said physician of his evil view with a thorn that does not cause blood to flow,[42] to excommunicate him and shun him until he reverts from his evil ways and repents completely and properly.

[הקהילות קודש] שכל הבשר הנשחט עי׳ [על ידי] האיש ההוא היא נבלה והכלים שנתבשלו בהם אסורים כי אפילו הלכות שחיטה לא למד ופלוני הרופא הנזכר עלה לראש המגדול באותה שעה ואמר בקול רם שלא ישגיחו על ההכרזה ההיא ושיאכלו הבשר עליו ועל נפשו וכן נעשה וממקצת העם לא יראו לנפשם ואכלו מהבשר נבלה: כל אלה הגיע לאזנינו בכתב משלשה רבנים מובהקים מעיר אמשטרדם ונתקיימה חתימתם בפני הרב אב״ד דק״ק [אב בית דין דקהילת קודש] לובלין. והנה תורף שאלת הרבנים החכמים לקנא קנאות ה׳ צבאות ודליפקיהו להאי דעתו בישתא דפלוני הרופא מאודניה בסילוא דלא מבע דמה להחרימו ולנדותו עד ישוב מדרכי הרעה ויעשה תשובה שלימה וראויה.

---

37   Lit., "on him and on his life."

38   Lit., "reached our ears."

39   There is general agreement that the three rabbis are R. Joseph Pardo, R. Ishac Uziel and R. Saul Levi Mortera ([Bodian], 53n28). Another reason Bodian maintains that this responsum refers to Abraham Farrar rather than David is that Mortera joined David's faction when the Bet Jacob congregation split, which was unlikely if he had been David's opponent in this dispute.

40   Isa. 9:6, and other verses.

41   Lit., "to take out from his ear," an expression that suggests that his ear is plugged against reason.

42   This expression is from *Bava Batra* 151b (also *Kᵉtubbot* 91a). According to R. Samuel ben Meir (Rashbam) (*Bava Batra* 151b) and Rashi (*Kᵉtubbot* 91a) the expression is a sobriquet for shunning and excommunication. See the chapter "On Excommunication."

[1][43] I say with a full heart[44] that there is no doubt that this man is deserving of "death":[45] shunning and excommunication—"death is there"[46]—for we excommunicate even Torah scholars about whom a bad word has been heard, as is [in] chapter "These may cut their hair" [*Mo'ed Qatan* 17a],[47] and the Rosh explained there,[48] such as one who engaged himself with heretical books, and so ruled [the *Shulḥan 'Arukh*] in *Yo-re De'a*.[49] Even more so one who scorns the words of the Sages and speaks slander about the wisdom of the Qabbala, which is a source of Torah and its essence, and is the containment of the awe of Heaven—it is obvious that he deserves to be shunned, as there is no one who shows contempt for the words of the Torah more deserving of shunning than such a person. Further, he was lured by philosophy, which is heresy itself—and [this is] the *alien woman* (Prov. 2:16), about whom Solomon warned, as R. Meir [ibn] Gabbai[50] wrote in the book *Mar'ot Elohim*.[51] And not only that, but he [also] drew others to himself and transgressed the negative [commandment] *do not put a stumbling block*

והנה חלקי אמרה נפשי דאין ספק שזה האיש חייב מיתה נידוי ושמתא שם מיתה דאפילו צורבא מרבנן דסנויה שומעניה משמתינן ליה כדאיתא פרק אלו מגלחין ופירש הרא״ש לשם דהיינו כגון שמתעסק בספרי מינות וכך פסק ביורה דיעה וכל שכן המלעיג על דברי חכמים ומדבר דופי על חכמת הקבלה שהוא מקור התורה ועיקרה וכולה יראת שמים דפשיטא דחייב נידוי דאין לך מזלזל בד״ת [בדברי תורה] דחייב נידוי גדול מזה ועוד דהלא נמשך אחר הפילוסופיא היא המינות בעצמה ואשה הזרה שהזהיר עליה שלמה כמ״ש [כמו שכתב] הר״מ [הר׳ מאיר] גבאי בספר מראות אלקים ולא זו בלבד אלא ממשיך אליו גם אחרים ועובר על לאו

---

43 Numbers are inserted to facilitate reading the discussion following the responsum.
44 Derived from Lam. 3:24.
45 Not literally, but figuratively, as his next words explain.
46 This is one of the creative suggestions of the etymology of the Aramaic word for shunning (*Mo'ed Qatan* 17a) *shamta*, derived from *sham mitta*, meaning "death is there."
47 See the chapter "On Excommunication."
48 *Mo'ed Qatan* 3:11. See the chapter "On Excommunication."
49 SA YD 334:42. See the chapter "On Excommunication."
50 R. Meir ben Ezekiel ibn Gabbai (1480–after 1540) was a kabbalist of the generation of the Spanish exiles.
51 III,19 (p. 78c in the Venice, 1567 edition). R. ibn Gabbai cites Rashi for this interpretation; see Rashi on Prov. 2:16. Also known as *'Avodat ha-Qodesh*, *Mar'ot Elohim* (the title is derived from Ezek. 1:1) is a book on the doctrine of the Qabbala.

before the blind (Lev. 19:14), which is punishable by shunning. Considering that he cast aside[52] the wisdom of the Qabbala and the words of the kabbalistic rabbis, it is appropriate to be stringent with him *with exceeding vigor* (Gen. 49:3) and to excommunicate him with all the stringencies of excommunication, with everything that can be said, and this needs no justification.

Further, because he defied the members of the *ma'amad* and the rabbis who proclaimed in their order that the meat is nonkosher, and he permitted what they had forbidden—for that, too, he is deserving of shunning, for even if [his] pronouncement is based on reason and deliberation, nevertheless we have taught in a *baraita* in chapter "These are the *t'refot*"[53] ([Ḥullin] 44[b]) [that if] a scholar has forbidden [something], his colleague is not permitted to allow [it]. The Rabad explained[54] that even if he [the second scholar] permitted, the [already forbidden matter] is not permitted, and even if [the second scholar] is greater in wisdom and in number [i.e., more than one scholar].[55] [Regarding] that [which

לפני עיור לא תתן מכשול דחייב נדוי ומאחר דמשליך חכמת הקבלה ודברי רז״ל [רבינו ז״ל] המקובלי[ן]ם] אחרי גיוו ראוי להחמיר עליו ביתר עוז להחרימו בכל החומרות החרם מכל מה שהפה יוכל לדבר וזה אין צריך פנים.

גם על מה שהתריס כנגד אנשי המעמד והחכמים שהכריזו בציווייהם שהבשר נבלה והוא התיר מה שאסרו הם גם על זה חייב נידוי דאפילו היתה הוראה התלויה בסברא ובשיקול הדעת הלא שנינו בברייתא פרק אלו טרפות (דף מ״ד) חכם שאסר אין חבירו רשאי להתיר ופי׳[רש] הראב״ד דאפילו התיר אינו מותר ואפילו היה גדול ממנו בחכמה

---

52 Lit., "cast behind his back," derived from Ezek. 23:35.

53 A *t'refa* (pl. *t'refot*) is an animal rendered forbidden to Jews to eat, either due to a fatal disease discovered upon slaughtering, or due to improper slaughtering.

54 R. Abraham ben David of Posquières, c.1125–1198. Most of his commentary on the Talmud has been lost since the fourteenth century, with only a few tractates in existence (see Israel M. Ta-Shma, *Ha-Sifrut Ha-Parshanit La-Talmud B'Eropa U-viTsfon Afriqa*, vol. 1 [Jerusalem: Magnes, 2000], 202). Still, there are numerous citations of his commentary in works by other medieval Jewish scholars and in compositions such as *Shitta M'qubbetset*, the compilation of glosses on the Talmud by R. Bezalel Ashkenazi (c. 1520–1591/1594). The explanation cited here is actually from Rabad's commentary on 'Avoda Zara (available since 1960), rather than Ḥullin. Sirkes is most likely citing it from a secondary source, such as *Shitta M'qubbetset* or from R. Solomon ben Abraham Adret (known as Rashba, c. 1235–c. 1310), who cites Rabad's commentary on 'Avoda Zara 7a (Rashba 'Avoda Zara 7a and Ḥullin 44b).

55 Rabad's commentary is on a *baraita* that appears in 'Avoda Zara 7a, which is a variant of the one cited here in Ḥullin 44b. The version in 'Avoda Zara states: "one who asks ... a scholar who forbids should not ask [another] scholar to permit."

is told] in chapter "[Cattle] should not be placed" (['Avoda Zara] 40[a]) about a boat with chopped fish that came to Sikhra,[56] etc.[57] Rava made an announcement[58] and forbade [the fish];[59] Rav Huna bar Ḥinnana made an announcement and permitted—[this is] not necessarily [a contradiction].[60] Rather, Rav Huna went out first,[61] and so explained the Rashba[62] and Naḥmanides.[63] Even more so [a second scholar would not contradict the first] if he is one versus many, and of lesser status than they; it is obvious that he is not permitted to permit what they have prohibited. And if it seemed to him [that he] could permit the meat for the reason [the author of] the Agudda[64] wrote, in the first chapter of Ḥullin [10a], [about] what we say there [ad loc.] the defect is in the knife, the defect is not in the animal: "From here is it proven that a ritual slaughterer who checked it [the knife] and it is found that he does

ובמנין וההיא דפרק אין מעמידין (דף מ׳) בארבה דצחנתא דאתא לסיכרא וכו׳[לי] נפיק שיפורא דרבא ואסר שיפורא דרב הונא בר חיננא ושרי לאו דוקא אלא לרב הונא נפיק תחלה כן פי׳[רשו] הרשב״יא והרמב״ן כ״ש [כל שכן] הכא דאיהו יחיד כנגד רבים וקטן כנגדם דפשיטא דאינו רשאי להתיר מה שאסרו הם ואם היה נראה לו להתיר הבשר מטעם שכתב האגודה פ״ק [פרק קמא] דחולין והא דקאמרינן התם סכין איתרע בהמה לא איתרע מכאן מוכח שוחט שבדקוהו ונמצא שאינו

---

56   A trading town on the Tigris.
57   The omitted text reads: Rav Huna bar Ḥinnana went out [to examine the fish] and saw scales, and permitted it. Rava said to him: "Is there any [one] who permits in such a case, in a place where scales are common [such as a fishing boat]?" Though the indications for kosher fish are fins and scales, the Mishna, Nidda 6:9 states "Every [fish] that has scales, has fins," so that the concern is how Rav Huna bar Ḥinnana can be certain that the scales he sees are from the chopped fish, and not from some other fish that was on the boat before.
58   Lit., "Rava's trumpets went out."
59   Since they were chopped, and it was not possible to be certain whether the scales were from this fish.
60   This incident does not contradict the statement from Ḥullin above that "[if] a scholar has forbidden [something], his colleague is not permitted to allow [it]."
61   Rav Huna bar Ḥinnana permitted and then Rava challenged him.
62   Rashba was a student of Naḥmanides. The version of Rashba found on the pages cited by Sirkes does not address this point. The explanation Sirkes presents is found in various sources (such as Ran [R. Nissim Gerondi, 1310?–1375?], 'Avoda Zara 1b-2a on the pages of the Rif [R. Isaac Alfasi, 1013–1103] at ha-nish'al l'ḥakham and 16b-17a at amar rav Pappa), but only in Naḥmanides's name.
63   Ḥiddushei Ha-Ramban 'Avoda Zara 40a at v'ha d'amrinan, and this explanation is consistent with the complete telling of the incident in 'Avoda Zara 40a.
64   R. Alexander Suslin Ha-Kohen of Frankfurt, d. 1349.

not know [the laws of ritual slaughter], [the meat] is not retroactively declared nonkosher, and it is not necessary to make the vessels kosher, because the defect is in the person, the defect is not in the animal, and when it was slaughtered it was under the status of being permitted, and the ritual slaughterer was in his status [of competence] and until now [his status was that] he knew [the laws]," and he thought that their [the community rabbis'] ruling was mistaken in a matter of accepted law,[65] and so he may permit what they forbade,[66] like that cow from Menaḥem's house in chapter "Cases concerning property" ([Sanhedrin] 33[a])[67]—in that case he should have discussed the halakhic issues with the rabbis who [were] forbidding [the meat], and perhaps they would have revoked their ruling, or he might have changed his mind, because it is clear that one could change a ruling of a prohibition, even if initially forbidden, according to reasoned examination [of the matter], like what the Ran wrote in the first chapter of ʿAvoda Zara [7a],[68] not as this man did in a manner of triumph and controversy, such that he went

יודע אין להטריף למפרע וגם אין צריך להכשיר הכלים דאדם איתרע בהמה לא איתרע וכשנשחטה בחזקת היתר עומדת ואוקי שוחט בחזקתו ועד עתה ידע עכ"ל [עד כאן לשונו] והיה סובר דדינים כטועה בדבר משנה דיכול להתיר מה שאסרו הם וכהאי פרה של בית מנחם בפ"א ד"מ [בפרק אחד דיני ממונות] (דף ל"ג) הנה היה לו לשאת ולתת עם החכמים האוסרין בדבר הלכה דאולי היו חוזרים מהוראותם או הוא היה חוזר מדעתו דפשיטא דיכול לחזור מהוראת איסור אפי'[לו] היה אוסרים מתחלה בשקול הדעת כמ"ש [כמו שכתב] הר"ן [הרב נסים] בפ"ק [בפרק קמא] דע"ז [דעבודה זרה] לא כאשר עשה האיש הזה בדרך נצחון

---

65   Lit., "a matter from the Mishna." This expression is understood to mean a legal matter for which the law has been previously decided. See *Sanhedrin* 33a.

66   A second scholar is permitted to contradict the first one, if the first made a clear error in a matter of accepted law, rather than having a different judgment.

67   There was a cow whose womb had been removed, and R. Tarfon fed the cow to the dogs, indicating his judgment that it was not kosher. But the matter was brought before the Sages in Yavne, who ruled that it was kosher, because the physician Theodos had said that no cow or sow leaves Alexandria without its womb cut out, to prevent them from giving birth. Thus, there is clear empirical evidence that an animal with a womb removed is not a *t'refa*. In fact, this is stated in the Mishna, *Ḥullin* 3:2, which R. Tarfon should have known. Thus, R. Tarfon erred in a matter of accepted law.

68   Ran, *ʿAvoda Zara* 1b-2a on the pages of the Rif at *ha-nish'al l'ḥakham* concluded his commentary there by saying: "but if the first [scholar] listened to the claims of the second and admitted that he erred in a matter of reasoning ... the second reverses the ruling of the first and permits what he [the first] forbade. Thus it seems to me that the halakha should be ..."

up to the pulpit and permitted without a reason, [according to] a lone [opinion], what all the many faultless rabbis forbid. And in Chapter "The obligation of ḥalitsa"[69] ([Yᵉvamot] 104[a]) it says: Rabba bar Ḥiyya of Ctesiphon did a deed [of officiating at a rite of ḥalitsa] with a [nonleather] slipper on his own and at night. Shmuel said [sarcastically]: "How great is his authority, that he acted as an individual!"[70] Rashi explained, "How great is his authority" [was said] derisively. Further, an even worse offense is that the members of the holy community accepted those rabbis and the members of the maʿamad as a religious court, in which case what was done was done, even if they forbade the meat not according to the law, [but to] safeguard[71] a matter, so that not everyone would go and slaughter for the community without permission of the religious court. [This is] as is found in the Mordekhai[72] in the first chapter of [Bava] Batra:[73] "from the JT[74] three [men] from a synagogue are like [all] the members of the synagogue;[75] seven from the residents of the city are like [all] the residents of the city. What is the case?[76] If it is that they accepted upon themselves [the authority of these], then even if it is an individual [he

ומחלוקת דעלה למגדול והתיר בלא טעם ביחידי מה שאסרו כל החכמים הרבים והשלמים. וב״פ [ובפרק] מצות חליצה (דף ק״ד) קאמר רבה בר חייא קטוספאה עבד עובדא במוק ביחידי ובלילה אמר שמואל כמה רב גובריה דעביד כיחידאה ופירש רש״י כמה רב גובריה בלשון גנאי ועוד רעה גדולה מזו שאנשי הקי״ק [הקהילה הקדושה] קבלו אותם החכמים ואנשי המעמד עליהם לב״ד [לבית דין] וא״כ [ואם כן] מה שעשו עשו אפילו היו אוסרים הבשר שלא מן הדין למגדר מילתא שלא יהא כל אחד הולך ושוחט לצורך הקהל בלי רשות ב״ד [בית דין] וכדאיתא במרדכי פ״ק [פרק קמא] בבתרא מהירושלמי שלשה מבית הכנסת כבני ב״ה [בית הכנסת] שבעה מבני עיר כבני העיר הא מה אנן קיימין אם שקבלו עליהן אפילו

---

69 Ḥalitsa is the rite for release of a widow whose deceased husband has no living descendants from the obligation to marry her brother-in-law.

70 Halakha requires a leather shoe, performing the rite in the daytime and having two authorities present. Using a nonleather shoe, performing ḥalitsa at night, and in the presence of only one authority are all consistent with minority opinions (Yᵉvamot 104a).

71 Lit., "to put a fence around."

72 Authored by Mordecai ben Hillel Ha-Kohen, 1240?–1298.

73 1:482 (in the edition of the Mordekhai that is printed in the Vilna edition of the Talmud).

74 JT Mᵉgilla 3:2 (74a).

75 Regarding the authority to make decisions about the synagogue.

76 Lit., "How are we standing?"

would have the authority]," etc. "therefore [continues the *Mordekhai*], in every case that the community selected and accepted upon themselves even one individual." Even more so in this case, for they are many faultless [rabbis], and this unworthy [person] disputed them, as a lone [voice], and also permitted what they forbade, and thereby led the public to desecrate the name of God, because they ate nonkosher meat on his word. For just this, too, he is deserving of shunning, because there is no doubt that it was clarified by the rabbis mentioned that he never learned the laws of ritual slaughter, as is apparent from what they wrote. According to this information, I am prepared to agree with the rabbis who have hastened me to excommunicate and shun said physician from Amsterdam, wherever Jews reside, his bread is to be treated like the bread of a heathen,[77] etc., until he returns from his evil ways. "I will forgive his sin."[78]

[2] However, since we have not seen a copy of said physician's writ [of his version of the events], it is incumbent upon

ביחיד וכו'/לי] אלמא דכל היכא שביררו הקהל וקיבלו עליהו אפילו יחיד וכש״כ [וכל שכן] הכא שהן רבים ושלמים וזה הקטן חלק עליהם ביחידי וגם התיר מה שאסרו והנה הביא את הרבים לידי חלול השם שאכלו נבלה על פיו דגם על זה חייב נידוי בפני עצמו כי אין ספק דנתברר אצל החכמים הנזכרים דמעולם לא למד הלכות שחיטה כאשר נראה מכתבם ועל פי הדברים האלה הנני מוכן ומסכים עם החכמים שזרזוני להחרים ולנדות את האיש פלוני הרופא מאמשטרדם הנזכר בכל גבול ישראל פתו פת כותי וכו'/לי] עד ישוב מדרכיו הרעים הנ״ז[כרים] ושב ורפא לו.

אמנם לאשר לא ראינו תמונות כתבו של פלוני הרופא יש לנו לדונו שלא בפניו באולי יאמר כי גם החכמים הנזכרים הם אנשי ריבו ומבקש להוציא לאור זכותו בפני איזה ב״ד [בית דין] חשוב שיברור בפניהם כי לא עשה מעשים כאלה אשר זממו ודימו בכתבים עליו הנה אין ספק שלא חל עליו נדוי וחרם מעתה דלא

us to litigate for him without his presence. Perhaps he would say that the rabbis mentioned are his antagonists, and [that] he requests to bring his innocence to light in some worthy court, and clarify in their presence that he did not do these things of which they have falsely accused him in their written account. Considering this, there is no doubt that shunning and excommunication should not be

---

77 See the chapter "On Excommunication."
78 Lit., *return and be healed* (Isa. 6:10). R. David Kimḥi (1160?–1235?) (Isa. 6:10 and 57:18) and other commentators interpret this to mean "I will forgive his sin." This phrase is commonly used in rabbinic literature and responsa to mean that if a person repents, he will be forgiven.

enacted, since the court in Amsterdam is not preferable [to another]. [We learn this] from Mar Ukva as is [found] at the end of chapter "One [litigant] chooses" [*Sanhedrin* 31b]:[79] A message was once sent [by the religious court in the Land of Israel] to Mar Ukva: "To him whose luster is like that of the son of Bitya, peace be with you! Ukvan the Babylonian has complained to us, saying: 'My brother Jeremiah has obstructed my path.' [Therefore], speak to him, and make sure that he meets us in Tiberias." And then the *gᵉmara* states: But is this not self-contradictory? [First] you say, "Speak to him," that is, you judge him [in Babylonia]; [and then] "make sure he meets us in Tiberias," which means "Send him here!" The *gᵉmara* resolves

עדיף ב״ד [בית דין] אמשטרדם ממר עוקבא דאיתא ס״פ [סוף פרק] זה בורר שלחו ליה למר עוקבא לדזיו ליה כבר בתי׳[ה] שלם עוקבן הבבלי קבל קדמנא ירמיה אחי העביר עלי את הדרך וא״ל [ואמרו ליה] השיאוהו ויראה פנינו בטבריא וקאמר בגמרא הא גופא קשיא אמרת אמרו לו אלמא דיינוהו אתון השיאוהו ויראה פנינו בטבריא אלמא שדרוהו הכא. ופריקו אלא ה״ק [הכי קאמר] אמרו להו דיינו אתון אי ציית ציית ואי לא השיאוהו הכא ויראה פנינו בטבריא. וכתבו התוספות וז״ל [וזה לשונם] אין לפרש אי לא ציית שלא תוכלו לכופו דכש״כ [דכל שכן] שלא יוכל נשיא

it: What they meant was: "Speak to him"—judge him; if he accepts your decision, well and good. If not, "make sure he appears before us in Tiberias." The Tosafot wrote: "One should not interpret [the instruction to Mar Ukva] 'if he does not accept your decision' to suggest that [the intention was] 'you would not be able to force him' [to accept the court's judgment]. A *Nasi*[80] would be even less able to force him—Here [in Babylonia] is the rod; there [in the Land of Israel] is the legislator,[81] and Mar Ukva was the exilarch [so he certainly had the

---

79   See Halakhic Background.

80   The head of the court in the Land of Israel, a scion of the family of Hillel. The Jewish courts in the Land of Israel had little power of enforcement under Roman rule in the time of Mar Ukva, a third-century *amora*.

81   *Sanhedrin* 5a (said from the perspective of a Babylonian Sage). The text there continues (5a–b): As is taught in a *baraita*: *The staff shall not depart from Judah* (Gen. 49:10)—these are the Exilarchs in Babylonia, who rule Israel with a rod; *nor the scepter from between his feet* (ibid.)—these are the descendants of Hillel, who teach Torah to the people (see, also, *Horayot* 11b). Hebrew *mᵉḥoqeq*, translated here as "scepter" (see also Num. 21:18) is a parallel in this poetic verse to the word *shevet*, translated here as "staff" or "rod." However, *mᵉḥoqeq* is primarily a word for a legislator or ruler (see Deut. 33:21). The *Nᵉsi'im*, descendants of Hillel, were considered to have less legal authority than the exilarchs, considered descendants of King David (traditionally considered a descendant of Judah). See *MT Hilkhot Sanhedrin* (The Laws of the Sanhedrin) 4,13-14.

authority to enforce a judgment]. Rather, Rabbenu Tam[82] explains, 'if he does not accept your position'—such as the defendant says to the court: 'I am going to the Supreme Court.'"[83, 84] The Rosh explained similarly.[85] We learn from this that even though Ukvan the Babylonian had a complaint against Jeremiah his brother in Babylonia, who castrated him according to one of Rashi's interpretations (may his memory be blessed),[86] and [for this] it is obvious that he was deserving of shunning, as for this Noah cursed Canaan,[87] and [furthermore,] Mar Ukva was the exilarch. Nevertheless, they wrote to him from the Land of Israel [to say] that if Jeremiah asserts "I am going to the Supreme Court in the Land of Israel," they listen to him, and do not shun him, nor do they inflict any punishment on him. Even more so, the physician mentioned may say, "I am going to a high[er] and [more] worthy court," and he should not be judged in Amsterdam.

לכופו דהכא שבט והתם מחוקק ומר עוקבא ראש גולה הוה אלא מפר״ת [מפרש רבינו תם] אי לא ציית כגון דאמר לב״ד [לבית דין] הגדול קאזלינא עכ״ל [עד כאן לשונם] וכן פי׳[רש] הרא״ש שמעינן מהכא דאעפ״י [דאף על פי] דעוקבן הבבלי הוה ליה דינא בבבל בהדי ירמיה אחיו שסירסו לפי פי׳[רוש] אחד של רש״י ז״ל ופשיטא דהיה חייב נידוי דעל זה אירר נח את כנען ומר עוקבא היה ראש גולה בבבל וא״ה [ואפילו הכי] כתבו אליו מארץ ישראל דאי טעין ירמיהו לבדה״ג [לבית דין הגדול] שבא״י [שבארץ ישראל] קאזלינא שומעין לו ולא ינדוהו ולא יעשה לו שום עונש כש״כ [כל שכן] דמצי אמר פלוני הרופא לבדה״ג [לבית דין הגדול] וחשוב קאזלינא ולא לידיינהו בית דין של אמשטרדם.

---

82 R. Jacob ben Meir Tam, c. 1100–1171.
83 The Great Sanhedrin in Tiberias.
84 *Tosafot Sanhedrin* 31b at *iy tsiyyet tsiyyet*.
85 *Sanhedrin* 3:41. Our version is not the same as the version that Sirkes alludes to.
86 *Sanhedrin* 31b at *'Ukvan Ha-Bavli*. Sirkes cites a fantastical interpretation of Ukvan's complaint against his brother (roughly, "he obstructed my path"), apparently to make the point that even someone who clearly deserves shunning can express his preference for a court. Rashi's other interpretation, that the complaint was about monetary matters, is more plausible.
87 One midrashic interpretation of Gen. 9:22-25 is that Ham castrated his father, who cursed Canaan when he became aware of what had happened; see *Sanhedrin* 70a; *B'reshit Rabba* 36:25 (Theodor-Albeck edition).

Regarding such a case, I saw a responsum of R. Samuel, son of R. Yoḥanan,[88] in the "long" *Mordekhai*,[89] [instructing] not to force judgment in someone's city if the important people and the leadership of the city are the ones who called him to judgment. Rather, they should go directly to a fair place so that a judgment in absolute truth will be rendered.[90] Maharik[91] alluded to this responsum in his responsa, principle 1,[92] and even though this responsum deals with monetary matters, I do not see any reason to differentiate between this [our case] and that [as far as getting a fair hearing in another court]. Therefore, if the physician mentioned claims "I am ready and willing to abide by whatever ruling is judged regarding the

וכיוצא בזה ראיתי תשובה הרב רבינו שמואל ב"ר יוחנן במרדכי הארוך שלא לכוף לנידון לדון בעירו כשגדולי העיר ופרנסיה הזמינוהו לדון אלא ילכו דרך ישרה למקום הגון כדי שיוציאו דין אמת לאמיתו ומהרי"ק רימז לתשובה זו בתשובותיו שורש א' ואע"פ [ואף על פי] דתשובה זו הוא בעסק ממון אין אני רואה לחלק ביניהם בין זו לזו וע"כ [ועל כן] אם פלוני הרופא הטוען הנני מוכן ומזומן להיות ציית דין על כל מה שמתרעמים עלי ואקבל עלי לקיים בכל אשר יפסקו הנה אין עליו עונש נדוי וחרם ובלבד שלא יהא שום צד ערמה בדבריו אלא תכף יקבע לה[ו]ם [ו]זמן לילך ולדון בפני ב"ד [בית דין]

complaints against me, and I will uphold whatever is decided," then there is no punishment of shunning and excommunication, so long as there is no deceit in his words. But he should immediately set a time for them to go and to be judged

---

88 This should be R. Samuel, son of R. Elḥanan (c. 1184–1230), a Tosafist and grandson of one of the leading Tosafists, R. Isaac (the Elder) ben Samuel of Dampierre.

89 "The history of the spread of the *Mordekhai* and the transmigrations of its many versions in manuscript and in print is one of the most complicated in all of rabbinic literature. ... [T]wo main compilations of extracts, the 'Austrian' and the 'Rhenish,' were made from it" (Israel Ta-Shma and Yehoshua Horowitz, "Mordecai ben Hillel Ha-Kohen," in *EJ*, 14:480-481). The Rhenish version is the shorter of the two, and is the version commonly found in printed editions of the Talmud. The responsum referred to here from the "long" *Mordekhai* is found in Yehoshua Horowitz and Eliyahu Waldman, eds., *The Complete Mordekhai—Sanhedrin* [Hebrew] (Jerusalem: Machon Yerushalayim, 2009), 111.

90 The phrase "judgment in absolute truth" appears in *Shabbat* 10a. Similar praise of a judge who judges in absolute truth is found in *Mᵉgilla* 15b, *Bava Batra* 8b, and *Sanhedrin* 7a.

91 The Italian halakhist, R. Joseph ben Soloman Colon, c. 1420–1480.

92 *Responsa of the Maharik*, principle 1 (Venice, 1519). Specific reference to the responsum written by R. Samuel, son of R. Elḥanan is found in Eliyahu Pines, ed., *Shᵉelot U-Tshuvot U-Fiskei Mahariq Ha-Ḥadashim*, 3rd ed. (Jerusalem: Machon Yerushalayim, 1999), 18.

at a worthy court that is near them, and there the law will be uncompromised[93] between them, to vindicate the innocent and to convict the guilty. But if he is stubborn[94] and dismisses them with a flimsy excuse,[95] then the shunning and excommunication will henceforth fall on him, until he repents completely and properly. As we say, peace to the judges of Israel[96] and to those who hearken to their voice.

חשוב הסמוך להם ולשם יקוב הדין ההר ביניהם לזכות את הזכאי ולחייב את החייב אבל אם יתן כתף סוררת לדחות אותם בקנה מעתה יחולו על ראשו נדוי וחרם שמתא שם מיתה עד ישוב בתשובה הגונה וראויה וכדאמרן ושלום על דייני ישראל והשומעים לקולם אני הקטן יואל פה קהלה קודש בריסק דליטא:

[Signed by] me, Joel, the insignificant,[97] here in the holy community of Brisk in Lithuania.

Discussion

There are two main themes in the response.[98]

[1] At the outset, it appears that Sirkes accepts the word of the plaintiffs, the leaders of the Amsterdam community who sent him their question. In fact, during most of the responsum, Sirkes writes as if the physician's guilt is unquestionable, and the only question is whether he is deserving of excommunication. Through presentation of many sources, Sirkes finds justification for such a punishment, unless the defendant is willing to retract his offending words and actions.

The justification is based on several points:
  i) He is guilty of various heresies, including scorning the words of the Sages, expressing heretical ideas, and engaging with heretical literature.
  ii) He defied the members of the *ma'amad* and the rabbis.
  iii) He led other people astray to eat nonkosher meat.

---

93 Lit., "the law will cut through the mountain," an expression that appears in *Y*ᵉ*vamot* 92a and *Sanhedrin* 6b about judging disputes without compromise.
94 Lit., turns *a stubborn shoulder* (Neh. 9:29, Zech. 7:11).
95 Lit, "a reed."
96 *K*ᵉ*tubbot* 50a.
97 A term used to describe oneself out of modesty.
98 See the section numbers in square brackets in the responsum.

[2] Then Sirkes takes a turn in his analysis and considers that the physician might have been framed! The accusations might, after all, be false, and the religious court in Amsterdam might not give a fair judgment. Just as in modern law a change in venue might be requested if a defendant might not get a fair trial in a local jurisdiction, Sirkes considers whether the religious court in Amsterdam might be biased against the physician and he might prefer to go before another court. Sirkes asserts that it is his right to choose that option. In fact, by citing Maharik as a precedent, Sirkes is recommending a change of venue so that the defendant will be judged in "absolute truth" in a "fair place."

R. Sirkes's tactic is quite wise. By initially accepting the plaintiffs' claims and expressing wrath at the presumed misdemeanors of the defendant, he placates the plaintiffs, leading them to believe that he is on their side, so that they would later be reluctant to question his opinion when he recommends that a fair trial be conducted in another locale. He also lets it be known that he cannot render a true judgment without hearing the defendant's version of events. He was not "born yesterday"—he realizes these could be false accusations, that there are often synagogue and communal politics, the stature of the plaintiffs notwithstanding.

One can only conjecture about the result of this judgment. The identity of the physician is not certain, nor do we know the outcome of the incident—whether he was excommunicated in Amsterdam, he retracted whatever he was accused of, or if he went to some other locale to be judged. But immersion in the case has provided a glimpse of life in the burgeoning Amsterdam Jewish community and a case study of the application of Jewish law at the beginning of the seventeenth century.

Questions for Further Discussion

According to Yosef Kaplan, "The Amsterdam Portuguese Jewish community frequently threatened to impose the punishment of excommunication even in fields where in other places, in other communities, less stringent measures were adopted."[99] Would Sirkes want to rule in light of the practices in Amsterdam, or would finding a less stringent approach be part of his agenda?

---

99   See [Kaplan], 124.

Uriel da Costa (residing at the time in Hamburg) was excommunicated first in 1618 by R. Modena of Venice, approximately the time of the case in Sirkes's responsum, and later in Amsterdam in 1623. Read about the accusations against him and his nonconformity, and compare his situation to that of the accused physician.[100]

Baruch Spinoza was excommunicated by the Portuguese Jewish community in 1656. Read about his relationship with the community and the record of censure,[101] and then compare his circumstances with those in this responsum. Why is his case the most glaring and outstanding of all? Discuss the thesis proposed by Nadler to explain Spinoza's harsh excommunication.

In his discussion of the defendant's behavior, Sirkes states that the physician was "lured by philosophy, which is heresy itself." Compare this attitude with that of R. Elijah ben Benjamin Ha-Levi (1481–after 1540), as presented in the chapter "Are You Calling Me a Heretic?!" Can you think of reasons for these vastly different attitudes? In his statement, does Sirkes reflect the view of only the Portuguese Jewish community in Amsterdam? Does he reflect his own view? Compare these views to the attitudes towards philosophy in Christian and Muslim societies in these periods. Did those attitudes influence the spectrum of views in Jewish society?

Further Reading

[Bodian] Bodian, Miriam. "Amsterdam, Venice, and the Marrano Diaspora in the Seventeenth Century." In *Dutch Jewish History, Proceedings of the Fourth Symposium on the History of the Jews in the Netherlands*, edited by Jozeph Michman, 47-65. Jerusalem: Institute for Research on Dutch Jewry, 1989.

[Bodian 2] ———. *Hebrews of the Portuguese Nation: Conversos and Community in Early Modern Amsterdam*. Bloomington: Indiana University Press, 1997.

[Huussen] Huussen Jr., Arend H. "The Legal Position of Sephardi Jews in Holland, circa 1600." In *Dutch Jewish History, Proceedings of the Fifth Symposium on the History of the*

---

100 See [Bodian 2], 118-121.
101 See "The Writ of Excommunication against Baruch Spinoza," in *The Jew in the Modern World: A Documentary History*, ed. Paul Mendes-Flohr and Jehuda Reinharz, 3rd ed. (Oxford: Oxford University Press, 2011), 62; [Nadler] and [Bodian 2], 123.

Jews in the Netherlands, edited by Jozeph Michman, 19-41. Jerusalem: Institute for Research on Dutch Jewry, 1993.

[Kaplan] Kaplan. Yosef. "The Social Functions of the *Herem* in the Portuguese Jewish Community of Amsterdam in the Seventeenth Century." In *Dutch Jewish History, Proceedings of the Symposium on the History of the Jews in the Netherlands*, edited by Jozeph Michman and Tirtsah Levie, 111-115. Jerusalem: Institute for Research on Dutch Jewry, 1984.

[Kaplan2] ———. "The Portuguese Community in 17th-Century Amsterdam and the Ashkenazi World." In *Dutch Jewish History, Proceedings of the Fourth Symposium on the History of the Jews in the Netherlands*, edited by Jozeph Michman, 23-45. Jerusalem: Institute for Research on Dutch Jewry, 1989.

[Kaplan3] ———. "The Jews in the Republic until about 1750: Religious, Cultural, and Social Life." In *The History of the Jews in the Netherlands*, edited by J. C. H. Blom, R. G. Fuks-Mansfeld, and I. Schoffer, 116-163. Oxford: The Littman Library of Jewish Civilization, 2002.

[Nadler] Nadler, Steven. "The Excommunication of Spinoza: Trouble and Toleration in the Dutch Jerusalem." *Shofar: An Interdisciplinary Journal of Jewish Studies* 19, no. 4 (Summer 2001): 40-52.

[Swetsch] Swetschinski, Daniel M. *Reluctant Cosmopolitans: The Portuguese Jews of Seventeenth Century Amsterdam*. London: The Littman Library of Jewish Civilization, 2000.

[Swetsch2] ———. "The Middle Ages to the Golden Age, 1516–1621." In *The History of the Jews in the Netherlands*, edited by J. C. H. Blom, R. G. Fuks-Mansfeld, and I. Schoffer, 44-84. Oxford: The Littman Library of Jewish Civilization, 2002.

[Vless] Vlessing, Odette. "New Light on the Earliest History of the Amsterdam Portuguese Jews" In *Dutch Jewish History, Proceedings of the Fifth Symposium on the History of the Jews in the Netherlands*, edited by Jozeph Michman, 43-75. Jerusalem: Institute for Research on Dutch Jewry, 1993.

8.

South of the Equator, in the New World

Torat Ḥayyim 3,3

Historical Background

If Holland was a haven to Jews and descendants of Jews[1]—whether Crypto-Jews or New Christians who wished to return to Judaism—what might have compelled some of them to emigrate from there to Brazil in the early seventeenth century, so shortly after becoming established in Amsterdam? Whether to expand their shipping and trade operations, or to satisfy a wanderlust cultivated among the generations of repeatedly migrating descendants of Spanish and Portuguese Jews, "from 1630 on and at different times, several hundred Jewish families migrated to Dutch Brazil."[2]

This migration began when the Dutch took Pernambuco, Brazil, from the Portuguese. The migrants were no doubt encouraged by article ten of the administrative rules of the West India Company, approved in 1629 by the States-General at The Hague, which stated:

> The liberty of Spaniards, Portuguese, and natives, whether they be Roman Catholics or Jews, will be respected. No one will be permitted to molest them or subject them to inquiries in matters of conscience or in their private homes; and no one should dare to disquiet or disturb them or cause them any hardship—under the penalty of arbitrary punishments or, depending upon circumstances, of severe or exemplary reproof.[3]

---

1 See Historical Background in the chapter "Excommunication in Amsterdam."
2 [Wiznitzer], 2. See [Wiznitzer 2], 58-60 for a description of the Jews in the Dutch expedition to Recife in 1630.
3 Cited from [Wiznitzer 2], 57. If this, however, sounds like the pinnacle of tolerance, see [Wiznitzer 2], 73-91.

The community of immigrant Jews in Brazil was joined by former Portuguese New Christians who returned to Judaism.⁴ By 1636 a synagogue had been established, and in 1642 R. Isaac Aboab was appointed Ḥakham. Aboab was himself a Crypto-Jew who had been baptized as a Catholic in Portugal in 1605. Following a sojourn in Saint-Jean de Luz, France, his family relocated to Amsterdam in approximately 1612 to be able to practice openly as Jews. There, having studied with R. Isaac Uziel of Fez, Aboab became the junior Ḥakham.

The following undated question about liturgy and the prayers concerning rain, responded to by R. Ḥayyim Shabbetai,⁵ was sent from Brazil,⁶ probably before Aboab's arrival in 1642,⁷ perhaps around the time of the establishment of the synagogue, when it would have been important to settle any liturgical uncertainties in order to maintain consistency and eliminate bickering.⁸

The exact year of composition is not essential, but the historical events of the time explain a portion of the text. In the responsum Shabbetai, in Salonica, refers to his many anxieties and also to the fact that he does not have access to his library. In 1620 there was a great fire in Salonica in which "thousands of the Jews' homes, twenty-eight synagogues, several study halls, a big *Talmud Torah* and a

---

4   Only some of the Portuguese Crypto-Jews chose to return openly to Judaism, while others felt uncertain about the permanence of the Dutch presence in Brazil. See [Wiznitzer], 2. Also see [Feitler].

5   Known by the acronym Maharḥash, before 1555–1647.

6   We are not certain how the question was sent to Shabbetai. Wiznitzer proposes that the last sentence ("Therefore, [please] instruct us, our teacher, if the law supports them, and in his [Shabbetai's] light we shall be enlightened") indicates that Shabbetai "did not receive the inquiry directly from Brazil, but rather through a rabbi in another city, probably Amsterdam" ([Wiznitzer 2], 67; reference to the congregants as "them" would suggest an intermediary rabbi composed the question). If the question was sent first to Amsterdam, why would it not have been sufficient for the senior Ḥakham there, R. Saul Levi Morteira, to respond? R. Saul Levi Morteira was certainly a competent rabbi, with R. Aboab serving as his assistant Ḥakham. If the inquiry was sent first to Amsterdam, it is most likely that it was R. Morteira who forwarded it to Shabbetai. Shabbetai was indeed "regarded as the outstanding halakhic authority of his time, questions being addressed to him from communities near and far" (Abraham David, "Ḥayyim (ben) Shabbetai," in EJ, 8:483-484). Perhaps the Brazilian Jews wanted a response from the most regarded authority, notwithstanding the additional delay of sending the question on to Salonica.

7   It is also possible that R. Aboab had already arrived and did make a decision, but congregants who were not satisfied demanded the opinion of a more renowned authority.

8   The congregation's detailed regulations, which can be found translated in [Wiznitzer], depict a congregation that was quite exacting in all its practices.

Mishne Torah were burned";⁹ other fires followed in 1630, 1636, 1640, and 1648.¹⁰ Due to these fires, many Jews emigrated from Salonica. In that same period, the city was stricken with plague several times. These misfortunes caused the flight of many Jews to the countryside, exacerbating the tax burdens on the community members who remained.¹¹

In addition, the responsum mentions "the royal garments." This refers to the woolen cloth that the Jewish community in Salonica was obligated to supply to the sultan, at first in lieu of taxes. The Jews in Salonica had become dominant in the production of wool in the Ottoman Empire following their arrival from the Iberian Peninsula,¹² and from approximately 1537 the community sold the sultan wool that was used primarily for the Janissaries' uniforms.¹³

For quite a while the contract was beneficial to the Jews, but by the end of the sixteenth century, the cost of production exceeded the payments received, so that provision of the wool became a heavy tax burden, in addition to the standard taxes, such as the poll tax. One of the most critical points in the travails of the community due to the demands for this fabric transpired when a delegation from the Salonica Jewish community, headed by R. Judah Covo, went to see the sultan in 1637 to negotiate the tax burden, only to result in the execution of Covo.¹⁴

We can now comprehend Shabbetai's reference to multiple anxieties: fires, plague, and the difficulty in supplying the woolen fabric demanded by the sultan. Wiznitzer believes that the responsum was written in 1637, after the disastrous expedition,¹⁵ but the reference to "the royal garments that overwhelmed us" could refer to the burden that existed even before the expedition.¹⁶

---

9   R. David Conforti, *Kore Ha-Dorot* (Berlin, 1845), 45a; see also R. Me'ir ben Shem Tov Melamed, *Mishpat Tsedeq* 3,35.

10 Jacov Ben-Mayor and Yitzchak Kerem, "Salonika," in EJ, 17:701.

11 Nükhet Varlik, "Plague, Conflict, and Negotiation: The Jewish Broadcloth Weavers of Salonica and the Ottoman Central Administration in the Late Sixteenth Century," *Jewish History* 28 (2014): 261-288, in particular 265n14 and 265n15 and fig. 3.

12 See Shemuel Avitsur, "The Woollen Textile Industry in Saloniki" [Hebrew], in *Sefunot: Studies and Sources on the History of the Jewish Communities in the East, The Book of Greek Jewry-II*, ed. Meir Benayahu (Jerusalem: Yad Izhak Ben Zvi, 1971), 145-168.

13 See Azriel Shohat, "'The King's Clothing' in Saloniki" [Hebrew], in *Sefunot: Studies and Sources on the History of the Jewish Communities in the East, The Book of Greek Jewry-II*, ed. Meir Benayahu (Jerusalem: Yad Izhak Ben Zvi, 1971), 169-188.

14 Ibid., 180.

15 [Wiznitzer 2], 66.

16 For example, Kohut [and Parry], cited by Wiznitzer [Wiznitzer 2], 66n12, suggested 1636.

Alas, the community remained in Brazil for only a short time. When Recife was retaken by the Portuguese in January 1654, any former Christians (and their descendants) would once again be subject to the Inquisition and were compelled to emigrate. Even Jews who were not subject to the Inquisition, having not been baptized or descended from conversos, chose not to remain.[17] Some of the community returned to Amsterdam, but a small number sought refuge in New Amsterdam (later New York).[18] Though the Recife community was disbanded, Shabbetai's responsum would serve as a resource when other Jewish communities arose south of the equator, even though his responsum did not settle the matter.[19]

Halakhic Background

The thrice-daily prayers in the Jewish liturgy[20] include both a request for rain and a "mention of rain," but only during a portion of the year. The request for rain is made only in weekday prayers (since no requests should be made on the Sabbath and holidays), while the mention of rain is made on all days. The request for rain is included in the benediction known as *birkat ha-shanim* (benediction of the years), a request for economic prosperity, expressed in agricultural terms,[21] so that plentiful rain in the desirable time is essential to the request. The mention of rain is included in the benediction known as *gᵉvurot* (the "powers" of God), among which is: "He causes the rain to fall."

The matter under discussion in the responsum written by Shabbetai is the location-dependence of the ideal season for rain and its relationship to the timing of these prayers. In all locales, the mention of rain is included from Shᵉmini Atseret through the first day of Passover, coinciding with what was considered the ideal season for rain in the Land of Israel, where there is a dry season and a

---

17 In fact, as related in [Bodian 3], a Jew in Portuguese hands might need to prove to the Inquisition that he was never baptized and therefore not subject to the Inquisition.

18 For a more nuanced history of the Jews who arrived in New Amsterdam in 1654, see Leo Hershkowitz, "By Chance or Choice: Jews in New Amsterdam 1654," *The American Jewish Archives Journal* 57, nos. 1-2 (2005): 1-13.

19 See [Lasker]: 164-169.

20 Specifically, the daily prayer unit known as the Eighteen Benedictions and the parallel Sabbath and holiday prayers.

21 The benediction includes a request to "bless our year like the good years," which is most likely a reference to Joel 2:23-25.

rainy season. In the Land of Israel the request for rain is from the 7th of Ḥeshvan until (but not including)[22] the first day of Passover, while in the (Babylonian) diaspora, the request for rain begins on the sixtieth day from the autumnal equinox,[23] presumably because rain was not needed in that region before that time, but also ends on the first day of Passover.

What about communities that were in neither locale? Though there were Jewish communities in places such as Egypt and Rome in Talmudic times, there is only one relevant discussion in the Talmud about a community that was neither in the Land of Israel nor Babylonia, but in the city of Nineveh.[24]

The question is presented in the Talmud following some discussion about communal fasts decreed by the rabbinic authorities in the event of drought, plague, or other afflictions.[25] When such a fast is decreed, an additional paragraph is inserted into the thrice-daily prayer. Nevertheless, almost all commentators interpret the question from Nineveh to be a general one, about the request for rain in the regular recitation of the thrice-daily prayer,[26] rather than about the additional paragraph when a fast is decreed, as is understood from the parallel narrative in the Jerusalem Talmud.[27]

---

22   Because *birkat ha-shanim* is not said on the holiday.

23   *Ta'anit* 10a. The date cannot be fixed in the Jewish calendar, which is lunar; in Jewish practice it has been fixed at December 4th (or 5th in a leap year) in the Gregorian calendar, due to a "calendrical miscalculation." See [Lasker2].

24   Nineveh was an Assyrian city. As to the actual location of this community, see [Lasker]: 143n8.

25   The classic religious view is that such afflictions are a punishment, so that repentance through prayer and fasting are enacted to request from God alleviation of the dire circumstances.

26   Rashi at *u-vshome'a' t'filla*; MT *Hilkhot T'filla* (The Laws of Prayer) 2,17; Rosh *Ta'anit* 20.

27   JT *Ta'anit* 1:1 (63d), where it is said that "the people of Nineveh needed to proclaim a fast day after Passover," suggesting that rain after Passover was a regular occurrence and desirable, but there was a drought when they inquired of Rabbi Judah Ha-Nasi if it was permissible to proclaim a fast (after Passover).

Ta'anit 14b

תענית י"ד ב'

The people of Nineveh sent Rabbi [Judah Ha-Nasi] [the following question]: [For ones] such as us, when even during the period of the summer solstice we need rain, what should we do? Are we like individuals [praying for rain], or are we like many [i.e., a community]? Are we like individuals and [request rain] in *shome'a' t'filla*?[28] Or are we like many and [request rain] in *birkat ha-shanim*? He sent them [the response]: You are like individuals, and [you request rain] in *shome'a' t'filla*.

שלחו ליה בני נינוה לרבי כגון אנן
דאפילו בתקופת תמוז בעינן מטרא
היכי נעביד כיחידים דמינן או כרבים
דמינן כיחידים דמינן ובשומע תפלה
או כרבים דמינן ובברכת השנים
שלח להו כיחידים דמיתו ובשומע
תפלה מיתיבי אמר רבי יהודה אימתי
בזמן שהשנים כתיקנן וישראל שרויין
על אדמתן אבל בזמן הזה הכל לפי
השנים הכל לפי המקומות הכל לפי
הזמן אמר ליה מתניתא רמית עליה
דרבי רבי תנא הוא ופליג מאי הוי

[The *g*ᵉ*mara*] challenges: R. Yᵉhuda[29] said: "When?[30] In the time when the [seasons of] the years are [as] usual, and [the People of] Israel are dwelling on their land, but in this time everything is according to the seasons, everything is according to the locations, everything is according to the period." He said to him:[31] You challenge Rabbi with a *baraita*? Rabbi is a *tanna*, and he [has a right to] differ [from a *baraita*]! What will be [the halakhic ruling] about it? Rav Naḥman says,

---

28 This is the prayer in the weekday Eighteen Benedictions that ends with "Blessed art Thou, Lord, who hears prayer" (*shome'a' t'filla*). It is considered appropriate to add any personal requests to this prayer.

29 This is R. Yᵉhuda bar Ilai, who preceded Rabbi Judah Ha-Nasi.

30 This *baraita* does not appear in the Tannaitic sources, so that we actually do not know the context in which R. Yᵉhuda made this statement, and we cannot be certain about what his "when?" is referring to. It is reasonable to understand it to refer to the dates between which it is appropriate to request rain in *birkat ha-shanim*, so that in his opinion the fixed dates only apply when the People of Israel all dwell in the Land of Israel, and therefore the people of Nineveh should request rain in that benediction and not in *shome'a' t'filla*. Though Rashi interprets "when?" to be referring to the order of fasts (and therefore some translations assume this to be the meaning), his interpretation is curious, as is stated by R. Arye Leib ben Asher in his commentary *G'vurat Ari*, *Ta'anit* 14b. He states: "It is difficult for me, because if it is referring to the order of fasts, then how is this challenging what Rabbi [says] about requesting rain in *shome'a' t'filla* as individuals? ... Therefore it seems [to me] that [one] should interpret 'when' to be referring to requesting rain in *birkat ha-shanim*, and so it appears from the words of the Tosafot [at *ha-kol lᵉfi ha-shanim*]."

31 "He said to him" does not appear in the most reliable manuscripts of *Ta'anit*, and, in fact, the text reads better without those words.

in *birkat ha-shanim*; Rav Sheshet says, in *shome'a' t^efilla*; and the law is, in *shome'a' t^efilla*.	עלה רב נחמן אמר בברכת השנים רב ששת אמר בשומע תפלה והלכתא בשומע תפלה

To understand the discourse about this passage in Shabbetai's responsum, it is necessary to look at two *mishnayot*, a related section of the *g^emara* and Maimonides's commentary on one of the *mishnayot*. A selection from Maimonides's *MT* is also relevant. Quite prominent in Shabbetai's responsum is also his reference to and quotation from a responsum from the Rosh,[32] of which a significant portion is presented here.

Mishna *Ta'anit* 1:2-3	**משנה תענית א,ב-ג**
[We] do not request rain unless it is close to the rainy season. R. Y^ehuda says on the last day of the Festival [of Sukkot], the last[33] prayer leader[34] mentions [rain], while the first[35] [prayer leader] does not mention [it]. On the first festival day of Passover, the first [prayer leader] mentions [rain], and the last [prayer leader] does not mention [it]. Until when do [we] request [rain]? R. Y^ehuda says until after Passover.[36] R. Meir [says] until [the month of] Nisan is over, as it says, *He has brought down*	אין שואלים גשמים אלא סמוך לגשמים ר׳[בי] יהודה אומ׳[ר] העובר לפני התיבה ביום טוב האחרון של חג האחרון מזכיר והראשון אינו מזכיר וביום טוב הראשון של פסח הראשון מזכיר והאחרון אינו מזכיר עד אמתי שואלין ר׳[בי] יהודה אומ׳[ר] עד שיעבור הפסח ר׳[בי] מאיר עד שיצא ניסן שנ׳[אמר] ויורד לכם גשם מורה ומלקוש בראשון

---

32 R. Asher ben Jehiel, c. 1250–1327.
33 Referring to the *musaf* prayer, which is a prayer on the Sabbath and festivals, in addition to the thrice-daily prayers, customarily recited after the morning prayers.
34 Lit., "the one who goes before the ark."
35 Referring to the leader for *shaḥarit*, the morning prayer.
36 The halakha is according to R. Y^ehuda, with the interpretation of "after Passover" to mean "after the time of the Passover sacrifice," so that the last request for rain is made in the afternoon prayer of Passover eve. See *Ta'anit* 4b.

for you the early [i.e., autumn] *rain and the late* [i.e., spring] *in the first* [*month*] (Joel 2:23).³⁷

On the third of Marḥeshvan [we] request rain. Rabban Gamliel says on the seventh of [the month], fifteen days after the Festival [of Sukkot],³⁸ so that the last of those in Israel [who came on pilgrimage] will reach the Euphrates [in Babylon, where they reside, before the rain begins].³⁹

בשלשה במרחשון שואלין גשמים רבן גמליא'[ל] אומ'[ר] בשבעה בו בחמשה עשר יום אחר החג כדי שיגיע האחרון שבישראל לנהר פרת

| Ta'anit 4b | מסכת תענית ד' ע"ב |

R. Asi said in the name of R. Yoḥanan: halakha is according to R. Yᵉhuda, [who said we begin to mention rain on the last day of Sukkot]. R. Zeira said to R. Asi: Did R. Yoḥanan say that? But we teach that we [begin to] request rain on the third of Marḥeshvan; [while] Rabban Gamliel says on the seventh, and R. Elazar says that the halakha is according to Rabban Gamliel! He [R. Zeira] said to him [R. Asi, in reply]: Are you pitting one man against another man?⁴⁰ If you want, [you can] say there is no contradiction: here [Rabban Gamliel refers to when] to request [rain], while here [R. Yᵉhuda refers to when] to mention [it]. But did R. Yoḥanan [who says halakha is according to R. Yᵉhuda] not say "when one requests, one mentions"? [He said] that [about when it is time] to cease [requesting, not about when it is time to begin]. It has been said: But did R. Yoḥanan not say "if he starts to mention,

אמר רבי אסי אמר רבי יוחנן הלכה כרבי יהודה אמר ליה רבי זירא לרבי אסי ומי אמר רבי יוחנן הכי והתנן בשלשה במרחשוון שואלין את הגשמים רבן גמליאל אומר בשבעה בו ואמר רבי אלעזר הלכה כרבן גמליאל אמר ליה גברא אגברא קא רמית איבעית אימא לא קשיא כאן לשאול כאן להזכיר והאמר רבי יוחנן במקום ששואל מזכיר ההוא להפסקה איתמר והאמר רבי יוחנן התחיל להזכיר מתחיל לשאול פסק

---

37 There are some significant differences among the many translations of this verse. I translated the verse to be consistent with R. Meir's use of it. In particular, the word *ba-rishon* (in the first) here refers, as in every other instance of its use in the Bible, to the month of Nisan.

38 This is for the Land of Israel, and the halakha is according to Rabban Gamliel.

39 So they would not get caught in the rain and be discouraged from coming in following years (*Ḥiddushei Ha-Ritva Ta'anit* 10a).

40 R. Elazar against R. Yoḥanan. Though R. Elazar was R. Yoḥanan's student, both men are Amora'im, in which case their opinions are equally valid.

then he starts to request; if he ceases to request, he ceases to mention"? Rather, [we reconcile the two opinions by saying] there is no contradiction: this one [Rabban Gamliel's opinion] is for us [in Babylonia,] while this one [R. Yᵉhuda's] is for them [in the Land of Israel]. What is different for us? We have crops in the field [which should not be damaged by rain before they are harvested]; they also have [a reason to delay requesting rain, in that] they have pilgrims [who need to return to Babylonia before it rains]. Rather, R. Yoḥanan was saying [that the halakha is according to R. Yᵉhuda] when the Temple is no longer in existence [and thus there are no pilgrims]. Now that you have reached this [conclusion], both this and this are for them [in the Land of Israel]: here [R. Gamliel's opinion applied] when the Temple was standing, here [R. Yᵉhuda's opinion applies] [now] when the Temple is no longer in existence.

מלשאול פוסק מלהזכיר אלא לא קשיא הא לן הא להו מאי שנא לדידן דאית לן פירי בדברא לדידהו נמי אית להו עולי רגלים כי קאמר רבי יוחנן בזמן שאין בית המקדש קיים השתא דאתית להכי הא והא לדידהו ולא קשיא כאן בזמן שבית המקדש קיים כאן בזמן שאין בית המקדש קיים

Maimonides's Commentary on the Mishna *Ta'anit* 1:2[41]

רמב״ם פירוש למשנה תענית א,ב

Halakha is according to Rabban Gamliel.[42] And all this [about the range of dates during which rain is requested] is in the Land of Israel and everywhere that is similar. Whatever will be said further about the seasons of the fasts [for rain] is only [applicable] to the Land of Israel and every place whose climate is like that, but in the other countries the request [for rain] should begin at the season that is appropriate for rain in that place. That time would be equivalent to the seventh of Marḥeshvan [in the Land of Israel]. If the rains are delayed after

והלכה כרבן גמליאל. וכל זה בארץ ישראל וכל שהוא דומה לה. וכן כל מה שייאמר הלאה בזמני התעניות אינו אלא בארץ ישראל וכל מקום שאוירו קרוב לאוירה, אבל בשאר הארצות הרי תהיה השאלה בזמן הראוי לגשמים באותו המקום, והרי אותו הזמן כאלו הוא שבעה במרחשון, ואם נתאחרו הגשמים

---

41 The Hebrew text is from the translation from the Arabic by Yosef Qafiḥ (Jerusalem: Mosad Ha-Rav Kook, 1963).

42 *Ta'anit* 4b.

that [local] time according to the corresponding times stated here, then those [people in those locations] would fast as is mentioned here.[43] This is because there are countries where the rainy season only begins in Nisan; and there are countries where in Marḥeshvan it is summer and rains at that time are not a blessing, but cause loss and destruction, so how could it be that the people in that locale would request rain in Marḥeshvan? Would this not be false? This matter is right and clear.

אחרי אותו הזמן לפי יחס זמנים אלו האמורים כאן, הרי אלו מתענים כמו שנזכר כאן, לפי שיש ארצות שאין זמן הגשמים מתחיל אלא מניסן, ויש ארצות שבמרחשון יהיה בהם קיץ, ואין הגשמים בו לברכה אלא מאבד ומשמיד, ואיך ישאלו אנשי אותו המקום גשמים במרחשון, האם אין זה שקר. זה דבר נכון וברור.

Maimonides *MT Hilkhot Tᵉfilla* (The Laws of Prayer) 2

רמב״ם משנה תורה הלכות תפילה ב

15 For the entire rainy season, one says "He causes the rain to fall" in the second benediction [that is, *gᵉvurot*], while during the summer [one says there,] "He causes the dew to fall."[44] From when does one say "He causes the rain to fall"? From the *musaf* prayer on the last day of the Festival [of Sukkot] until the morning prayer of the first day of Passover. And from the *musaf* prayer of the first day of Passover one says "He causes the dew to fall."

16 Rains are requested in *birkat ha-shanim* from the seventh of Ḥeshvan, the whole period that rain is mentioned. To what does this refer? To the Land of

טו כל ימות הגשמים אומר בברכה שניה מוריד הגשם, ובימות החמה מוריד הטל. מאמתי אומר מוריד הגשם, מתפלת המוספין של יום טוב האחרון של חג, עד תפילת שחרית של יום טוב הראשון של פסח. ומתפלת המוספין של יום טוב הראשון של פסח אומר מוריד הטל.

טז משבעה ימים במרחשון שואלין את הגשמים בברכת השנים, כל זמן שמזכיר הגשם. במה דברים אמורים, בארץ ישראל, אבל בשנער ובסוריא ומצרים, ומקומות הסמוכות לאלו

---

43 The *mishnayot* that follow present a schedule of dates and fasts such that if it does not rain by a certain date, the fasts are decreed. Each later date in the schedule is associated with more restrictions on the corresponding fasts. Maimonides is stating here that the schedule would be in accordance with the seasons in a particular locale.

44 The Ashkenazi liturgy does not "mention dew" (see the Rma [R. Moses Isserles] in *SA OḤ* 114:3), though in modern Israel it is generally customary for Ashkenazim to say it, too.

Israel. But in Babylonia, Syria and Egypt, and places that are close and similar to them, rain is requested from the sixtieth day of the autumnal equinox.

17 [In] locales that are in need of rain in the summer, such as the far islands in the sea, rain is requested when it is needed in *shome'a' t^efilla*.⁴⁵

Responsum

Rosh Responsa, Principle 4,10⁴⁶	שאלות ותשבות הרא"ש כלל ד, סימן י

It happened in the year 5073⁴⁷ since the creation of the world that the rains stopped, and there was no rainfall the entire winter, only a negligible amount. They [the rabbis] decreed a fast to beseech God to provide rain on the earth. On the first night of Passover, after the evening prayer, my master and father the Rosh⁴⁸ was sitting at the entrance to his house, and we, some of his colleagues, were standing to his right and to his left. He said: "Now it would be [a] good [time] to raise the matter that I always wondered about:

why should they [the people] not mention and request rain until Shavuot?" This group of colleagues replied that it would be good to notify the elders of this, and they did so. It was agreeable to them [the elders], and they sent [instruc-

---

45   The second part of this halakha is omitted here as it is not relevant for us.
46   Only selected excerpts of this responsum are included.
47   1313 CE.
48   Some of the Rosh's responsa were recorded by some of his sons. See Shmuel Glick, *Quntres ha-T^eshuvot he-Ḥadash* (Jerusalem: Schechter Institute for Jewish Studies, 2006), 3:1011.

tion] to the cantor of the synagogue to mention rain on the following day. They did so, ... but then some of the rabbis who were not consulted on this matter voiced their objection and said it was not appropriate to mention it [rain] because it is a sign of a curse.[49] My master and father the Rosh contained himself and did not say a word [about it] on that day, until the eve of *hol ha-moʻed*.[50] He wrote a treatise to back up his words as follows:

Because I heard that there are those who were bewildered by my words, I will explain what I said. ... It is not just now but rather quite a while ago, in Ashkenaz, that I complained about two things I saw being done in those days. The first is that they do not request rain properly. [I say this] even though we say in the first chapter of *Taʻanit* [10a]: It is taught in a *baraita*: Ḥananya says, in the diaspora on the sixtieth day from the autumnal equinox, and Rav Huna bar Ḥiyya said in the name of Shmuel that the law is according to Ḥananya. Further, in all matters we follow [the rulings of] the Sages of Babylonia, and we do as they do whenever there is a difference of opinion between the Sages of Babylonia and the Sages of the Land of Israel, because the Babylonian Talmud is considered the essential one. [However], these words [apply] to a matter of forbidden or permitted [foods, etc.], liable or not liable, impurity and purity. But in a matter that is dependent upon the needs of the time and there is no alteration that would result in transgressing the words of the Torah, it is fitting to go according to the seasons, locations, and time. Babylonia is located where there is much water, and they did not need rain

וישר בעיניהם וישלחו לחזן הכנסת להזכיר למחר הגשם ויעשו כן ... והנה רעש מקצת החכמים אשר לא היה הדבר בעצתם ויוציאו קול לאמר שלא היה ראוי להזכירו שסימן קללה הוא ויתאפק א״א [אדוני אבי] הרא״ש ולא דבר ביום ההוא מאומה עד ליל חולו של מועד. ויכתוב מגלת ספר לחזק דבריו וזה תרפה.

על כי שמעתי כי יש תמהים על דברי באתי לפרש מה שאמרתי ... ולא מן כדו אלא מכבר ימים רבים באשכנז נתרעמתי על שני דברים שראיתי שנוהגים בימים הללו. האחד שאינן שואלים הגשמים כתיקון. ואף על גב דאמרינן בפרקא קמא דתענית תניא חנניא אומר ובגולה עד ס׳ יום לתקופה ואמר רב הונא בר חייא אמר שמואל הלכה כחנניה. ואנן בכל מילתא אזלינן בתר חכמי בבל ועבדינן כוותייהו היכא דפליגי אהדדי חכמי בבל וחכמי ארץ ישראל דתלמוד בבל חשבינן עיקר, ה״מ [הני מילי] בדבר איסור והיתר וחיוב ופטור

---

49 *Taʻanit* 2b.
50 The intermediate days of the festival.

until the sixtieth day from the autumnal equinox, or the sowing season was late in Babylonia. But in Ashkenaz, where the sowing season is from the middle of Tishrei and on, it is known that if there would not be any rainfall immediately after sowing, then it [the seed] would be ruined, because the birds and mice would completely eat it. Why [then] should we not do as the people of the Land of Israel, who request rain from Ḥeshvan, according to Rabban Gamliel? [After all,] in this matter there is no disagreement between those in Babylonia and those in the Land of Israel. ... Rather, in Babylonia they did as they needed, and the *mishna* that states that [to] request rain in Ḥeshvan[51] is taught in the Land of Israel according to their needs. ... If the people in Babylonia act according to their location and needs, but not according to the *mishna*, even more so should the people in Ashkenaz do according to their needs without departing from the *mishna*.[52] ...

טומאה וטהרה אבל דבר התלוי בצורך השעה ואין בו שינוי לעבור על דברי תורה ראוי לילך אחר השנים והמקומות והזמן דבבל שוכנת על מים רבים ולא היו צריכין גשמים עד ס' לתקופה או היה זמן הזרע מאוחר בבבל. אבל בארץ אשכנז שזמן הזרע הוא מחצי תשרי ואילך הדבר ידוע שאם לא ירדו גשמים מיד אחר הזרע שהוא מתקלקל שהעופות והעכברים יאכלוהו כלו למה לא נעשה כבני ארץ ישראל ששואלין הגשמים במרחשון כרבן גמליאל, כי בדבר הזה אין מחלוקת בין בני בבל ובין בני ארץ ישראל ... אלא שבבבל היו עושים כפי הצריך להם, והמשנה שאומרת ששואלין במרחשון נשנית בארץ ישראל כפי הצריך להם. ... אם בני בבל עושים כפי מקומם וכפי צרכם בשינוי המשנה כל שכן שבני אשכנז יעשו כפי צרכם שלא בשינוי המשנה.

...

והמנהג השני שנוהגין לפסוק מלשאול ולהזכיר ביום טוב הראשון של פסח והדבר ידוע שבאשכנז עיקר

And the second practice [that I challenged] is that they cease to request or mention [rain] on the first festival day of Passover. But it is known that in Ashkenaz the wheat depends primarily on the rain between Passover and Shavuot, while the *mishna* that states that [we] cease

---

51   See Halakhic Background.

52   The text as found in the printed editions and what is considered the best manuscript, National Library of France MS Hebrew 420 has this sentence convoluted ("If the people in Babylonia act according to their location and needs without departing from the *mishna*, even more so should the people in Ashkenaz do according to their needs not according to the *mishna*"), so that the logic of a fortiori does not make sense. It is the practice in Babylonia that was not in accordance with the *mishna*. It can be assumed that a corruption to the text occurred. See Haym Soloveitchik, *Use of Responsa as Historical Source: A Methodological Introduction* [Hebrew] (Jerusalem: Zalman Shazar Center for Jewish History, 1990), 11.

from the first festival day of Passover is taught for the people of the Land of Israel, as I have proven. ... For [in] every country, according to its needs, [the people] request [rain] and mention it, and just as the Land of Israel and Babylonia each have distinct practices for the request and mention [of rain], and these do according to their needs and these do according to their needs, so is the law for the rest of the lands, for what is the difference?

Another proof is from this: The people of Nineveh sent Rabbi [the question] ...[53] Therefore, [I conclude] that Rabbi differs only [in the case] of the people of a single city, but Ashkenaz is a spacious land, and Rabbi would concede that [the people] request [rain] whenever they are in need [of it], and since they request [it] because of the need, all the more so they mention [it], ... as Rabbi Yoḥanan said, "Whenever one requests, one mentions."[54] All of this I explained to my teachers in Ashkenaz, and no one

קיום התבואה היא על ידי הגשמים שבין פסח לעצרת והמשנה שאומרת שמפסיקין מיום טוב הראשון של פסח לבני ארץ ישראל נישנית כאשר הוכחתי ... שכל ארץ וארץ לפי צרכה שואלת ומזכרת דכמו שארץ ישראל ובבל חלוקים במנהגם בשאלה והזכרה ואלו ואלו עושין לפי צרכן ואלו לפי צרכן הוא הדין שאר ארצות דמאי שנא.

ועוד ראיה מהא דשלחו ליה אנשי נינוה ... אלמא דר' לא פליג אלא בבני עיר אחת. אבל ארץ אשכנז שהיא רחבת ידים מודה ר' דשואלין כל זמן שהם צריכין, וכיון ששואלין מפני הצורך כ"ש [כל שכן] שמזכירין ... דאמר ר'[בי] יוחנן כל זמן שהוא שואל הוא מזכיר. כל אלו הדברים דנתי לפני רבותי באשכנז ולא היה אדם מערער לדברי אלא שאמרו אין אנו צריכין לשנות המנהג באשכנז כי אין עצירת גשמים מצוי שם והרבה פעמים התבואה מתקלקלת מפני רוב הגשמים. כשיצאתי מאשכנז ועברתי

disputed what I said, but they said that they do not need to change the custom in Ashkenaz because there is no drought there, and [in fact] many times the wheat is damaged due to heavy rain. When I left Ashkenaz and traveled through Provence,[55] I heard in Montpellier that they would mention rain[56] on the seventh of Ḥeshvan, and I was very pleased with this. So I told the rabbis in Montpel-

---

53 The Rosh quotes the excerpt from *Taʿanit* 14b presented in Halakhic Background, until "he [has a right to] differ."
54 *Taʿanit* 4b; see Halakhic Background.
55 On his way to Spain.
56 Considering that the 7th of Ḥeshvan is named, we can understand him to mean "request rain," rather than "mention rain," which would begin on Shʿmini Atseret regardless of when they begin to request it.

lier: You solved one of my questions, but what do you do as far as stopping [to mention rain]? They said that they do as [is taught] in the *mishna* and cease on the first festival day of Passover. I said to them: Do you not need rain between Passover and Shavuot? They said that they need it very much, and the wheat cannot survive without rain. I told them everything as I wrote it above, and they thought it quite agreeable, but they said: "Our requesting rain on the seventh of Ḥeshvan is how the earlier rabbis were accustomed [to do]. As far as ceasing [such a request], we cannot do a thing to change the custom if all the rabbis in the land do not join [in agreement]." And I left there without knowing what they agreed to do. When I came here [to Spain], I saw that they need rain between Passover and Shavuot more than other places, and I said several times to my colleagues that it would be appropriate not to stop requesting and mentioning [rain] until Shavuot, because now I know that [in] all the lands that I know their essential rain [occurs] between Passover and Shavuot, and certainly there are many [such lands]. But I did not dare to say such things as to change the custom. But now that I have seen that, due to our sins, the rains have stopped, and the seeds are ruined, and the [people] are fasting for rain ... I said to myself that now the time has come to correct what I have desired for a quite a while, because they certainly would listen in such a time of distress as this, and if they do it this year, then they will find it pleasing and would not revert [to their previous custom]. They certainly would have done

דרך פרובינצא שמעתי במונפישליר שהיו מזכירים הגשמים בז' במרחשון ויושר מאוד בעיני. ואמרתי לחכמי מונפישליר תרצתם לי קושיא אחת ולעניין הפסקה מה אתם עושין, ואמרו שעושין כמשנה מיום טוב הראשון של פסח פוסקים. אמרתי להם שמא אינכם צריכים מטר בין פסח לעצרת אמרו לי שהרבה הם צריכים ואי אפשר לתבואה להתקיים בלא מטר, ואמרתי להם כל דברי כאשר הם כתובים למעלה וישרו מאד בעיניהם אלא שאמרו מה שאנו שואלין בשבעה במרחשון כך הנהיגו חכמים הראשונים. ועל ההפסקה לא נוכל לעשות דבר בשנוי מנהג אם לא שיתקבצו חכמי הארץ ויצאתי משם ולא ידעתי מה הסכימו לעשות. ובבואי הנה ראיתי שיותר צריכין גשמים בין פסח לעצרת משאר מקומות ואמרתי כמה פעמים לחברי שראוי היה שלא להפסיק מלשאול ולהזכיר עד עצרת כי עתה אני יודע שכל הארצות שאני יודע עיקר גשמיהם הם בין פסח לעצרת ובודאי רבים נינהו. אלא שלא מלאני לבי לדבר כדברים הללו לשנות המנהג.

ועתה שראיתי כי בעונותינו הגשמים נעצרו ונתקלקלו הזרעים ומתענין בשביל הגשמים ... אמר לי לבי עתה הגיע העת לתקן מה שנתאויתי זה

so, but they turned their hearts and their minds aback. ... Maimonides (may his memory be blessed) wrote in his Commentary on the Mishna [what is consistent] with what I say, and this his formulation: "...".[57] And in his composition [the *MT*] he wrote "...".[58] Cursorily,[59] this would [seem to] mean that the Commentary on the Mishna contradicts what he wrote in his composition, because in the Commentary on the Mishna he wrote "but in the other countries the request [for rain] should begin at the season that is appropriate for rain in that place. That time would be equivalent to the 7th of Marḥeshvan [in the Land of Israel]." Therefore, they request [rain] in *birkat ha-shanim*. But in his composition he wrote that "[in] the far islands in the sea, rain is requested ... in *shomeʿaʿ tʿfilla*." Whoever examines his words with scrutiny will find them to be precise, because in the Commentary on the Mishna he wrote "lands," since there is a distinction between the Land of Israel and Babylonia in the matter of requesting and mentioning [rain]. From this we deduce that [a group of people] are not called "many" unless [we are referring to] one [whole] land, and about such people we say that the request [for rain] is in *birkat ha-shanim*. But in his composition he wrote "In locales that are in need of rain in the summer, such as the far islands in the sea," but they are not themselves called "lands." Thus they are like individuals, and they say [the request for rain] in *shomeʿaʿ tʿfilla*. So here

ימים רבים כי בודאי שישמעו לך בעת צרה כזאת ואם יקיימו עליהם בשנה הזאת יערב עליהם ולא ישובו ממנה. וכן בודאי היו עושים אלא שהטו את לבבם והסבו את דעתם אחורנית. ... והרמב״ם ז״ל כתב בפירוש המשנה כדברי וזה נוסחו. ... עכ״ל [עד כאן לשונו]. ובחבורו כתב ... ולפום ריהטא משמע שפירוש המשנה סותר מה שכתב בחבורו כי בפירוש המשנה כתב ובשאר ארצות צריכה להיות השאלה בזמן שהן צריכין לגשם באותה הארץ ויעשו אותו זמן כאלו הוא שבעה במרחשון אלמא ששואלים בברכת השנים. ובחבורו כתב שאיי הים שואלים הגשמים בשומע תפלה. והמדקדק בדבריו ימצאם מכוונים כי בפי[רוש] המשנה כתב ארצות לפי שיש חלוק בין ארץ ישראל לבבל לענין שאלה והזכרה מזה נלמוד שאין נקראין רבים אלא ארץ אחת ואותם אומרים בזמן הצריך להם שאלה בברכת השנים. אבל בחבורו כתב ומקומות שהם צריכין גשמים בימות החמה

---

57 The Rosh quotes Maimonides's Commentary on the Mishna *Taʿanit* 1:2; see Halakhic Background.
58 The Rosh quotes *MT Hilkhot Tʿfilla* 2,16-17; see Halakhic Background.
59 Lit., "according to the running," i.e., "hastily."

I proved [my point], and it is known that in Ashkenaz, which is a very large land, and France and all the lands from Ashkenaz to this land [Spain], and this [land] included with them all, require rain between Passover and Shavuot, and certainly they are many [people] and can request in *birkat ha-shanim* and can mention rain like the people in the Land of Israel in the winter.

But when I saw that the heart of the congregation was turned from accepting the words of the living God, I, too, withdrew [my practice of] requesting and mentioning [rain] in the synagogue in which I pray, even though I could have requested [in *birkat ha-shanim*] in spite of the fact that I am an individual, because it is the need of many. But nevertheless I did not want to make "separate sects."[60] I would not have written on the intermediary days of the festival because it is not my practice, but for the immediate need, to avoid the desecration of God's name, and also this matter does contain something of need for the festival.

Asher ben R. Jehiel.

כגון איי הים ואינם נקראים ארץ בפני עצמן הילכך כיחידים דמו ואומרים בשומע תפלה. והרי הוכחתי והדבר ידוע שבאשכנז שהיא ארץ גדולה מאד וצרפת וכל הארצות שמאשכנז עד הארץ הזאת וזאת בכלל כלם צריכות מטר בין פסח לעצרת ובודאי רבים הם ויכולים לשאול בברכת השנים ולהזכיר הגשמים כבני ארץ ישראל בחורף.

ובראותי כי הטו את לב הקהל לבלתי קבל ממני דברי אלהים חיים גם אני חזרתי בי מלשאול ולהזכיר בבית הכנסת שאני מתפלל בו, אע״פ [אף על פי] שהייתי יכול לשאול אע״פ [אף על פי] שאני יחיד כיון שצורך רבים הוא, מכל מקום לא רציתי לעשות אגודות אגודות. ולא הייתי כותב בחול המועד כי לא הורגלתי בכך אלא שצורך שעה הוא מפני חלול שם שמים, וגם יש בדבר הזה קצת מצורך המועד. אשר בן ה״ר [הרב] יחיאל

Discussion

A critical question that arose in the Rosh's exposition on the halakhic sources is: Does Maimonides's Commentary on the Mishna contradict his ruling in the

---

60 A midrash on Deut. 14:1 derives from *lo titgodᵉdu* (lit., "do not gash yourselves," a prohibition against certain mourning practices) the additional command "do not form separate sects" (*Yᵉvamot* 13b). This exegesis is frequently used as an instruction to maintain conformity within a community.

MT? Considering that they were composed at different stages in his life, and with different purposes, it is certainly feasible, though never considered by scholars to be likely. Rather, scholars tend to reconcile the two compositions. Is the Rosh's method of reconciling the two citations—that in the Commentary on the Mishna Maimonides wrote about whole large countries, while in the *MT* he was referring to more local areas—convincing?

The twentieth century scholar R. Yosef Qafiḥ wrote the following explanation of the difference between the Maimonidean texts:

> Our rabbi's words [in the Commentary on the Mishna] are clear and straightforward, that the subject of discussion here is climates that are the total reverse, that is, the months Ḥeshvan, Kislev [and] Tevet are summer, and the months Iyyar, Sivan and Tammuz are winter, so that in the months Kislev [and] Tevet the wheat is totally ripe, and that is the time of harvest of the wheat and barley, and rain in this period would destroy the crops and cause them to perish, as is the case in the Land of Israel in the months Iyyar and Sivan. Regarding those lands Maimonides wonders "and how could it be that the people in that locale would request rain in Marḥeshvan? Would this not be false?"[61] This reasoning, which he emphasized with the words "this matter is right and clear," he did not mention in his great composition, the *Yad Ha-Ḥazaqa*,[62] not here in The Laws of Prayer, nor in The Laws of Fasts. Rather, he ruled as we have before us.[63]
>
> And the matter is clear from the preciseness of his language [in the *MT*] "that are in need of rain in the summer." That is to say, that the winter for them is winter, and the summer is summer, the rainy season is the natural rainy season for most of the world, and the dry season is the dry season for most of the world. Rather, they also need rain in the dry season, in addition to the natural rainy season. The matter is, again, straightforward and clear that such is his intention from what he said: "the dry season."[64]

According to Qafiḥ, the Commentary on the Mishna addresses a situation of a locale south of the equator, while the *MT* does not. He also explains why the *MT* does not:

---

61   Maimonides, Commentary on the Mishna *Ta'anit* 1:2; see Halakhic Background.
62   This, "The Strong Hand," is an alternate name for the *MT*. The numerical values of the letters *yud-dalet* that make up the word *yad* also add up to fourteen, referring to the fourteen volumes in the *MT*.
63   *MT Hilkhot T'filla* (The Laws of Prayer) 2,16-17; see Halakhic Background.
64   Maimonides, *Mishne Torah*: Yosef Qafiḥ (Qiryat Ono: Mekhon Mishnat Ha-Rambam, 1984–1996) *Hilkhot T'filla* 2,17n36; translation from the Hebrew is mine.

So now the matter is straightforward, why Maimonides did not rule according to the reasoning that he offered in the Commentary on the Mishna: because it is not his method to codify in his great composition, *Mishne Torah*, anything other than what is expounded upon in the basic sources, that is the words of the Tanna'im and Amora'im, and as such. But matters that are not stated clearly in the sources—it is not his method to include them in his composition, as is well-known and accepted among all of his commentators. His reason is as I commented in my introduction to the Book of Knowledge.[65] According to what is said there, these are two distinct things, that is to say, what Maimonides wrote in the Commentary on the Mishna and what he wrote here [in the *MT*], and they have no connection,[66] and there is no possibility to consider that there is, seemingly, a contradiction between them.[67]

Therefore, Qafiḥ challenges the Rosh's reconciliation of the "contradiction":

So now it is most difficult for us to comprehend the Rosh's difficulty with the Commentary on the Mishna [in comparison] to his composition [the *MT*], so that the Rosh saw, at first glance, a contradiction between them that he needed to explain. ... The matter is very surprising, that he formed a contradiction that never was and was never created, and needed a tenuous explanation for something that needed no explanation.[68]

Shabbetai will also address the two different Maimonidean texts and quote extensively from the Rosh, and refute him, in this responsum.

Responsum

Torat Ḥayyim 3,3	תורת חיים חלק ג סימן ג
Question: [The following question] was sent from a far off land, Brazil, which is a place that is far from the equator in the Southern Hemisphere,[69]	שאלה שלחו מתם מארץ רחוקה ממלכות בראזיל שהוא מקום רחוק מהקו השוה לצד דרום שקוטב

---

65 The first volume of the *MT*.
66 Referring specifically to the topic of request and mention of rain.
67 *MT*: Yosef Qafiḥ, *Hilkhot T^efilla* 2,17n36 (my translation).
68 Ibid.
69 Actually, Recife is only about 8° south of the equator.

such that the south celestial pole is more than twenty degrees high [i.e., above the horizon], and the north celestial pole is hidden beneath the horizon by more than twenty degrees. The days of the year and the entire order of the winter and summer seasons are different there: the summer is from Tishrei until Nisan, and the rainy season is from Nisan until Tishrei. The rain is necessary from Nisan until Tishrei, and from Tishrei until Nisan they have no need for rain, in that the seeds and the fruits of the trees need rain from Nisan until Tishrei, but from Tishrei until Nisan, they do not have a need for it. Not only that, but if they had rain from Tishrei until Nisan it would be very bad for them, because the air in that place is not good as we, the northern dwellers, have in our place. If there were rain from Tishrei until Nisan, the air would become damp and bring about bad diseases.[70] For these reasons they want to change the order of the prayers in the matters of requesting [rain][71] and mentioning [it.[72] They wish] to request rain from Nisan until Tishrei and not request [it] from Tishrei until Nisan. Similarly, they wish to mention rain from Nisan until Tishrei and not request[73] [it] from Tishrei until Nisan. Therefore, [please] instruct us, our teacher, if the law supports them, and in his [Shabbetai's] light we shall be enlightened.

דרומי גבוה שם עשרים מעלות ויותר וקוטב צפוני נסתר להם תחת האופק עשרים מעלות ויותר וימות השנה וכל סדר זמנים משתנה שם מקיץ לחורף שימות החמה להם מתשרי עד ניסן וימות הגשמים מניסן עד תשרי והגשמי[ם] הם צורך להם מניסן עד תשרי ומתשרי עד ניסן אין להם צורך בהם באופן שלצורך הזרעים ולפירות האילנות צריכים גשמים מניסן עד תשרי ומתשרי עד ניסן אין להם צורך בהם וגדולה מזאת שאם יהיו להם גשמים מתשרי עד ניסן הוא רע להם הרבה שבהיות שאין אויר אותו מקום טוב כמו מקומנו אנחנו יושבי צפון אם יהיו גשמים מתשרי עד ניסן ירטיב האויר ונהפך לחולאים רעים ומפני אלו הסיבות רוצים לשנות סדר תפלה בענין שאלה והזכרה ולשאול גשמים מניסן עד תשרי ושלא לשאול מתשרי עד ניסן וכן בהזכרה להזכיר גשמים מניסן עד תשרי ושלא לשאול מתשרי עד ניסן על כן יורנו מורנו אם הדין עמהם ובאורו נראה אור

---

70 See [Lasker]: 163n73 for comments about this depiction of the rainfall in Recife.
71 See Halakhic Background.
72 See Halakhic Background.
73 It is certain that he meant to write "mention."

Response: It is true that my anxieties are many, [coming] from several fronts, on top of which [there is difficulty] in our city due to the "royal garments"[74] that overwhelmed us,[75] and *the city was bewildered,*[76] and [so] I do not have in my possession the books of the authorities for reference, as I would wish.[77] But to [respond] to the request of the questioner, I will state with extreme brevity only the essence of the law, according to what is recorded in my memory.

[1][78] First of all, I'll state that it is already known that the Rosh (may his memory be blessed) wrote in principle 4,10 that it is his opinion that even in the summer when there is a need for rain for many [people], they [should] request rain in *birkat ha-shanim,* even though we say in the g*e*mara at the end of the first chapter of *Ta'anit* [14b] that the people of Nineveh were in need of rain during the period of the summer solstice, and they asked Rabbi, and he answered that you are like individuals and [should request rain] in *shome'a' t*e*filla.* Specifically there [continues the Rosh] [it refers to] when it is one city, but [with regard to] a whole country, such as Spain in totality or Ashkenaz in totality, if they are in need of rain, they can request it in *birkat ha-shanim,* according to their needs. The Tur[79] (may his memory be blessed) cited his words in *Oraḥ Ḥayyim,* 117. Further, the

---

74 See Historical Background.
75 Lit., "have knit together and came up upon our necks," derived from Lam. 1:14.
76 Derived from Esther 3:15.
77 Lit., "as is in my heart" (Josh. 14:7), a phrase frequently used in responsa.
78 Numbers are inserted to facilitate reading the discussion following the responsum.
79 R. Jacob ben Asher, son of the Rosh.

Rosh wished to interpret the words of Maimonides (may his memory be blessed) in a manner that agrees with his [the Rosh's] words, [explaining] that in his Commentary on the Mishna, regarding what Rabban Gamliel said—we request for rain on the seventh of Ḥeshvan, and [the *gᵉmara* teaches that] R. Elazar said that the halakha is in accordance with Rabban Gamliel—he [Maimonides] wrote:[80] "And all this [about the range of dates during which rain is requested] is only in the Land of Israel and the lands whose climate is like their climate [in the Land of Israel]. Whatever will be said further about the seasons of the fasts [for rain] is only [applicable] to the Land of Israel and every place whose climate is like that climate, etc. But in the other countries the request [for rain should begin] at the season that they need rain in that country. That time should be set [for that place] to be equivalent to the 7th of Marḥeshvan [when the request is begun

קי״ז וגם רצה הרא״ש לפרש דברי הרמב״ם ז״ל [זכרונו לברכה] באופן מסכים לדבריו וזה שבפירוש המשנה כתב עלה דההיא דר״ג [דרבן גמליאל] דאמר בשבעה במרחשון שואלים על הגשמים וא״ר [ואמר רבי אלעזר] הלכ׳[ה] כר״ג [כרבן גמליאל] וז״ל [וזה לשונו] וכל זה אינו אלא בא״י [בארץ ישראל] ובארצות שאוירם כאוירם כו׳[לי] אבל בשאר ארצות צריכה להיות השאלה בזמן שהם צריכים לגשמים באות׳[ה] הארץ ויעשו אותו זמן כאילו הוא ז׳ במרחשון ואם ישהו הגשמי׳[ם] מלירד אחר אותו זמן צריך להתנהג בתעניו׳[ת] כפי זה לפי שיש ארצות אין מתחילים הגשמים אלא מניסן ויש ארצות שיהיו במרחשון הקיץ והגשמים אינם להם טובים אלא ממיתים ומאבדים והיאך ישאלו אנשי אותו המקום גשם במרחשון והלא זה שקר ואולת ע״כ [עד כאן] ובחבורו כתב משבעה ימים במרחשון שואלים הגשמי׳[ם] בברכת השני׳[ם]

in the Land of Israel]. If the rains are delayed after that time [the beginning of the local rainy season], then those [in those locations] would fast in accordance, because there are lands where the rains only begin in Nisan, and there are lands where the summer is in Ḥeshvan, and rain is not good for them, but only destroys [the crops and causes them] to perish. How could the people request rain in such a place in Ḥeshvan? Is that not falsehood and folly?!" [The Rosh continues:] "However, in his composition [*MT*, Maimonides] wrote 'Rains are requested in *birkat ha-shanim* from the seventh of Ḥeshvan, the whole period that rain is men-

---

80 The Hebrew text (and therefore the translation) here are not identical to the Hebrew text (and its translation) in the citation from Maimonides's commentary in Halakhic Background, due to the variations among the translations to Hebrew from Arabic.

tioned. To what does this refer? To the Land of Israel. But in Babylonia, Syria, etc., rain is requested from the sixtieth day of the autumnal equinox. [In] locales that are in need of rain in the summer, such as the far islands in the sea, rain is requested when it is needed in *shome'a' t'filla*.'" The Rosh wrote about this: "Cursorily, this would [seem to] mean that the Commentary on the Mishna contradicts what he wrote in his composition, because in the Commentary on the Mishna he wrote 'but in the other countries the request [for rain] should begin at the season that is appropriate for rain in that place. That time would be equivalent to the 7th of Marḥeshvan.' Therefore, they request [rain] in *birkat ha-shanim*. But in his composition he wrote '[in] the far islands in the sea, rain is requested ... in *shome'a' t'filla*.' Whoever examines his words with scrutiny will find them to be precise because in the Commentary on the Mishna he wrote 'lands' since there is a distinction between the Land of Israel and Babylonia, etc. [From this we deduce that a group of people] are not called 'many' unless [we are referring to] one [whole] land, and about such people we say that the request [for rain] is in *birkat ha-shanim*. But in his com-

כל זמן שמזכיר הגשם בד״א [במה דברים אמורים] בארץ ישראל אבל בשנער וסוריא וכו׳[לי] שואלים הגשמי׳[ם] ביום ששים אחר תקופת תשרי מקומות שהם צריכים לגשמים בימות החמה כגון איי הים הרחוקים שואלים הגשמים בעת שצריך להם בשומ׳[ע] תפלה וכת׳[ב] הרא״ש על זה דלפום ריהטא משמע שפירוש המשנ׳[ה] סותר למה שכתב בחבורו כי בפירוש המשנה כתב ובשאר הארצות צריכה להיות השאלה בזמן שהם צריכים לגשם באותה הארץ ויעשו אותו זמן כאילו הוא ז׳ במרחשון אלמא ששואלים בברכת השנים ובחבורו כתב שבאיי הים שואלים בשומע תפלה והמדקדק בדבריו ימצאם מכוונים כי בפירוש המשנה כתב ארצות לפי שיש חלוק בין ארץ ישראל לבבל וכו׳[לי] שאין נקראים רבים אלא ארץ ואותם אומרי׳[ם] בזמן הצרי׳[ך] להם שאלה בברכת השנים אבל בחבורו כתב ומקומות שהם צריכים גשמי׳[ם] בימות החמה כגון איי הים שאינם נקראים ארץ בפני עצמם הילכך כיחידים דמו ואומרים בשומע תפלה ע״כ [עד כאן] ולי הדיוט ופעוט נר׳[אה] פירוש זה לדברי הרמב״ם דחוק מאד דבכי הא הוה ליה לפרושי ובחבור נר׳[אה] מדבריו דבין בהזכרה בין בשאלה

position [*MT*] he wrote 'In locales that are in need of rain in the summer, such as the far islands in the sea,' but they are not themselves called 'lands.' Thus they are like individuals, and they say [the request for rain] in *shome'a' t'filla*."

[2] But to me, amateur and insignificant that I am, this explanation of Maimonides's words seems very tenuous. Rather, he should have interpreted it thus:

In the composition it appears from his words that regarding mentioning [rain] or requesting [it] in *birkat ha-shanim*, from the *musaf* prayer of the first day of Passover and onward, we neither mention nor request [rain], but only dew, because he [Maimonides] wrote, "For the entire rainy season, one says 'He causes the rain to fall' in the second benediction, while during the summer [one says there] 'He causes the dew to fall'" etc. "And from the *musaf* prayer of the first day of Passover, one says 'He causes the dew to fall.'" Note that he wrote in [the matter of] "mentioning" that one says "He causes the dew to fall" from the *musaf* prayer of the first day of Passover and onward, but regarding the request in *birkat ha-shanim* he wrote, "Rains are requested in *birkat ha-shanim* from the seventh of Ḥeshvan, the whole period that rain is mentioned, etc." Therefore, so long as one does not mention rain, that is from the *musaf* prayer of the first day of Passover, we do not request rain in *birkat ha-shanim* anymore. If there were [substance to the interpretation of the Rosh], then [Maimonides] should not have omitted to state that also after the *musaf* prayer of the first day of Passover we [both] mention and request rain in those places that need rain. Rather, it certainly seems that according to Maimonides we do not mention [rain] or request [it] in *birkat ha-shanim* in any location after the *musaf* prayer of the first day of Passover, but if they [in some location] require rain, they request it in *shome'a' t'filla*. [This is] as he wrote "[In] locales that are in need of rain in the summer ... rain is requested when it is needed in *shome'a' t'filla*."

בברכת השנים מתפלת המוספין של יום טוב א׳ של פסח ואילך אין מזכירין ואין שואלים אלא טל שהרי כתב וז״ל [וזה לשונו] כל ימות הגשמים אומר בברכה ב׳ מוריד הגשם ובימות החמה מוריד הטל כו׳ ומתפלת המוספין של י״ט [יום טוב] הראש[ון] של פסח אומר מוריד הטל הרי שכתב בהזכרה שמתפלת המוספי[ן] של י״ט [יום טוב] הראשון של פסח ואילך אומר מוריד הטל וגבי שאלה בברכת השנים כתב מז׳ ימים במרחשון שואלים את הגשמים בברכת השנים כל זמן שמזכיר הגשם כו׳ הא כל זמן שאינו מזכיר גשם דהיינו מתפלת המוספין של י״ט [יום טוב] א׳ של פסח שוב אין שואלין גשם בברכת השנים ואם איתא לא לישתמיט לומר דגם אחר תפלת המוספין של י״ט [יום טוב] א׳ של פסח מזכירים ושואלים גשמים במקומות הצריכים גשם אלא נראה ודא[י] דלהרמב״ם אחר תפלת המוספין של י״ט [יום טוב] הראשון של פסח אין מזכירים ואין שואלים בברכת השנים בשום מקום גשם אך אם צריכים מטר שואלים בשומע תפלה וכמו שכתב מקומות הצריכים מטר בימות החמה כו׳[לי] שואלים את הגשמים בעת שצריכים להם בשומע תפלה והרמב״ם מעת

Maimonides calls the period from the *musaf* prayer on the first day of Passover and onward [until the end of Sukkot] summer, which is similar to what we see at the beginning of his words, where he wrote "during the summer [one says] 'He causes the dew to fall.'" He further wrote "And from the *musaf* prayer of the first day of Passover [and on,] one says, 'He causes the dew to fall,'" and thus is [also] seen from the simplicity of the statements of the other authorities. [Regarding] what Maimonides (may his memory be blessed) wrote in his Commentary on the Mishna, he intended only to say that even in the rainy season, so long as the rain is detrimental to them, they [should] not request [it], because a person should not request something that is detrimental to him. It also is [thus] seen from the start of his words and from their end, regarding what we learned [in a *mishna*], On the third of Marḥeshvan [we] request rain. Rabban Gamliel says on the seventh. He [Maimonides] wrote, "Halakha is according to Rabban Gamliel. And all this [about the range of dates when rain is requested] is in the Land of Israel and where it is similar in climate, but

תפלת המוספין של י"ט [יום טוב] א' של פסח ואילך קרי ליה ימות החמה וכמו שנראה מתחלת דבריו שכתב ובימות החמה מוריד הטל וכתב עוד ומתפלת המוספין של י"ט [יום טוב] הראשון של פסח אומר מוריד הטל וכן נר'[אה] מסתמיות דברי שאר הפוסקים ומה שכתב הרמב"ם ז"ל [זכרונו לברכה] בפירוש המשנה לא נחית אלא לומר דאף בימות הגשמים כל זמן שהגשם רע להם אין שואלים שאין לאדם לשאול דבר שהוא רע לו וכן נראה מתחלת דבריו ומסופם דעלה דההיא דתנן בג' במרחשון שואלים את הגשמים רבן גמליאל אומר בז' בו כתב וז"ל [וזה לשונו] והלכה כרבן גמליאל וכל זה בארץ ישראל ומה שהוא קרוב לאוירם אבל בשאר ארצות השאלה בזמן שהמטר טוב והגון באותו מקום וניתן אותו זמן כאילו הוא ז' במרחשון כלומר דוקא בזמן שהמטר טוב והגון לאפוקי אם הוא רע הגשם ומה שכתב שיש ארצות לא יתחילו הגשמים אלא מניסן וארצות שיש להם במרחשון הקיץ כלומר שיש ארצות שמתחילים הגשמים מניסן וקודם לכן הוא רע וגם יש ארצות שיש בהם במרחשון הקיץ והגשמים אינם טובים אלא ממיתים

in the other countries the request [for rain] should begin at the season that is appropriate for rain in that place. That time would be equivalent to the 7th of Marḥeshvan [in the Land of Israel]," that is to say, specifically when the rain is appropriate, excluding [times] that the rain is detrimental. Regarding what he wrote: "there are countries that the rainy season only begins in Nisan, and there are countries where in Marḥeshvan it is summer," that is to say, there are countries where the rain begins in Nisan and prior to then it would be detrimental, and there are also countries where it is summer in Marḥeshvan and rains at that time [in those places] are not beneficial, but rather "cause loss and destruction, and how could it be that the people in that locale would request rain in Marḥeshvan" which is detrimental to them?—[this can be understood] in a manner that Maimonides (may his memory be blessed) intended only to say that they do not request rain, even in the rainy season [of the Land of Israel] when it is detrimental to them, but only when it is beneficial to them, and then they request according to the corresponding law, so that when it is before the *musaf* prayer on the first day of Passover they mention and request rain in *birkat ha-shanim*, and if it is after *musaf* of the first day of Passover but they need rain, they request it in *shome'a' t'filla*. This appears correct to one who recognizes the truth, and I saw it similarly [explained] upon examination of *Kesef Mishne*,[81] [where R. Joseph Caro] wrote somewhat in this vein.

ומאבדים והיאך ישאלו הגשם במרחשון שהוא רע להם באופן דלא נחית הרמב״ם ז״ל [זכרונו לברכה] שם רק לומר שאין שואלים גשמים אף בימות הגשמים בזמן שהוא רע להם אלא בזמן שהוא טוב להם ואז שואלים כפי דינם שאם הוא קודם תפלת המוספין של יום טוב ראשון של פסח אז מזכירין ושואלים גשם בברכת השנים ואם הוא אחר מוסף של יום טוב ראשון של פסח וצריכים להם הגשם שואלים בשומע תפלה וזה נראה נכון למודה על האמת וכן ראיתי אחר העיון להרב כסף משנה שכתב קצת כעין זה.

ואגב עיוני בזה עמדתי על מה שאמרו בגמרא ובגולה עד ששים בתקופה אם אירע ששאל גשם בברכת השנים בתוך זמן זה מה דינו אם מחזירין אותו ויראה לי שאין מחזירין אותו שהרי באותו זמן הגשם לאו סימן קללה הוא אלא שאין צורך וראיה

By way of my examination of this, I considered what they said in the *g'mara*— in the (Babylonian) diaspora, [the request for rain begins] on the sixtieth day from the autumnal equinox[82]—if it happened that someone [in the diaspora] requested rain in *birkat ha-shanim* during this time [i.e., the period when rain is requested in the Land of Israel, but before the sixtieth day], what is the law in his regard, and must he repeat [the prayer]?[83] It appears to me that he is not required to repeat, because at that time rain is not a sign of a curse, rather there is [simply] no need [of it]. Evidence for this [opinion] is that in the matter of mentioning

---

81 *Kesef Mishne Hilkhot T'filla* 2,17.
82 *Ta'anit* 10a. See Halakhic Background.
83 Lit., "do we return him," i.e., make him go back and start again.

[rain,] they [the Sages] said that rain is mentioned in the *musaf* prayer of the last day of the Festival [of Sukkot], even in the diaspora; and if it were a sign of a curse they would not mention it, for [as with] what we say about the summer days, if one mentions rain, he is required to repeat [the prayer,] because it is a sign of a curse. Rather, it is seen that [in] the whole period after the Festival of Sukkot, it is not a sign of a curse, but they [the Sages] said that since there is no need, it is not requested until the sixtieth day from the autumnal equinox. But in [the matter of] mentioning, which is merely praise, we mention it [rain] in the *musaf* prayer of the Festival [of Sukkot], and since it is not a sign of a curse, if it happened that one requested rain, he need not repeat, because the request is merely an addition that he added. I have proof [of this] from what the Ran[84] (may his memory be blessed) wrote. *Bet Yosef*[85] quoted him in section 114[86]

לזה שהרי בהזכרה אמרו שמזכירין גשם בתפלת המוספין של יום טוב אחרון של חג אף בגולה ואם היה סימן קללה לא היו מזכירין דהא אמרינן בימות החמה אם הזכיר גשם מחזירין אותו מפני שהוא סימן קללה אלא שנר'[אה] שכל אותו זמן אחר חג הסכות אינו סימן קללה אלא שאמרו שאחר שאין צורך אין שואלים עד ס' יום מתקופת תשרי רק בהזכרה שאינו אלא שבח בעלמא מזכירין אותו בתפלת מוספין של חג וכיון שכן שאינו סימן קללה אף בברכת השנים אם אירע ששאל אין מחזירין אותו שאינו אלא הוספה בעלמא שהוסיף לשאול ויש לי ראיה מדכתב הר"ן ז"ל [זכרונו לברכה] הביא דבריו הרב בית יוסף בסימן קי"ד וז"ל [וזה לשונו] על ההיא דירושלמי דהתפלל ואינו יודע מה הזכיר כו'[לי] איכא למדק דבימו'[ת] החמה נמי למה מחזירי'[ן] אותו כל שלשים יום אם הזכיר גשם והלא אינו סימן קללה אלא א"כ

as follows: "Regarding that [which is written] in the Jerusalem Talmud[87] about one who prayed but does not know what he mentioned, etc.—it should also be examined why he must repeat it [the prayer] for the full thirty days in the summer if he mentioned rain, when it is not a sign of a curse unless the month of

---

84 R. Nissim Gerondi, 1310?–1375?.
85 R. Joseph Caro.
86 *Bet Yosef OḤ* 114,4. The citation of the Ran is found in his commentary on the Rif (R. Isaac Alfasi, 1013-1103), *Ta'anit* 1b at *tu garsinan*.
87 JT *Ta'anit* 1,1 (63d). The relevant citation is: "It is taught: He prayed and does not know what he 'mentioned'—R. Yoḥanan says that for thirty days there is the presumption that whatever he was accustomed to is what he 'mentioned' [meaning that if he has 'mentioned' rain all winter, for example, he most likely did so by force of habit, for up to thirty days]; after that period [we can assume] that he 'mentioned' what is required [for the season]."

Nisan has ended. [...] And even though he added and said what is not established [as the obligatory text]—after all, 'He causes the wind to pass and brings forth the dew' is not established—but if he said [it,] he is not required to repeat. It should be said [to explain this] that since most of the time one [is supposed to] refrain from mentioning rain, it is a sign of a curse, the Sages did not dispute, but [all] said that from the moment that one [is supposed to] refrain from mentioning rain, if he did mention rain, he is required to repeat [the prayer]." But in this case, it is the opposite [situation], because from the moment one [is supposed to] stop mentioning dew, which is from the *musaf* prayer of the Festival [of Sukkot], it is not a sign of a curse, and therefore if he mentioned[88] rain in *birkat ha-shanim*, he does not need to repeat.

[3] Now I shall come to the matter of the decision about the law in our matter. According to what was told, that there were only a small number of individuals who gathered in one city, and what I wrote that is understood from the words of Maimonides is not even necessary, for even according to the words of the Rosh, who was inclined, etc.[89]—even he wrote that specifically in a whole land like all of Spain or all of Ashkenaz, but in one city alone, even a large city like Nineveh, I will conclude like the *g'mara* that they should only request [rain] in *shome'a' t'filla*. Further, even the Rosh wrote in the cited responsum that his opinion was not accepted and he did not want to perform an individual act, and wrote: "But when I saw that the heart of the

[אם כן] יצא ניסן ואעפ״י [ואף על פי] שהוסיף ואמר מה שלא נתקן הרי מעביר הרוח ומפריח הטל שלא נתקן ואם אמר אין מחזירין אותו יש לומר כיון שרוב הזמן שפוסק מלהזכיר גשם הוא סי׳[מן] קללה לא פלוג רבנן ואמרו משמעה שפוסק מלהזכיר גשם אם הזכיר מחזירין אותו ע״כ [עד כאן] והכא הוא להיפך שמשעה שפסק מלהזכיר טל שהוא ממוספין של חג ואילך אינו סימן קללה ולהכי אם הזכיר גשם בברכת השנים אין מחזירין אותו

ועתה אבוא לענין פסקי[נא] דדינא בנדון דידן כפי מה שהוגד שלא היו אלא קצת יחידים שנתאספו בעיר אחת ולא מבעיא למה שנר[אה] מדברי הרמב״ם דכתיבנא אלא אף לדברי הרא״ש שהיה נוטה כו׳[לי] הרי כתב דדוקא בארץ אחת כולה כמו ספרד בכללה או אשכנז בכללה אבל בעיר אחת לבד אף בעיר גדולה כמו נינוה אסיק כגמרא דלא ישאלו אלא בשומע תפלה ומה גם דאף הרא״ש כתב בתשובה הנז׳[כרת] שלא קבלו דבריו וגם לא רצה לעשות

---

88 It is certain that he meant to write "requested," as that is the purpose of *birkat ha-shanim*.
89 Shabbetai is referring to the opinion that the Rosh expressed in his responsum.

congregation was turned from accepting the words of the living God from me, I, too, withdrew [my practice] of requesting for and mentioning [rain] in the synagogue in which I pray, even though I could have requested [in *birkat ha-shanim*] in spite of the fact that I am an individual, because it is the need of many. [But] I did not want to make 'separate sects.'" All this is regarding the summer, which is from the festival of Passover until the festival of Sukkot, [during which period] they are not to mention or request rain in *birkat ha-shanim*. But if they require rain, they are to request it in *shome'a' t'filla*. However, from the time of the festival of Sukkot until the festival of Passover, according to what is in the question (that the rain is detrimental to them and brings sickness), certainly they should not mention or request rain at all, in any manner, so long as it is detrimental, as Maimonides wrote in his Commentary on the Mishna, and we also say in the *g'mara* in the first chapter of *Ta'anit* [4b]: Rabbi Asi said that Rabbi Yoḥanan said that halakha is according to Rabbi Y'huda, etc. But did R. Yoḥanan [really] say that? But we teach [in a *mishna*] etc., and R. Elazar said that the halakha is according to Rabban Gamliel!, etc. ... Rather, [we shall reconcile the two opinions by saying] there is no contradiction—this one [of Rabban Gamliel] is for us [who dwell in Babylonia,] while this one [of R. Y'huda] is for them [who dwell in the Land of Israel]. What is different for us? We have crops in the field, meaning, those who live in Babylonia have grain and fruit in the field all of Tishrei, [therefore] they do not mention [rain], and [the *g'mara*] refutes: They also have [a reason in that] they have pilgrims! Rather, R. Yoḥanan was saying [that the halakha is according to R. Yᵉhuda] when the Temple was no longer in existence. Now that you have reached this [conclusion], this and this are both for them [in the Land of Israel]—here [R. Gamliel's opinion applied] when the Temple was standing, here [R. Yᵉhuda's opinion applies] when the Temple is no longer in existence. It is seen from all this that so long as there is damage from the rains, we do not request [rain], and likewise we say that on the festival of Sukkot we request rain in *musaf* of the last day of the festival but not the first, as on the festival of Passover, because rain on the holiday is a sign of a curse on the first days of the festival.

In conclusion, we see that in that location named in the question they should neither, in any year, mention [rain] nor request rain in *birkat ha-shanim*; rather, if they need rain during the summer, from Passover and on, they should request it in *shome'a' tᵉfilla*. [This is] according to my humble opinion, Ḥayyim Shabbetai, the young.⁹⁰

נמי אית להו עולי רגלים כי קאמר ר' יוחנן בזמן שאין בית המקדש קיים השתא דאתית להכי הא והא לדידהו ולא קשיא כאן בזמן שב״ה [שבית המקדש] קיי'[ם] כאן בזמן שאין ב״ה [בית המקדש] קיי'[ם] נר'[אה] מכל זה כל שיש נזק מצד הגשמי'[ם] אין שואלים והכי נמי אמרי'[נן] דבחג הסוכות שואלי'[ם] מטר במוסף י״ט [יום טוב] אחרון ולא בראשון כמו בחג הפסח משום דבחג הגשמים סי'[מן] קללה בימים הראשונים של חג

כלל הדברים שנר'[אה] שבאותו מקו'[ם] הנז'[כר] בשאלה אין להם להזכיר ולשאול גשם בברכת השני'[ם] בכל השנה מטעמא דכתי'[בנא] אלא אם יצטרכו גשמים בימות החמה מפסח ואילך ישאלו בש״ת [בשומע תפלה] הנלע״ד [הנראה לעניות דעתין] הצעיר חיים שבתי

---

90 An expression of humility.

Discussion

To Shabbetai, the question is fairly straightforward, with his goal being to present his interpretation of the two citations from Maimonides, in contrast with the interpretation offered by the Rosh. Shabbetai then applies his interpretation to the matter at hand.[91]

[1] Shabbetai quotes extensively from the responsum written by the Rosh on whether the liturgy should reflect the climate of the location of any given Jewish community, including the Rosh's explanation of the two citations from Maimonides.

[2] Shabbetai's purpose in quoting the Rosh is clear. He refutes the Rosh's interpretation and explains that according to Maimonides rain is not mentioned, nor is it requested in *birkat ha-shanim*, in any location after the *musaf* prayer of the first day of Passover, but if in some location there is a need for rain, it is requested in *shome'a' t'filla*. He further explains that in his Commentary on the Mishna, Maimonides intended only to say that even in the rainy season according to the Land of Israel, so long as the rain is detrimental to a particular locale, rain should not be requested, because a person should not request something that is detrimental to him. Shabbetai includes several arguments to justify his explanation of Maimonides's two citations, and informs the reader that the *Kesef Mishne* interpreted Maimonides similarly.

[3] When he gets to the matter at hand, Shabbetai writes that in the situation under consideration, the Rosh would agree with Maimonides, because the situation is one of a small number of people in one city, and not an entire land, and therefore requesting rain in *birkat ha-shanim* between Passover and Sukkot would not be permitted, but rather should be requested in *shome'a' t'filla*. Further, between Sukkot and Passover, if rain is detrimental, then it should neither be mentioned nor requested. The result is that for a community in the Southern Hemisphere, rain is never requested in *birkat ha-shanim*, nor is it ever mentioned, but only prayed for in *shome'a' t'filla*.

A. and D. Lasker concluded:

> In his responsum, Shabbetai obviously chose a middle path. On one hand, he could not authorize the Jews in Recife to say *tal u-matar*[92] in

---

91 See the section numbers in square brackets in the responsum.
92 "[Give us] dew and rain" (1 Kings 17:1), which is said in the winter.

the Blessing of the Years during their winter (his own summer) because tradition, as represented in this case by Maimonides, restrained him from such a ruling. On the other hand, he could not in good conscience demand from this community that they pray for rain when such rain, according to their testimony, would be harmful to them. His only recourse, or so it seemed to him, was to suggest, in effect, that the Jews of Recife ignore the prayer for rain. If they had a particular need for rain during their winter, these Jews, like those of Nineveh, could always pray for it in Shomeʻa Tefilah.[93]

Questions for Further Discussion

We saw three different approaches to harmonize (or reconcile) the citation of Maimonides in the MT with his statement in the Commentary on the Mishna: 1) that of the Rosh, 2) that of Shabbetai (similar to that of *Kesef Mishne*), and 3) that of Qafiḥ. How would you harmonize those texts?

Maimonides has two versions of *birkat ha-shanim*—one for the summer months and one for the winter months.[94] Jews from the Yemenite, Sephardic, and Middle Eastern communities follow this tradition of two formulas, while Ashkenazic Jews only vary a few words. Review all versions of the entire text of *birkat ha-shanim*. Qafiḥ maintains that the reason that Rabbi Judah Ha-Nasi ruled in *Taʻanit* 14b that the people of Nineveh should request rain in *shomeʻaʻ tᵉfilla* and not in *birkat ha-shanim* is that Rabbi had two formulas, and if the people of Nineveh recited the one in which rain is requested in both the winter and the summer, then the summer formula would fall into disuse.[95]

Is it such a terrible thing if people who need rain in both what are the winter and summer seasons in Babylonia (not in the Land of Israel) would include only the winter formula, with its request for rain, in their daily prayers? Does your opinion change in the case of Ashkenazi Jews, such that only a few words would be different?

For Jews who live in the Southern Hemisphere, where "summer is winter and winter is summer" and they need rain in the "summer," but in the "winter" it would damage the crops—the seasons are named according to Babylonia—fol-

---

93 [Lasker]: 164.
94 See MT *Sefer Ha-Ahava, Seder Ha-Tᵉfillot* (Yitzhak Shilat, *Rambam Mᶜduyyaq* [Maale Adumim: Mᵉkhon Maʻaliyot, 2006], 170-171.
95 MT: Yosef Qafiḥ, *Hilkhot Tᵉfilla* 2,17n36.

lowing the ruling of Shabbetai would result in never requesting rain in *birkat ha-shanim*. Would *birkat ha-shanim* be devoid of its purpose if rain is never requested in that part of the liturgy? Would it be better to say the formula that is appropriate at the time in the Southern Hemisphere, that is, request rain in *birkat ha-shanim* when it is winter there, rather than abstain from requesting it because it is summer in Babylonia?[96] Do you see any disadvantages to such an approach?

In their discussion about the beginning date for requesting rain in the diaspora, A. and D. Lasker state: "It would seem that, once the decision was made to follow the Babylonian practice to the exclusion of local needs, the prayer for rain became trivialized."[97] In light of the previous questions and the "calendrical miscalculation" explained in [Lasker2], do you see a conflict between the imperative to pray with intent and the actual practice of the request for rain? If so, how would you resolve the conflict?

How might Shabbetai have ruled had he been asked not about one small community in Brazil, but about the entire Southern Hemisphere?

Why didn't the Rosh succeed in his approach of modifying the timing of the slight seasonal liturgical modifications in his Ashkenazi custom to be consistent with the actual climate?

Why was this matter so important to the community in Recife, as to send inquiries—and to distant authorities, no less? Is it a trivial matter and not worthy of so much discussion, or is it vital to the Jewish community? And if the latter, why?

Further Reading

[Bodian 3] Bodian, Miriam. "Baptized or Not? The Inquisitors' Dilemma in Trials of Portuguese Jews from Dutch Brazil, 1645–1647." In *Portuguese Jews, New Christians, and 'New Jews': A Tribute to Roberto Bachman*, edited by Claude B. Stuczynski and Bruno Feitler, 123-144. Leiden: Brill, 2018.

[Feitler] Feitler, Bruno. "Jews and New Christians in Dutch Brazil, 1630–1654." In *Atlantic Diasporas: Jews, Conversos, and Crypto-Jews in the Age of Mercantilism, 1500–1800*, edited by Richard L. Kagan and Philip D. Morgan, 123-151. Baltimore: Johns Hopkins University Press, 2009.

---

96 See [Lasker]: 165-170.
97 [Lasker2]: 96.

[Lasker] Lasker, Arnold A., and Daniel J. Lasker. "The Jewish Prayer for Rain in the Post-Talmudic Diaspora." *AJS Review* 9, no. 2 (Autumn 1984): 141-174.

[Lasker2] ———. "The Strange Case of December 4: A Liturgical Problem." *Conservative Judaism* 38, no. 1 (Fall 1985): 91-99.

[Wiznitzer] Wiznitzer, Arnold. *The Records of the Earliest Jewish Community in the New World*. New York: American Jewish Historical Society, 1954.

[Wiznitzer 2] ———. *Jews in Colonial Brazil*. New York: Columbia University Press, 1960.

Index

Aboab, Isaac, 210
Abraham ben David of Posquières
 (acr. Rabad), 196
'aguna (pl. 'agunot), viii, xi, 9, 11–13, 18n41,
 21–23, 26–28, 33–34, 36–37, 39–41, 43
Alfasi, Isaac (acr. Rif), 29nn69–70, 70n98,
 75n116, 131n25, 145n26, 170n42,
 183n92, 197n62, 198n68, 235n86
Amsterdam, vii-viii, xiii–xiv, xvi, 1n2, 8, 47n2,
 139, 155, 157, 188–89, 192, 194, 200–2,
 204–6, 209–10, 212
Aquinas, Thomas, 99n72
Arye Leib ben Asher, 214n30
Asher ben Jehiel (acr. Rosh), xvi–xvii, 5–6, 68,
 109n126, 124n33, 134, 141, 146, 151,
 176–79, 183, 191, 195, 202, 213n26, 215,
 219–20, 222n53, 224nn57–58, 225–27,
 229–32, 236, 239–41
Ashkenazi, Bezalel, 196n54
asmakhta, xii, 52–58, 63, 67–68, 78–79, 82
Assaf, Simha, 85n2
Avitsur, Shemuel, 211n12

Ba'al ha-Tur(im). See Jacob ben Asher
Baḥ. See Sirkes, Joel
Bareket, E., 59n46, 193n35
Barfat. See Isaac ben Sheshet Perfet
Barski, Leonid, 184n95
Baumgarten, Elisheva, viiin3
Bedershi, Yedaiah, 108n123
Beer, Moshe, 143n18
Beinart, Haim, xviii, 119nn2–3

Ben-Mayor, Jacov, 211n10
Ben-Sasson, Haim Hillel, 114, 117
Berav, Jacob (Mahari Berav), 13n27
Berenbaum, Michael, xvn7
Berger, David, 108n123, 114, 117
birkat ha-shanim, 212–15, 217, 223–25,
 228–34, 236–41
Blau, Jacob Isaiah, 13n30
Blidstein, Gerald J., 89n15, 117
Bloch, Abraham Isaac, 87n9
Bodian, Miriam, vii, 189n13, 192n26,
 193n31, 194n39, 206, 212n17, 241
Bowen, Barbara C., 107n118
Boyce, Mary, 143n16
Brazil, vii, xiv, 209–10, 212, 227, 241
Broadie, Alexander, 99n72
Brulez, W., 156n7, 159n18

Caro, Joseph, xvii, 33n79, 149n40, 169,
 183n92, 234, 235n85. See also Shulḥan
 'Arukh (SA)
Carter, Jimmy, 43n116, 44
Cohn, Haim Hermann, 8n18
Constantinople (Istanbul), xii, xvii, 85

da Costa, Uriel, 206
David, Abraham, 210n6
de Medina, Samuel (acr. Maharashdam),
 xiii, xvi, 139–40, 142, 144n20, 145n26,
 150n42, 151nn43–44, 152–53
de Modena, Leon, 189n13, 192n26-27,
 193n31, 206

de Nis, Filippo (Marcus, Salomon), xiii, 156–59, 164–65, 168n36, 178n77, 181–82
Derovan, David, 174n50
Diem, Werner, 64n76
di Trani, Moses ben Joseph (acr. Mabit), xii, xvi, 13n27, 119–20, 128, 133n29, 135n38, 136–37
divorce, conditional, xi, 10–11, 13–14, 21, 25, 32–34, 36n90, 38–43, 44n, 75n115
divorce by proxy, xi, 10, 14, 22
Dorff, Elliot N., 160n19
Draper, John William, 114n
Dratch, Mark, 154

Edels, Samuel (acr. Maharsha), 12n19, 12n21
Ehrlich, Uri, 173n48
Elazar of Verona (Eliezer), 13, 25
Eisenstadt, Abraham Hirsch ben Jacob, 12n20
Epstein, Mark Alan, 83
excommunication, viii, xi, xiii–xiv, 1–2, 4–5, 7–8, 12, 25n58, 47n2, 73, 76, 80, 94n34, 97, 187, 194n42, 195–96, 200, 203–6. See also ḥerem

Farrar, Abraham, 192n26, 193n31, 194n39
Farrar, David, 189n13, 192nn26–27, 193n31, 194n39
Feitler, Bruno, 210n4, 241
Fermaglich, Kirsten, 153n51, 154
Fixler, Dror, 43n117, 44
Frank, Ẓevi Pesaḥ, 13n30
Freehof, Samuel, ixn3, xn5
Frye, Richard N., 189n17
Furstenberg, Yair, 162n26

Galilei, Galileo, 114, 117
Gerondi, Nissim (acr. Ran), 29–30, 75, 145–47, 170, 197n62, 198, 235
Gitlitz, David, 119, 120n4, 138, 140
Glick, Shmuel, 85n2, 86n8, 219n48
Goitein, S. D., 21n49, 22nn50–51, 44
Goldish, Matt, viii–ixn3
Goldman, Israel M., viiin3, 44
Golinkin, David, 135n38, 180n79
Goodblatt, David M., 143n17, 144n18
Goodblatt, Morris S., viiin3, 1n2, 47nn3–4, 48n5, 60nn47–48, 83
Grant, Edward, 114, 117
Greenberg, Jason H., 153n51
Greenberg, Moshe, 8n18
Grossman, Avraham, viiin3

Ḥabiba, Joseph, 69n93, 131n25, 145n25
Hacker, Joseph, 86nn3–4, 109n127, 117
Hai Gaon, 69n94, 98, 176
Ha-Kohen of Salonica, Solomon ben Abraham (acr. Maharshakh), xiii, xvi, 155–56, 159–60, 163–66, 171n43, 176n61, 176n65, 180–84
Ha-Levi, David ben Samuel (acr. Taz), 12n19
Ha-Levi, Elijah ben Benjamin, xii, xvi, 85–88, 92, 94n36, 95n42, 95nn46–47, 99n69, 99n71–72, 100n76, 101n80, 104n96, 104n101, 105n109, 105n110, 106n111, 106n115, 107n119, 108n123, 108n124, 109n127–29, 110n133, 111n136, 112–14, 116, 206
Halevi, Judah, 99
ḥalitsa, 11, 18n41, 22, 38, 40, 42, 43n119, 199. See also levirate marriage
Halkin, A. S., 108n123, 117
Ḥazon Ish. See Karelitz, Avraham Y.

Henkin, Joseph Elijah, 12n22, 21n49
ḥerem, 1, 12. *See also* excommunication
Hershkowitz, Leo, 212n18
Herzog, Isaac, 13nn28–30
Higger, Michael, 105n107
Hirsch, Abraham, 12n20
Holland, 187–88, 209
Holocaust, 114, 153
Horowitz, Yehoshua, 203n89
Huussen Jr., Arend H., 188n10, 206

Iberia, xii–xiii, 140, 155
Iberian Peninsula, vii, 120, 211
ibn Abi Zimra, David ben Solomon
    (acr. Radbaz), xi, xvi, 9–10, 14–15, 20,
    22, 25n58, 31n73, 36n90, 40, 85n2
ibn Ezra, Abraham, 99
ibn Gabirol, Solomon ben Judah, 99
ibn Gabbai, Meir, 103, 195, 215, 216n37
ibn Ḥabib, Jacob, 182
ibn Lev, Joseph (Mahari ibn Lev), xi, xvi, 47–48,
    58–59, 60n48, 62n62, 67n83, 72n107,
    73n109, 74n110, 74n112, 75n116, 78–80
ibn Tibbon, Samuel, 101n78
Inalcik, Halil, 60n48, 83
inheritance laws, vii–viii, xii, 103n90, 120–32,
    135–38
Isaac ben Abba Mari of Marseilles, 35n88,
    71n101
Isaac ben Joseph of Corbeil, 148n35
Isaac (the Elder) ben Samuel of Dampierre
    (acr. Ri), 41n106, 76, 177, 179, 203n88
Isaac ben Sheshet Perfet (acr. Ribash), 133,
    173–74
Isserlein, Israel, 34–35
Isserles, Moses (acr. Rma), 12n20, 13n30,
    218n44

Istanbul (Constantinople), xii, xvii, 85
Italy, 120, 156–57

Jacob ben Asher (aka Tur, Ba'al ha-Tur(im)),
    20n47, 41–42, 140, 142–43, 152,
    176–78, 189n16, 229n79
Jacob ben Meir Tam, 176–77, 202
Jacob ben Moses Moellin (acr. Maharil),
    34n86
Jastrow, Marcus, 151n45
Jehiel of Paris, 12
Jerusalem, xi, 9–10, 22–26, 40
John Paul II, 115n149
Joseph ben Solomon Colon (acr. Maharik
    or Mahari Colon), 72, 147, 148n35,
    149–50, 153, 203, 205
Jospe, Raphael, 117
Jotkowitz, Alan, 184n95

Kagan, Richard L., 139n2
Kaplan, Yosef, 1n2, 8, 205, 207
Karelitz, Avraham Y. (aka Ḥazon Ish), 44n
Katz, Jacob, viiin3
Kellner, Menachem Marc, 89n15, 118
Kerem, Yitzchak, 211n10
Kimḥi, David, 200n78
Kook, Avraham Yitzḥak Ha-Kohen, 183n92
Kohut, George Alexander, 211n16
Koren, Debby, 156n6, 159n17, 185
Krochmal, Menahem Mendel ben Abraham,
    12n21, 13n30

Lamdan, Ruth, 21n49, 22n50, 44
Landau, Ezekiel, 13n30
Langer, Ruth, 173n48
Lasker, Arnold, 212n19, 213nn23–24, 228,
    239–42

Lasker, Daniel, 212n19, 213nn23–24, 228, 239–42
levirate marriage, 11–12, 18n41, 22, 36, 38–43. *See also* ḥalitsa
Levy, Avigdor, 83
Lieberman, Saul, 14n32, 67n85
Lisbon, 158n14
Lithuania, 10n5, 204
London, 155
Lopes, Maria, 157
Low Countries, 156
Lublin, 194

Mabit. *See* di Trani, Moses ben Joseph
Macuch, Maria, 144n19, 145n26
Maggid Mishne, 20n47, 35n88, 126–27, 130, 135n40
Maharam of Rothenberg. *See* Meir ben Baruch
Maharashdam. *See* de Medina, Samuel
Maharḥash. *See* Shabbetai, Ḥayyim
Mahari Berav. *See* Berav, Jacob
Mahari Colon. *See* Joseph ben Solomon Colon
Mahari ibn Lev. *See* ibn Lev, Joseph
Maharik. *See* Joseph ben Solomon Colon
Maharil. *See* Jacob ben Moses Moellin
Maharsha. *See* Edels, Samuel
Maharshakh. *See* Solomon ben Abraham Ha-Kohen of Salonica
Maimonides (acr. Rambam), xvi–xvii, 3, 4n7, 11n13, 14–16, 17n37, 18, 29, 44n, 49n15, 50, 74n110, 87, 89n15, 97, 99, 102n88, 104–5, 111, 114, 116, 117n152, 124, 127, 133, 134n32, 137n44, 141n11, 160, 163n27, 165, 169n40, 182, 183n92, 215, 217–18, 224–27, 230–34, 236–37, 239–40

Mamluk sultanate, vii, 10, 21n48
Margaliyot, Mordecai, 156n5
Marx, Alexander, xviii, 119n2
Meir ben Baruch (Maharam of Rothenberg), 66, 67n85, 72
Meir, R., 103, 215, 216n37
Meiri, Menachem ben Solomon, 94n40
Melammed, Renée Levine, 155n2, 156n7, 185
Mizraḥi, Elijah, xii, 40, 85, 182n87
Mordecai ben Hillel Ha-Kohen, 41, 66, 67n85, 199n72
Morteira (or Mortera), Saul Levi, 194n39, 210n6
Murad III, Sultan, 47

Nadler, Steven, 206–7
Nagid, 10
Naḥmanides (acr. Ramban), 197
Nathan ben Jehiel of Rome, 97n58
Netherlands, the, xiii, xiv, 187n4, 188n8
Neusner, Jacob, 143n18
New Amsterdam, 212
New York, 153–54, 212
niddui, 1. *See also* shunning

Ottoman Empire, vii, xii–xiii, 10, 47–48, 60n48, 86, 109n137, 120, 155–56, 158, 159n15, 181, 211
Ovadiah, Yosef, 13n29

Palestine, vii, 21n48
Pamuk, Sevket, 60n48, 62n62, 83
Pardes, S. A., 21n49, 44n120
Pardo, Joseph, 194n39
Parry, Peter, 211n16
Pérez, Joseph, xviii, 119n2

Perez of Corbeil, 12
Pernambuco, 209
Pines, Eliyahu, 203n92
Poland, xiv, 10n5
Popper, William, 104n101, 111n136, 140n9
Portugal, vii, xi–xiii, 9, 10n5, 85, 109n127, 109n129, 119, 139, 142, 155–57, 181, 182n85, 188, 210
prayer for rain. *See birkat ha-shanim*
Pseudo-Rashi, 144n19
Pullan, Brian, 155n2, 157n9, 158n13, 168n36, 185

Qafiḥ, Yosef, xvi, 217n41, 226–27, 240
qiddush ha-Shem, 160. *See also* sanctification of the name of God
qinyan, 48–49, 51, 58–59, 67–72, 78
qinyan d'varim, 49–52, 54, 57n38, 58–59, 70–71, 72n102, 78–79, 82n132
qinyan sudar, 49, 72
Quataert, Donald, 83

Rabad. *See* Abraham ben David of Posquières
Rabbenu Samson. *See* Samson ben Abraham of Sens
Rabbenu Tam. *See* Jacob ben Meir Tam
Radbaz. *See* ibn Abi Zimra, David ben Solomon
Radzyner, Amihai, 44
Rakover, Nahum, 10n8
Rambam. *See* Maimonides
Ramban. *See* Naḥmanides
Ran. *See* Gerondi, Nissim
Rapoport, Yossef, 13n30, 21nn48–49, 42n115, 45
Rashba. *See* Solomon ben Abraham Adret
Rashbam. *See* Samuel ben Meir

Rashi (R. Solomon ben Isaac), 6, 50, 51n22, 52n25, 69n92, 75n114, 75n116, 89n15, 91n23, 94n34, 94n40, 97nn58–59, 101n81, 104, 106, 108, 109n126, 110, 143, 144n19, 149n38, 151, 152n48, 194n42, 195n51, 199, 202, 213n26, 214n30
Ravid, Benjamin, 157n12
Ray, Jonathan, viin1, xviii, 185
Recife, xiv, 209n2, 212, 227n69, 228n70, 239–41
Reiss, Yona, 43nn118–19, 45
Ri. *See* Isaac (the Elder) ben Samuel of Dampierre
Ribash. *See* Isaac ben Sheshet Perfet
Rif. *See* Alfasi, Isaac
Rma. *See* Isserles, Moses
Roman law, 11
Rosh. *See* Asher ben Jehiel
Roth, Cecil, 158n14
Rothkoff, Aaron, 144n19
Rozen, Minna, 47n3, 48n6, 83, 86n7, 118

Saadiah Gaon, 98
Sadan, Joseph, 101n78
Saint-Jean de Luz, 210
Salonica, xiii, xvi–xvii, 120n6, 156, 182, 210–11
Samson ben Abraham of Sens (aka Rabbenu Samson), 170
Samuel ben Elḥanan, 203n88, 203n92
Samuel ben Meir (acr. Rashbam), 52, 53n27, 94n34, 194n42
sanctification of the name of God, 160, 162. *See also qiddush ha-Shem*
Sandel, Michael J., 160n20, 184n97, 184nn97–99, 185

Sasanian Empire, 144n19
Savello, Cardinal, 168n36
Schacter, Jacob J., 87–88, 118
Schwartz, Dov, 117
Selim II, Sultan, 47n5
Shabbetai, Ḥayyim (acr. Maharḥash), xiv, xvii, 210–12, 215, 227–28, 236n89, 238–41
Shakespeare, William, 81
shamta, 1, 195n46. *See also niddui*
Shevaḥ, Yosef, 85n2
Shilat, Yitzhak, xvi, 240n94
Shimon bar Yoḥai, 91
Shmuelevitz, Aryeh, 47n4, 60n48, 83
Shohat, Azriel, 211n13
shome'a' t'filla, 214–15, 219, 224, 229, 231–32, 234, 236–40.
Shulḥan 'Arukh (SA), xvii, 6–7, 35n86, 49n10, 50, 195, 218n44. *See also* Caro, Joseph
shunning, xiv, 1–4, 6, 73, 76, 94n34, 110n133, 111, 113, 194n42, 195–96, 200, 202–4. *See also ḥerem*
Simeon ben Zemaḥ Duran, 109n126
Singer, Isidore, xvn8
Sirkes, Joel, (acr. Baḥ), xiii–xiv, xvii, 12n19, 187, 189, 191–92, 193n31, 196n54, 197n62, 202nn85–86, 204–6
Six-Day War, 21n49
Skolnik, Fred, xvn7
Solnica, Amy, 184n95
Solomon ben Abraham Adret, (acr. Rashba), 58, 70, 74, 108n123, 126n16, 127, 131, 135, 145n22, 146n27, 174n55, 175n58, 196n54, 197n62
Soloveitchik, Haym, 221n52
Soyer, François, viin1, xviii

Spain, vii, xi–xiii, 9, 10n5–6, 85, 109n127, 109n129, 119–20, 139, 155–56, 181, 182n85, 187, 222n55, 223, 225, 229, 236
Sperber, Daniel, 104n101
Spinoza, Baruch, 206
Stein, Peter, 11n9, 45
Steinsaltz, Adin, 75n114, 100n75
Sulaiman, Sultan, 47n5
Suslin, Alexander, Ha-Kohen of Frankfurt, 197n64
Swetschinski, Daniel M., 139, 187n4, 188nn9–10, 189nn14–15, 192n26, 207

Tam. *See* Jacob ben Meir Tam
Tamar, David, 85n2
Tanukhi, al-Muhassin ibn ʿAli al-, 64n76
Ta-Shma, Israel M., 196n54, 203n89
Taz. *See* Ha-Levi, David ben Samuel
Torah, obligation to study, 87–88, 91–92
Torat Ḥayyim, 209
Trani, 120n6
Tsadok Gaon, 94n40
Tsits Eli'ezer. *See* Waldenberg, Eliezer
Tur. *See* Jacob ben Asher
Turkey, 166, 168
Tyson, Neil deGrasse, 115n148

Union of Utrecht, 187
Urbach, E. E., 13n28
Uziel, Isaac (Ishac), 194n39, 210

Varlik, Nükhet, 211n11
Vatican, 115n149, 124n9
Venetian Inquisition, viii, xiii, 155–57, 158n16, 159n16, 166, 168n36, 182

Venice, xiii, xvi, 81–82, 156–59, 166, 181, 189n13, 192n26, 206
Vidal Yom Tov of Tolosa. *See Maggid Mishne*
Vlessing, Odette, 207

Waldenberg, Eliezer, 12n22, 13nn29–30, 21n49, 41
Waldman, Eliyahu, 203n89
Wehberg, Hans, 82–83
Westreich, Avishalom, 21n48, 42n114, 45
White, Andrew Dickson, 115
Wiznitzer, Arnold, 209nn2–3, 210n4, 210n6, 210n8, 211, 242

World Trade Center attacks, xi, 43
Wygoda, Michael, 10n8

Zeitlin, S., 111n136
Zᶜqan Aharon, 85
Zilberstein, Yitzchok, 153
Zimmels, Hirsch Jacob, 174n50
Zorattini, Pier Cesare Ioly, 156nn7–8, 157nn9–11, 158nn13–14, 159n16, 168n36
Zsom, Dora, 139n1, 140n5, 154
Zukermandel, 14n32

www.ingramcontent.com/pod-product-compliance
Ingram Content Group UK Ltd.
Pitfield, Milton Keynes, MK11 3LW, UK
UKHW020738250226
468390UK00008B/160